Volkswagen 411/412 Owners Workshop Manual

by J H Haynes
Associate Member of the Guild of Motoring Writers
and K F Kinchin

Models covered

UK: 411/412 Saloon 2 and 4 door. 1679 cc
411/412 Estate (Variant). 1679 cc

USA: 411/412 Sedan 2 and 4 door. 103 cu in
411/412 Wagon. 103 cu in

Including automatic transmission

ISBN 0 900550 91 0

Printed in England

**J H HAYNES AND COMPANY LIMITED
SPARKFORD YEOVIL SOMERSET ENGLAND**
distributed in the USA by
**HAYNES PUBLICATIONS INC.
9421 WINNETKA AVENUE
CHATSWORTH LOS ANGELES
CALIFORNIA 91311 USA**

Acknowledgements

Thanks are due to Brian Horsfall and Les Brazier who took the vehicle to pieces, photographed it and put it together again, also to Tim Parker.

The assistance of the VW organization and permission to use some of their illustrations is most appreciated.

About this manual

The aim of this book is to help you get the best value from your car. It can do so in two ways. First it can help you decide what work must be done, even should you choose to get it done by a garage, the routine maintenance and the diagnosis and course of action when random faults occur. But it is hoped that you will also use the second and fuller purpose by tackling the work yourself. This can give you the satisfaction of doing the job yourself. On the simpler jobs it may even be quicker than booking the car into a garage and going there twice, to leave and collect it. Perhaps most important, much money can be saved by avoiding the costs a garage must charge to cover their labour and overheads.

The book has drawings and descriptions to show the function of the various components so that their layout can be understood. Then the tasks are described and photographed in a step by step sequence so that even a novice can cope with complicated work. Such a person is the very one to buy a car needing repair yet be unable to afford garage costs.

The jobs are described assuming only normal spanners are available, and not special tools. But a reasonable outfit of tools will be a worthwhile investment. Many special workshop tools produced by the makers merely speed the work, and in these cases guidance is given as to how to do the job without them, the oft quoted example being the use of a large hose clip to compress the piston rings for insertion in the cylinder. But on a very few occasions the special tool is essential to prevent damage to components, then their use is described. Though it might be possible to borrow the tool, such work may have to be entrusted to the official agent.

To avoid labour costs a garage will often give a cheaper repair by fitting a reconditioned assembly. The home mechanic can be helped by this book to diagnose the fault and make a repair using only a minor spare part. The classic case is repairing a non-charging dynamo by fitting new brushes.

The manufacturer's official workshop manuals are written for their trained staff, and so assume special knowledge; detail is left out. This book is written for the owner, and so goes into detail.

The book is divided into twelve chapters. Each chapter is divided into numbered sections which are headed in bold type between horizontal lines. Each section consists of serially numbered paragraphs.

There are two types of illustration: (1) Figures which are numbered according to Chapter and sequence of occurrence in that Chapter. (2) Photographs which have a reference number on their caption. All photographs apply to the Chapter in which they occur so that the reference figure pinpoints the pertinent section and paragraph number.

Procedures, once described in the text, are not normally repeated. If it is necessary to refer to another Chapter the reference will be given in Chapter number and section number thus: Chapter 1/16.

If it is considered necessary to refer to a particular paragraph in another Chapter the reference is eg, 'Chapter 1/5:5'. Cross references given without use of the word 'Chapter' apply to sections and/or paragraphs in the same Chapter, eg, 'see Section 8' means also in this Chapter'.

When the left or right side of the car is mentioned it is as if looking forward.

Great effort has been made to ensure that this book is complete and up to date. The manufacturers continually modify their cars, even in retrospect.

1973 VW412 Sedan (North America version)

1973 VW412 Sedan (USA version)

1971 VW411 Variant LE (UK version)

Introduction

The 411/412 is a most happy car, pleasant to look at, comfortable to sit in, and without being spectacular, a joy to drive. It is a precision piece of engineering and like all such machines will not respond to uninformed attempts to adjust it.

This manual is designed to help the owner understand his car, and to overhaul it as far as possible without special tools.

The Type 4 is a departure from the traditional Beetle. MacPherson struts at the front and trailing wishbones with coil spring at the rear replace the torsion bar suspension.

The steering box is a recirculating ball worm and nut, and the transmission has been redesigned. The larger engine, although a traditional "flat four" is not just a bored out 1500 but a completely new set of castings.

The body style, available as a Sedan or an Estate changed in August 1972 with extensive modifications to the front and rear of the vehicle, which gave reason to change the title from 411 to 412.

Initially produced as a twin carburettor model in 1969 the fuel system was changed to low pressure fuel injection and so remained until 1974.

Like many precision machines the vehicle is best serviced with special tools and jigs. The power unit is easily removed, and most of the work to be done on it can only be done when it is away from the car. Certain of the parts are not repairable, and some only with special gauges. With this fact in mind we dismantled and rebuilt the major portions of a Variant and the manual relates the way in which this was achieved. It also recommends limits beyond which it is thought the owner should not go. Even the best machines wear out or suffer accident, and should this befall it is hoped that the owner may be helped in his decision of what to do by "getting out the book".

Contents

Vehicle identification and ordering spare parts

The identification plate is under the front hood near the lock. A photo of it is given. The 411 and 412 use the same identification code.

Type 41 – 2 door saloon
Type 42 – 4 door saloon
Type 46 – Variant

The chassis number is on a long plate under the rear seat between the anchor points for the safety belt.

The engine number is on the top of the right hand half of the crankcase below the breather (photo). The 1st letter indicates the type of engine.

V and Z – Carburettor engines
W – Fuel injection
EA or EB – Fuel injection with emission control

When ordering spares give the model identification, chassis and engine numbers to the storeman and take the vehicle, or the old part with you.

It is as well to ascertain spares availability before taking things to bits, the scaling is generous but not 100% replacement, and railing at the Storeman will do no good, he can only give what is on the shelves.

The UK organization of VW is most helpful and efficient but even they find the impossible a little difficult, be it demand or customer, so a little thought, a plan of repair and a check of stores availability before the overhaul starts may avoid a lot of heartache and trouble.

Identification plate

Engine number

Routine maintenance

The term "routine maintenance" was probably invented by an Army Transport Officer to keep the drivers busy. The amount of maintenance a car requires depends entirely upon the life it leads. There is a basic minimum below which the car becomes unsafe, the remainder depends on how much the owner expects to get when he sells the car. VW have built into the Type 4 a most elaborate system whereby maintenance requirements may be ascertained comprehensively in a remarkably short time by a technician using an electrical circuit. He does not do the maintenance, that is still done by mechanics with spanners and lubricating devices. The computor diagnosis service is discussed at the end of Chapter 10. For the man who uses his car a lot it would seem stupid not to use this service exactly as it is designed; for the owner who uses the car only on fine Sundays it could be a 'once a year' affair like the English MOT inspection. It is not the diagnosis that costs the money, it is for the work to do afterwards that costs mount up. A lot of these costs may be

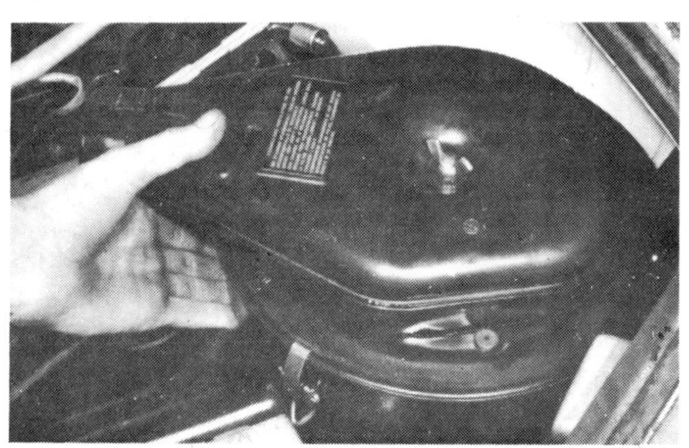
R.M.1 Removing the air cleaner (fuel injection model)

avoided by reading carefully the excellent instruction manual and the service record supplied with the car and doing just what the book says.

Basic maintenance may be divided into two parts, **lubrication** and **inspection.** Lubrication requirements are shown on pages 8 to 10 and should be observed in the same spirit with which you clean your teeth, essential if pain is to be avoided. Inspection starts by observing the garage floor; if there is oil on it then it is leaking out of your car and something needs doing right away. So find where the oil is coming from and deal with the leak.

Every week

Check the battery for electrolyte level and signs of corrosion. Check the level of the fluid in the brake/clutch fluid reservoir in the forward luggage compartment. If it has sunk appreciably in a week then urgent repairs are required. Check that all the lights are working properly, and do something if they are not. Check the level of the fluid in the windscreen washer tank and the tyre pressure in the spare wheel (this should be between 42 and 28 psi). Check that the jets hit the screen in the right place (Chapter 10). Inspect the tyres, check pressures, and remove any flints from the treads.

Once every month

Get underneath the car with an inspection lamp. Check the brake and petrol lines for leaks and damage. Look at all the steering joint rubber covers to see that they are not split. Do the same for the boots on the Constant Velocity joints of the drive shafts. Check that the shock absorbers (dampers) are not leaking. Do not worry about the master cylinders, if they are leaking the fluid will be all over your feet, so you will know about them, but check the clutch slave cylinder for leaks and look to see if there are signs of oil or brake fluid coming from the rear brake drums. Repeat this on the disc calipers.

Now look in the engine compartment. Signs of oil mist mean leaks from hoses, find the leak and cure it. Check the wiring for signs of fraying and loose connections. Check the tension of the alternator belt. Service the air cleaner (Chapter 2 or 3). (If the car is working in dusty conditions this must be done more often).

Finally give everything a wipe round, and shut the lid for another month.

Once every six months

Preferably in the spring and the fall, remove the plugs from the rear brake drums and inspect the linings. Check the state of wear of the front brake pads, lubricate the distributor change the spark plugs for new or reconditioned ones do the same for the CB points, and check the free play on the clutch and brake pedals. Look at the top of the front spring struts and check for rust in the body anchorage. Look for signs of rust around the wishbone brackets on the rear axle carrier and check the state of the hollow bump stops. Measure the free play at the steering wheel rim and compare it with that of six months ago.

If you carry out all this inspection and lubricate properly the car should survive. If the repairs described in the manual are done when faults are found then the car may be kept in a roadworthy condition. However, remember that you need the VW agent as a friendly ally not as a business rival, and you can do little if he doesn't supply the parts.

Preventative maintenance

As stated above the car will survive on Basic maintenance but it certainly will not be a saleable asset for long, if kept on this

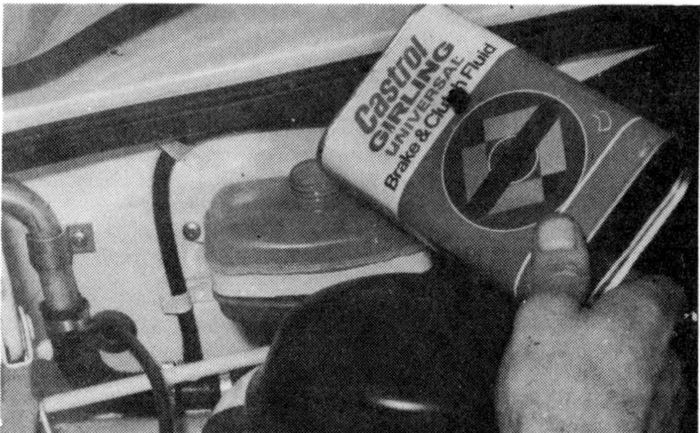

R.M.2 Filling the brake/clutch header tank

R.M.3 Filling the engine with oil

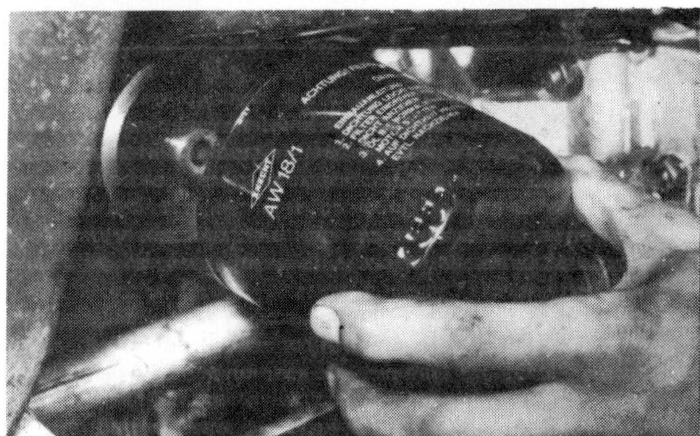

R.M.4 Changing the oil filter

R.M.5 Filling the gearbox

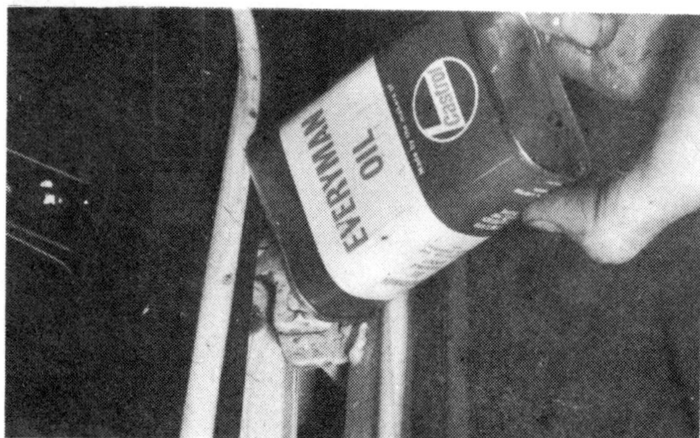

R.M.6 Oiling the door hinge

basis. The car should be washed and polished once a week, particular care being given to locate and deal with minor scratches and abrasions (Chapter 12). The interior needs a good clean and polish just as often as the rooms of a house if it is to maintain its appearance. The underside of the car should be rust proofed and checked freguently to make sure rust does not get a hold anywhere.

Windows should be washed clean and polished, as should

R.M.7 Oiling the filler flap

lamp lenses and reflectors.

A good coat of wax twice a year preserves the paint, and the bright work, and makes the removal of tar much easier.

If the car must travel on snow covered roads where salt has been used then the sooner the underside is pressure hosed the better to get the salt away.

Finally, it lasts much longer if it is kept in a garage and dried when it is put away.

Lubrication

(Capacity measure in Imperial pints, for U.S. pints multiply by 1.2).

ENGINE

Check the oil level every time the car is filled with petrol, top up as necessary with the recommended brand
Change the oil at 600 miles, 3000 miles, and then every 3000 miles thereafter. Capacity 6 pints with filter change, 5¼ without. Change the oil filter at 600 miles, 6000 miles and then every 6000 miles thereafter (once every two oil changes). Do not use additives.

AIR CLEANER

See Chapter 2 or 3.

MANUAL TRANSMISSION

Change the oil in the transmission at 600 miles (new car or new box), thereafter top up only (photo). Capacity of transmission 3.5 pints. Fill until the oil runs out of the filter hole. Note: Unless a leak is observed the gearbox rarely requires oil, but if a leak is seen top up right away.

AUTOMATIC TRANSMISSION

The transmission fluid (ATF) acts as the lubricant. ATF should be checked by the dipstick (Chapter 7) at the front of the engine compartment every 6000 miles. This should be done with the engine warm and running at idling speed with the selector at N. The difference between the marks is 0.7 pints Imp (0.84 US) and the level must be in between the marks. Use a funnel and 20" of plastic hose as a filler. Every 30,000 miles the ATF must be changed (18,000 if towing). Remove the plug (Chapter 7) and drain, fill with between 5.25 to 7 pints (Imp). Do not overfill.

There is quite a business about this. The oil pan should be removed and cleaned, then reinstalled with a new gasket. Do not move the vehicle or start the engine with no ATF in the transmission. Put in 4½ pints, start the engine, select all the gear positions (vehicle stationary) in turn, check the oil level with the gear lever at N, add fluid until the fluid shows on the dipstick, run the vehicle 2 miles then add ATF to the correct level. Check the oil pan gasket to torque 7 lb/ft.

LOCK CYLINDERS

Dip the key in graphite powder and insert into the lock every 3 months.

HINGES, LOCKS

Oil every 3 months.

DISTRIBUTOR

2 drops of engine oil on the felt of the shaft once a month, and a little grease on the cam.

FINAL DRIVE AND STEERING GEAR

No action required.

FRONT HUBS, REAR HUBS AND CV JOINTS

Depending on the nature of the work of the vehicle repack every two years, or more often (6 months) if used on very rough terrain, or at constant high speeds (motorways).

Recommended lubricants and fluids

Component	Grade	Castrol Grade
ENGINE	(Summer) SAE 30 or (Winter) SAE 20W - 50	CRI 30 (Summer), CRI 20 (Winter) or GTX (all seasons)
MANUAL GEARBOX	SAE 90 Hypoid oil to MIL-L 2 105B Specification. Use SAE 80 in Arctic	Castrol Hypoy B
AUTOMATIC GEARBOX	Dexron R B10100	Castrol TQ Dexron R
HUBS AND CV JOINTS	Multi purpose HMP Grease	Castrol LM Grease
AIR CLEANER	As engine	CRI 20, 30 or GTX
DISTRIBUTOR	As engine	CRI 20, 30 or GTX
LOCK CYLINDERS	Graphite powder	
HINGES AND LOCKS	As engine	Everyman Oil or CRI 20 or 30
BRAKE FLUID	Exceeds all required specifications	Castrol Girling Universal Brake and Clutch Fluid
CONTACT BREAKER AND BATTERY TERMINALS	Petroleum jelly	Vaseline

Lubrication chart

Frequencies are based on an average monthly mileage of 1000

ENGINE

Weekly: Check level and if necessary replenish with Castrol

3 Months: Drain off old oil while warm and refill with fresh, clean, Castrol.
Owners are advised that more frequent sump draining periods are derivable if the operation of the car involves:-
1) Frequent start/stop driving.
2) Operation during cold weather, especially when appreciable engine idling is involved, i.e. town operating conditions.
Capacity – 4.4 pints (2.5 litres).

TRANSMISSION

3 Months: Check level and if necessary top up to the edge or the filler plug hole with Castrol Hypoy Gear Oil.

2 Years: Drain off old oil while warm from the drain plug and refill with fresh Castrol Hypoy Gear Oil to the edge of the filler plug hole.
Capacity – 4.4 pints (2.5 litres).
5.25 pints (3 litres) from dry.

FRONT AND REAR WHEEL BEARINGS

2 Years: Remove hub clean out and re-pack with Castrol LM Grease

for VEHICLES WITH AUTOMATIC TRANSMISSION use Castrol TQ Dexron R for torque converter – Capacity 7.8 pints (3.6 litres)

Chapter 1 Engine, exhaust and cooling system

Contents

Specifications

Engine - general

Type	Horizontally opposed flat 4 cylinder air cooled, push rod overhead valve
Weight	277 lbs/126 kg
Bore	90 mm
Stroke	66 mm
Capacity	1679 cc

	Carburettors	**Fuel Injection**
Compression ratio	7.8 : 1	8.2 : 1
Power output DIN bhp/rpm	68/4500	80/4900
Torque mkg/rpm	12.7 din/2800	13.5 din/2800
ft lbs/rpm	93.3 SAE/3300	99.5 SAE/3500
Compression pressure - normal	114 - 142 psi	128 - 156 psi
(warm engine turned by starter) - minimum	100 psi	100 psi
Fuel octane	90	98

No. 1 cylinder location	Right front
Firing order	1 4 3 2

Engine EB Series (USA California August 1972 on)

Compression ratio	7.3 : 1 recessed crown pistons
Power output DIN bhp	72 at 5000 rpm
Torque DIN mkg	12.3 at 2700 rpm
Compression pressure - normal	85 - 132 psi
- minimum	71 psi
Fuel octane	91

Cooling system

Type	Radial fan on crankshaft
Air quantity	28.5 cu ft/800 litres per second at 4600 rpm
Thermostat opening temperature	65 - 70° C/149 - 158° F

Lubrication system

Type ...	Wet sump - pressure and splash	
Filter ...	Full floor - replacable cartridge	
Capacity - with filter change ...	3.5 litres/6.1 pints Imp/7.3 pints US	
- without filter change ...	3.0 litres/5.25 pints Imp/6.3 pints US	
Oil required to fill from the lower to upper marks of the dipstick ...	1 litre/1.75 pints Imp/2.1 pints US	
Oil pressure ...	SAE 30 70° C at 2500 rpm/42 psi	
Oil pressure ...	SAE 30 70° C at minimum/28 psi	
Oil warning light comes on between ...	2 - 6 psi	
Oil cooler ...	Pressurized, multi tube, air cooled	
Oil pump ...	Twin gear	
Oil pump gear/body end clearance ...	Nil	
Oil pump gear/backlash ...	Nil	
Oil pressure relief valve spring ...	Prior to March 1971, length 40 mm (1.57") at a loading of 4.2 to 5.1 kg (9.2 - 11.2 lb) After March 1971, length 39 mm (1.53") at a loading of 6.8 to 8.8 kg (15 - 19.4 lb)	
Oil pressure regulating valve spring ...	26 mm (1.02" at 1.7 - 2.0 kg (3.7 to 4.4 lb)	

Crankshaft and main bearings

No. of bearings ...	4	
Journal diameters - Nos. 1, 2, 3 ...	59.97 - 59.99 mm	2.3609 - 2.3617 in
- No. 4 ...	39.98 - 40.00 mm	1.5739 - 1.5748 in
Undersize main bearing shells ...	.25, .50, .75 mm	
Bearing shells - type Nos. 1, 3, 4 ...	Aluminium, lead coated	
- No. 2 ...	Split, 3 layer steel backed	
Bearing clearances - Nos. 1, 3 ...	.04 - .18 mm	.0016 - .007 in
- No. 2 ...	.03 - 17 mm	.0011 - .0066 in
- No. 4 ...	.05 - .19 mm	.0019 - .0074 in
Crankshaft end float limits ...	.07 - .15 mm	.0027 - .0051 in
Journals - maximum ovality ...	.03 mm	.0011 in

Crankcase

Main bearing bore diameters Nos. 1, 2, 3 ...	70.00 - 70.03 mm	2.7560 in 2.7580 in 2.7580 in
No. 4 ...	50.0 - 50.04 mm	1.9685 - 1.970 in
Oil seal bore diameter (flywheel end) ...	95.00 - 95.05 mm	3.7401 - 3.742 in
Oil seal bore diameter (fan pulley end) ...	62.00 - 62.05 mm	2.4410 - 2.4429 in
Camshaft bearing bore diameter ...	27.5 - 27.52 mm	1.0825 - 1.0852 in
Oil pump housing bore diameter ...	70.00 - 70.03 mm	2.7560 - 2.7580 in
Tappet (cam follower) bore diameters ...	24.00 - 24.05 mm	.9448 - .9467 in

Camshaft and bearings

Camshaft drive ...	Right alloy gear from crankshaft	
Bearings ...	White metal steel backed shells	
Journal diameters ...	24.99 mm -25.00 mm	.9837 - .9842 in
Bearing radial clearance ...	.02 - .12 mm	.0008 - .0047 in
End float ...	.04 - .16 mm	.0016 - .0063 in
Gear backlash ...	0 - .05 mm	0 - .0019 in

Connecting rods and bearings

Type ...	Forged steel	
Big end bearings ...	3 layer thin wall shells	
Crankpin diameter ...	54.98 - 55.00 mm	2.1644 - 2.1648 in
Small end bush ...	Steel bush lead bronze coated	
Undersize big end shells ...	.25 mm, .50 mm, .75 mm	
Big end clearance limits ...	.02 - .15 mm	.0008 - .006 in
Crankpin end float limits ...	.1 - .7 mm	.004 - .0016 in
Gudgeon (wrist) pin/bush clearance ...	.01 - .04 mm	.004 - .0016 in
Connecting rod weight (brown/white) ...	746 - 752 grams	
(grey/black) ...	769 - 775 grams	
Crankpin - maximum ovality ...	.03 mm	.0011 in

Cylinders

Type	Single barrel, finned, cast iron	
Oversizes	0.5 mm, 1.00 mm	.020 in, .040 in
Distance between centres	124.5 mm	4.9 in

Cylinder heads

Type	Aluminium alloy, 1 per pair of cylinders	
Combustion chamber capacity	51.6 - 52.6 cc	
Depth of cylinder seating	5.4 - 6.5 mm	.212 - .255 in

Pistons and rings

Type	Light alloy with steel inserts, domed crowns for fuel injection, flat crowns for carburettors	
Cylinder clearance limits	.04 - .20 mm	.0015 - .008 in
Ring/groove clearance - top compression	.06 - .12 mm	.0023 - .0047 in
- lower compression	.04 - .10 mm	.0015 - .0039 in
- oil control	.02 - .10 mm	.0008 - .0039 in
Piston oversizes	.05 mm, 1.0 mm	
Gudgeon (wrist) pin	Fully floating, steel tube	
Gudgeon pin diameter - carburettor	22.996 - 23.00 mm	.9052 - .9055 in
- fuel injection	24 mm	.9455 in
Top compression ring gap limit	.35 - .90 mm	.014 - .035 in
Lower compression ring gap limit	.30 - .90 mm	.012 - .035 in
Oil control ring gap limit	.25 - .95 mm	.010 - .037 in

Tappets (cam followers)

Type	Cylindrical, flat based	
Diameter	23.96 - 23.98 mm	.9422 - .9440 in

Pushrods and valve rockers

Pushrod type	Hollow cylindrical with hemispherical ends	
Rocker shaft diameter	19.95 - 19.97 mm	.7854 - .7862 in

Valves, valve seats and timing

Inlet - head diameter (carburettor)	37.5 mm	1.476 in
(fuel injection)	39 mm	1.536 in
- stem diameter	7.94 - 7.9 mm	.3125 - .3109 in
- seat width	1.8 - 2.2 mm	.07 - .086 in
- seat angle	30°	
- guide bore diameter	8.00 - 8.06 mm	.3149 - .3156 in
- maximum rock in guide	.9 mm	.035 in
Exhaust - head diameter	33 mm	1.299 in
- stem diameter	8.91 - 8.87 mm	.3507 - .3491 in
- seat width	2.0 - 2.5 mm	.08 - .098 in
- seat angle	45°	
- guide bore diameter	9.0 - 9.06 mm	.3543 - .3566 in
- maximum rock in guide	.9 mm	.035 in
Seat width correction angle - inner	75°	
- outer	15°	
Springs - loaded length	29 mm	1.14 in
- load	80 kg 176 lb	
Valve clearances (all)	.15 mm	.006 in

Valve timing (Code V, early engines)

Inlet opens	4° BTDC
Inlet closes	39° ABDC
Exhaust opens	40° BBDC
Exhaust closes	3° ATDC

Valve timing (Code Z, later engines)

Inlet opens	12° BTDC
Inlet closes	42° ABDC
Exhaust opens	43° BBDC
Exhaust closes	4° ATDC

Torque wrench settings:	lb ft	mkg
Fan screws (M8)	14	2.0
Fan hub screws	23	3.2
Oil pump nuts	14	2.0
Oil drain plug	16	2.2
Oil strainer cover nuts	9	1.3
Rocker shaft standard nuts	10	1.4
Cylinder head nuts	23	3.2
Engine carrier to crankcase nuts	22	3.0
Flywheel screws	80	11.0
Crankcase screws M8	14	2.0
Crankcase nuts	22	3.0
Connecting rod screws	24	3.3
Engine mounting to body screws	18	2.5
Torque converter drive plate screws	61	8.5
Torque converter screws	14	2.0

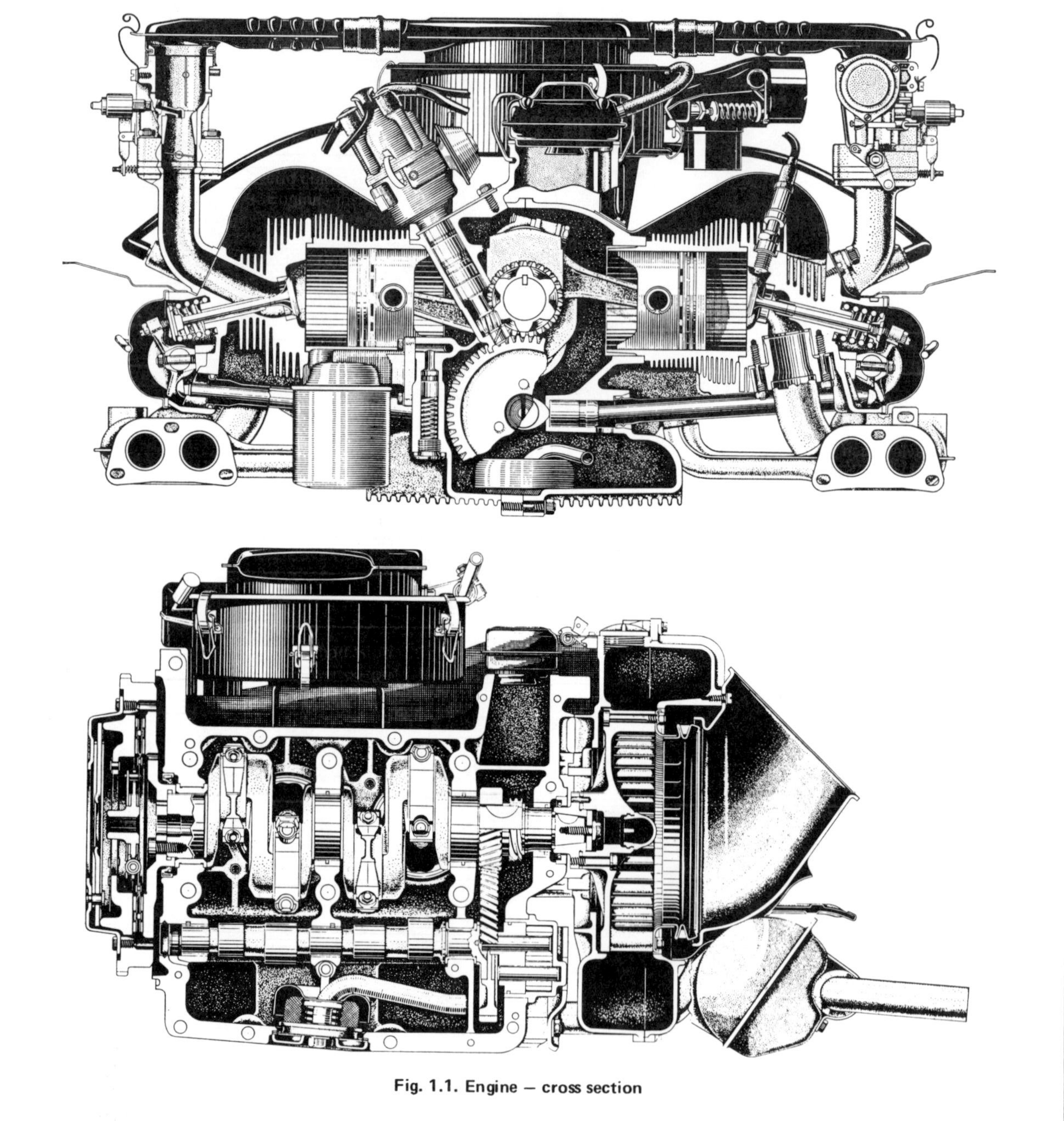

Fig. 1.1. Engine — cross section

1 General description

1 The four cylinder air cooled engine is bolted to the transmission unit and the whole power pack is held in the car by four mountings. When the two drive shafts have been taken off and various air and petrol hoses disconnected and a number of electrical connections unplugged, the mounting bolts may be withdrawn and the whole unit lowered away from the rear of the car and taken away underneath.

Alternatively the engine may be taken out without moving the gearbox and thus without having to remove the drive shafts, although it is more difficult to install by this method.

With the engine comes the exhaust system and all the cooling and heating arrangements. It is not possible to discuss engine overhaul and cooling/heating/exhaust system repair separately so the whole unit is covered in this Chapter.

The detailed overhaul of the gearboxes is discussed in other Chapters, as is the fuel system, both carburettor and fuel injection and the ignition system. These are therefore not included in this Chapter except for passing reference.

2 The engine is a flat horizontally opposed fourstroke, a larger version of the 'suitcase' fitted to the Type 3 VW. It is totally enclosed in sheet metal and aluminium castings in such a way that the cooling may be thermostatically controlled to small limits. The fan, mounted on the end of the crankshaft sucks air from a ducted system and blows it over the engine in a guided and variable system of ducts allowing the engine to warm up quickly and then opening flaps to provide a cooling air stream which increases in volume as the speed of the engine increases.

3 The layout of the engine is normal VW style, a split crankcase containing the crankshaft, camshaft, and oil pump; camshaft, oil pump and distributor being driven by gearing off the end of the crankshaft.

The cylinders are finned castings arranged in pairs with one cylinder head for each pair. Overhead valves (although in VW engines these are at the side!), are operated by pushrods bearing on followers activated by the camshaft, and the conventional rocker gear and valve springs.

4 Alloy pistons have steel inserts and are fitted with two compression and one spring loaded scraper ring. The gudgeon (piston) pins are fully floating and retained in place by circlips.

5 Split shell bearings are fitted to the big ends, camshaft bearings and one of the main bearings. The other main bearings are circular shells in one piece.

6 Lubrication is by pressure feed from the pump, the pressure regulated by a relief valve at the end of the circuit. An oil cooler is fitted and for the first time on this type of engine a renewable filter with a bypass valve. The usual VW strainer is fitted to the pump suction. A warning light operates from a pressure switch which lights the lamp at pressures below 6 pounds/square inch.

7 The engine is much heavier than the Type 3, it provides a lift for which four men are required in its unit form, so if you are thinking of moving it by yourself, think again.

A cross section drawing is shown at Fig.1.1 and two photographs show the front and rear views of the engine removed from the vehicle without the gearbox. (photos)

8 Although no work may be carried out on the engine itself, other than routine maintenance, without removing it from the car, this does not include those items classed as ancillaries and forming part of the electrical, ignition or fuel systems. For details of these refer to the appropriate Chapter.

The tables below give an idea of the degree of dismantling required once the engine is removed in order to renew or repair various items.

a) Not necessary to split the crankcase.
   Cylinder heads and valves
   Oil cooler
   Fan and cooling systems
   Oil pump
   Cylinders
   Pistons and rings

1.7a The engine as it comes from the chassis without the gearbox The inlet manifolds are the large pipes on the top.

1.7b The rear view of the engine. The 'big mouth' is the air inlet to the fan casing. The exhaust and rear engine mountings are still in place but the front mounting is still in the vehicle supporting the gearbox.

   Flywheel
   Crankshaft oil seals

b) Necessary to split the crankcase.
   Camshaft
   Crankshaft and main bearings
   Distributor drive gear
   Camshaft bearings
   Big end bearings

2 Engine removal - preparation

Removal is quite straightforward but some basic tools are essential if accidents and damage are to be avoided. As the engine is quite shallow it is not necessary to raise the rear of the car more than 24 inches in order to draw the engine out once it has been lowered. If the engine is resting on a trolley jack, or blocks, then the depth of this must also be taken into account. Suitable ramps on to which the rear wheels may be stood are the safest way of raising the rear of the car. At a pinch, two VW car jacks can be used to raise the car but these must be supplemented by blocks under the rear wheels to hold the car up.

A trolley jack is ideal for lowering the engine. Otherwise use two scissor jacks with a piece of stout plank between them.

If the car is very dirty underneath it would be well worthwhile getting it thoroughly cleaned off away from the removal area first. The lower mounting stud nuts call for a certain amount of reaching around. If you are working on your back at floor level dirt falling in the eyes can be a major irritation.

It is better to remove the engine and transmission together although this entails more work. Reassembly is much easier this way. However both methods are given.

It is possible to get the engine out and clear single-handed if all the foregoing equipment is available but the trickiest part is lowering the engine to floor level. Assistance is insurance against dropping it. Even a few inches fall could crack the aluminium crankcase - there being no conventional sump. Note that the engine is back-to-front as compared with a conventional layout so that the flywheel is at the front. All references to front and rear of the engine will, therefore, be in relation to its position in the car.

At first sight the engine is a little frightening, however if you remove the parts enumerated in Sections 5 or 7 depending on the type of engine, the engine can be unbolted and taken out with or without the gearbox. It isn't really as hard as it looks. It is a good idea to label the parts of the F.I. system so that you can put your hand on them more or less automatically.

Drain all the oil from the engine while it is hot and on a level keel if you can. The oil drain plug is in the centre of the sump, a 19 mm socket spanner is required.

3 Engine removal - carburettor engine - preparatory work

1 This Section concerns the removal of those parts connecting the power unit with the chassis before the engine, with or without the gearbox can be removed from the vehicle.
2 Disconnect the battery (Chapter 10) and pull off the plug from under the voltage regulator (Chapter 10).
3 Remove the cooling air duct with the warm air fan and hose.
4 Disconnect the oil filler hose and the dipstick hose.
5 Remove the ignition coil and bracket.
6 Disconnect the cables from the oil pressure switch.
7 Remove the air cleaner (Chapter 2).
8 Disconnect the accelerator cable.
9 Remove the engine compartment seal.
10 On the automatic gearbox model remove the three M8 screws from the convertor through the access holes and remove the gearbox oil dipstick and rubber boot.
11 Now lift the vehicle and from underneath remove the muffler shield.
12 Working underneath the vehicle disconnect the heat exchanger control boxes with hoses and cables.
13 Pull off the fuel hose from thepump and seal the hose (on the automatic take the vacuum hose off the balance pipe).
14 Remove the heater booster exhaust pipe.
15 Pull the accelerator cable and the heater blower cable out of the engine compartment.
16 The engine is now ready for removal. Now turn to Section 5 or 7, depending whether the engine or the engine and gearbox are to be removed.

4 Engine removal - Fuel injection engine - preparatory work

1 Disconnect the battery.
2 Remove the cooling air duct, air intakes, bellows, warm air fan and hoses.
3 Remove the hoses to the air cleaner and take out the air cleaner (Chapter 3).
4 Remove the oil filler boot and the dipstick tube boot.
5 Take away the cooling air bellows from the body.
6 Now look around at the various wires connecting the engine to the chassis. Remove them and hang them on one side but label each one as you do it. Get a small piece of mirror and look under the voltage regulator (Chapter 10) and pull out the plug.
7 Remove the coil and its bracket. Locate the oil pressure switch, label the connections and pull them off.
8 Disconnect the accelerator cable and feed it back through the bulkhead. Take the vacuum hose off the warm air distributor.
9 The pressure sensor stays behind up on the left of the engine compartment, remove the hose from it.
10 Disconnect the heat exchangers at the front end.
11 On the automatic gearbox model remove the screws from the converter through the access holes.
12 Remove the fuel hoses from the injection ring main and the return line. Remove the heater booster exhaust pipe.
13 The power unit is now ready for removal.

5 Engine removal without gearbox

1 It is necessary to remove the drive shaft from the clutch. This is done by removing the rear seat and the cover over the drive shaft access hole. Refer to Chapter 6, Fig. 6.5. Screw the drive shaft plug out, remove the hexagon nut from the drive shaft, screw VW tool 796 (which is a universal joint wrench) onto the shaft and push the circlip out of the groove by tapping lightly on the wrench. Pull the shaft forward about 4 inches (100 mm).
2 If you do not have a tool VW 796 then it is possible to do it this way. Use a 15 mm socket and slacken back the circular nut three or four threads. Tap the top of the socket, then remove the socket and wrench and using a pair of long nosed pliers pull the shaft and the nut forward. The circlip can then be removed and put in a safe place. Now pull the shaft out until it has come forward a total of 4 inches.
3 Remove the screws securing the transmission carrier to the body. (photo) To do this first support the engine on a trolley jack with a suitable piece of wood packing. (photo) On the Variant the muffler shield fairing should also be removed. (photo) The screws are in the top of the bulkhead behind rubber plugs and can be seen on Fig.6.1, Chapter 6. There is an M.10 nut on the inside and a second person will be needed to hold a spanner on them. If they are difficult it may be necessary to lift the car and then ease the engine weight again.
4 The engine is now firmly on the jack so make sure the jack cannot move.
5 Now support the gearbox with a jack. Make sure it is firm and then remove the two bolts securing the top of the gearbox to the engine. This can be done from inside the engine compartment. In effect now the transmission carrier beam is neither connected to the vehicle or the gearbox so that the carrier will move down with the gearbox as the gearbox is juggled to do the next bit. It is possible to do the job with the carrier still bolted to the body but much harder to get the engine off the lower studs. This is the next job.
6 First remove the four screws holding the engine cross beam to the vehicle. (photo) The engine is now held only by the lower studs to the gearbox. These are quite long studs, so be careful. Remove the nuts. By carefully lowering the engine and manipulating the gearbox the engine can be drawn off the studs to the back. If the stud threads are damaged they will have to be rethreaded or replaced.
7 It is quite a tricky business to guide the F.I. engine out of the compartment as the injectors are close to the lip on one side. Hold the engine all the way down and when it is on the floor pull it out to the rear. (photo)
8 As soon as the engine is safely parked put a piece of wood across the engine compartment aperture and sling the gearbox (see Chapter 6, photo 2.3).
9 The weather seal may now be removed.

6 Engine replacement - gearbox in vehicle

1 Lift the engine onto the trolley jack supported by suitable packing.
2 Clean the transmission case and engine flanges carefully.
3 Install the engine compartment seal to the cover plates with the water deflecting side downwards. Put a strong thin (nylon ?) cord in the slot. Remove the sling from the gearbox.
4 Push the engine under the car and lift it until it is about 4 inches from the body. Feed the accelerator cable through the hole in the bulkhead as the engine goes up. Now feed the engine into position over the lower gearbox studs. When it is in position install the nuts, now install the two upper gearbox bolts and tighten them.
5 Ease the engine carrier upwards into the slots in the brackets so that the screws are at the top of the elongated holes. Watch that the transmission carrier beam does not foul the mountings and prevent the engine from going up. If it does, move to paragraph 6. Fit new locking tabs and torque to 18 lbs ft.

5.3a The bolts holding the transmission carrier to the rubber mountings come out through the bulkhead.

5.3b Engine supported on trolley jack for lowering. This picture is showing the engine half way down

5.3c The snuffler shield must be removed on the Variant

5.6 The screws holding the engine carrier to the body brackets.

5.7 Engine safely lowered and removed to the rear.

6 It now remains to feed the transmission carrier beam into place. It may be that it prevented the engine from going up, in which case slacken off the studs holding the rubber mountings to the body and remove the packing pieces. This will give enough play to enter the carrier beam, and allow the engine to go into place. Replace the packing pieces and tighten up everything as soon as the carrier has entered.

7 Now replace the bolts holding the clutch housing to the carrier beam from inside the engine compartment, and fit the nuts from underneath the car. Tighten up all round and check that the engine carrier is vertical and parallel to the fan housing and that the two rubber mountings do not touch the housing. If necessary the brackets on the body must be adjusted. Lower the vehicle to the ground.

8 Work underneath and check that the gearbox shift lever is correctly placed in the hole through the rear axle carrier. It should be 23 mm from the bottom of the hole to the bottom of the shaft and equidistant (25.5mm) from each side. If it isn't then the transmission carrier must be repositioned to give sideways movement, and the engine carrier to give vertical movement. The distances can best be checked by cutting out a sheet metal gauge and slipping it between the shaft and the carrier.

9 Now reconnect all the bits and pieces. If everything was labelled then life is easy. If it was not refer to Chapter 3 for the fuel ignition system reconnection.

10 Push the drive shaft forward until it touches the clutch splines then turn it until the splines enter. Refit the circlip and tighten the nut. Install the cap and cover and replace the back seat.

11 Refit the accelerator cable and adjust it, Chapters 2/3.

12 Tuning of the carburettors is discussed in Chapter 2, Ignition in Chapter 3.

7 Engine and transmission - removal as a unit

1 Depending upon whether the engine is fitted with a carburettor or Fuel Injection remove the top hamper as in Section 3 or 4.

2 Working underneath the car disconnect the gearbox shift rod from the gear lever shift rod at the connection in front of the rear axle carrier. Remove the locking wire, undo the square headed nut and pull out the joint. There are photos of this in Chapter 6.

3 Remove the cables from the starter. Label them and note which terminal they come from. This is a patient job done mostly by feel.

4 Now remove the bolts connecting the drive shafts to the final drive flanges. This is described in detail in Chapter 8. Cover the C.V. joints with polythene bags to keep them clean.

5 Undo the clip which holds the hydraulic pipe for the clutch slave cylinder so that the pipe may be moved easily. Remove the slave cylinder. Do not disconnect it. See Chapter 5.

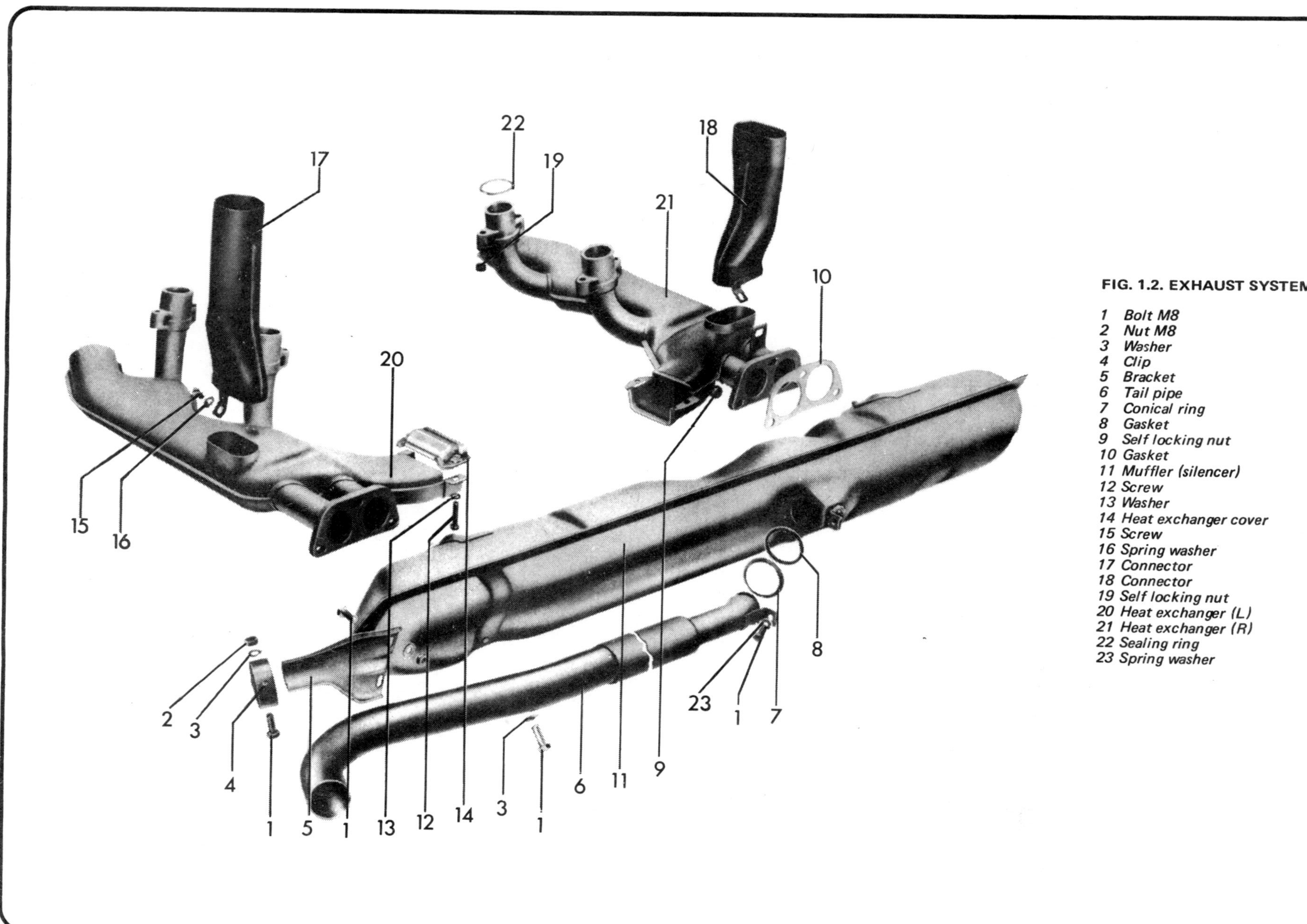

FIG. 1.2. EXHAUST SYSTEM

1 Bolt M8
2 Nut M8
3 Washer
4 Clip
5 Bracket
6 Tail pipe
7 Conical ring
8 Gasket
9 Self locking nut
10 Gasket
11 Muffler (silencer)
12 Screw
13 Washer
14 Heat exchanger cover
15 Screw
16 Spring washer
17 Connector
18 Connector
19 Self locking nut
20 Heat exchanger (L)
21 Heat exchanger (R)
22 Sealing ring
23 Spring washer

6 On the automatic gearbox model take the cables from the kick down switch to the control solenoid off at the lower end.
7 At this stage the engine and gearbox unit is disconnected from the chassis except for the transmission carrier and the engine carrier. Remove the plugs from the front cover plate so that the bolts for the transmission carrier are visible, undo the nuts from underneath the car and with-draw these bolts. (photo 5.3a). It will be necessary to support the engine on a jack to take the weight so that the bolts will come out. Use suitable wood packing and position the jack as shown in photo 5.3b. If the carrier bolts are still obstinate loosen the screws holding the rubber mountings to the body and remove the packing pieces. Replace them as soon as the carrier is clear of the rubber mountings and retighten the screws.
8 The four screws holding the engine carrier should now be removed (photo 5.6). On the Variant the muffler fairing must also be removed (5.3c) before you can get at the engine carrier.
9 Lower the engine gently, as soon as it is clear of the mounting withdraw it to the rear so that the gear shift rod comes out of the hole in the rear axle carrier, and then lower it to the ground.
10 Keep a good look round as you lower. The fuel injection engine is a fairly close fit through the engine compartment aperture. If anything seems to be holding up, raise the engine a little and find out what it is, clear it, and then lower again.
11 Once the engine is on the ground remove it to the rear and support it on blocks. Blank off the hole from which the clutch slave cylinder came and get to work cleaning off all the dirt from the transmission and engine unit . It will not be possible to get underneath at this stage but get as must as possible off before splitting the transmission from the engine.
12 The transmission carrier is still in place. Undo the nuts and remove the bolts. Watch where the various plastic washers and spring washers come from (Fig.6.1 refers). Put the bolts, washers and nuts back in the carrier after it has been cleaned so that they will be to hand for reassembly.
13 Undo the lower nuts and draw the transmission off the studs leaving the engine ready for overhaul.

8 Engine and transmission - reinstallation as a unit

1 This is dealt with at the end of the engine overhaul section. The installation described is for the fuel injection engine; the carburettor engine is identical except that of course the final assembly after installation is much more simple. For the Carburettor type engine reinstall the fuel supply and then refit the carburettor and air cleaner as described in Chapter 2. The fuel pump should be assembled before the engine is installed (Chap. 2). Connection and tuning of the linkages is described in Chapter 2.

9 Exhaust system and heat exchangers

1 The removal and reassembly of the exhaust system and the heat exchangers is discussed in the engine sections but it is as well to understand the system before going further.
2 The whole exhaust system comes away with the engine . It is built of much heavier material than the average system and can be welded or repaired if split. Refer to Fig. 1.2.
3 The tail pipe may be removed with the engine in situ, as can the muffler (silencer) itself, although the screws are difficult to get at. There the matter stops. For the remainder the dismantling of the heat exchangers and connectors, is possible only when dismantling the engine. The heat exchangers must be disconnected at the front end before running the engine.
4 The pipes from the exhaust ports pass through the heat exchangers and discharge their contents direct into the muffler. Fresh air passes round these pipes and suitably warmed is supplied to the engine and body under controlled arrangements.

10 Lubrication system

1 The oil is drawn from the crankcase by the suction tube via a strainer which removes the larger impurities. Fig.1.3 refers.
2 The gear type pump delivers the oil to a filter (the first time this type of engine has had such a device) which is fitted with a spring loaded valve bypass. From the filter (or bypass) the oil goes to a cooler which again has a bypass valve, depending upon the pressure, which in turn depends on the temperature. The cold high pressure oil thus does not go through the cooler.
3 From the cooler (or bypass valve) the oil is distributed to the various bearings from which it returns to the sump. At the end of the pressure line is yet another pressure valve which controls the pressure in the bearing circuit.
4 An oil pressure switch is included in the system. For SAE 30 at 70°C (158°F) the pressure at the switch for engine revolutions of 2500 rpm should be 42 lbs per square inch. If this pressure sinks below 28 lbs sq. inch then remedial action in the bearing circuit or pump is indicated.
5 A cross section of the oil filter is given at Fig. 1.4. When changing the filter ensure that the sealing surface on the oil filter flange is clean, oil the seal lightly and screw in the filter by hand as far as it will go. For tightening further a special wrench is required, but doubtless the owner will manage to improvise. Start the engine and check for leaks, top up as required.

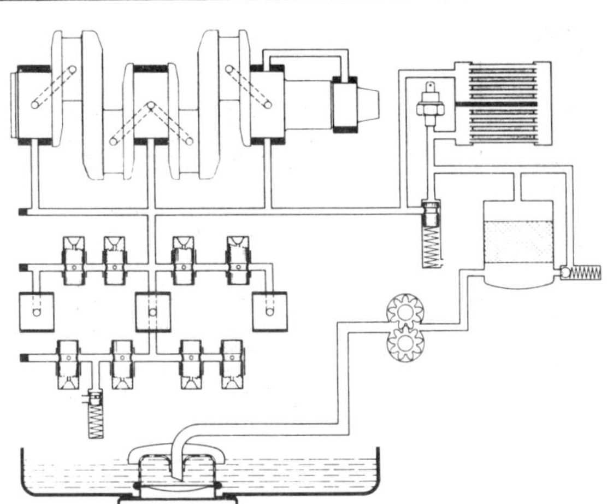

Fig. 1.3. Diagrammatic layout of the Lubrication System

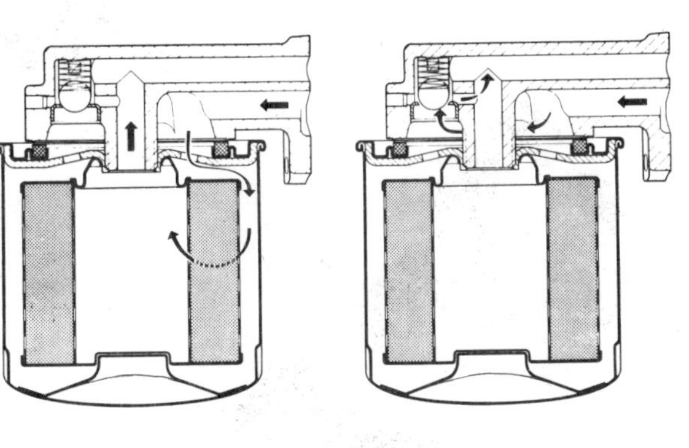

Fig. 1.4. Oil filter — cross section
When the filter is blocked the ball valve in the flange opens ensuring a supply of oil (unfiltered) to the engine bearings. (Left) normal oil circuit (Right) oil circuit through bypass valve

11 Cooling system and cover plates

1 Refer to Figs. 1.5 and 1.6.

2 The various pieces of metal which cover the engine are divided into those which have a function guiding the air, and those which fill in the remainder of the spaces. They all seem to supply the same function, however it is important to realize what the names are if the engine is to be assembled correctly.

3 Fig.1.7 shows the layout of the fan and fan casing together with the alternator and the flaps which either exclude, or allow air to blow round the engine from the fan housing. These flaps are actuated by a thermostat set inside the engine compartment which moves a wire connected to a lever.

4 It is most important that all of these plates are in good order and are fitted correctly with good air seals so that the air passing over the engine does not penetrate the interior of the body. Any such fumes, apart from being offensive, can be dangerous to the health of the driver and passengers.

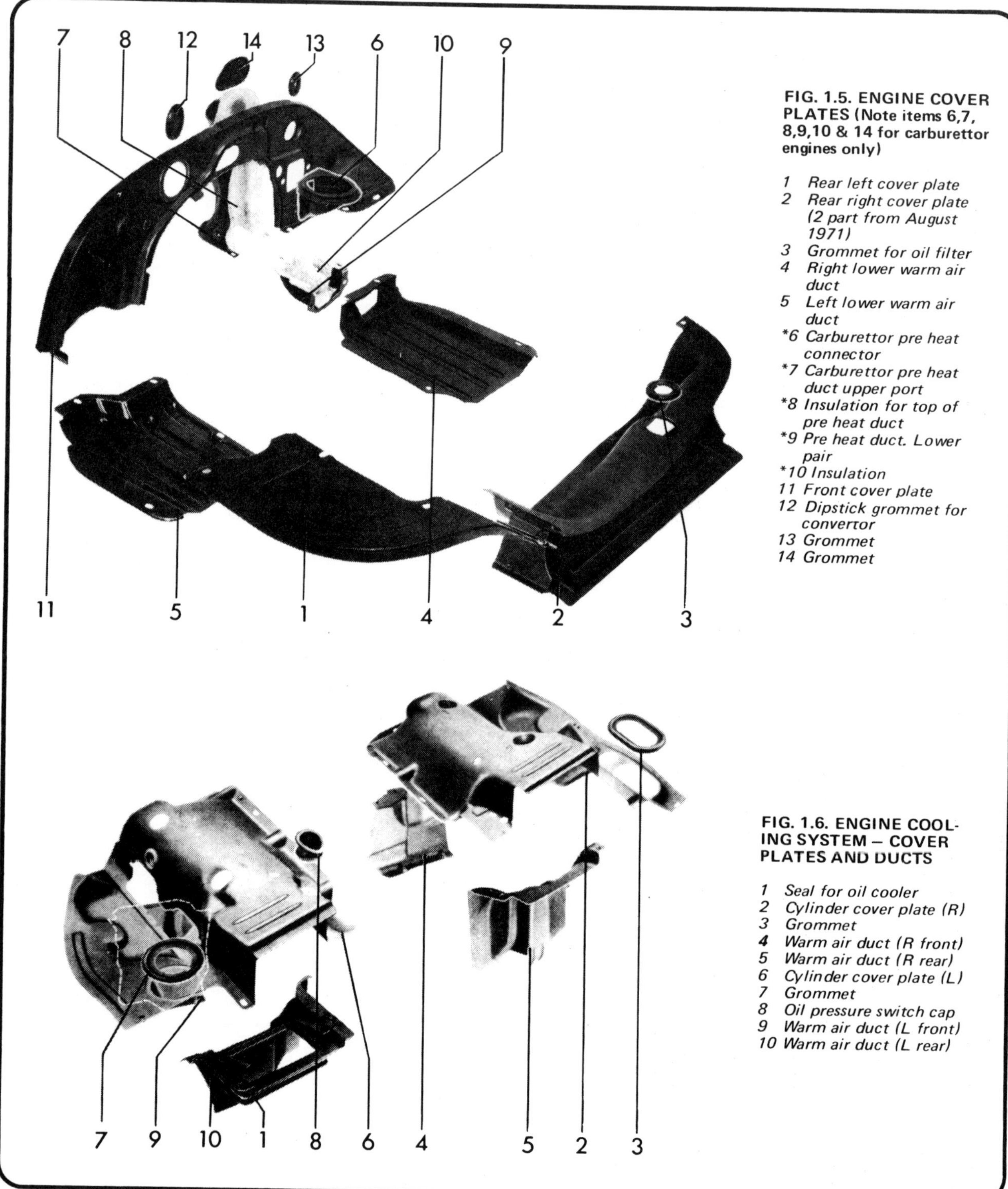

FIG. 1.5. ENGINE COVER PLATES (Note items 6,7, 8,9,10 & 14 for carburettor engines only)

1 Rear left cover plate
2 Rear right cover plate (2 part from August 1971)
3 Grommet for oil filter
4 Right lower warm air duct
5 Left lower warm air duct
**6 Carburettor pre heat connector*
**7 Carburettor pre heat duct upper port*
**8 Insulation for top of pre heat duct*
**9 Pre heat duct. Lower pair*
**10 Insulation*
11 Front cover plate
12 Dipstick grommet for convertor
13 Grommet
14 Grommet

FIG. 1.6. ENGINE COOLING SYSTEM – COVER PLATES AND DUCTS

1 Seal for oil cooler
2 Cylinder cover plate (R)
3 Grommet
4 Warm air duct (R front)
5 Warm air duct (R rear)
6 Cylinder cover plate (L)
7 Grommet
8 Oil pressure switch cap
9 Warm air duct (L front)
10 Warm air duct (L rear)

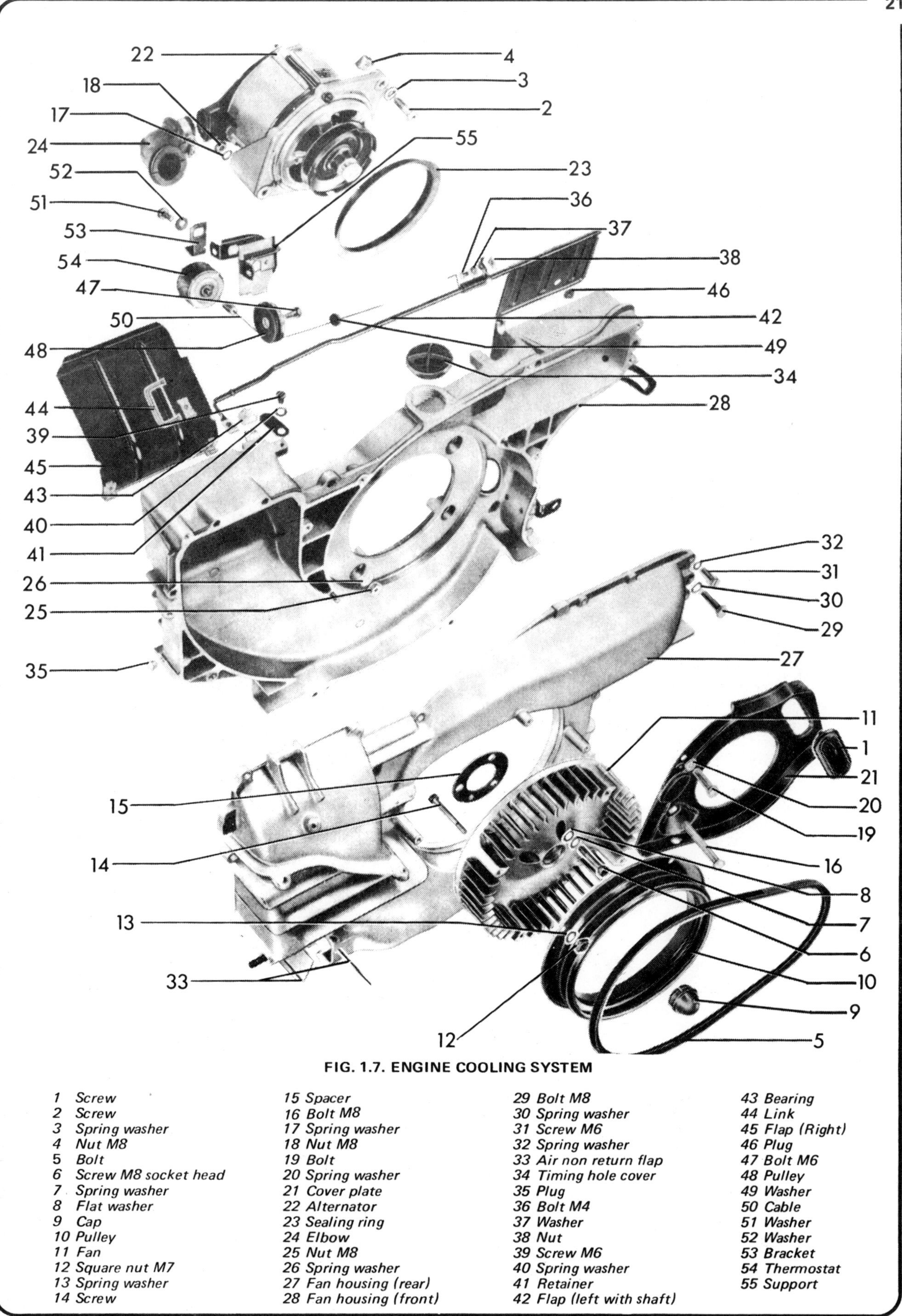

FIG. 1.7. ENGINE COOLING SYSTEM

1 Screw
2 Screw
3 Spring washer
4 Nut M8
5 Bolt
6 Screw M8 socket head
7 Spring washer
8 Flat washer
9 Cap
10 Pulley
11 Fan
12 Square nut M7
13 Spring washer
14 Screw
15 Spacer
16 Bolt M8
17 Spring washer
18 Nut M8
19 Bolt
20 Spring washer
21 Cover plate
22 Alternator
23 Sealing ring
24 Elbow
25 Nut M8
26 Spring washer
27 Fan housing (rear)
28 Fan housing (front)
29 Bolt M8
30 Spring washer
31 Screw M6
32 Spring washer
33 Air non return flap
34 Timing hole cover
35 Plug
36 Bolt M4
37 Washer
38 Nut
39 Screw M6
40 Spring washer
41 Retainer
42 Flap (left with shaft)
43 Bearing
44 Link
45 Flap (Right)
46 Plug
47 Bolt M6
48 Pulley
49 Washer
50 Cable
51 Washer
52 Washer
53 Bracket
54 Thermostat
55 Support

12 Engine dismantling - heads, cylinders, pistons; cooling, exhaust and lubrication systems

1 The engine as removed from the vehicle, with the gearbox taken away is cleaned and set up on a suitable bench.
2 Plenty of containers, a tray to catch surplus oil, metric spanners ring, socket, and open end are required, together with drifts, screwdrivers, a suitable extractor, hide and ball peen hammers, and a set of Allan keys (metric). Other useful tools are a blow lamp and a mole grip.
3 Plenty of clean non-fluffy rag and a paraffin cleaning bath are necessary.
4 Remove the injectors and manifold complete (Chapter 3) (photo).
5 Next the silencer. This requires a little patience to remove the six screws which are sure to be rusted in. (photo).
6 Now remove the right rear cover plate unscrewing four screws from underneath. (photo)
7 Using the correct tools slacken the fan adjuster nut and remove the fan belt. If the nut is obstinate remove the stay at the back of the fan adjuster and ease the cover for the alternator away so that you can get a mole wrench on the nut.
8 Remove the right lower warm air duct (Fig. 1.5) (photo).
9 Now the right hand heat exchanger may be removed using a socket spanner from underneath. This will probably be a stiff fit and a little tapping with a hide hammer may be necessary. (photo)
10 Now remove the alternator completely. Undo the nut at the back and remove the bolt. (photo), then the alternator; (photo) and finally the cover plate. The grommet round the dipstick pipe may be stuck and require easing away (photo).
11 The remainder of the cover plates should now be removed, noting carefully where they go and which flange goes over which. Now remove the left hand heat exchanger and set it to one side. (photos).
12 The engine proper is now exposed. Look around and mark the cylinder heads, cylinders, crankcase etc., in such a way as to be able to reassemble them in the same place after overhaul. Use paint, centre punch marks, sticky tape, or any other method, but mark them.
13 Remove the clutch, six bolts, which comes away in one piece (photo).
holding the fan to the crankshaft and draw off the fan (photos).
15 Remove the cable from the flap control lever (photo).
16 Undo the four bolts holding the fan housing and wriggle the fan housing off past the oil filler tube (photos).
17 Remove the engine carrier from the crankcase and examine the rubber mountings very carefully. The one we dismantled had a broken rubber mounting. Replace if necessary.
18 Undo the three nuts and remove the oil cooler (photo). Preserve the seals and note carefully how they fit. The cooler pulls off sideways.
19 Now undo the five bolts from the centre of the flywheel, remove the spacer and tap the flywheel gently off the crankshaft (photo). Take care not to damage the locating pin which remains in the crankshaft hub.
20 Start with the L.H. head. Remove the valve covers and rockers complete with rocker shaft. Pull out the push rods, watch what you are doing because they are hollow and will be full of oil which is a trap for the unwary. Note how the spring fits under the rocker shaft.
21 Refer to Fig. 1.8 for details of the cylinder heads. Refer to Fig. 1.12 which gives the tightening sequence for cylinder head bolts and using a reverse sequence slacken and remove the cylinder head nuts. Remove the screw from the deflector plate to the cylinder head; and then the two screws holding the deflector plate to the crankcase and the head may be drawn off with the deflector plate (photos). Note the sealing rings at the top and bottom of the cylinders. Remove the gaskets from the exhaust ports. Pull out the push rod tubes marking them to ensure correct assembly.
22 Now repeat the process for the other cylinder head.

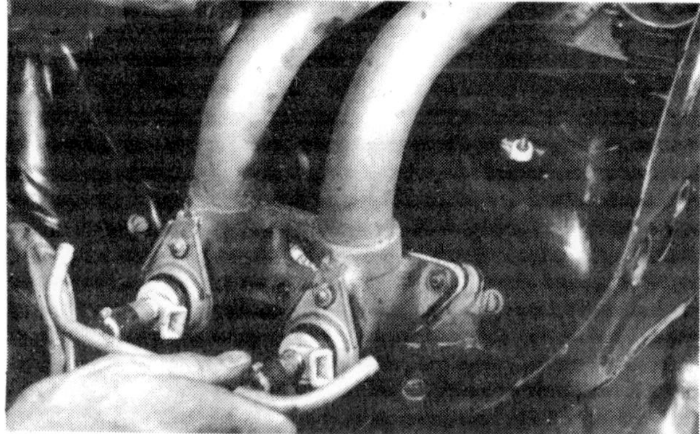

12.4 Remove the injectors complete with manifolds.

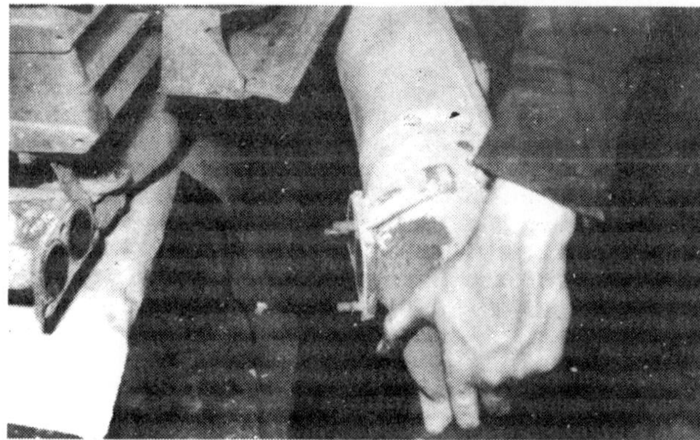

12.5 Remove the silencer

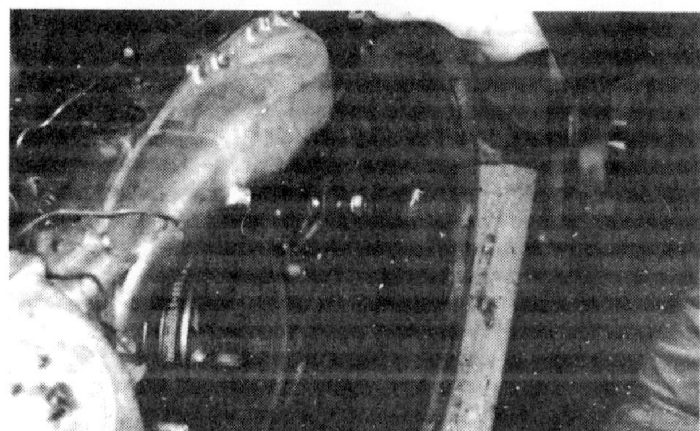

12.6 ... and the right rear cover plate

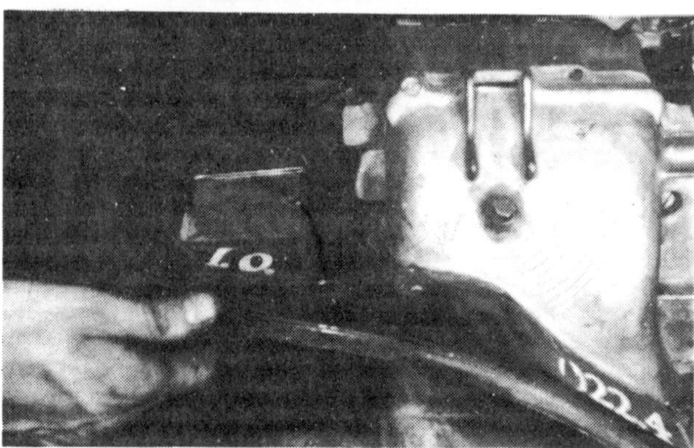

12.8 Remove the right lower warm air duct

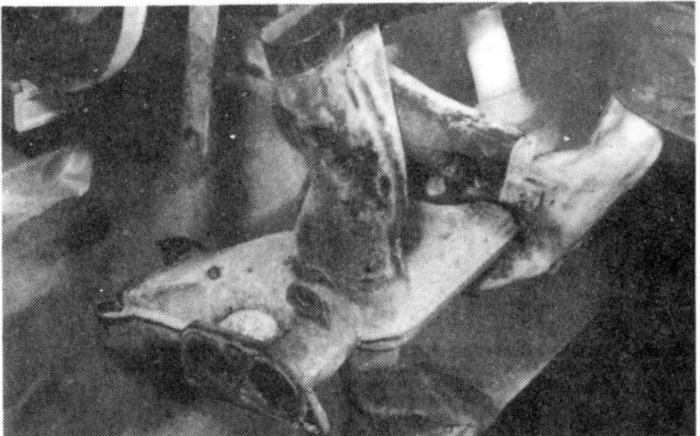
12.9 Remove the right hand heat exchanger

12.10a Remove the alternator bolt

12.10b ... then the alternator ...

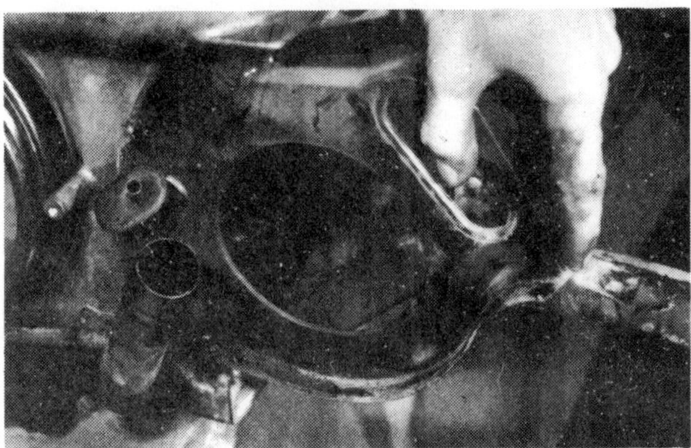
12.10c ... and finally the alternator cover plate (watch for the dip stick tube grommet)

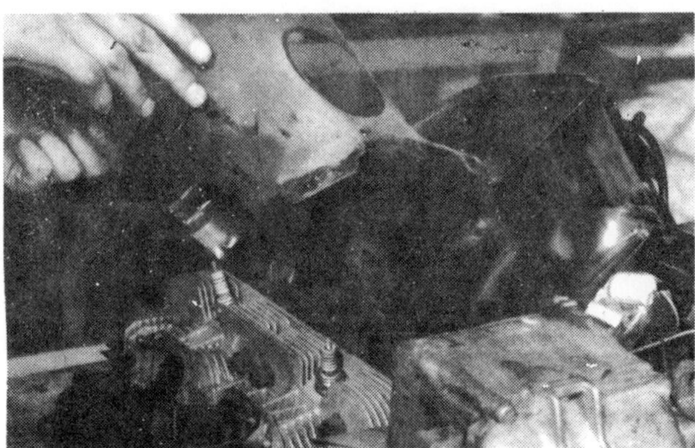
12.11a Removing the left cylinder cover plate

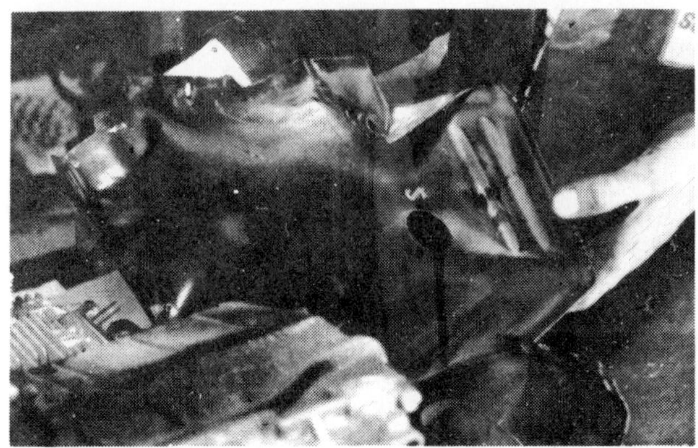
12.11b Removing the right cylinder cover plate

12.13 Remove the clutch (six bolts)

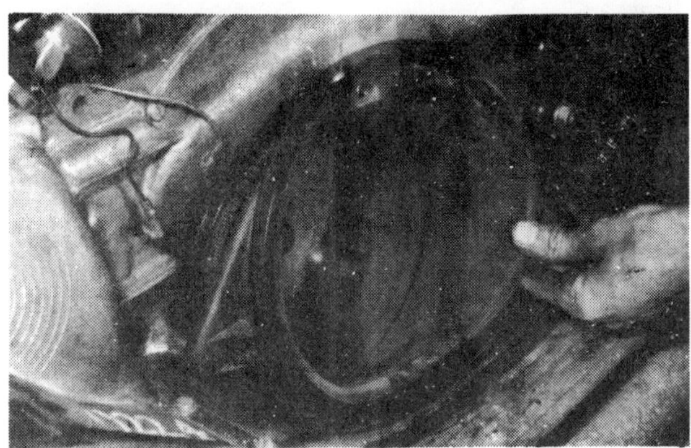
12.14a Remove the air intake grommet

12.14b Remove the fan

12.15 Remove the cable from the flap control lever

12.16a Remove the fan housing bolts

12.16b and wiggle the fan housing away

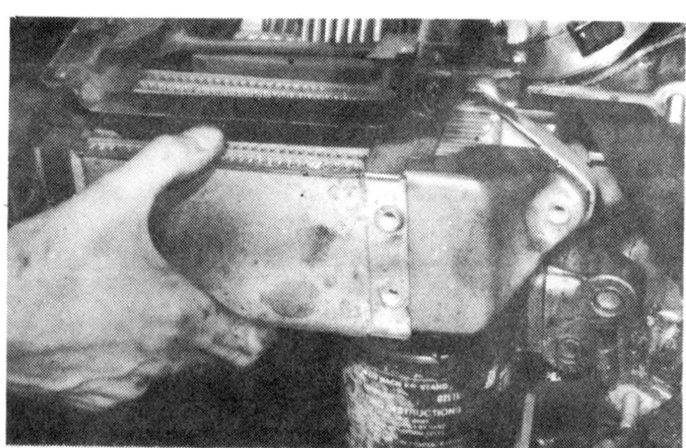
12.18 Removing the oil cooler

12.19 ... and tap the flywheel off the crankshaft

12.21a The screw holding the deflector plate to the cylinder head

12.21b Withdrawing the head with the deflector plate

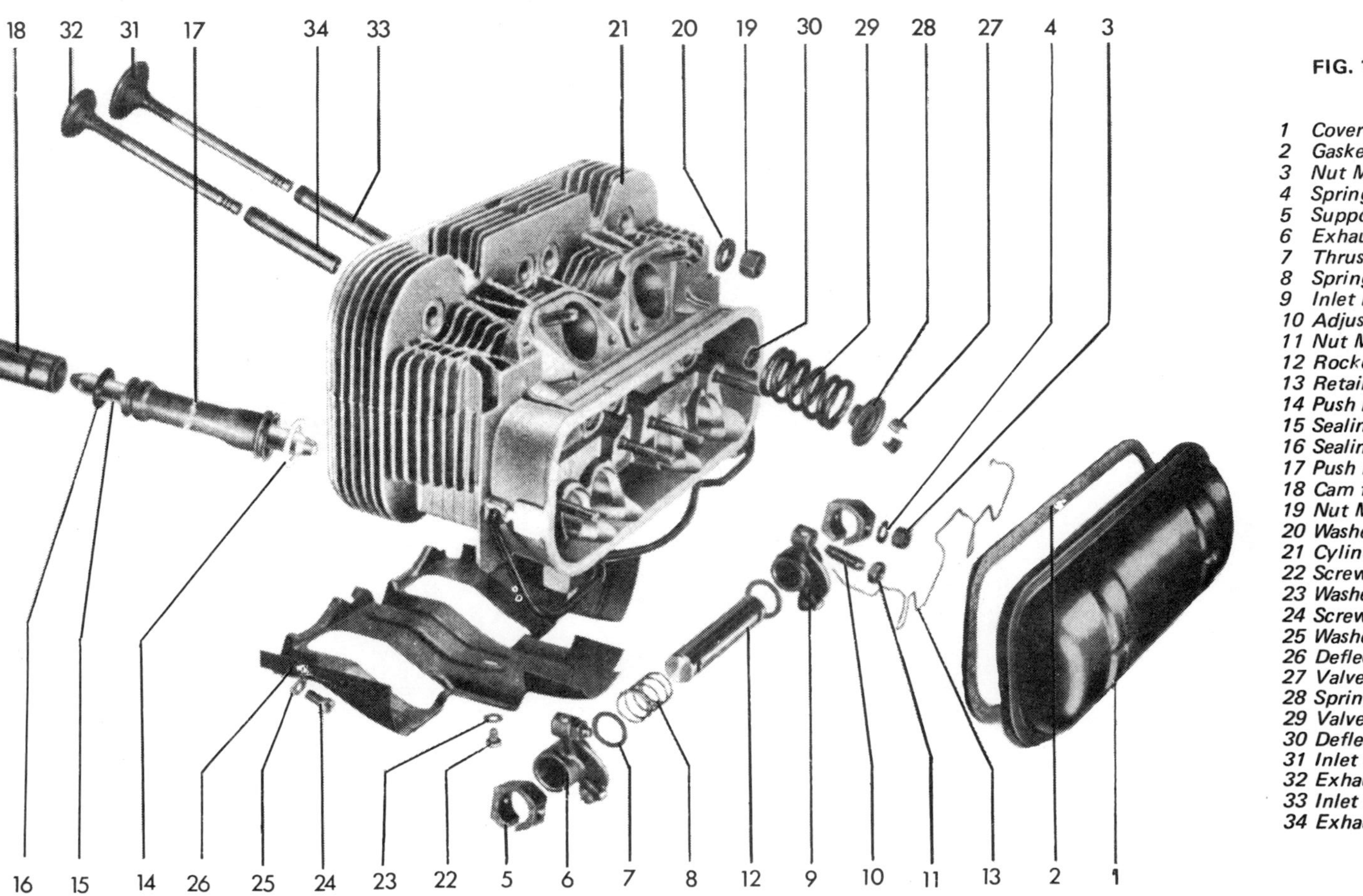

FIG. 1.8. CYLINDER HEAD AND VALVE GEAR

1 *Cover*
2 *Gasket*
3 *Nut M7*
4 *Spring washer*
5 *Support*
6 *Exhaust valve rocker arm*
7 *Thrust washer*
8 *Spring*
9 *Inlet rocker arm*
10 *Adjusting screw*
11 *Nut M8*
12 *Rocker shaft*
13 *Retainer*
14 *Push rod*
15 *Sealing ring*
16 *Sealing ring*
17 *Push rod tube*
18 *Cam follower*
19 *Nut M10*
20 *Washer*
21 *Cylinder head*
22 *Screw M5*
23 *Washer*
24 *Screw M6*
25 *Washer*
26 *Deflector plate*
27 *Valve collar*
28 *Spring cap*
29 *Valve spring*
30 *Deflector ring*
31 *Inlet valve*
32 *Exhaust valve*
33 *Inlet valve guide*
34 *Exhaust valve guide*

23 It is now convenient to remove the thermostat before it gets damaged. There are two screws, one is behind the control wire (photo).
24 Take off the oil filler pipe and elbow and the oil filter complete with elbow. Be careful because the filter is full of oil.
25 Draw off the cylinders in turn (photo).
26 Remove the circlips from the gudgeon pins (photo) and holding the piston firmly tap out the gudgeon pin and remove the piston from the connecting rod. If the pin will not come out easily, warm the piston to 100°C (no more). No 4 gudgeon pin presents a little difficulty as it can be taken out only one way and the casing gets in the way.
27 Take the nut off the stud holding the distributor clamp and remove the distributor. Do NOT undo the clamp - unless you want to retime the ignition. (Chapter 4).
28 Remove the square sheet metal oil breather box from the top of the engine crankcase. It is held only by a clip.
29 Now undo the four screws holding the oil pump, and using a lever on each side, ease the pump away and set it on one side. Replace the nuts on the studs. (photo).

12.23 Removing the thermostat

13 Engine dismantling - splitting the crankcase - camshaft and crankcase dismantling

1 Refer to Fig. 1.9 and 1.10.
2 Undo the nuts and remove the bolts holding the crankcase halves together. There are 24 in all, 16 x 7 mm, 2 x 5 mm, and 6 x 10 mm. Work methodically using wooden blocks to support the crankcase while removing the bolts as there are studs sticking out in all directions.
3 Tap the halves apart, but do not tap too hard. If it wont come apart look for more studs or bolts. When all of these are out it does come easily. Do NOT push the faces apart with a wedge. Tap the right hand half and lift it off the left hand half leaving the crankshaft and camshaft in the lower half.
4 There will be a gentle tinkle as the cam followers fall into the lower half. Remove them, noting if possible which bore they came from.
5 Put the right hand half of the crankcase safely away and turn to the left hand half. Lift out the camshaft (photo), and remove the white metal shell bearings from both halves of the crankcase noting which way they came out. Unless there are signs of wear there is no need to remove the bearings for more that a careful inspection, when they may be replaced right away.
6 With camshaft removed remove the shims from the end of the crankshaft (photo), next remove the crankshaft (photo).
7 The distributor drive shaft is still in the crankcase. It may be removed at this point if necessary. First remove the preload (anti-rattle) spring.
8 Remove the screw from the end of the crankshaft and pull off the cap (photo). The No 4 main bearing may now be removed.
9 Now using the puller remove the skew gears from the end of the crankshaft. Pull on the camshaft drive gear. Remove the circlip before starting to pull and if a lot of force seems necessary warm the distributor drive gear a little (photo).
10 The circular main bearing (No 3) may now be removed for inspection. The woodruff key from the camshaft drive gear should be stored safely.
11 No. 1 main bearing, the circular one at the clutch end of the crankshaft, may be removed for inspection, and of course the shell bearings of No 2 main bearing.
12 All that remains is to remove the big ends and inspect them and the crankshaft. Mark the bearing caps so that they go back in the same place, the same way round. Remove the nuts from the connecting rod bolts and ease the cap from the rod. Remove the rod from the shaft and replace the cap on the connecting rod.
13 It is now all in pieces. The next job is inspection.

14 Engine - inspection and overhaul of components contained in crankcase

1 All the parts should now be cleaned again and oiled lightly.
2 Examine the two halves of the crankcase. Look for cracks, burrs, loose studs and any sign of rotating parts fouling the crankcase. If all is well set the two halves on one side.
3 Next examine the crankshaft. If it can be run between centres the main bearing surfaces may be checked to ensure the shaft is straight.
4 All bearing surfaces of the crankshaft must be checked for scoring or signs of overheating. Measure them accurately with a micrometer for ovality and diameter against the specification or replacement.
5 The connecting rods should be examined for twist and bending. Unless special tools are available this is beyond the scope of the keen owner driver, but unless something drastic has occured the rods will not be distorted. If it has (a seizure or a sudden stop) then take the rods along for checking. If rods are replaced they must be matched for weight. This again is a job for the agent.
6 Assuming the rods are in good order, and the shaft is satisfactory next examine the big end shells. With the shells fitted correctly and the caps torqued to the right amount, the roundness or ovality of the bearing may be measured with an inside micrometer. Discolouration, scoring or ovality beyond the limit condemn the shells. Indeed if the shaft measures up to the standard specification it is a false economy not to fit new big ends right through.
7 If the shaft has to be reground then special shells must be fitted to both the big ends and mains. Leave this job to the firm who do the grinding and make sure the shaft is assembled and runs freely when returned to you.
8 A reasonable test for a new big end when assembled is that the rod should fall slowly under its own weight from just off top dead centre. If it doesn't it is too tight, but it must descend slowly or the clearances are too great.
9 The main bearings may only be examined and measured against specification.
10 End play, both of mains and big ends should be checked when the crankshaft is reassembled to the crankcase before the two halves of the crankcase are joined.
11 The camshaft must show no signs of wear or overheating on the cam surfaces. The gear must be firmly rivetted to the shaft. If either of these do not seem right the shaft must be replaced. It is not a scheduled spare as we found to our annoyance.
12 The camshaft bearings must now be checked. They are all different so make sure the right partners go together. Check them against specification and for superficial damage. Again, if there is the least doubt, renew the whole lot. The cost is small compared with the total work of the job.

15 Engine - inspection of cylinders, pistons and rings

1 The main components to inspect next are the pistons, rings

12.25 Removing the cylinders

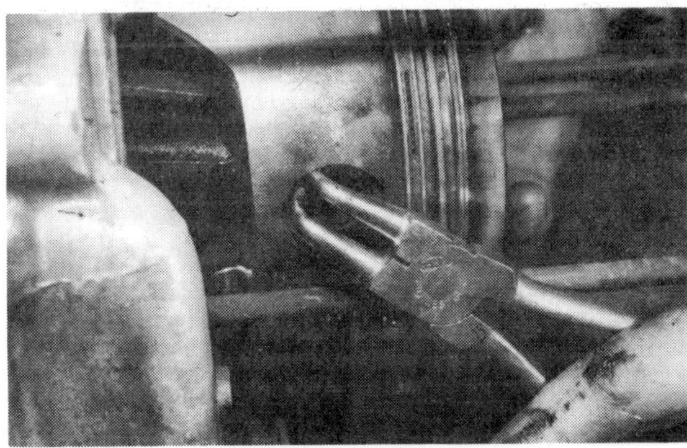
12.26 Removing the circlips from the pistons

12.29 Removing the oil pump

13.5 Removing the camshaft

13.6a Removing the shims from the end of the crankshaft

13.6b Removing the crankshaft

13.8 Removing the cap from the end of the crankshaft

13.9 Pulling the drive gears off the crankshaft. The distributor drive may require a little warming

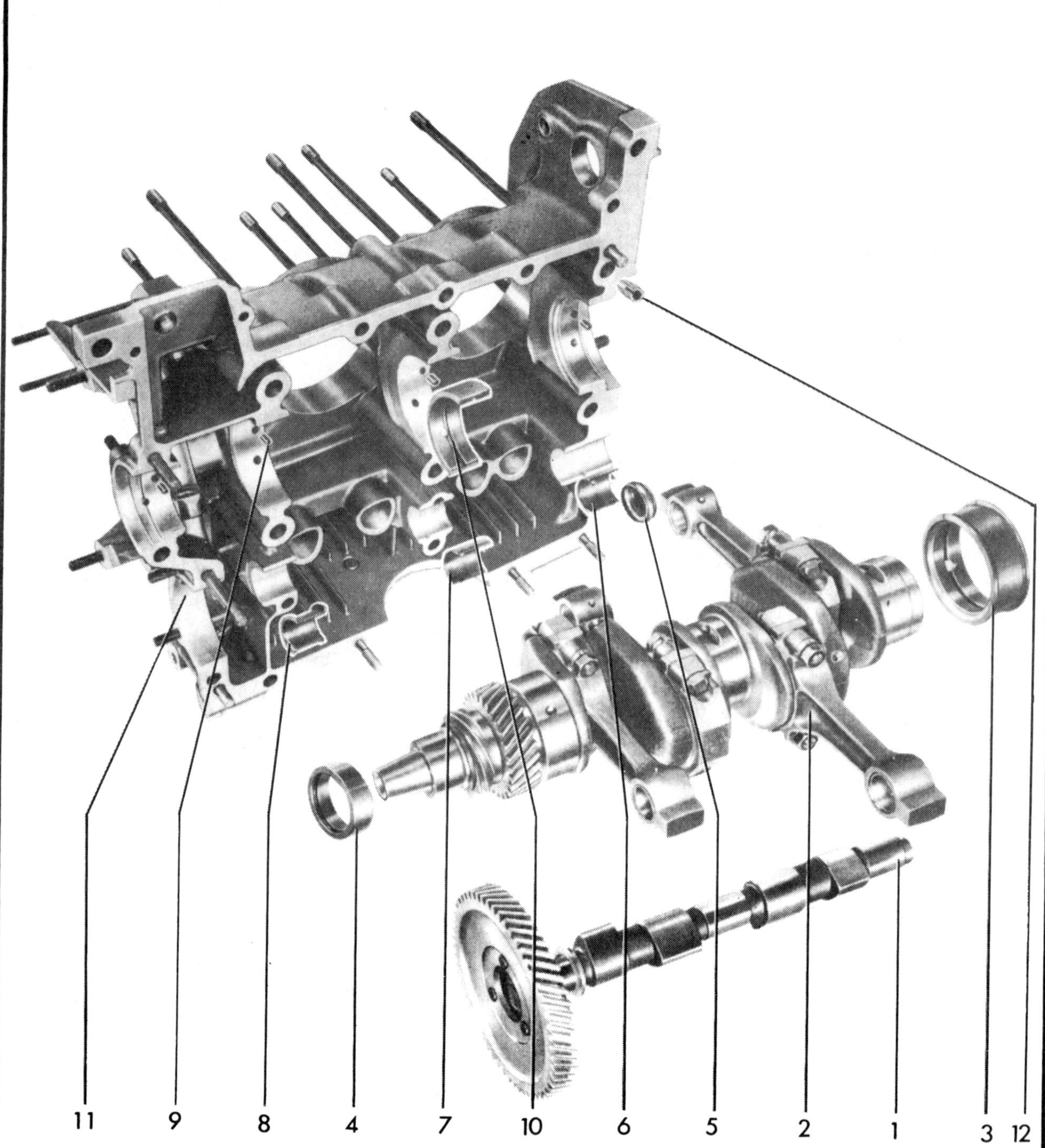

FIG. 1.9. CRANKCASE, CAMSHAFT AND CRANKSHAFT

1 Camshaft
2 Crankshaft assembly
3 Main bearing No. 1
5 End cap for camshaft
6 Camshaft bearing No. 1
7 Camshaft bearing No. 2
8 Left shell for camshaft No. 3 bearing
9 Dowel pin
10 Shell bearing No. 2 main
11 Crankcase left half
12 Vibration limiter

Note – the right hand half of the crankcase is not shown. This contains the dowel pin for No. 2 bearing, a shell for No. 2 main, a shell for each of Nos. 1, 2 and 3 camshaft bearings, the oil suction pipe with its sealing ring, and the oil deflector plate.

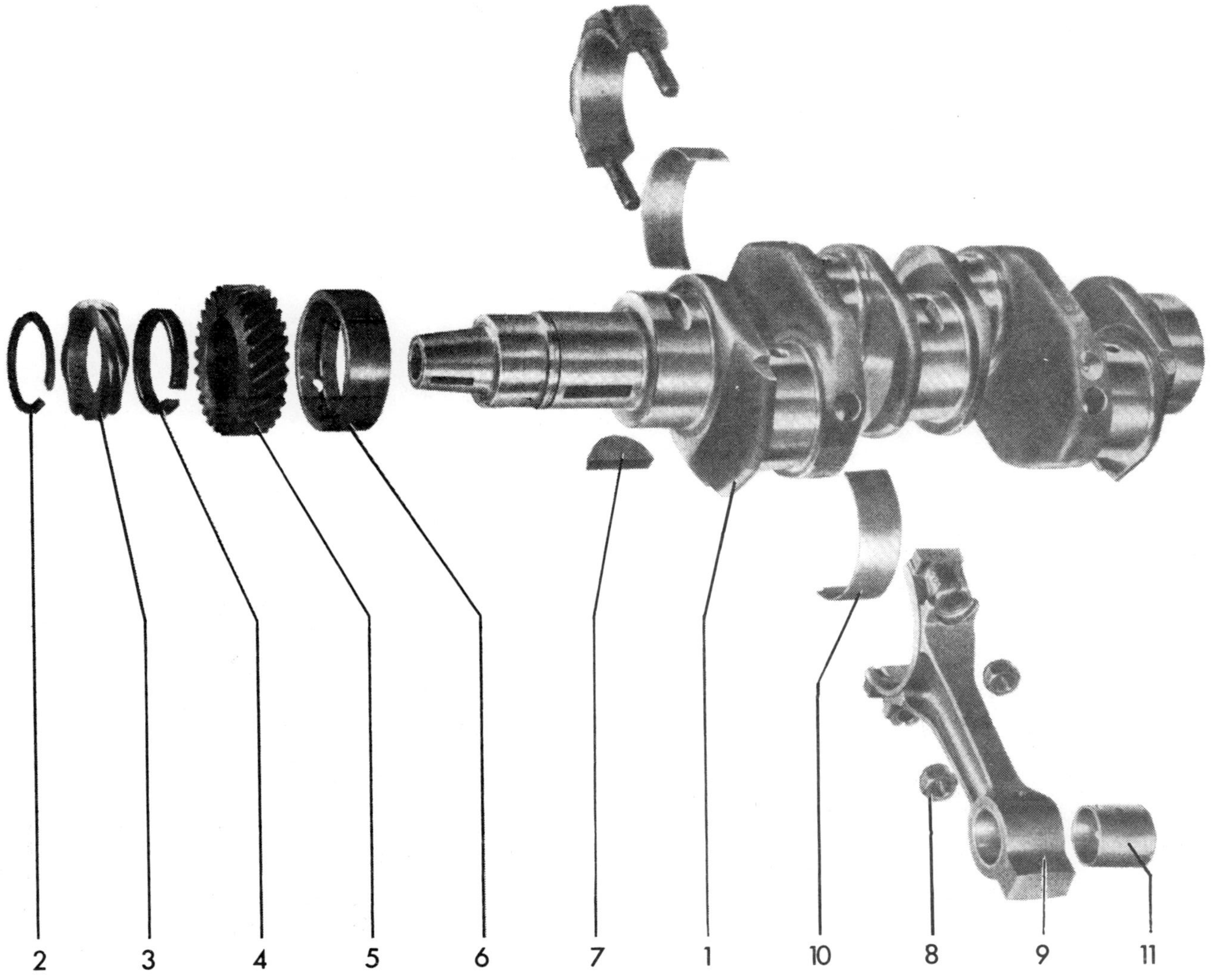

FIG. 1.10. CRANKSHAFT ASSEMBLY

1 Crankshaft
2 Circlip
3 Distributor drive gear
4 Spacer
5 Camshaft drive gear
6 Crankshaft No. 3 bearing
7 Key
8 Nut
9 Connecting rod
10 Connecting rod shell bearing
11 Gudgeon pin bush

and cylinders. The cam followers, push rods and guides, and the valves and valve mechanisms are also on the list.
2 Cylinders should be measured with an internal micrometer for wear and ovality. The danger point is the top of the piston stroke on the thrust side of the bore. A ridge tends to wear here. Cylinders may be reground and fitted with oversize pistons and rings.
3 However there is a snag to this. There are two sizes of oversize. The nominal size is 90 mm. The oversizes are nominally 90.5 mm and 91 mm. So that if one cylinder is reground to 91 mm and the others remain at 90 mm, the piston may be several grams different in weight, with vibration and wear problems ahead.

Cylinders must not be bored and installed with standard cylinders. All four must have the same dimensions. This means that if one cylinder only is scored, it should be replaced, not rebored.

Again, if there are problems of this nature it is better for a reputable firm to sort them out and set the engine to rights rather than risk an out of balance torque.
4 Piston rings should be replaced if the engine has done 30,000 miles since the last overhaul. There are two dimensions to check. The first one is the wear in the groove. The upper ring wear limit is 0.005 ins. (0.12 mm) nd the lower ring and scraper rings 0.004 ins., (0.10 mm). The gap, when cold, measured with the ring installed in the bore should be less than 0.035 ins. (0.90 mm) and more than 0.014 ins (0.35 mm) for the upper ring. The lower ring figures are 0.035 ins (0.90 mm) and 0.012 ins. (0.30 mm) for the lower ring, and for the scraper ring 0.038 ins. (0.95 mm) and 0.010 ins. (0.25 mm).
5 This means that the rings must be removed from the pistons for measurement. They should be placed in the bore and pushed down approximately 0.20 ins. from the BOTTOM of the bore. Make sure they are square to the bore when measured.
6 Pistons should be measured for ovality, but seldom require renewal unless the cylinder does as well. The fit of the piston pin is important. The wear limit is 0.0015 ins. (0.04 mm) in other words it should be a stiff fit or there will be small end knock.

16 Inspection - valve gear and cylinder head

1 The cam followers should be checked for wear on the flat surfaces. Any with other than flat surfaces should be replaced. Do not attempt to grind out indentations.
2 Push rods should be checked for distortion. The maximum bend (or run out between centres) should be 0.3 mm (0.012 ins.)
3 Valve guides seldom require replacement. As the valves work in a horizontal plane the problem of oil running down worn guides is not nearly so serious. The rock at the end of the stem is 0.45 mm (0.017 ins.) for a new valve and guide, and a wear limit of 0.900 mm (0.035 ins.) is permitted.
4 Inside diameters vary somehwat but the 'rock' test will decide whether replacement is required.

If new guides are required this is a job for the VW agent. The old guides must be drilled out partially before removal and the new ones reamed to size after installation.
4 If the valves cannot be ground in satisfactorily by hand using the traditional method of a rubber sucker and paste, then, again the agent must be consulted. Exhaust valves may only be ground in, not refaced on a machine, inlets may be refaced but the owner is unlikely to possess a machine so the agent must again be sought. The correct loaded length for a valve spring is 29 mm (1.14 ins.) at 80 kg (176 lb).
5 Cylinder head inserts may be installed where valve seats are damaged but this is a factory job. Check the head for cracks between seats, and check the threads of the plug sockets.

17 Inspection - lubrication system

1 All oilways and passages should be checked carefully for blockages. An engine with a blocked oilway in the crankcase is a disheartening, expensive sight — it does happen, so check that rag, grease and sludge are absent from oilways.
2 If the oil cooler is functioning satisfactorily when the engine is dismantled, leave it alone; if it isn't, replace it with a new one. The old cooler will be tested by the agent to a pressure of 6 kg/cm^2 on a special rig. This is 85 lbs per square inch. It is unlikely that a suspect cooler will stand up to this. If there has been a bearing failure and the bearing has broken up then it is essential to fit a new oil cooler as the oil cooler may harbour metal particles which will start the process all over again.
3 The oil pump is not easy to dismantle. An extractor (VW tool 803), is required to pull the cover off. When this is done the only inspection is a visual one of the housing and cover for scoring, particularly where the gears may rub on the housing and cover. If there is any scoring a new pump is required.
4 The pressure relief valve should be free from ridges and the spring checked for length. Those fitted before March 1971 are 40 mm (1.57 ins.) long at a loading of 4.2 to 5.1 kg (9.2 to 11.2 lbs). Those fitted after March 1971 are 39 mm (1.53 ins.) at a loading of 6.8 to 8.8 kg (15 lbs to 19.4 lbs). Replace if necessary.
5 The spring loadings for the oil pressure regulating valve are 26 mm (1.02 ins) at 1.7 to 2.0 kg (3.7 to 4.4 lbs) for all models.
6 Never refit an old dirty oil filter, replace it with a new one.
7 Check the oil strainer for cleanliness.

18 Inspection - cooling system

1 There is nothing to dismantle and measure in the cooling system other than to test the thermostat. This should be immersed in water at 70°C and the length should then be at least 46 mm measured across the bellows.
2 Check that the flaps work, the pulley goes round on its axis and that the cable is in good order.
3 Finally have a look at all the 'tin ware' to check for rust, bent flanges or other damage, and that it fits together properly. The boot for the dipstick must fit tightly on both tubes.

19 Reassembly - general

1 Everything has been checked and rectified and it is all laid out neatly ready for reassembly. Start with a clean bench top, an oil can of light oil, all the tools clean, plenty of clean non-fluffy rag, and clean hands and overalls.
2 Gaskets, 'O' rings and seals should be replaced by new ones and the set should be laid out conveniently on a clean flat surface.
3 Finally — take your time. The 1700 engine is a well made piece of machinery which goes together in a most satisfactory way, but each job must be completed properly and checked before going on to the next one.

20 Assembly of the crankshaft, camshaft, connecting rods and crankcase complete

1 Lay the crankshaft on a clean surface and lubricate the bearing surfaces. Assemble the No.3 main bearing. The blind hole must be next to the crankshaft web (photo).
2 Heat the camshaft drive pinion to 100° and slide it into position, the chamfer edge of the bore leading (photo), and then fit the spacer (photo).
3 Now heat the distributor drive pinion to 100°C, slide it on (photo) and then fit the circlip (photo).
4 Assemble a shell bearing to the cap, making sure that each cap goes back to its own rod the right way round. (Centre punch marks) (photos). Repeat with the other three rods and then torque the nuts to 3.3 mkg (24 lb ft) (photo). Check the centre punch marks to see that the rods and caps are in the right place.
5 Measure the axial play of the connecting rods with a feeler gauge. This should be 0.004 ins. to 0.016 ins. It must not be

20.1 No. 3 main bearing. The blind hole must be next to the crankshaft web ...

20.2a ... fit the crankshaft drive gear ...

20.2b ... followed by the spacer

20.3a Fit the distributor drive gear ...

20.3b ... and the circlip

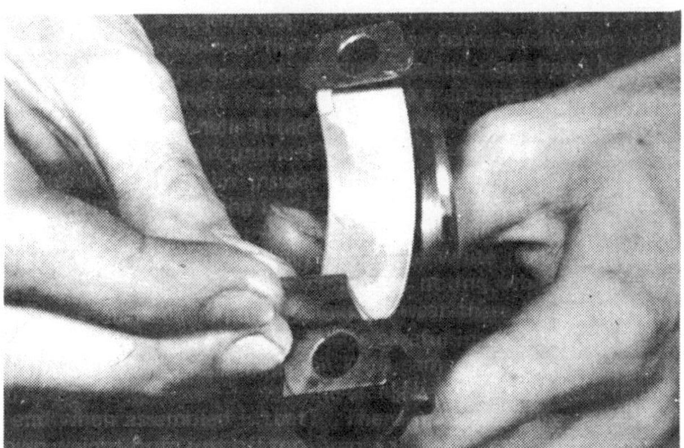

20.4a Assemble a shell bearing to the con rod

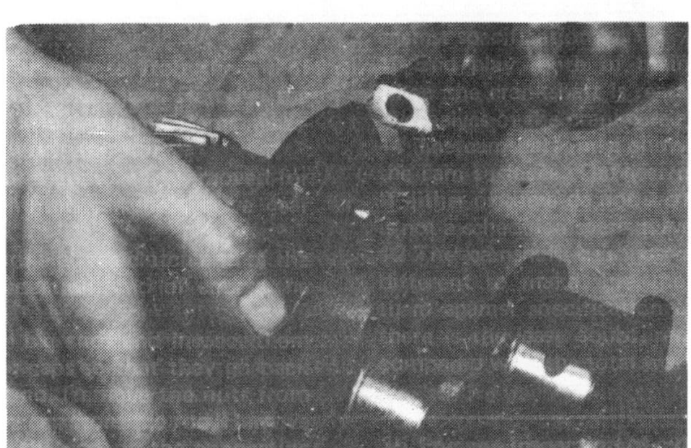

20.4b Assemble the rod to the shaft

20.4c Torque the nuts to 24 lb ft.

more than 0.028 ins. Now lock the nuts with a peening tool.

6 Now layout the crankshaft as shown in the photo with No. 1 main bearing, the two shells for No. 2 main bearing, and the No. 4 main bearing.

7 Add the two halves of the crankcase and the camshaft with its bearing, and the stage is set to assemble the crankcase. (Fig.1.11).

8 Assemble the No. 2 (shell bearing) to both halves of the crankcase (photo).

9 Fit the camshaft bearings to the crankcase, try the camshaft in position and remove it. Note that the flanged thrust bearing goes at the distributor end (photo).

10 Oil all the bearing surfaces of the mains and the crankshaft and camshaft, lift the crankshaft by the 2nd and 4th cylinder cam rods and lower it into the crankcase, feeding No. 1 and 3 cam rods through the holes in the crankcase (photo). Check that Nos. 1,3 and 4 mains have located properly with the dowels in place and that No. 2 shell main is in place.

11 Rotate the crankshaft so that the two punch marks on the side of the camshaft drive gear are horizontal and install the camshaft so that the pip mark on the camshaft gear fits between the two marks on the drive gear. (photo). This is all there is to valve timing. Check all the bearing shells again.

12 Fit the sealing plug for the end of the camshaft into position (photo). This should be coated with V W jointing compound, or with Hylomar before installation.

13 Wipe carefully round the two mating surfaces of the crankcase and coat the one in which the crankshaft is installed with jointing compound. Use this sparingly.

14 Now turn to the other half of the casing. Install the oil suction pipe and the strainer (photo). Use a new seal ring.

15 Check that the shell bearing for No.2 main bearing is in place correctly, and that the camshaft shells are safely in position, oil the bearing surfaces, and holding the crankcase by the cylinder bolts lower it carefully into position over the crankshaft and camshaft, feeding the connecting rods through the cylinder openings as the case is lowered (photo).

16 Install the six M.10 bolts with the washer and sealing nuts, coating the heads of the bolts with sealing compound. The sealing rings of the nuts should be outwards. Install all the other nuts and bolts and tighten them slightly. Do not forget the bracket with the thermo-switch for cold starting (photo). Now stop to think:

1 Are all the connecting rods protuding from their right holes?
2 Did you fit all the bearings (or are some still on the bench)?
3 Was the camshaft timing meshed correctly?
4 Is the camshaft sealing plug in position?

17 Turn the crankshaft through 360° to make sure that nothing is fouling and now tighten the M.10 nuts to 15 lb ft, working diagonally as for a cylinder head. Check the rotation of the shaft again. If it is stiff in anyway undo the nuts, split the case and search for the reason. It will probably be a bearing not seating properly. It is essential to find the reason before pressing on as damage will ensue if the casing is tightened further.

18 When all is correct tighten the large (M.10) nuts to 25 ft lbs and all the smaller ones to 14 ft lbs working diagonally all the while. Check the rotation frequently (at the end of each round of tightening).

19 Now fit the rest of the oil strainer (photos) and cover to the bottom of the sump and torque the nut to 10 lb ft. Refit the oil pressure relief valve and screw home the plug. Check that the oil

Fig. 1.11. Crankcase, camshaft, crankshaft assembly, and bearings laid out for assembly

20.6 Crankshaft assembly with main bearings

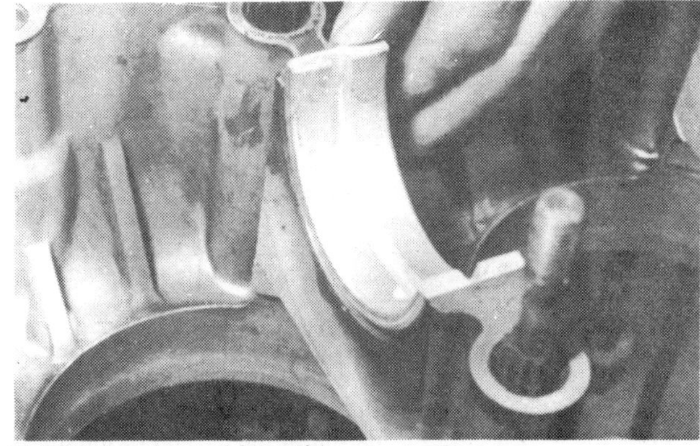
20.8 Fitting the shell (No. 2) bearing to the crankcase

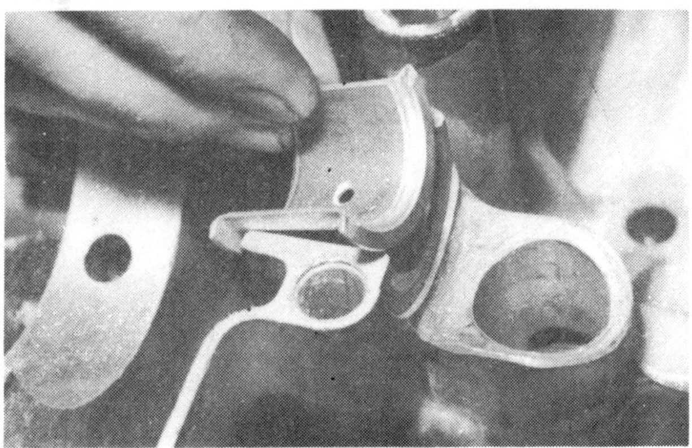
20.9 The flanged camshaft thrust bearing

20.10 Lowering the crankshaft into position

20.11a Match the timing marks on the drive and driven gears for the camshaft

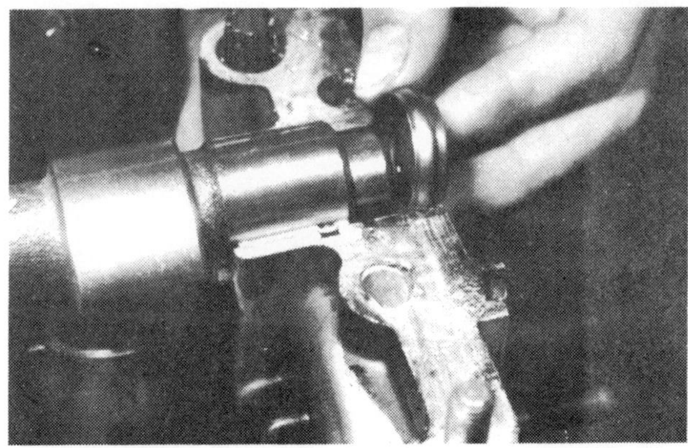
20.12 Installing the camshaft sealing plug

20.14 Install the strainer ...

20.15 Fitting the second half of the crankcase

pressure switch is in place.
20 Reasssemble the oil pump to the crankcase. Use a new gasket. The tab on the drive gear shaft should be aligned with the slot in the camshaft gear. Centre the pump by turning the crankshaft two revolutions and tighten the nuts to 15 lb ft. (photo).

21 Fitting the crankshaft oil seals, fan hub and flywheel

1 The oil seals will have been removed and the seats cleaned. It is not necessary to split the crankcase to do this job.
2 Cover the seats with a thin coat of sealing compound. If necessary make a small lead in the seat, and remove all burrs.
3 Press the oil seal into the housing at the fan end of the shaft, and place the sealing ring in turn. Oil them both lightly. The seal is 62 mm (2.59 ins) diameter. (photos).
4 Fit the woodruff key, then the fan hub and finally the bolt with the large washer. Torque the M8 bolt to 23 lbs ft. (photo).
5 The hub is now ready for the fan to be installed.
6 Going to the other end, install the flywheel with two shims behind it. Do not fit the seal yet.
7 Now measure the axial play of the crankshaft. If it is possible to obtain a dial gauge read the play of the dial gauge, otherwise you will have to rig up an arrangement to use feelers. The axial play should now have 0.004 (0.10 mm) subtracted from it and this will give the thickness of the third shim required. Shims of 0.012 and 0.015 ins. are available. Unless major repairs have been done the reinstallation of the old shims will usually meet the requirement. Having settled the shim problem remove the flywheel, install the shims (photo) with the seal and sealing ring; then refit the flywheel. (photo)
8 Be careful, the small dowel must not be damaged, it locates the flywheel correctly and ensures the correct dynamic balance of the crankshaft and flywheel. The seal must be bedded squarely in the crankcase recess. It can be driven in but it is better pressed in using VW tool 204b.
9 When refitting the flywheel, first fit the spacer and then the five bolts and torque them to 80 lb ft. (11 mkg) (photos).

22 Valves and springs - assembly to the cylinder head

1 The clean cylinder head minus all carbon and other fouling should now be assembled with the valves. The valves have been serviced, either machined or ground in and are ready for fitting (Section 16.4).
2 Refer to Fig. 1.8. Insert the valve into the guide, fit the oil deflector ring, slip the spring over the stem, fit the spring cap, compress the spring with a valve lifter and fit the cotters in place. (photos).
3 If the cotters are difficult hold them on the end of a screwdriver with a blob of grease and poke them into place that way.
4 When the valve is assembled compress the spring to open the valve and let it go sharply. This will indicate whether the cotters are properly seated.
5 Clean off the flange of the cylinder head, and repeat for the second cylinder head.

23 Assembly of pistons to connecting rods, cylinders and cylinder heads

1 First replace the cam followers in their bores (photo). They should go into the bore from which they came. Unlike the Type 3 which are flanged and must be fitted from the inside the Type 4 followers are cylindrical throughout their length.
2 The rings should be fitted to the pistons before assembly to the connecting rod. Gapping is discussed in Section 16.4 Ease the rings over the piston carefully for they are brittle. Use a piston ring expander, or slide them over a thin piece of metal wrapped round the piston. The rings are marked TOP on one surface near the gap. This surface should point to the piston crown. The lower compression ring (middle of the three) has a

20.16 Do not forget the bracket with the thermo switch

20.19a Refit the remainder of the oil strainer ...

20.19b ... and fit the nut to the cover (Torque to 19 lb ft)

20.20 Fit the oil pump

21.3a Fit the oil seal ...

21.3b ... and the sealing ring

21.4 ... the woodruffe key, the hub, and the bolt and washer

21.7a Install the shims with the seal

21.7b and then the flywheel

21.9a Fit the spacer and then the five bolts

21.9b Torque the bolts to 80 lbs ft.

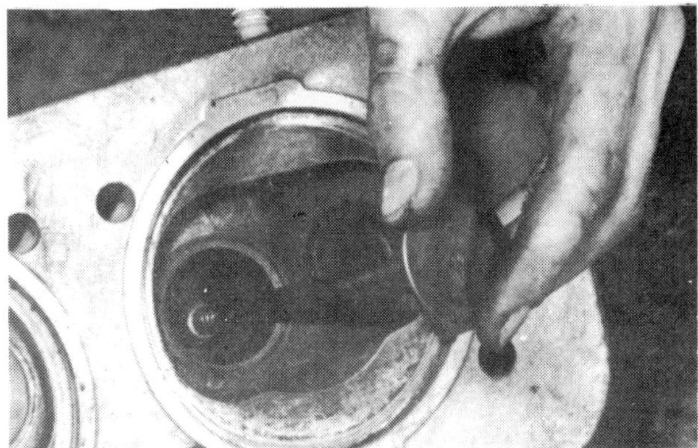
22.2a Install the valve ...

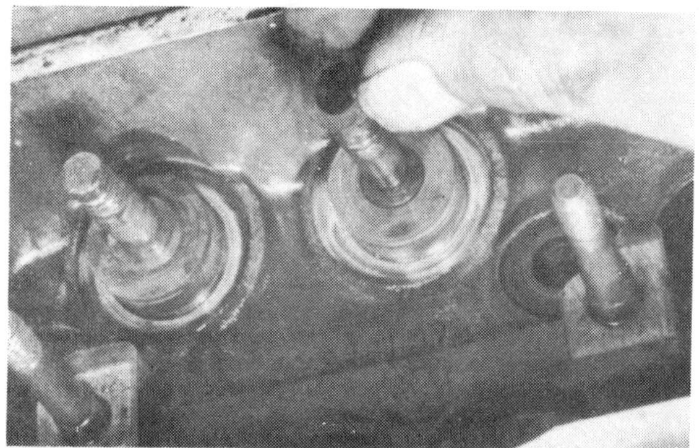
22.2b ... then the seal washer ...

22.2c. . . . followed by the spring and cap

22.2d... and compress the spring to insert the cotter

23.1 Replace the cam followers

23.3 Fit the pistons to the con rods

23.4 Replace the circlips

23.6a Using a home made clamp to compress the rings

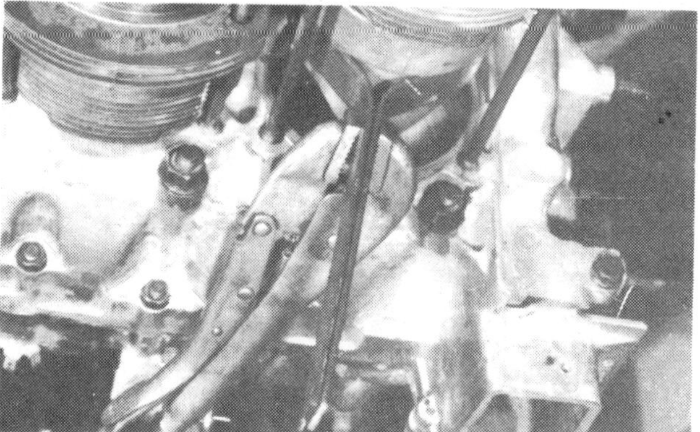
23.6b push the clamp off the piston using the cylinder remove the mole wrench and then the clamp

step on the lower edge. Space the gaps 120° apart.

3 The gudgeon pin is a push fit in the piston. Heat the piston with an electric lamp and fitting the piston over the small end bush push the gudgeon pin through the bush. (photo).

4 Install the circlips. It is advisable to use new circlips. (photo).

5 As each piston is installed to the connecting rod, slide the cylinder over the piston installing the cylinder over the studs. Do not forget the sealing ring at the bottom of the cylinder. Lightly oil the piston and the cylinder before installation.

6 Getting the piston into the cylinder is not as easy as it might be. Various methods are recommended from proprietary piston ring compressors to jubilee clips. We had none of the right size so a piece of 1" x 1/8" mild steel was bent to form a circle about 1/16" larger than the piston and was then sawn opposite the open end to form two half circles, each with a long stem. These were clamped round the rings and held with a mole wrench. It was then simple enough to push the clamp off the piston with the cylinder until all the rings were in the cylinder, and by removing the mole wrench extract the clamp in two parts. (photos).

7 When all four cylinders are in place install the sealing rings in over the cylinders and gently ease the heads over the studs (photo). Take care not to pinch the sealing rings.

8 Fit the M.10 nuts and washers to the studs and torque the head down using the sequence in Fig. 1.12. Tighten down progressively a little at a time to 25 lbs ft. (photo).

9 Fit the deflector plates next. The right hand one is the smaller of the two. There is one screw in the cylinder head and two in the crankcase.

23.7 Fitting the cylinder head

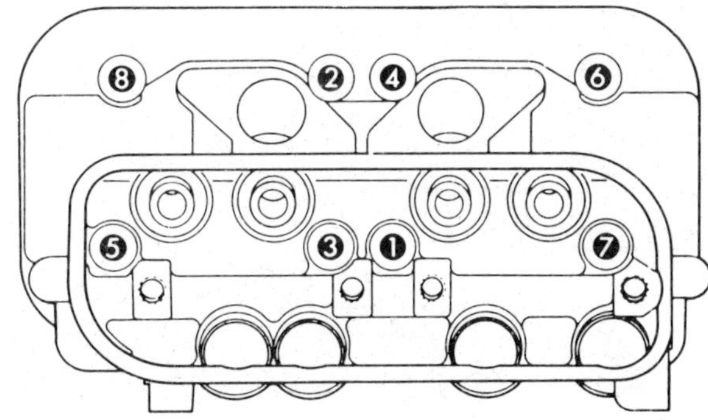

Fig. 1.12. Sequence for tightening cylinder head nuts
Note - tighten first to 10 lb ft and then to 25 lb ft in easy stages

24 Fitting the push rods and rocker gear

1 The cam followers are in place. Now install the push rod tubes; fit a new red or green sealing ring at the top and a black one at the bottom (photo) and push the tubes into place through the rocker box (photo). Make sure the seals are firmly installed (photo).

2 Now install the push rods (photo) and assemble the rocker gear. The spring retainer for the tubes goes on first (Fig.1.8). This is a much bent piece of wire which fits round the studs and across the top of the push rod tubes. Fit the rocker gear on top of the retainer, engaging the tops of the push rods in the cups while so doing. (photo). Tighten the nuts on the rocker studs to 10 ft lbs. (1.4 mkg).

23.8 Torque the head down to 25 lb ft. (see Fig. 1.12)

25 Refitting the oil cooler, breather and filter

1 Fit a new cork gasket and install the oil breather in the top of the crankcase. (photo).

2 Bolt the bracket for the oil filter to the side of the crankcase (photo). Do not forget to fit a new gasket. Install a new oil filter and tighten it.

3 Install new seals for the oil cooler (photo) and fit the oil cooler (photo 12.18). The seals should not be too soft or they will 'blow', and the engine must come down again. On the other hand do not tighten them so much that they are squashed. Do not forget the washers between the cooler and the crankcase. Watch out for residual oil if the old cooler is being replaced, it can make a mess.

26 Engine cooling system, warm air ducting, fan and alternator - refitting

1 Refit the thermostat (see photo 12.33). It goes on the two studs. The control wire should be in line with the pulley.

2 Refit the oil filler pipe (photo).

3 Place the fan housing in position taking care to fit the boot over the dipstick housing (photo).

4 Fit the cowl round the oil cooler (warm air duct left rear) and the counterpart on the other pair of cylinders (warm air

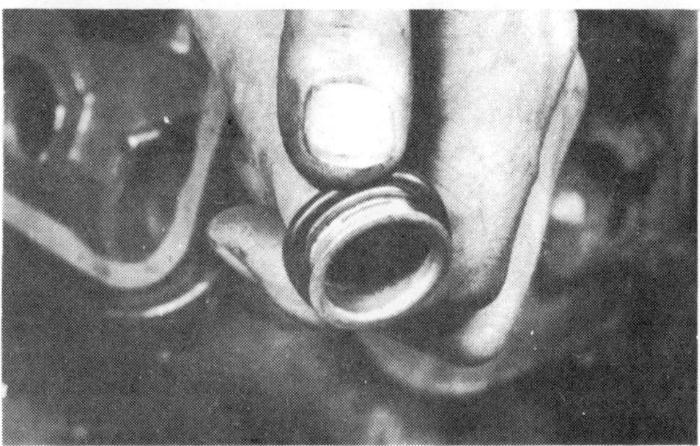

24.1a Fit a sealing ring

24.1b Install the push rod tube

24.1c The box should look like this

24.2a Install the push rods ...

24.2b ... and fit the rocker assembly

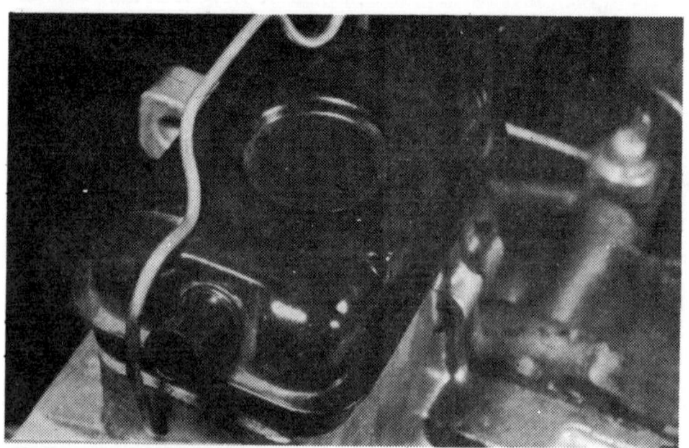
25.1 Refit the oil breather

25.2 Fitting the bracket for the oil filter

25.3 Fit new seals to the oil ports for the cooler

26.2 Fit the oil filler pipe

duct right rear) but do not screw them down yet (photos).

5 Fit the cylinder cover plate left and the cylinder cover plate right but do not bolt them down yet (photos).

6 Manoeuvre the fan housing into position finally and tighten the nuts. Put all the screws in the tin ware and fasten it up so that it fits snugly. By doing it this way, any minor adjustments can be done with the whole cover system in place. (Fig. 1.6 refers also).

7 The cylinder cover plate right has a hole in it for the thermostat control wire to pass through before it connects to the flap control. Put the wire over the pulley and connect it up so that the flaps are shut when the thermostat is cold (photo).

8 Put the warm air duct right front and the left front in position but do not tighten them yet.

9 Assemble the bracket to the back of the alternator and the sheet metal cover over the alternator. Offer it up to the fan housing. Insert the coach head type bolt at the bottom and the alternator and cover are held loosely in place. Now fit the adjusting bracket inside the cover, put your hand behind the alternator cover and fit the rubber ducting to the fan housing. Feed the wires through the top cover grommet and fit the two cheese headed screws to the alternator cover. The long one goes in the fan housing. (photos).

10 Now fit the fan spacer, and then the fan. It will only go on one way. There are four socket screws for the fan which are tightened to 15 lbs ft. (photos).

11 Fit the alternator belt set to the correct tension and lock the alternator in position with the socket head screw (Fig. 1.7). Tighten the nut on the back of the coach head screw (photo).

27 Heat exchangers and engine bearer - assembly

1 Tip the engine so that it rests on the flywheel, support it with wooden blocks. Fit the left hand heat exchanger (do not forget the very solid little gaskets). Slide the metal tube through the grommet in the engine cover and make sure the grommet fits snugly, there is also a clamp connecting the heat exchanger to the fan housing. Tighten all the nuts correctly. (photos).

2 Before fitting the right hand heat exchanger fit the engine bearer. If it is not fitted before the heat exchanger it is not possible to get it in. Check that the bonded rubber mountings are in good condition, replace them if not: tighten up all the nuts and bolts. (photo).

3 Now fit the right hand heat exchanger in the same way as the left one.

28 Fitting the distributor

This is discussed in detail in Chapter 4. It should be done now when reassembling the engine.

29 Setting the valve clearances

1 The clearance for both inlet and exhaust valves is 0.006 ins. cold. Turn the engine so that the valve is completely closed, slacken off the locknut and screw the tappet screw in until a 0.006 feeler is just held. Keep the tappet screw steady and tighten the locknut. Check the clearance and reset if necessary (photo).

2 Repeat for each valve in turn. It is much easier to rotate the engine if the plugs are taken out.

3 When the clearances are satisfactory clip on the valve covers. Fit new gaskets to them before assembly.

4 Replace the spark plugs.

30 Engine cover plates and exhaust - refitting

1 The remainder of the 'tin-ware' may now be fitted.

2 The front cover plate (Fig.1.5) may be installed (photo).

3 Now fit the left and right lower warm air ducts (photos).

26.3 Fit the fan housing into position

26.4a ... the warm air duct right rear ...

26.4b ... and the warm air duct left rear

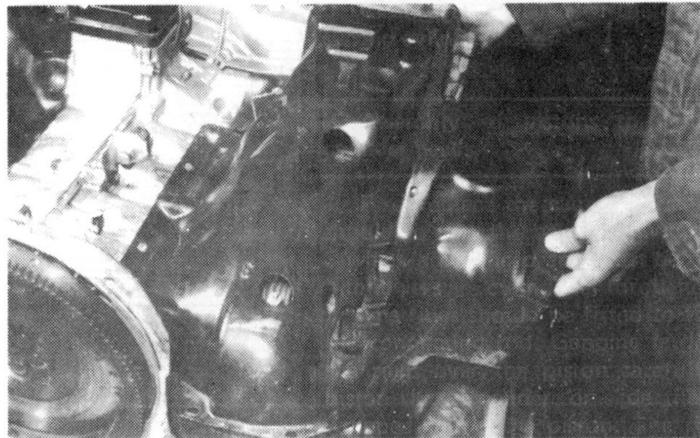

26.5a The cylinder cover plate left...

26.5b ... and the cylinder cover plate right

26.7 Connecting the thermostat wire to the flaps

26.9a The adjusting bracket for the alternator

26.9b Fitting the coach head bolt through the alternator cowling

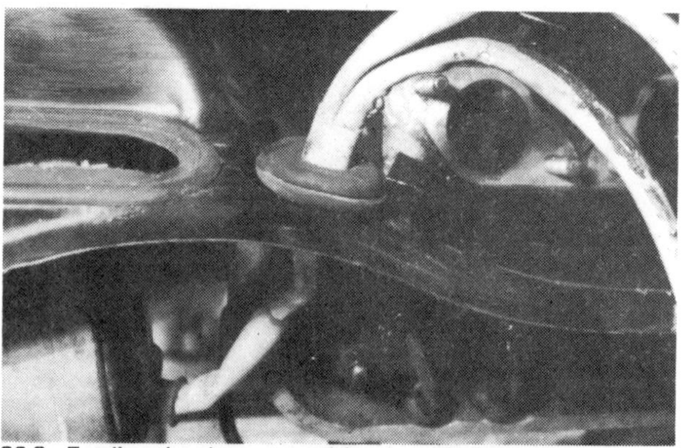

26.9c Feeding the alternator cables through the grommet

26.9d The sealing ring for the alternator

26.10a Fit the fan spacer

26.10b and then the fan

26.11 Tighten the nut on the back of the alternator pivot

27.1a Fitting the heat exchanger

27.1b The cover for the heat exchanger

27.2 Fitting the engine carrier

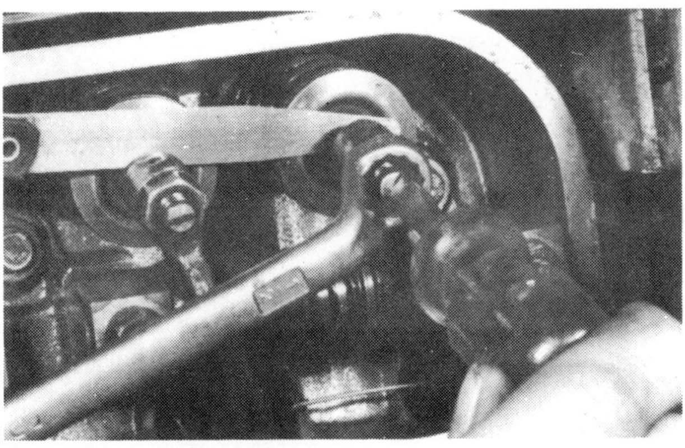
29.1 Adjusting valve clearance

30.2 The front cover plate

30.3a The left lower warm air duct

30.3b The right lower warm air duct

4 The exhaust system may now be installed. Tighten the six bolts with a good nip. (photo).
5 Refer to Fig.1.5 and fit the left and right rear cover plates. Fit the large one first. Make sure the rubber grommet is in place or it will foul the alternator drive belt. Slide the cover plate over the oil filler tube after installation but before screwing the plate down. Fit the small plate. (The one with the valve clearance notice on it. This may be out of date, if so, cancel it). The screw at the back of the alternator belt may be a bit of a fiddle. It is fitted from the outside into a fixed nut and has to be worked past the heat exchanger. Tighten all the screws.
6 Now fit the air trunking (the large elliptical plastic mouth and its rubber partner). This fits onto the body air duct when the engine is installed. (photo).

31 Engine assembly - final details before installation

1 Fit the air intake distributor to the top of the crankcase (photo). It is complete with a throttle valve and pressure switch.
2 Fit new gaskets (photo) and replace the injectors complete with the air intake manifolds (see photo 12.4).
3 Install the distributor cap and plug leads and run the plug leads conveniently to the plugs.
4 Fit the vacuum control hose from the distributor to the air intake throttle valve. Be careful how this is routed or it will foul the accelerator cable connector and lever.
5 Install the clutch. Centre the friction plate using the main drive shaft from the gearbox and tighten up the six bolts to a torque of 18 lbs ft. using a diagonal method of tightening. The long boss of the friction plate must face away from the engine or the assembly will not bolt up (photo).
6 Arrange two suitable blocks of wood about 7 ins. deep and 36 ins. long spaced about 24 ins. apart on a clean hard floor. Recruit four strong helpers and lift the engine on to the blocks (photo).
7 Slide the gearbox over the studs, engage the starter pinion in the flywheel teeth. Enter the main shaft through the gearbox to the clutch splines. Fit the two top bolts to the gearbox/engine joint and tighten all four nuts and bolts. Install the circlip and nut at the gearbox end of the main shaft, tighten, and fit the end plug (see Chapter 6). The gearbox should now look like photo 31.7.
8 Now fit the plastic bushes to the clutch housing and install the transmission carrier (photos). See also Fig 6.1. The power unit is now ready for installation to the car.

32 Installation in the car

1 The rear of the car should be lifted so that there is 24 ins. clearance from the ground to the bumper bar.
2 Lift the engine/transmission assembly on the trolley jack, be careful to pack it to avoid damage and move the unit into place under the car. Thread the accelerator cable into the front engine cover.
3 Lift the assembly until the gear change shaft goes into the hole in the rear axle carrier. Now move the whole unit forward raising it steadily until the jaws of the transmission carrier engage in the rubber mounting blocks. If there is difficulty in doing this slacken off the screws holding the rubber blocks and remove the packing pieces (see Fig. 6.1). This will give enough play to enter the jaws. Replace the packing pieces and tighten the screws as soon as the carrier is in position. Fit the bolts to the carrier from inside the engine compartment as the holes line up (photo 5.3a).
4 Raise the engine still further and enter the engine carrier into the brackets at the side. Raise the carrier until the bolts are at the top of the elongated slots (photo).
5 The whole process requires some careful manoeuvre, and two people are necessary. Do not rush, and do not force anything or the unit will become jammed with all sorts of dire trouble. Softly - softly is the motto.
6 Check the centricity of the gear shift rod in the hole of the rear axle carrier (Sections 6 and 8 of this Chapter). With the shift rod correctly positioned tighten all the bolts. New tabs should be fitted to the enginge transmission carrier bolts, to lock the bolts in place.
7 At the most convenient stage of assembly reinstall the clutch slave cylinder (if it has been removed). If the slave cylinder was not removed connect the pipe and bleed the slave cylinder (Chapter 5).
8 During installation the engine compartment seal must be fitted. A used one goes in readily with a little thought and patience, but a new one must be installed, before the engine is in place, with a cord threaded in it so that the lip may be pulled into place rather in the way a windscreen seal is fitted.
9 Pull the shaft into position and reconnect the shift lever mechanism,. Lock the square headed screw with wire (photo).
10 Reconnect the cables to the starter (photo). Reinstall the ignition coil (Chapter 4).
11 The accelerator cable was threaded through the front engine cover. Now fit the cable to the throttle valve arm and re-install the spring (photos).
12 Replace the stiff hoses to the heat exchanger (photo).
13 Refit the CV joints to the transmission hubs. Remember the plates under each pair of bolts, and the serrated washers. Remember also to pack the joints with grease (Chapter 8).
14 Now lower the vehicle to the ground and go to the engine compartment.
15 Reconnect the air hoses between the various components and connect up the petrol ring main. If you labelled everything then life is simple. If you did not consult Chapter 3.
16 Reconnect the electric wiring. Again if you tagged it as it was dismantled then there is no trouble. If not the various wires are coded in colour and the pins are fairly obvious. If in difficulty turn to Chapter 3 and consult the wiring and hose diagrams.

The circuits are divided into:–

a) The ignition to the coil and distributor.
b) The alternator with its control in the right rear corner. A mirror is needed to see how to fit the plug.
c) The wiring connecting the various sensors, valves, and switches.
d) The wire from the 'back-up' light which comes from the rear of the car, joins the plastic bottle fuse and goes out from the fuse to the starter - cut-off switch located on the side of the gearbox. A further wire from the plastic fuse bottle is connected to the terminal.

17 Check that the engine and gearbox are filled with oil. Before pouring oil into the engine see that the filter pipe is securely connected to the engine extension pipe or there will be a puddle. Check also the dipstick connection. The gearbox should have 5½ pints of SAE 90 Hypoid oil, the engine 6 pints of fortified detergent engine oil (Castrol CR120 or CR130).
18 Replace the battery (negative earth) and now for the big moment. It should start (ours did).
19 Run the engine and look around for leaks. If all is correct stop the engine and go on with assembly.
20 Refit the air cleaner with hoses , and connect the hoses from the cleaner to the air auxiliary switch and the engine breather box. The short hose goes to the auxiliary air switch from the throttle valve, the long hose to the breather from the elbow on the air cleaner proper.
21 Install the air heater trunking from the heat exchangers to the water for intake. These are the long flexible hoses (photo).
22 Start the engine and adjust the slow running screw to a sensible tick-over speed. (Chapter 3).
23 Two photographs are included at Figs. 1.13 and 1.14 to show the engine installation top view.

See page 46 for Fault diagnosis .

30.4 The exhaust system may now be installed

30.6 The air trunking connecting the engine to the body air ducts

31.1 Fitting the air intake distributor

31.2 A new gasket for the injectors

31.5 The clutch correctly assembled

31.6 Engine and gearbox ready for assembly

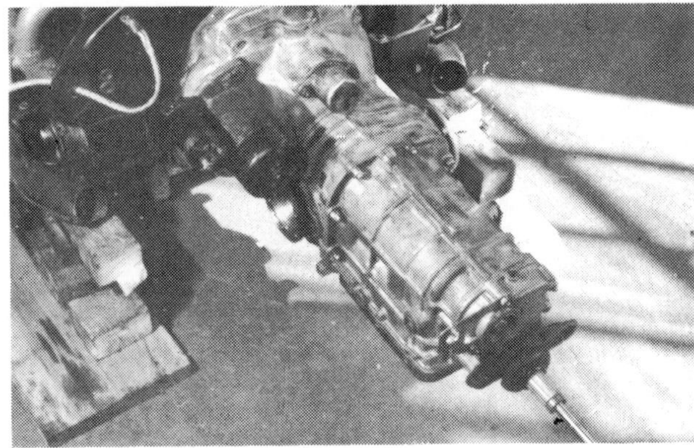
31.7 Gearbox fitted to the engine

31.8a Fit the plastic washers ...

31.8b ... and install the engine carrier

32.4 The bolts for the engine carrier

32.9 Wire the gear shift clamp screws

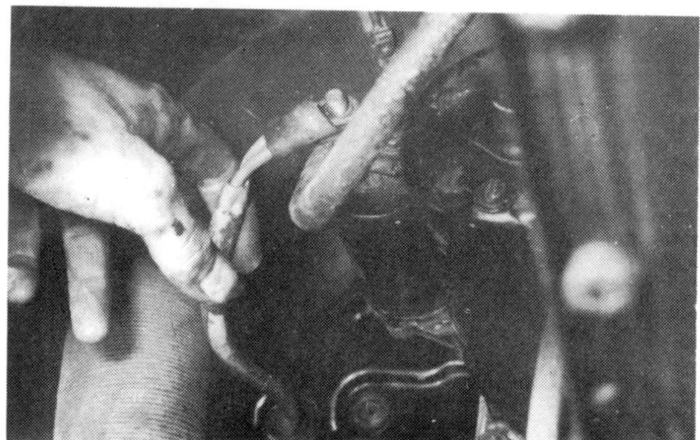
32.10 Reconnect the cables to the starter

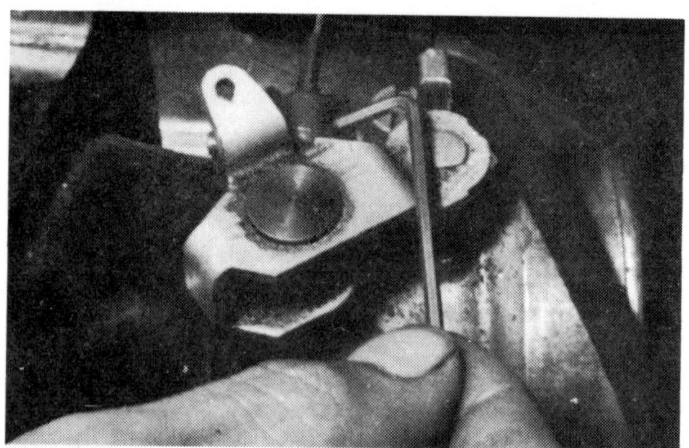
32.11a Fit the accelerator cable to the throttle valve

32.11b Do not forget the spring

32.12 The hoses to the heat exchangers

32.21 The air heater hoses from the heat exchangers to the fan connection

Fig. 1.13. Engine installed but no air cleaner fitted yet

Fig. 1.14. Air cleaner and trunking fitted

33 Fault diagnosis

NOTE: When investigating starting and uneven running faults do not be tempted into snap diagnosis. Start from the beginning of the check procedure and follow it through. It will take less time in the long run. Poor performance from an engine in terms of power and economy is nor normally diagnosed quickly. In any event the ignition and fuel systems must be checked first before assuming any further investigation needs to be made.

Symptom	Reason/s	Remedy
Engine will not turn over when starter switch is operated	Flat battery Bad battery connections Bad connections at solenoid switch and/or starter motor	Check that battery is fully charged and that all connections are clean and tight.
	Starter motor jammed	Rock car back and forth with a gear engaged. If ineffective remove starter.
	Defective solenoid	Remove starter and check solenoid.
	Starter motor defective	Remove starter and overhaul.
Engine turns over normally but fails to fire and run	No spark at plugs	Check ignition system according to procedures given in Chapter 4.
	No fuel reaching engine	Check fuel system according to procedures given in Chapters 2 and 3.
	Too much fuel reaching the engine (flooding)	Slowly depress accelerator pedal to floor and keep it there while operating starter motor until engine fires. Check fuel system if necessary as described in Chapters 2 and 3.
Engine starts but runs unevenly and misfires	Ignition and/or fuel system faults	Check the ignition and fuel systems as though the engine had failed to start.
	Incorrect valve clearances	Check and reset clearances.
	Burnt out valves	Remove cylinder heads and examine and overhaul as necessary.
Lack of power	Ignition and/or fuel system faults	Check the ignition and fuel systems for correct ignition timing and carburettor settings.
	Incorrect valve clearances	Check and reset the clearances.
	Burnt out valves	Remove cylinder heads and examine and overhaul as necessary.
	Worn out pistons or cylinder bores	Remove cylinder heads and examine pistons and cylinder bores. Overhaul as necessary.
Excessive oil consumption	Oil leaks from crankshaft oil seal, rocker cover gasket, oil pump, oil cooler, oil strainer cover plate, or oil filter	Identify source of leak and repair as appropriate.
	Worn piston rings or cylinder bores resulting in oil being burnt by engine (Smoky exhaust is an indication)	Fit new rings or rebore cylinders and fit new pistons, depending on degree of wear.
	Worn valve guides and/or defective valve stem seals	Remove cylinder heads and recondition valve stem bores and valves and seals as necessary.
Excessive mechanical noise from engine	Wrong valve to rocker clearances	Adjust valve clearances.
	Worn crankshaft bearings Worn cylinders (piston slap)	Inspect and overhaul where necessary.
Unusual vibration	Misfiring on one or more cylinders	Check ignition system.
	Loose mounting bolts	Check tightness of bolts and condition of flexible mountings.

Chapter 2 Fuel system - twin carburettors

Contents

Specifications

Twin carburettors

Type	Solex 34 PDSIT - 2/3	
	PDSIT - 2 (left)	PDSIT - 3 (right)
Venturi diameter (mm)	26	26
(in)	1.024	1.024
Main jet	135	135
Air correction jet	150	175
Pilot jet with cut off valve	55	55
Float needle diameter (mm)	1.2	1.2
(in)	0.047	0.047
Float valve washer thickness (mm)	0.5	0.5
(in)	0.020	0.020
Float weight (grams)	7	7
Pump capacity cc/stroke	0.90 to 1.10	0.90 to 1.10
Pump capacity cc/stroke - automatic	0.70	0.70
Throttle valve gap - manual (mm)	0.6 - 0.8	0.6 - 0.8
(in)	0.024 - 0.031	0.024 - 0.031
- automatic (mm)	0.9	0.9
(in)	0.035	0.035
Distance from pump injection to joint surface	12.5 mm/0.5 in	12.5 mm/0.5 in

Fuel pump ... Mechanical/diaphragm

Pump pressure at 3800 rpm	5.0 lb sq in	(0.35 kg/cm^2)
Delivery capacity at 3800 rpm	0.7 Imp. pint/0.8 US pint/400 cc per minute	

Fuel tank

Capacity	11 gallons (50 litres) (US gallons)

Note: 1.3 gallons (6 litres) is in reserve.

1 General description

1 The tank at the front supplies petrol to the engine and to the heater unit. Fuel to the engine is piped via a strainer (in the tank) through the length of the car to the petrol pump situated in the engine compartment at the right hand side of the clutch housing. Petrol is piped from the pump to twin SOLEX PDSIT 34 carburettors. The twin air cleaners are supplied with air through vents in the rear of the body.

The fuel pump is mechanically operated from the cam shaft.

2 Air cleaners (with preheating)

1 There are two brackets on the top of the crankcase to which the air cleaner is secured by quick release clips. The air cleaner consists of an upper and lower part which are held together by quick release clips. The lower part has an air intake elbow which contains a thermostat which operates a flap to regulate the flow of warm air from No 1 cylinder or cold air from outside depending upon the temperature of the outside air. A second flap in the elbow regulates the manifold vacuum for crankcase ventilation. At either end of the upper part the ducts terminate in bosses which fit over the carburettor intakes. These are held in position with clamping springs. Figure 2.1 refers.

2 Refer to Figure 2.2. To remove the air cleaners pull off the flexible pipe and the crankcase ventilation hose. Release the spring clips holding the end pieces to the carburettors and lift off the end pieces. Release the clips securing the air cleaner to the bracket and lift the air cleaner away.

3 Undo the clips holding the upper and lower halves together. Lift the top away from the bottom. DO NOT place the top half on the bench upside down or dirty oil will run up into the filter.

Scrape any sludge adhering to the top half away and wipe it clean. Empty the oil and sludge from the bottom half and clean the container. Refill with 0.8 pints of SAE 30 engine oil.

4 Refitting is the reverse of removal. Make sure the embossed marks on the top and bottom coincide. Check that all seals and sleeves are correctly fitted.

5 The frequency of servicing depends largely on local conditions. In very dusty places weekly or even daily. In normal conditions monthly or even longer periods may suffice. There must be a minimum of 3/16in (5mm) of oil on top of the sludge for efficient working. Experience will soon dictate the time interval required but it is better to clean too often than not soon enough.

Fig. 2.1. Air cleaner showing halves divided (Secs. 1 and 2)

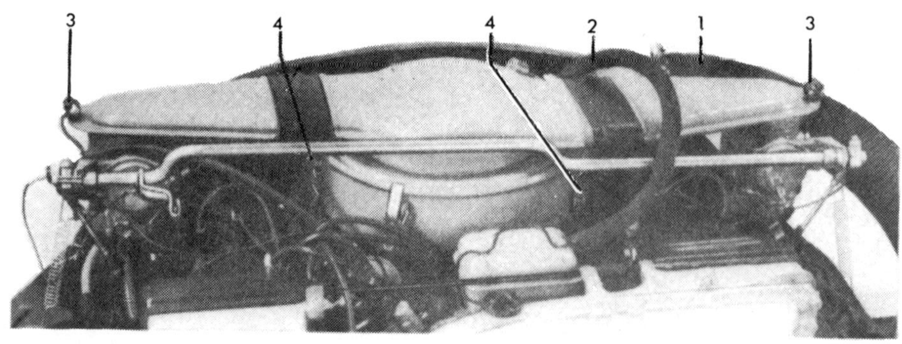

FIG. 2.2. AIR CLEANER INSTALLED (SEC. 2)

1 Intake flexible pipe 2 Crankcase ventilation hose 3 End piece spring clips 4 Securing clips

3 Solex carburettors (description)

Refer to Figure 2.3. The carburettor is basically a tube through which air is drawn into the engine by the action of the pistons and en route fuel is introduced into the air stream in the tube due to the fact that the air pressure is lowered when drawn through the 'tube'.

The main fuel discharge point is situated in the 'tube' - choke is the proper name for the tube to be used from now on - between two flaps which can block off the tube. One of these is the throttle flap - operated by the accelerator pedal and positioned at the engine end of the choke tube. The other is the strangler - which is operated by an automatic device.

When the engine is warm and running normally the strangler is wide open and the throttle open partially or fully - the amount of fuel/air mixture being controlled according to the required speed.

When cold the strangler is closed - partially or fully and the suction therefore draws more fuel and less air, i.e. a richer mixture to aid starting a cold engine.

At idling speeds the throttle flap is shut so that no air and fuel can get to the engine in the regular way. For this there are separate routes leading to small holes in the side of the choke tube, on the engine side of the throttle flap. These 'bleed' the requisite amounts of fuel and air to the engine for slow speeds only.

The fuel is held in a separate chamber alongside the choke tube and its level is governed by a float so that it is not too high or low. If too low it would only be drawn in at a higher suction than required for proper operation.

The main jet, which is simply an orifice of a particular size through which the fuel passes, is designed to let so much fuel flow at particular conditions of suction (properly called depression) in the choke tube. At idling speed the depression draws fuel from orifices below the throttle which has passed through the main jet and after that a pilot jet to reduce the quantity further.

Both main and pilot jets have air bleed jets also which let in air to assist emulsification of the eventual fuel/air mixture.

The strangler flap is controlled by an electrically operated bi-metal strip. This consists of a coiled bi-metal strip connected to the choke flap spindle. When the ignition is switched off the coiled metal strip is cold and the flap is shut. When ignition is switched on current flows through the strip which heats up and uncoils - opening the choke flap after some minutes. If anything should go wrong with this electrical arrangement the flap will return to the closed position.

With the flap closed there are two features which partially open it immediately the engine starts. The flap spindle is offset so one side tends to turn around the spindle under the depression in the choke tube. Also there is a diaphragm valve connected to another rod attached to the flap spindle. Depression in the choke tube also operates this. If these devices did not exist no air at all would get through with the fuel. This would then flood the engine.

Also there is the accelerator pump This is a diaphragm operated pump which is directly linked to the accelerator controls. When sudden acceleration is required the pump is operated and delivers neat fuel into the choke tube. This overcomes the time lag that would otherwise occur in waiting for the fuel to be drawn from the main jet.

The fuel in the float chamber is regulated at the correct height by a float which operates a needle valve. When the level drops the needle is lowered away from the entry orifice and fuel under pressure from the fuel pump enters. When the level rises the flow is shut off. The pump delivery potential is always greater than the maximum requirement from the carburettor. Another device fitted is an electro magnetic cut-off jet. This somewhat unhappy feature is designed to positively stop the fuel flow when the engine is stopped. Otherwise the engine tends to run on - even with the ignition switched off - when the engine is hot.

4 Solex carburettor - removal, replacement and overhaul

Refer to Figure 2.3. The carburettor should not be dismantled without reason. Such reasons would be for cleaning or renewal of the float and needle valve assembly and in rare circumstances, the jets. Partial dismantling would also be necessary for checking and setting the float chamber fuel level. Where statutory exhaust emission control regulations are in force it must be remembered that any disturbance of the carburettor (and ignition) setting may result in unacceptable exhaust gas emission. Such emissions will need checking with the proper equipment.

2 Remove the air cleaner and then detach the accelerator cable from the throttle control lever. Undo the screw which holds the cable end to the link, withdraw the cable and remove the link so that it does not fall out and get lost. Pull off the wire connection clips from the automatic choke and electro magnetic cut-off. Also pull off the fuel pipe and vacuum pipe.

3 Undo the two nuts which hold the carburettor to the inlet manifold and lift the carburettor off.

4 The first stage of dismantling should be to remove the screws holding the top to the base. Separate the two halves carefully and remove the paper gasket taking care to keep it from being damaged. It can be re-used.

5 To clean out the float chamber, remove the float pin and the float can then be taken out. Do not under any circumstances strain it in such a way that the pin or bracket is bent. When the float is removed the bowl may be flushed out and sediment removed with a small brush.

6 The needle valve is screwed into the top cover and when taking it out note the washer mounted underneath it. The simplest way to check this for leaks is to try blowing through it. It should not be possible to do so when the plunger is lightly pushed in. If in doubt, then renew the assembly, as a leaking valve will result in an over-rich mixture with consequent loss of performance and increased fuel consumption.

7 The accelerator pump diaphragm may be examined when the four cover securing screws and cover have been removed. Be careful not to damage the diaphragm. Renew it if there are signs of holes or cracks which may reduce its efficiency.

8 The electric automatic strangler may be removed for cleaning. If any part is suspected of malfunction the whole unit must be renewed. When refitting the bi-metal spring the looped end must be positioned so that it hooks over the end of the lever. Then the cover should be turned so that the notch lines up with the notch on the carburettor.

It is easy for the hook to disengage from the spring loop when refitting this so see that when it is in position finally that the choke flap is in the closed position. If it is not then you know the hook has jumped out. Do not overtighten the securing screws.

9 The main jet is situated behind a hexagonal headed plug in the base of the float chamber. This can be removed without taking the carburettor off the car. Remove the plug and then unscrew the jet with a screwdriver. The pilot jet is fixed similarly in the body alongside the accelerator pump housing on down draught versions. In the side draught model it is incorporated in the top cover. When cleaning jets do not use anything other than air pressure. Any poking with wire could damage the fine tolerance bores and upset the fuel mixture. The electro-magnetic cut-off valve may be simply unscrewed from the carburettor body. Do not grip the cylinder when doing so - use a suitable spanner. Never clamp the valve or carburettor body in a vice.

10 The air correction jet and emulsion tube is mounted vertically in the body of the carburettor. This too may be unscrewed for cleaning. Blow through the passageway in the carburettor also when it is removed.

11 Before reassembly check that the float is undamaged and unpunctured. It can be checked by immersion in hot water. If it is punctured bubbles of air will then come out as the air inside expands.

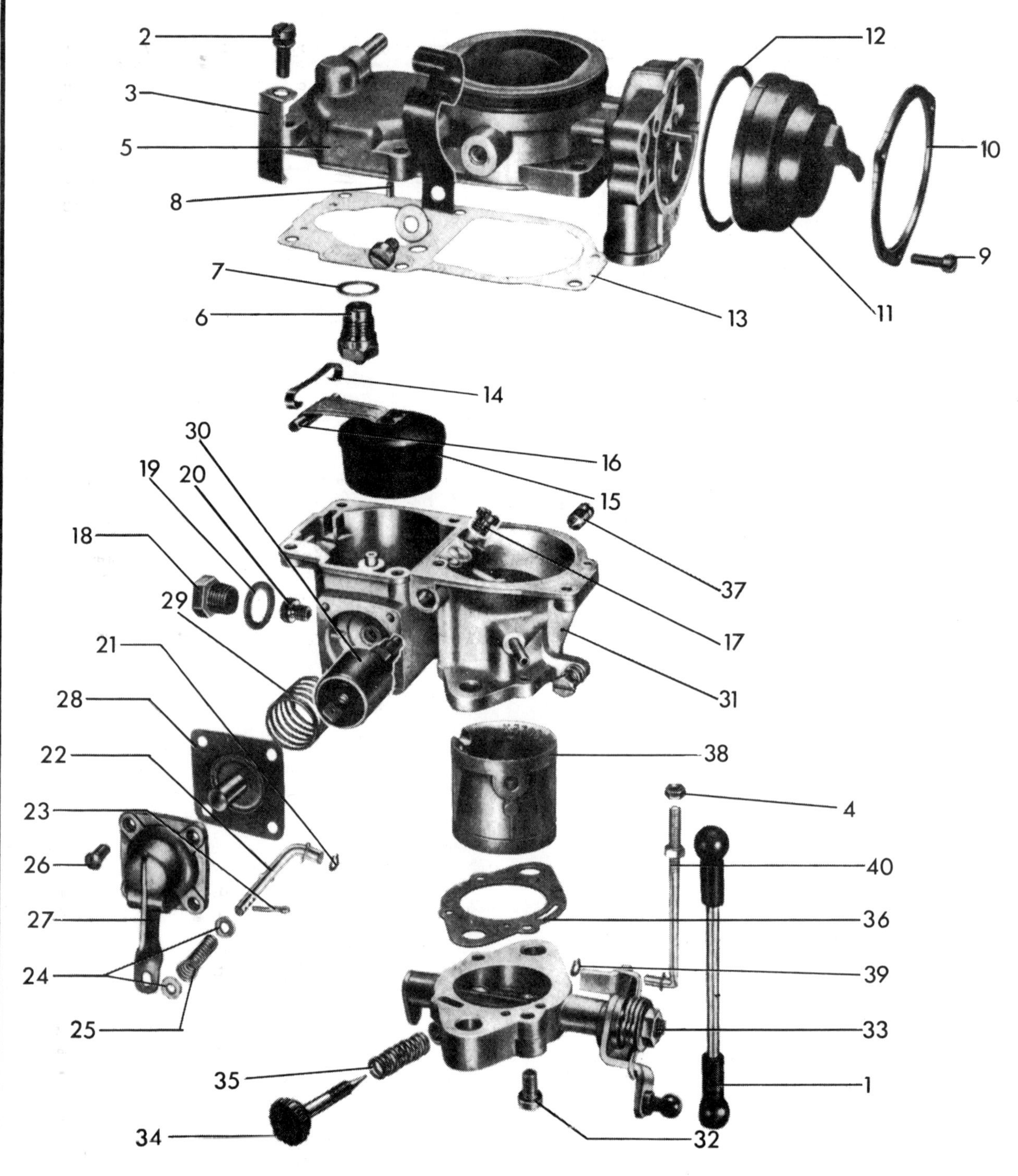

FIG. 2.3. CARBURETTOR – SOLEX PDSIT 34.2/3 EXPLODED VIEW (SECS. 3 AND 4)

1 Pull rod
2 Top cover screw
3 Adjusting nut
5 Top cover
6 Needle valve
7 Washer
8 Hollow screw for injector tube
9 Screw
10 Retaining ring
11 Auto choke cover with heating element
12 Gasket
13 Top cover gasket
14 Float pin retainer
15 Float
16 Float pivot pin
17 Air correction jet
18 Plug
19 Washer
20 Main jet
21 Clip
22 Connecting link
23 Clip
24 Washer
25 Link spring
26 Screw
27 Accelerator pump lever and cover
28 Pump diaphragm
29 Spring
30 Pilot jet cut off valve
31 Carburettor body
32 Screw
33 Throttle sector (Automatic only)
34 Volume control screw
35 Spring
36 Gasket
37 Venturi screw
38 Venturi
39 Clip
40 Connecting rod

12 If the throttle flap spindle should be very loose in its bearings in the main body of the carburettor then air may leak past and affect the air to fuel ratio of the mixture. In such cases the easist remedy is a new carburettor. An alternative is to drill and fit bushes to suit but this needs expertise and time.
13 Reassenbly is a reversal of the dismantling procedure but the following points should be watched carefully. Do not forget the washer when replacing the needle valve. Make sure that the gasket between body and cover is correctly positioned. When refitting the accelerator pump cover, the screws should be tightened with the diaphragm centre pushed in. Do not bend or distort the float arm when replacing it into the float chamber.

5 Solex carburettor 34 PDSIT/2/3 - checking float level

1 With the carburettor replaced in the car and connected up, and with the vehicle on a level surface, start the engine and run for a minute and then switch off.
2 Remove the fuel pipe from the upper part of the carburettor and take the top half of the carburettor off. Hold the feed pipe shut so that fuel does not flow into the float chamber as the top half is removed. Take off the gasket.
3 Now measure the fuel level with a depth gauge (not too near the cylinder wall as capilliary attraction will give a false reading there), from the body joint. The tip of the depth gauge should just touch the surface of the fuel when the depth gauge reading is 0.51 $\pm$ 0.04 in. (12 - 14 mm).
4 Adjustment is by shim washers under the needle valve, level too high - increase the thickness of the washers, too low - decrease the thickness. Washers may be obtained in thicknesses 0.5, 0.8, 1.0, and 1.5 millimetres.

6 Solex carburettor 34 PDSIT/2/3 - adjusting throttle gap

1 With the carburettor installed in the car and the choke valve open turn the idle running adjusting screw out until the throttle valve is fully closed; now turn the screw in until it just touches the throttle lever.
2 Close the choke valve fully, (flip the throttle valve and press the choke) adjust the automatic choke connecting rod by turning the two nuts until the gap between the idler adjustment screw and the throttle valve lever is 0.10 in. A number 40 drill is 0.098 in. diameter and is near enough to be used as a gauge.
Lock the nuts and check that the connecting rod and throttle valve lever move freely.

7 Adjusting the twin carburettors

1 Having checked the adjustments in Sections 5 and 6 the next thing is to adjust the carburettors so that they synchronise.
2 Unless the owner has access to a revolution counter and a synchro tester this task cannot be completed successfully. Some measure of success can be achieved, but not the final refinement.
3 Run the engine until it is warm, check that the throttle valve on each carburettor is in the idle position and both volume control screws are open about 1½ turns.
4 Lift up the end-pieces of the air cleaner and check that the starter flaps are open - they must remain open throughout the operation.
5 Take off the springs and remove the connecting rods from both sides. Set the left hand connecting rod to a length of 4.1 in measured between the centres of the spherical balls. The right hand rod is not adjustable.
6 Fit the non adjustable rod and spring to the right hand carburettor.
7 Slacken the lever for the left hand carburettor and fit the connecting rod and return spring.
8 Now back off the idle adjusting screw of each carburettor until the throttle valves are closed completely. Then screw in the idle adjusting screws until they just touch the stop lever. Now screw them in 1¼ turns each.
9 Screw in the volume control screws until they just touch the seating and then turn them out one turn.
10 This is as far as the adjustments can be done without a rev counter and synchro tester.
11 If these are available then the intake air depression of each carburettor may be balanced exactly. Measure the left hand one first and adjust the right hand one by altering the throttle stop screw setting as required.
12 Tighten the operating lever on the left hand carburettor. The axial play in the linkage shaft should be about 0.08 in., the overhang at the ends of the linkage shaft should be equal and the pivot locations must fit in the bearing brackets.
13 Finally with the engine stopped and the acceleration fully depressed there must be a gap of 0.040 in. between the throttle valve stops and the levers. Adjust the acceleration cable if necessary.

8 Carburettor linkages - removal and installation

1 Figure 2.4 refers. The accelerator cable moves a lever welded to the cross shaft. At the outer ends of the cross shafts levers are bolted to the shaft and are joined to the throttle valve shafts with pull rods. The levers are held in the closed position by return springs. The mechanism to the left hand carburettor is adjustable, the right hand one is not.
2 To remove the linkage disconnect the cable and springs, and separate the pull rods from the throttle levers.
3 Undo the screws holding the cross shaft brackets to the carburettor, remove the hose connecting the air cleaner and

FIG. 2.4. TWIN CARBURETTOR LINKAGE (SEC. 8)

1 Accelerator cable *2 Cross shaft* *3 Levers* *4 Pull rods* *5 Return springs*

crankcase breather and lift the linkage out.
4 Check all parts and renew as necessary.
5 To reassemble proceed the reverse way. Assemble the various parts but do not tighten the screws and nuts.
6 Adjust the left hand pull rod to a length of 4.1 in. between the centres of the ball socket centres and tighten the locknuts.
7 Refit the pull rods and return spring. Press the levers at the ends of the cross shaft down holding the throttle valve levers in the rolling position - push the shaft sideways to the left and with the lever pressed hard down tighten the nut securing it in position. Fit the axial play control spring on the lever.
8 Now press the cross shaft to the right and slide the right hand lever so that there is a clearance of 0.06 in. to 0.08 in. between it and the support bracket. Lock it in this position with the securing nut.
9 Set the carburettors as in Section 7.11. On automatic transmission vehicles the accelerator cable should be adjusted so that the pedal still has enough travel to work the kickdown switch in full throttle position.

9 Dual carburettors - balance pipe

1 On all models fitted with twin carburettors a balance pipe runs between the intake manifolds of each carburettor. This enables the induction manifold pressure to be equalised from side to side thus ensuring uniformity of carburettor setting.
2 If the connecting hoses at each end of the balance leak - or the pipe itself is fractured the engine will not run properly because secondary air will be let in. One can usually hear hissing sounds when this happens. Make sure that the balance pipe and connections are in good condition.

10 Fuel pump

1 A simple mechanical pump is operated by a push-rod from the camshaft. Figure 2.5 refers. The push-rod impinges on the operating lever and draws the diaphragm downwards. Fuel is drawn in through the suction non-return valve, and as the spring faces the diaphragm upwards, the fuel is expelled through the outlet pipe via the pressure valve. A cut-off diaphragm stops the fuel flowing into the diaphragm when at rest.
at rest.
2 An exploded view of the pump is given at Figure 2.6.
3 The pump can be checked whilst the engine is still in the vehicle given suitable apparatus. The delivery capacity is 400 cc/min at 3800 rpm at which speed the pressure should be 5 lbs. sq.in.
4 To remove the pump loosen the clamp on the heat control box on the left hand heat exchanger and pull the box off the exchanger, remove the lower part of the deflector plate, remove the left upper screw of the upper deflector plate and loosen the right upper screw (photo).
5 Push the left upper deflector plate to one side pivoting round the screws, then with a ratchet wrench angled at 120° remove the two socket head cap screws and the pump with gasket and flange will come away. (photo).
6 Before re-installing the pump check the push rod stroke. This should be 5mm clear of the flange at its highest point. If necessary adjust by fitting extra or less gaskets. (photo). The smaller

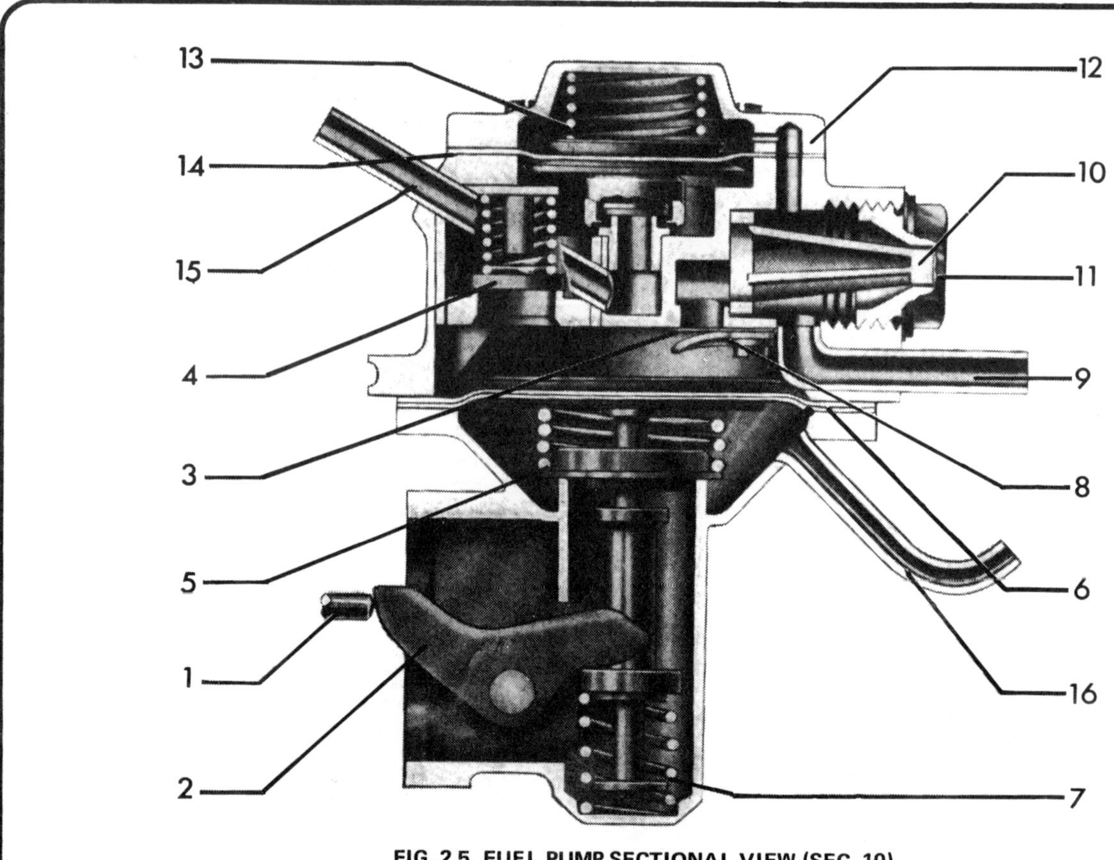

FIG. 2.5. FUEL PUMP SECTIONAL VIEW (SEC. 10)

1 Push rod
2 Operating lever
3 Suction valve
4 Pressure valve
5 Diaphragm spring
6 Diaphragm
7 Lever return spring
8 Suction valve retainer
9 Inlet pipe
10 Fuel filter
11 Plug
12 Upper cover
13 Spring
14 Cut off diaphragm
15 Outlet pipe
16 Breather

10.4. The fuel pump showing screws to be removed before it can be extracted

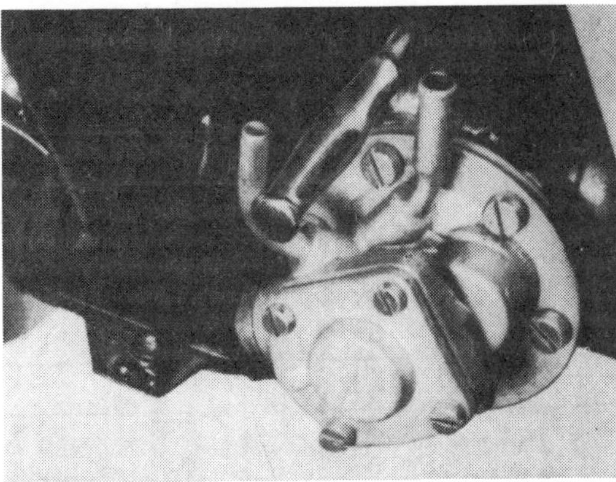

10.5. A clear view of the fuel pump, hoses have been removed

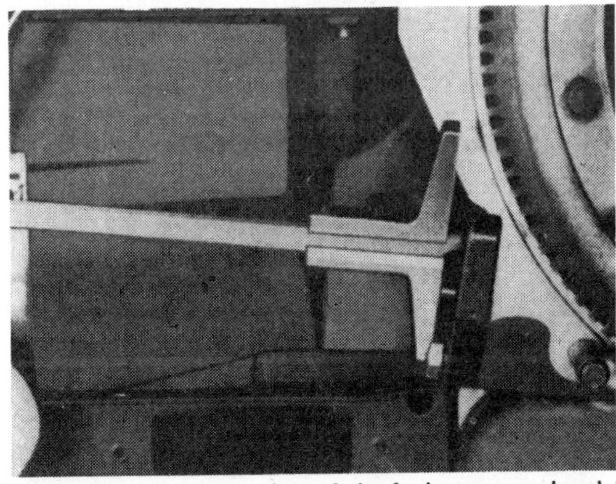

10.6. Measuring the protrusion of the fuel pump pushrod. This should be 5 mm and must be brought to this dimension with suitable gaskets

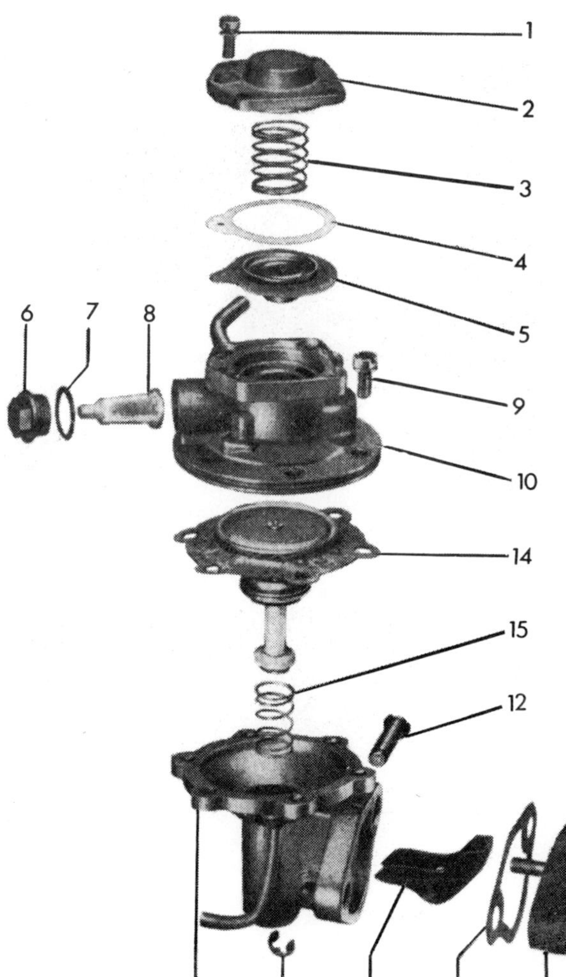

FIG. 2.6. FUEL PUMP EXPLODED VIEW (SEC. 10)

1 Screw
2 Cover
3 Spring
4 Gasket
5 Cut off diaphragm
6 Plug
7 Washer
8 Filter
9 Screw (6 off)
10 Pump upper part
11 Circlip
12 Lever shaft
13 Operating lever
14 Diaphragm and spring
15 Spring
16 Pump lower casing
17 Gasket
18 Flange
19 Gasket
20 Push rod

end of the push rod bears on the camshaft.
7 The lower portion of the pump should be packed with multi-purpose grease and the cap screws tightened uniformly but not overtightened.
8 Should it be necessary to replace the diaphragm mark the upper and lower parts of the pump before dismantling so that correct alignment may be obtained on reassembly. The pump base must be held securely during dismantling and reassembly. When fitting a new diaphragm the operating lever should be depressed 5mm to set the diaphragm in the correct position.

11 Fuel tank

1 The fuel tank should not give trouble but if persistent signs of rust are found in the fuel filter then the tank should be removed for cleaning. It is a very big job.
2 Drain off the fuel from underneath and clip the outlet pipe to prevent any further oil discharge (photo).
3 Pull the luggage compartment lining away and remove the covers from the access holes. (photo).
4 Detach the fuel gauge cable.
5 Loosen the clip securing the hose to the tank filler neck and remove the boot for the filler neck. Pull the filler neck out. (photo).
6 Remove the front axle carrier complete with track control arms tie rods, steering box and bracket for steering idler arm, detach the stabilizer from the track control arm. (See Chapter 11).
7 Remove two nuts and brackets and remove the tank out from underneath the car. (photo).
8 Installation is the reverse of dismantling. In view of the large amount of derusting fluid required and the type of chemical to be used (11 Imperial/13 US gallons of ANTOX Extra M Derusting phosphate agent) plus the important rinsing and sealing procedure it is thought that an expert firm should be employed to clean and derust the tank, especially in view of the large amount of work to extract it from the vehicle.

11.2. Clip off the fuel hose

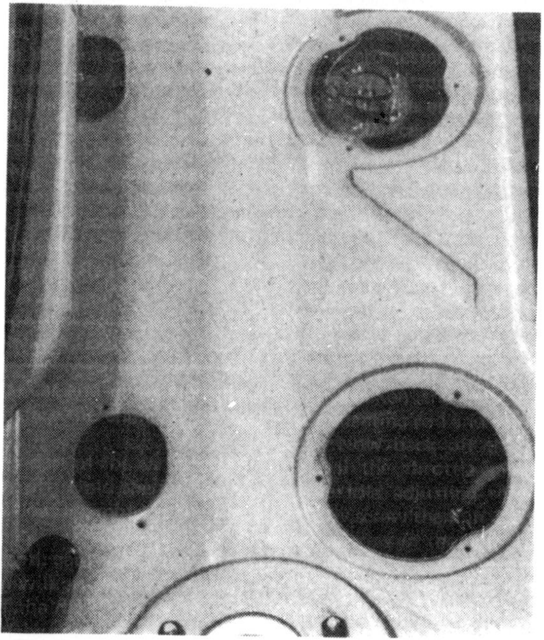

11.3. Access holes to the fuel tank under the luggage compartment lining

11.5. The filler neck

11.7. The nuts and retainers must be removed before the tank will come out

12 Fuel strainer

1 Fortunately the fuel strainer can be removed while the tank is installed by screwing out the threaded ring. When refitting the strainer fit a new sealing ring (photo), between the flange and the metal plate on the pipe. The tabs must engage the slots before the ring is tightened.
2 As the strainer is incorporated in the outlet pipe union it is necessary to drain the tank before removing the sealing ring.

13 Accelerator pedal

1 A layout of the accelerator pedal fitted to all models left hand and right hand drive is given in Fig 2.7. The cable in the right hand drive models is routed differently and is thus longer, so that if it is necessary to replace the cable note should be taken of its length.
2 If the cable is worn or frayed it should be replaced. As and when necessary detach the cable and pull the cable out to grease the inner wire.
3 When installing note the precaution in Section 7.13 of this Chapter.

14 Exhaust emission control equipment

1 The legislation forecast for the next two years on atmospheric pollution will vary with different countries, from none in some places to a great deal, particularly in the USA.

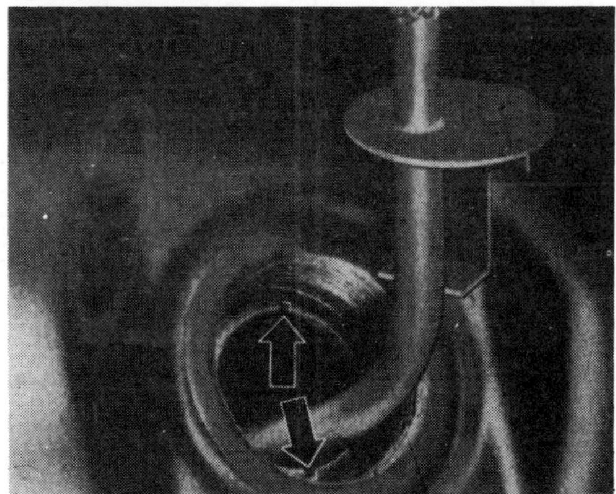

12.1. The outlet pipe and joint. The recesses are marked. This picture has been taken with the tank out of the chassis.

2 Charcoal filters, recirculating exhaust gas devices, over run cut-off switches, crankcase fume recirculation systems and many more attempts to solve the problem are already with us.
3 This manual does not propose to go in depth into the subject as the situation is changing rapidly. Owners of VW 411/412 are advised to consult their VW agents as to the local legal programme and the VW solution to cope with it. Also they will be able to analyse the specific fitment to your vehicle. Rest assured that little can be undertaken in the way of overhaul; rather that replacement will be necessary. Nevertheless, the VW dealer is the best placed person to help.

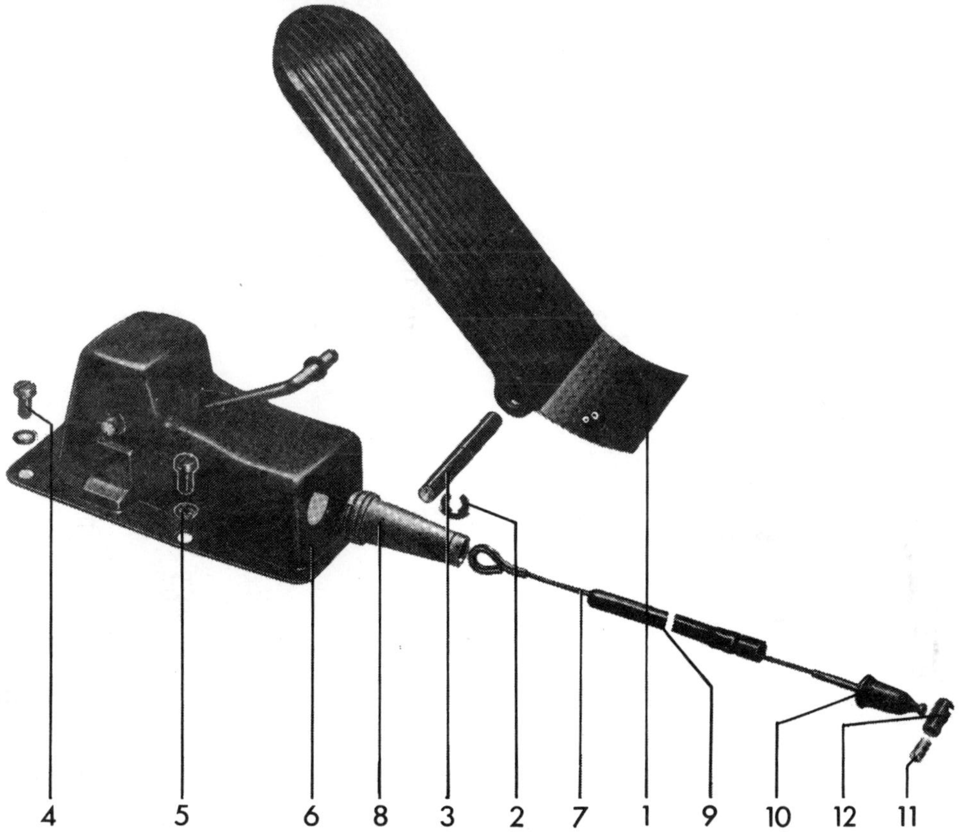

4 5 6 8 3 2 7 1 9 10 12 11

FIG. 2.7. ACCELERATOR PEDAL (ALL MODELS) (SEC. 13)
Note: Vehicles with automatic transmission have a kick down device on the pedal bracket

1 Pedal
2 Circlip
3 Pin
4 Screw M6
5 Spring washer
6 Bracket
7 Cable
8 Sleeve
9 Outer cable
10 Grommet
11 Pin (threaded)
12 Roller

15 FAULT DIAGNOSIS

As many owners will know (some to their cost) snap diagnosis of faults due to "carburettor problems" can result in an irritating flutter being transformed into near complete immobility.

Prior to the design changes brought about by exhaust emission control systems the check procedures were reasonably straightforward and the table below should suffice if followed logically through. More recently there are additional matters to worry about and all engine parts must be in good condition if adequate performance and acceptable exhaust emission levels are to be maintained.

Before acting on the fuel system it is necessary to check the ignition system first. Even though a fault may lie in the fuel system it will be difficult to trace unless the ignition is correct. The table below therefore, assumes that the ignition system is in order.

Symptom	Reason/s	Remedy
Smell of petrol when engine is stopped	Leaking fuel lines or unions	Repair or renew as necessary.
	Leaking fuel tank	Fill fuel tank to capacity and examine carefully at seams, unions and filler pipe connections.
Smell of petrol when engine is idling	Leaking fuel line unions between pump and carburettor	Check line and unions and tighten or repair.
	Overflow of fuel from float chamber due to wrong level setting or ineffective needle valve or punctured float	Check fuel level setting and condition of float and needle valve and renew if necessary.
Excessive fuel consumption for reasons not covered by leaks or float chamber faults	Worn jets	Renew jets.
	Sticking strangler flap	Check correct movement of strangler flap.
Difficult starting, uneven running, lack of power, cutting out	One or more jets blocked or restricted	Dismantle and clean out float chamber and jets.
	Float chamber fuel level too low or needle valve sticking	Dismantle and check fuel level and needle valve.
	Fuel pump not delivering sufficient fuel	Check pump delivery and clean or repair as required.
	Intake manifold gaskets leaking, or manifold fractured	Check tightness of mounting nuts and inspect manifold connections.
	Balance pipe between twin carburettors leaking	Check pipe for fractures and hose connections for tightness and splits.
	Twin carburettors out of balance	Balance carburettors.

Chapter 3 Fuel injection equipment

Contents

Specifications

System - low pressure	VW - Bosch (28 psi)	
Petrol pump	Electric	
Filter	Sealed, renewable every 12000 miles	
Injectors	Electrically operated	
Opening gap	0.15 mm (not adjustable)	
Air cleaner		
Up to 1973	Oil bath	
1973	Paper type	
Slow running adjustment - manual gearbox	850 - 900 rpm	
- automatic gearbox	Up to engine No. WO 105248	700 - 750 rpm
	After engine No. WO 105248	650 ± 50 rpm
Torque wrench settings:	**lb ft**	**mkg**
Injector/manifold bolts to cylinder head	4	0.6

1 General description

1 Introduced in August 1969 the system is a low pressure (28 p.s.i) constant pressure system. The fuel is supplied from the tank in the front of the vehicle by an electric pump fitted under the fuel tank. The fuel pipes conduct fuel via a filter to the injectors, one for each cylinder, fitted in the engine compartment. In effect the fuel system is a ring main, fuel in excess of that required being returned to the fuel tank via a second line. Pressure is maintained by a pressure regulator (photo). Fuel is also supplied from the ring main to a cold starting valve.

1.1 The fuel pressure regulator which is mounted on the forward engine plate

2 Air is supplied from the louvres in the rear side of the vehicle via hoses and an air cleaner to the air intake distributor at the inlet of which is situated the throttle valve controlled by the accelerator pedal. Four pipes lead away from the air intake, one to each cylinder head. A short flexible connection joins each pipe to the air distributor and at the other end each pair of pipes form an integral part of a casting which bolts to the cylinder heads. This casting carries an injector for each cylinder and it is at this point that the petrol is injected onto the back of the inlet valve.

3 The injector is controlled electronically by a solenoid, the armature of which opens the injection and a spring which closes the nozzle when the current to the solenoid is switched off. Since the injection is either fully open or shut and the pressure of the fuel is constant it follows that the amount of fuel injected is completely governed by the length of time the nozzle remains open. This is determined by the control unit, which in the Type 4 is behind the arm rest in the right rear seat (photos). The control unit is a mini computer .

4 To determine the length of injection time the control unit is supplied with information from various sources. Certain of these control the basic quantity of fuel required. These are the pressure sensor (photo) which supplies the information concerning the pressure conditions in the intake distributor, and the trigger contact mechanism in the distributor which passes electrical impulses to the control unit measuring the engine speed and supplying the information as to the exact moment injection should open.

5 In addition there are a number of correction devices supplying information to the control unit. Temperature Sensor One in the intake distributor and Temperature Sensor Two in the

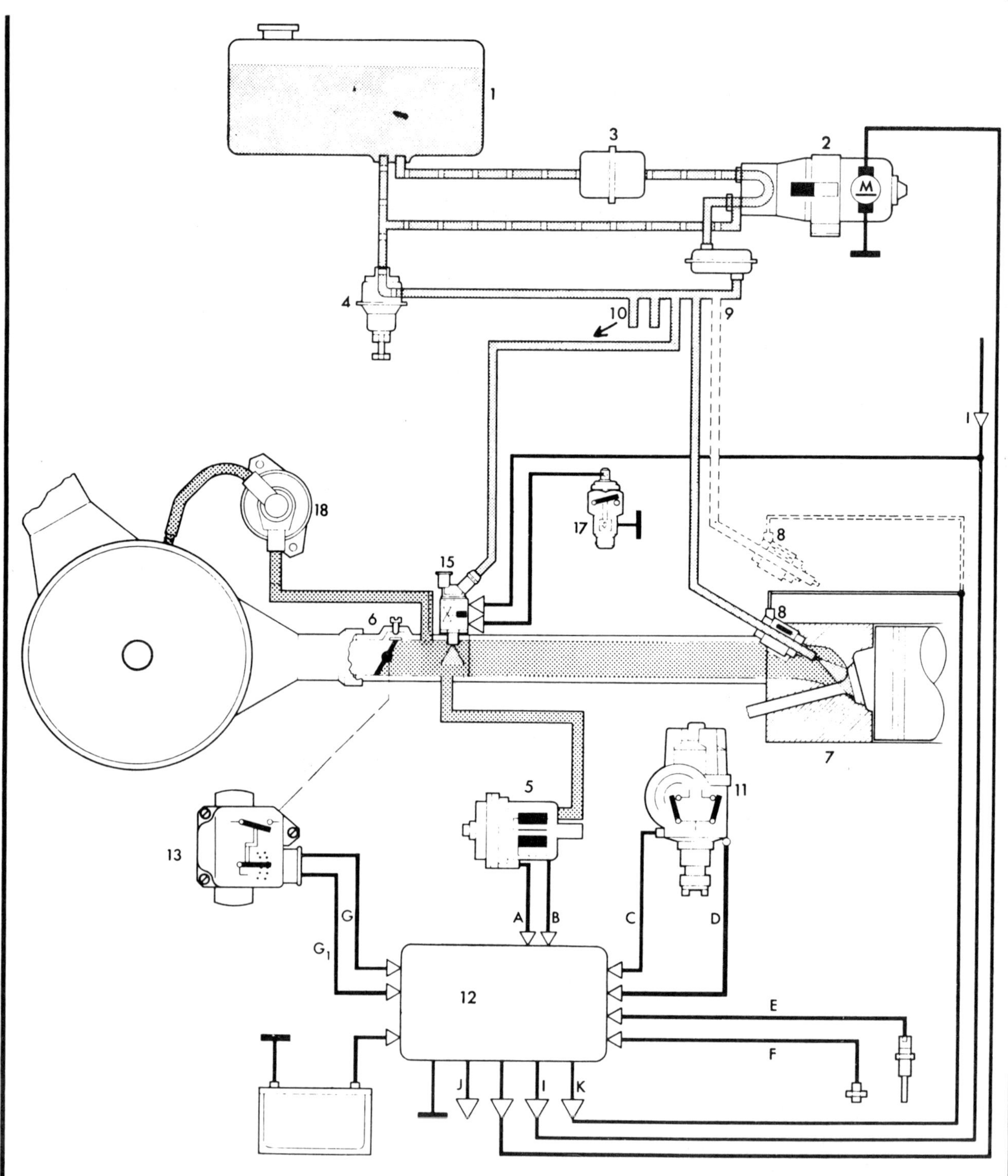

FIG. 3.1. FUEL INJECTION SYSTEM – DIAGRAMMATIC LAYOUT

1 Fuel tank
2 Fuel pump
3 Fuel filter
4 Fuel pressure regulator
5 Air pressure sensor
6 Air intake distributor and throttle valve
7 Cylinder head
8 Fuel injectors
9 Fuel distribution pipes to injectors
10 Fuel distribution pipes to cold start valve
11 Ignition distributor with trigger contacts
12 Control unit (mini-computer)
13 Throttle valve switch (with acceleration enrichment)
15 Cold starting fuel valve
17 Cold start temperature sensor switch
18 Auxiliary air regulator
A Outside air pressure signal
B Air manifold vacuum signal
C RPM signal
D Timing signal
E Warming up temperature signal
F Cold start temperature signal
G Fuel cut-off signal
H Acceleration enrichment signal
I From starter solenoid terminal 50 (cold start enrichment)
J Injector valve opening signal-cylinders 1 and 4
K Injector valve opening signal-cylinders 2 and 3

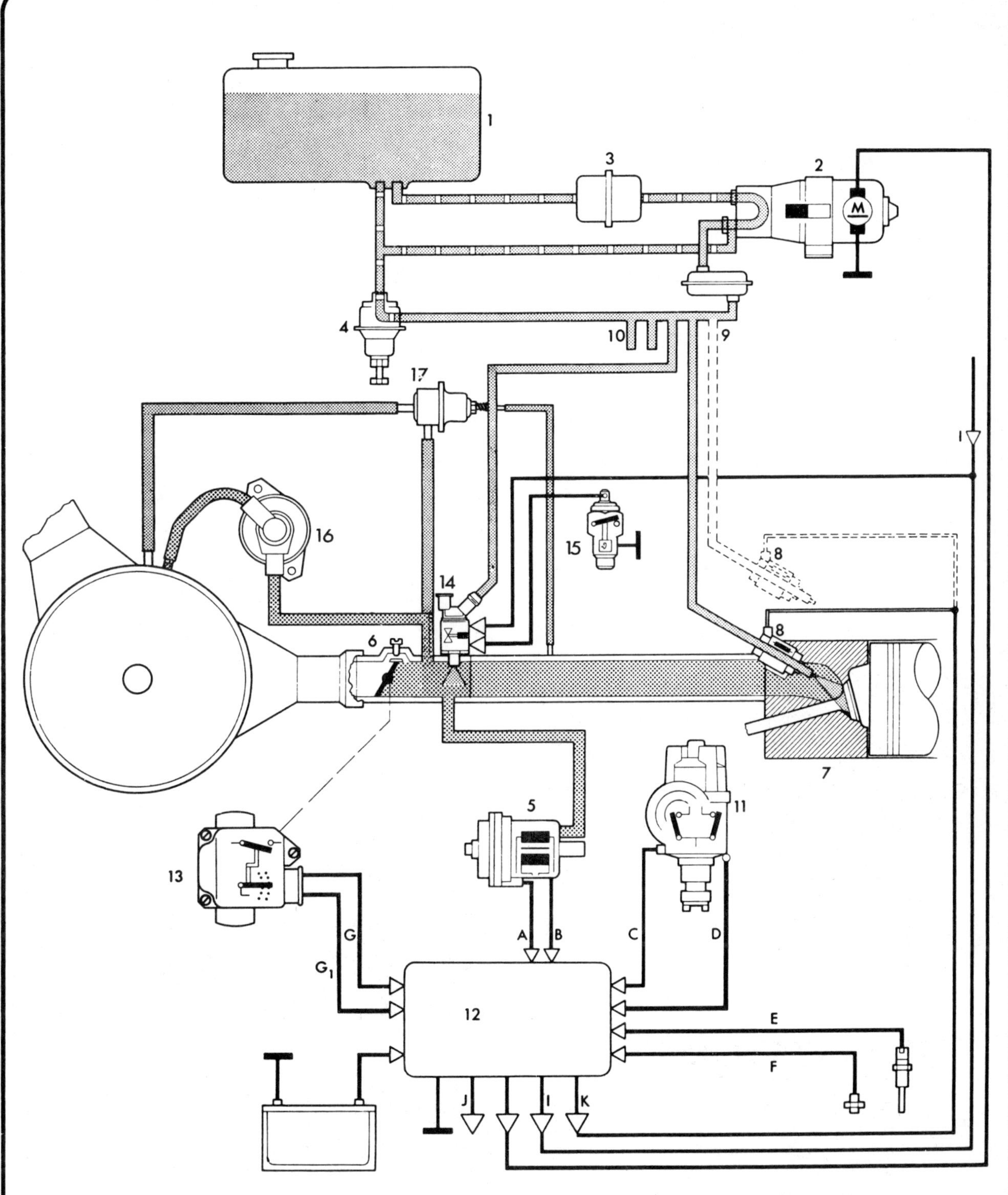

FIG. 3.2. FUEL INJECTION SYSTEM – DIAGRAMMATIC LAYOUT CALIFORNIA VERSION FROM AUGUST 1971 (SECS. 1 AND II

1 Fuel tank
2 Fuel pump
3 Fuel filter
4 Pressure regulator
5 Pressure sensor
6 Intake air distributor with throttle valve support
7 Cylinder head
8 Injector
9 Fuel ring main
10 Fuel ring main with connection for cold starting
11 Trigger contacts
12 Control unit
13 Throttle valve switch
14 Cold starting valve
15 Thermo switch (cold start)
16 Auxiliary air regulator
17 Deceleration valve (USA only)
A&B Pressure sensor signals
C&D From ignition trigger mechanism
E&F Temperature sensors
G Extra fuel for acceleration
I From starter solenoid terminal 50
J&K To injectors

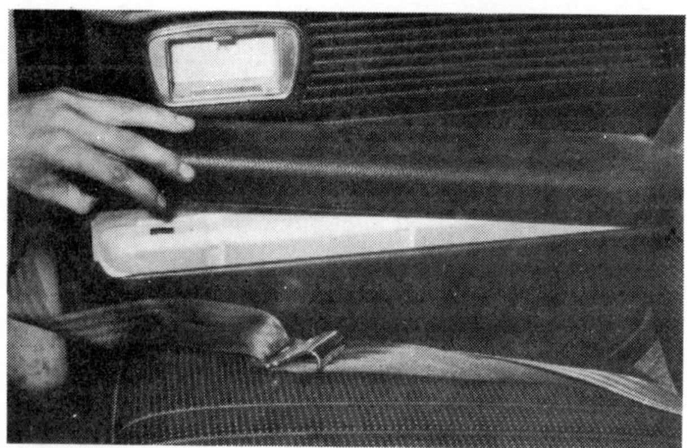

1.3a Lift up the top of the arm rest

1.3c and the control unit is visible

1.5a Temperature sensor 1 (arrow) measuring the air temperature in the intake distributor

1.6 Picture taken during assembly shows the air intake distributor. The fitter has the auxiliary air intake in his left hand and his right hand points to the throttle valve switch on the bottom of the air intake control valve. The slow running adjusting screw is on the top right of the air intake.

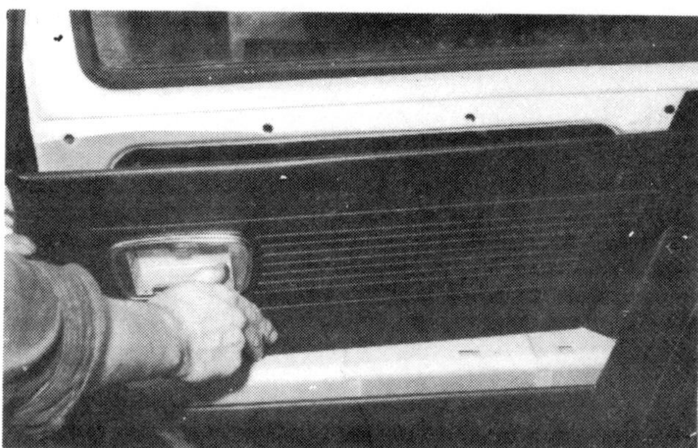

1.3b Ease the trim away

1.4 The pressure sensor mounted under the left hand side of the engine compartment which supplies information about pressure in the manifold. Hose is disconnected

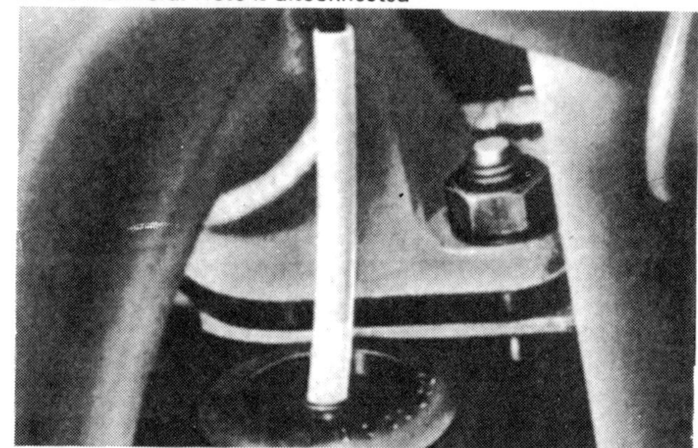

1.5b Temperature sensor 2 measuring the cylinder head temperature. When replacing make sure the raised figures are as shown in the picture. The nut is holding the injector housing

1.7 The thermo switch which regulates the cold starting valve at the back of the air intake and allows extra fuel when necessary.

cylinder head supply information governing the starting and warming up period. These are resistances; as the temperature rises the resistance increases and this in turn alters the signal to the control unit and has an influence on the opening period of the injectors. They cannot be adjusted. (photos).

6 During the warming up period the engine requires an extra amount of air. On the Type 4 this is arranged by the auxiliary air regulator which is situated by the air intake distributor. (photo). This has an electric heater element which warms up as the engine warms up and causes a bi-metal spring to expand closing the regulator and cutting off the auxiliary supply of air as the engine reaches operating temperature.

7 For cold starting a valve situated on the back of the intake distributor injects fuel into the air distributor. This is regulated by a thermo switch placed adjacent to it and held by a bracket to the crankcase. (photo).

8 When the accelerator is depressed (for increased speed) an extra amount of fuel is required as well as extra air. This is provided by a switch contact which moves across two contact strips and is actuated by the throttle valve. It is enclosed in a black plastic case bolted to the bottom of the throttle housing, (photo 1.6). The four pin plug connects wiring to the control unit which in turn signals a longer opening time to the injectors.

This works in reverse on deceleration cutting off the fuel as the accelerator is lifted and giving engine braking without the over-run pollution normal to carburettor type engines.

9 The control unit, the heart of the business, situated away from the engine compartment in the side of the car is connected by a multi-pin plug to the sender units. Even this plug requires a special tool to extract it.

The control unit main components are the two output stages, the time stage, and the logic stage. The warm up and acceleration enrichment stages (WL and BA) are correction devices. The pressure sensor and the two trigger contacts are in the time stage. The speed switch, (DS) and throttle valve switch (DKS) work together to cut off the fuel supply on deceleration. A fuel cut-off (AF) was installed until August 1971. The time circuit (VSI) ensures that the electric fuel pump is switched on only when the starter is operated or the engine speed is greater than 100 rpm. A diagram (Fig 3.3) is appended.

10 Injection timing is controlled by two trigger contacts in the

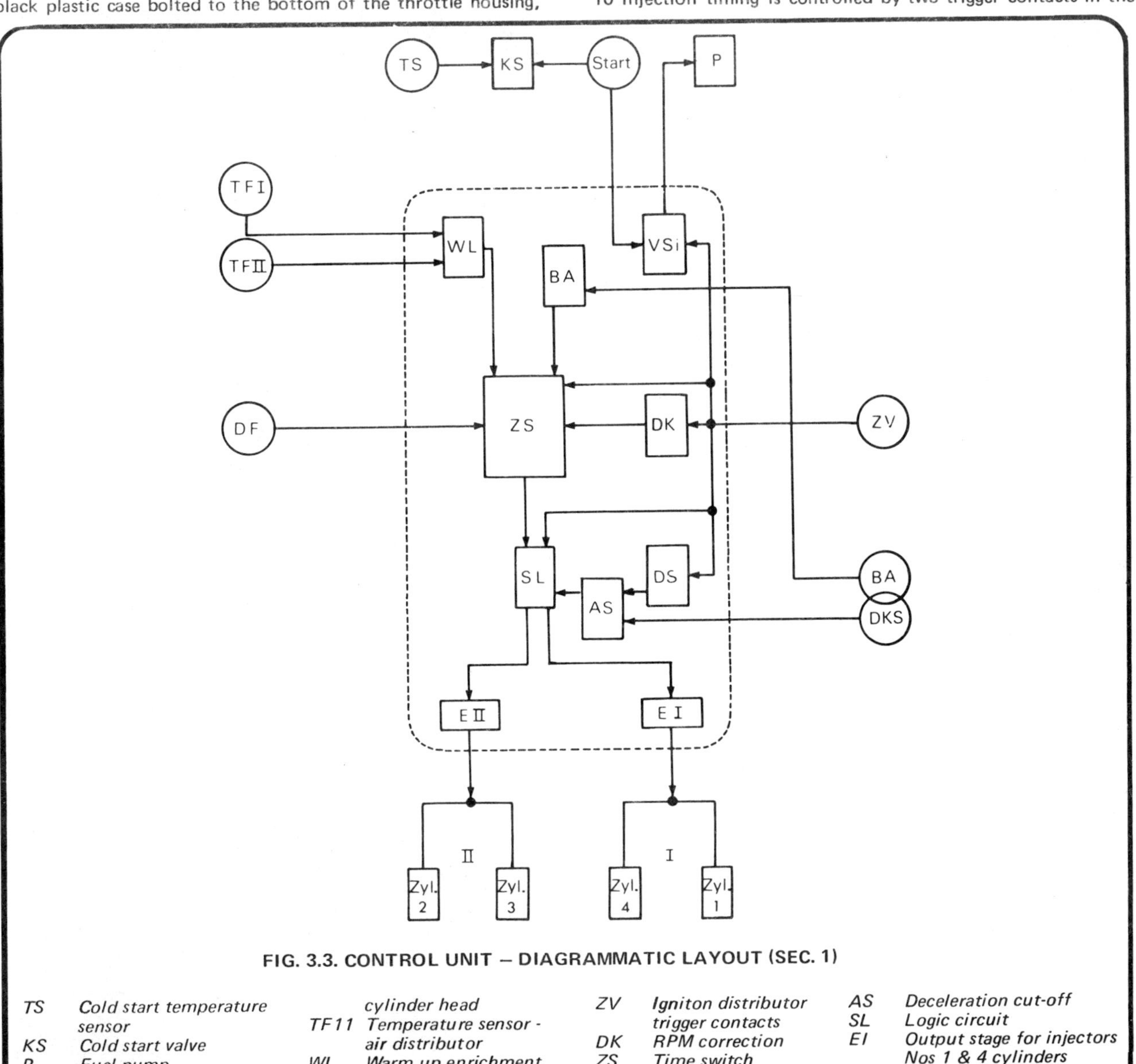

FIG. 3.3. CONTROL UNIT – DIAGRAMMATIC LAYOUT (SEC. 1)

TS *Cold start temperature sensor*
KS *Cold start valve*
P *Fuel pump*
VS1 *Overflow cut-off*
TF1 *Temperature sensor - cylinder head*
TF11 *Temperature sensor - air distributor*
WL *Warm up enrichment*
BA *Acceleration enrichment*
DF *Pressure sensor*
ZV *Igniton distributor trigger contacts*
DK *RPM correction*
ZS *Time switch*
DKS *Throttle valve switch*
DS *Speed switch*
AS *Deceleration cut-off*
SL *Logic circuit*
EI *Output stage for injectors Nos 1 & 4 cylinders*
E11 *Output stage for injectors Nos 2 & 3 cylinders*

lower half of the distributor. Two screws hold the contacts in place. A three pin connector carries the signals (photos). The contacts are 180° apart (photo). No adjustment is possible. The contacts are operated by a cam on the distributor shaft so that the injection timing is controlled by the same shaft as the ignition timing.

11 Two photographs show the left hand and right hand halves of the engine compartment with the fuel injection equipment located. The air cleaner and hoses are removed as are several of the smaller hoses to give a clearer view.

2 Maintenance and adjustment - general remarks

1 There are two schools of thought on this subject. The first recommends the owner driver not to touch anything but to go to the agent at the first sign of trouble. This is alright for rich owners. The second school very sensibly says there is no black magic in this and prepare to do all tests and adjustments at home. For such an enthusiast there is a very good publication on the fuel injection system written by an American author who has a great deal of experience in VW fuel injection systems. This goes into the subject much more deeply than is intended in this manual. The main problem is that although the system may be dismantled and reassembled quite easily, unless a great deal of test gear is available little can be done to test and adjust the various components. The manual therefore discusses only what can be done by a keen owner driver with a reasonable tool kit, which should include a voltmeter to measure 12 volts.

3 Air cleaner

1 Regular maintenance of the air cleaner is essential. In very dusty conditions weekly or even daily checks must be done, but under normal conditions once a month is sufficient.

2 To remove the air cleaner pull off the crankcase breather hose, loosen the clip and pull off the hose between the intake air distributor and the upper part of the air cleaner (photo). Using a phillips screwdriver loosen the clip on the hose connecting the cleaner lower part and the air duct. Undo the clip on the intake air preheating and pull the hose off. Remove both hoses for load and temperature - sensitive intake air preheating from the connections on the upper part of the cleaner.

3 Remove the wing screw from the centre of the cleaner (photo) and lift the heater out in a horizontal position.

4 Undo the clips and take the top part of the cleaner away from the bottom half. DO NOT lay the top down with the filter element upwards or dirty oil will run into the duct from the filter. (photo).

5 There should be a layer of oil in the lower part. This will be on top of a layer of sludge formed by dust extracted from the intaken air. There MUST be at least 3/16 in (5 mm) of oil on top of the sludge for efficient working. Clean out the oil and sludge from the lower half and replace it with 0.8 pints of engine oil (0.45 litres). Use SAE 30 in temperate climates and SAE 10 in very cold ones.

6 Unless the cleaner has been neglected the top half will not need attention. However check it for blockage of air holes and remove any dirt with a piece of wood.

7 Reassembly is the reverse of removal but do not tighten the wing nut until the hoses are assembled satisfactorily. Make sure that the '4L' mark on the top half and the arrow on the bottom half are aligned correctly.

8 In October 1972 the filter was changed from an oil bath type to a paper filter type in a plastic housing. The filter element should be replaced every 18000 miles or two years whichever is the sooner.

4 Air hoses

1 Apart from the large rubber hoses which carry the main air

1.10a Removing the lead from the distributor trigger contact. Distributor in engine

1.10b Removing the trigger contact after the two screws have been taken out. This can be done with the distributor in the engine. We took it out to get a better picture.

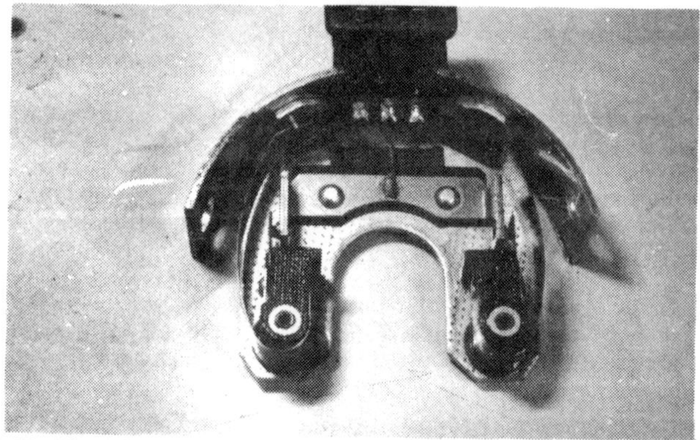

1.10c The trigger contact points. These are not adjustable and if worn or damaged must be replaced with a new set.

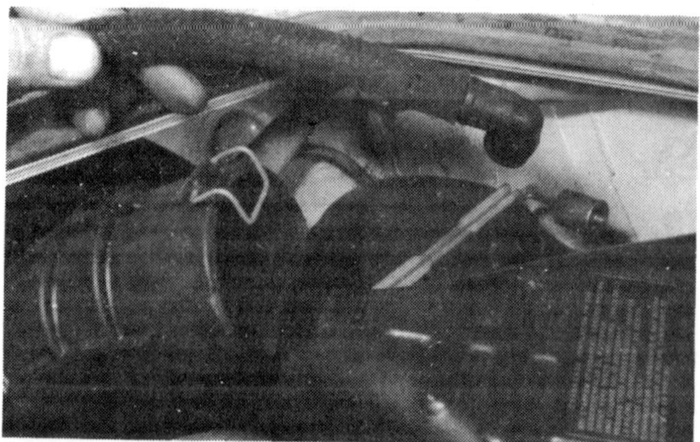

3.2 Remove the hose connections from the top of the air cleaner

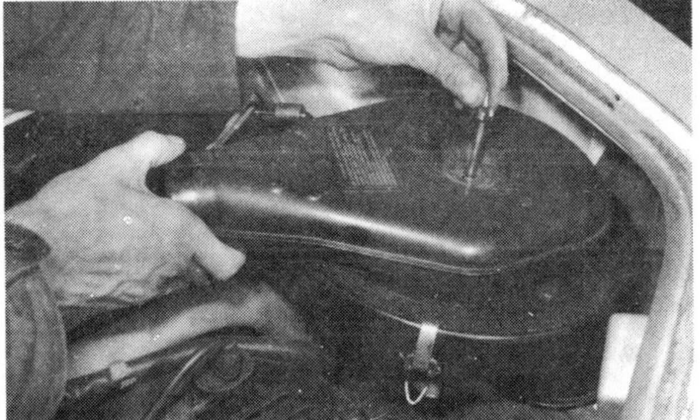

3.3 Take out the centre bolt and the cleaner may be lifted out

3.4 Undo the clips and the top can be lifted out of the base. This one has been emptied and cleared ready for refilling (0.8 pints) with S.A.E. 30

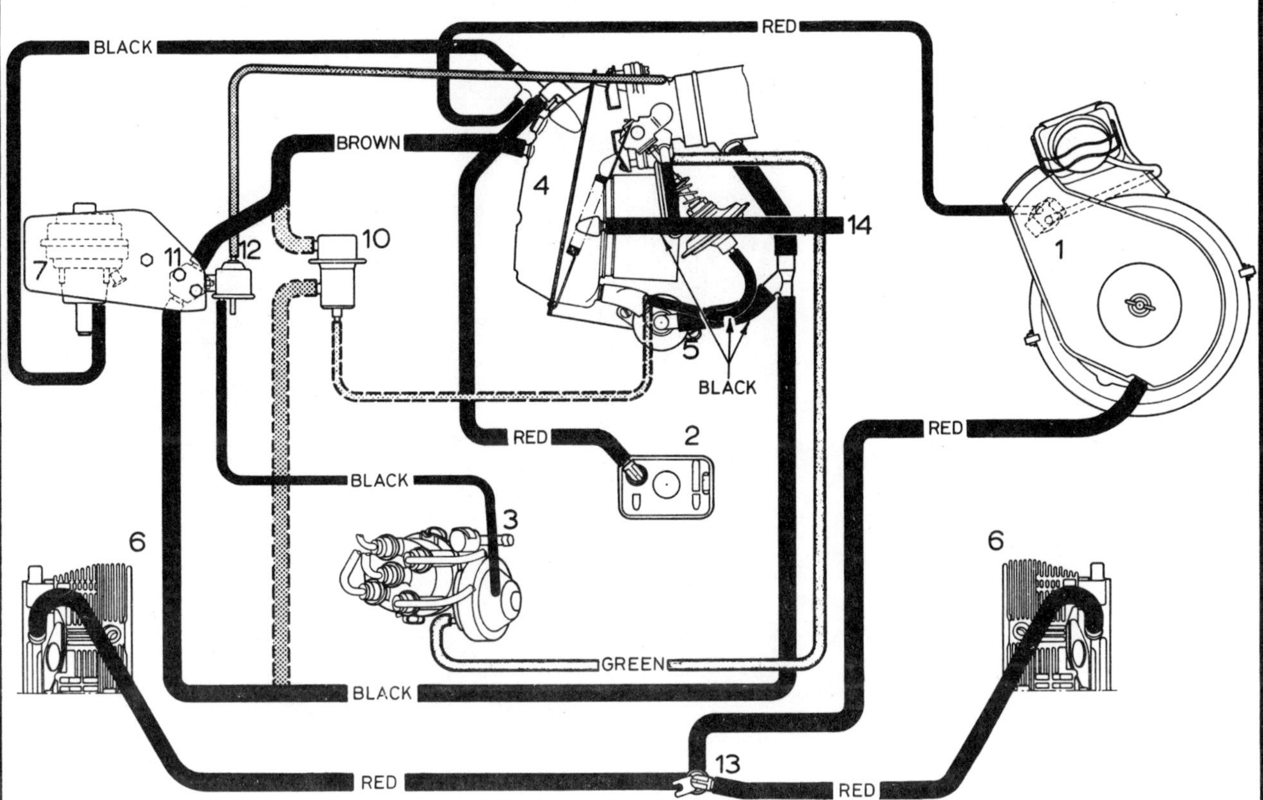

FIG. 3.4. ENGINE COMPARTMENT – HOSE CONNECTIONS (SEC. 4)

1 Air cleaner
2 Crankcase breather
3 Distributor
4 Air intake distributor
5 Auxiliary air regulator
6 Cylinder head
7 Pressure sensor
10 Deceleration valve (only USA) (pneumatic for manual transmission)
11 Deceleration valve (auto transmission - electro magnetic) (only USA)
12 Valve (two way) for ignition vacuum (only California)
13 Flame arrester
14 To automatic transmission

1.11a A view of the left hand side of the engine

1 *Inlet air pressure sensor* 2 *Fuel pressure regulator* 3 *Inlet air distributor* 4 *Crankcase breather cover* 5 *Timing mark plug* 6 *Heat exchanger connection*

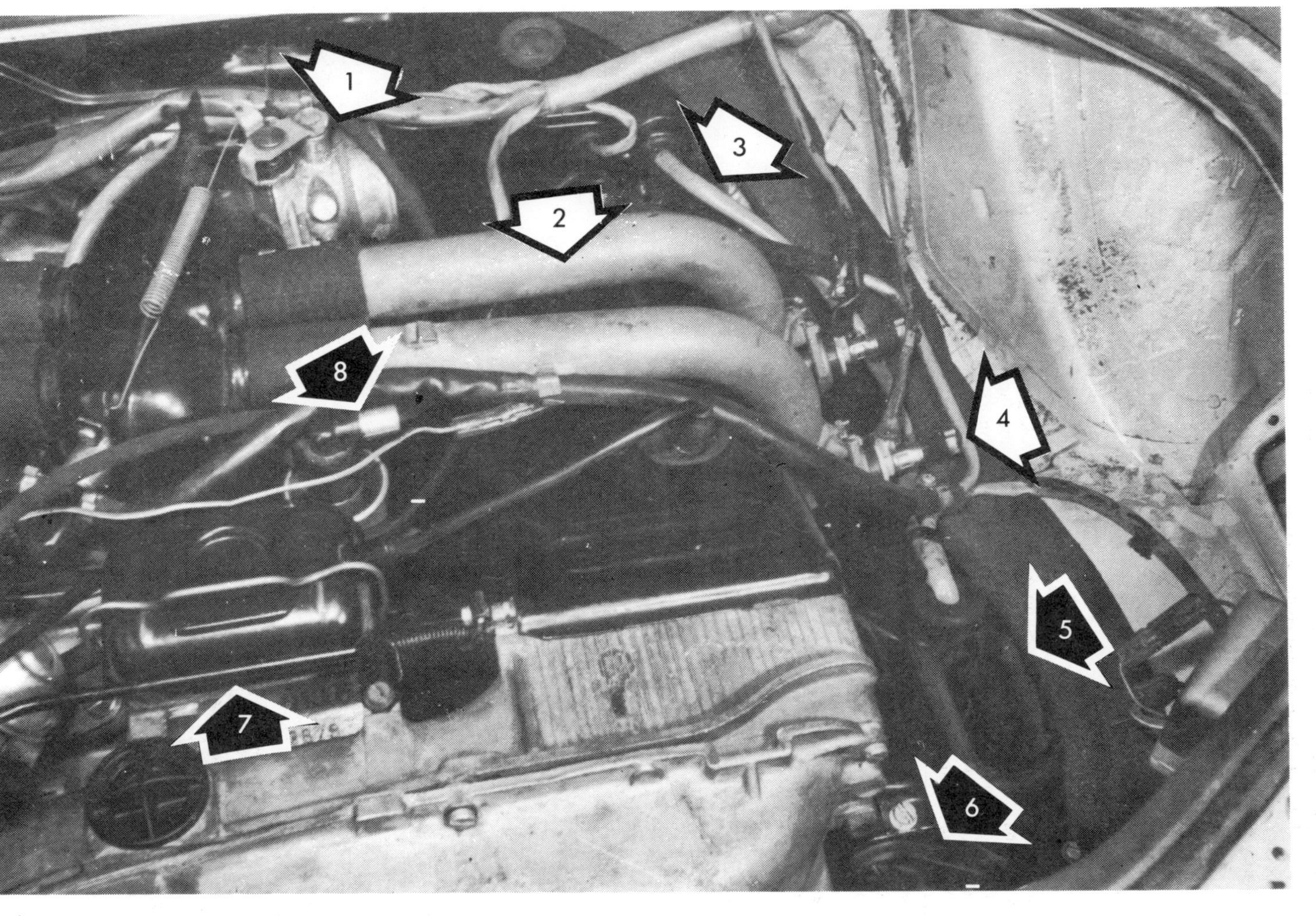

1.11b A view of the right hand side of the engine

1 *Air inlet throttle valve*
2 *Inlet manifold*
3 *Fuel ring main*
4 *Injectors*
5 *Heat exchanger inlet*
6 *Access hole to fan belt adjuster*
7 *Spindle for air flaps*
8 *Auxiliary air regulator*

supply to the air distributor there are a number of smaller hoses which interconnect the various part of the air system. A diagram (Fig.3.4) is given. It will be noted that certain of the hoses are on US (California) models only.

2 The only maintenance required is to keep the layout clean, tidy and free from grease. Make sure hoses do not chafe or fray at the ends. If it is necessary to remove a number of them at the same time label the ends so that they go back the right way round.

5 Fuel pump

1 Situated under the petrol tank the pump can be serviced from under the car.

2 To remove it clamp the fuel hoses to avoid fuel leaks, remove the electric connector, unbolt the clamp and lower the pump from its housing. Pull off the fuel hoses and the pump may be taken for testing and servicing.

3 The pump motor field is composed of permanent magnets (sinter magnets) which are sensitive to shock. The pump must not be dropped or hammered or the magnets will disintegrate and a new pump will be required.

4 A simple rig can be made to test the pump if required supplying petrol to inlet S (photo) and connecting the electrical contacts to a 12v supply. The pump requires about 2 amps to operate it. However if it is not working correctly it should be exchanged rather than dismantled. The electric motor is actually submerged in fuel during operation and the repair is a specialist business.

5 Replacement is the reverse of removal, Make sure the pressure line hose is clipped firmly to inlet D and that the protective cover is fitted to the electric plug. Remove the clamps from the hoses.

6 Fuel filter - replacement

1 The fuel filter is located at the front of the car close to the petrol pump (photo).

2 The filter must be replaced (on the same principle as the oil filter) every 12000 miles.

3 Cut off the fuel supply to it by clamping the hose on both sides, ease the filter out of the bracket and fit the replacement. Reconnect the hoses and remove the clamps.

7 Fuel pipes - inspection and maintenance

1 Although the system is labelled low pressure it is as well to remember that the operating pressure is 28lbs per square inch. The recommended rear tyre pressure is 26 p.s.i; the comparison should give you food for thought. Even more thought provoking is the fact that the pressure originates at the pump and the pressure line runs the full length of the car, through the engine compartment to the pressure regulator situated on the engine front bulkhead.

2 It is suggested therefore that the petrol pressure line is traced through the car while it is in good order rather than later when an emergency arises, as there is no tap.

3 The only maintenance required is to see that the pipes are not corroded or squashed and that the various joints do not leak. Any such defects can only be remedied by replacement, and only with the correct type of pipe or hose. It is recommended that the VW agent is consulted if replacement action is contemplated.

4 There are various types of pinch clamps obtainable, a mole wrench can be used in an emergency, and each enthusiast will have his own solution. VW agents usually make their own, but

5.4 The petrol pump S = Suction line, D Pressure line, R return line

6.1 The fuel filter which must be replaced every 12000 miles

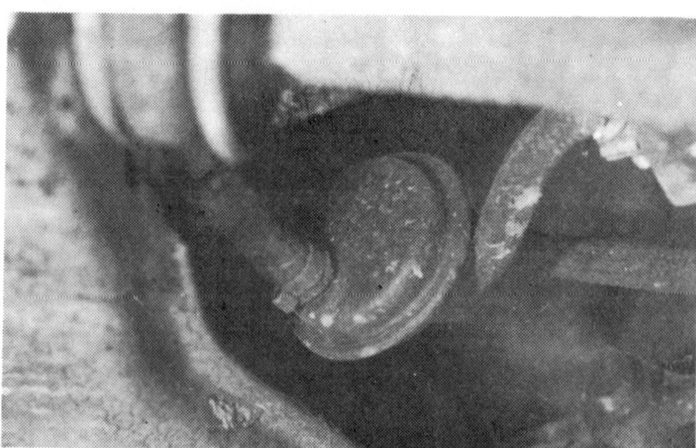
7.5 The muffler (damper) mounted near the petrol filter

the thing is to have a pair in the tool box, for as stated there is no tap in the system.

5 There is one small component of the fuel system which puzzles most people. It is a muffler, or damper, to iron out the impulses in the system. It is mounted forward near the petrol filter (photo). It should give little trouble and will require replacing only if it leaks or becomes ineffective due to damage.

8 Injectors

1 Removing and replacing the injectors is a simple task but the injector cannot be overhauled, only replaced with a new one.

2 There are three things which may go wrong with the injector itself.

a) The orifice may have become blocked (the gap is only 0.15 mm).

b) The solenoid may cease to operate.

c) The return spring may not function correctly.

3 Defects (a) and (b) will prevent fuel getting to the cylinder and cause misfiring, defect (c) will cause the nozzle to dribble and again affect the smooth running of the engine. The problem is to know which injection is causing the trouble. The simple way to find out is to short out each spark plug in turn. Shorting out a cylinder which is firing correctly will make matters worse, shorting out the faulty cylinder will make no difference.

4 Injectors must be removed from the engine in pairs. If the right hand pair is in trouble the air cleaner must be removed plus the heater hose. Seal off the petrol ring main either side of the the metal pipe and disconnect the fuel line distributor (the metal pipe). Pull off the electrical connections (photo).

5 Undo the four manifold securing nuts and remove the manifold (photo). The trunking to the air intake distributor will come away with the manifold.

6 A drawing of the manifold and injectors is given (Fig 3.5). Each injector is held into the manifold with a retainer, remove the nut and ease the faulty injector out of the manifold together with the inner and outer locating bushes.

7 When replacing the new injector push the inner locating bush into the manifold before installing the injector, install the injector, push the outer locating bush over the injector then the injector retainer and then tighten the retainer nut in place.

8.4 Removing the electrical connection from an injector

8.5 The ring main hoses have been removed and the inlet manifold with the injectors can be removed once the four retaining nuts are taken off

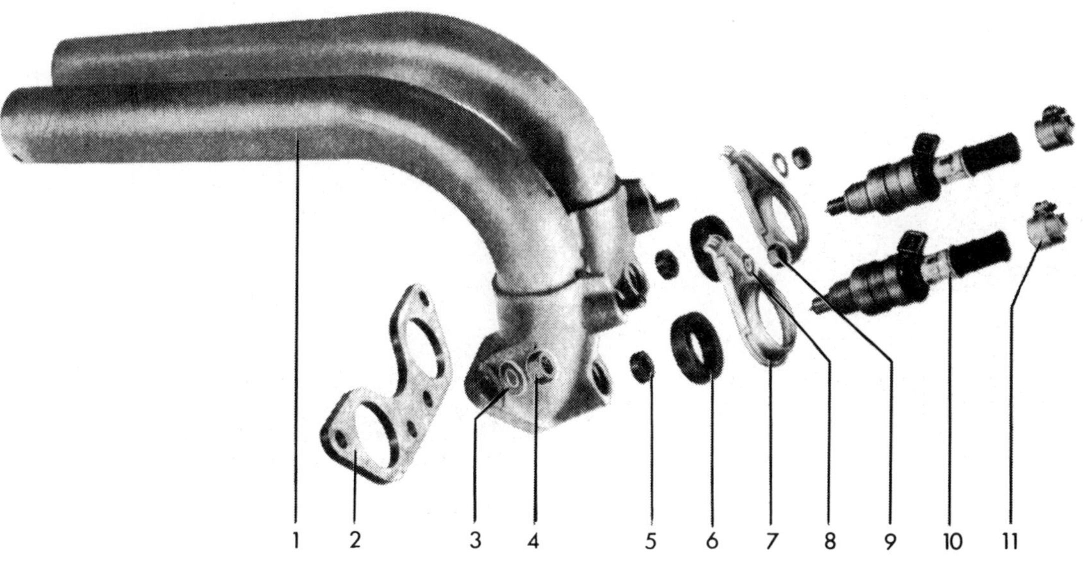

FIG. 3.5. INJECTOR – EXPLODED VIEW (SEC. 8)

1 Inlet manifold
2 Gasket
3 Spring washer
4 Nut
5 Locating bush inner
6 Locating bush outer
7 Retainer
8 Spring washer
9 Nut
10 Injector
11 Hose clip

8 Reinstall the injector manifold to the engine, tightening the manifold bolts to 4 ft.lb. (0.6 kgm).
9 Reconnect the petrol ring main and electrical connections, replace the air cleaner and hoses as necessary.

9 Ignition/injection timing and control wiring

1 Reference has already been made to the fuel injection timing device in Section 1.10 of this chapter. No maintenance of the contact unit is possible except replacement of the trigger contact.
2 The control wiring for the various parts of the system is colour coded and should present no problem. Each wire has a junction plug which enables the various units to be removed easily. Spade terminals are crimped on to the wires to fit the junction plugs. If a terminal is detached then a new one should be crimped on properly or faults will occur. Give the roll of insulating tape away!
3 Although trepidation may be felt about reconnecting the wiring on reassembly of the engine to the vehicle in fact the colour coding is so good that on the vehicle dismantled and reassembled for this manual the fitter was able to reconnect the wiring correctly first time without recourse to the wiring diagram even though he had no experience of the circuit. Nevertheless it is wise to put your own labels on disconnected wire and make certain.
4 Wiring diagrams for models up to 1971 and after 1971 are given plus the additional wiring for the USA version from 1971 onwards, Figs. 3.6, 3.7, and 3.8.

10 Slow running adjustment

1 This is really the only adjustment that can be done. The adjustment screw is on the top rear of the throttle valve casting. It is spring loaded and has a slot in the head to take a screwdriver (photo). The idling speed for the 4/1700E engine is 850-900 rpm., for both manual and automatic transmission. In the case of the automatic the engine should be warmed up before adjustment. (Engine oil temperature 50° - 70°C).
2 In 1971 the automatic gearbox model was fitted with an engine idling speed limiter. A vacuum operated diaphragm type mechanism is connected to the air intake distributor (photo). Adjustment of the locknut (arrowed) will move the rod and adjust the clearance 'a' between the screw head and the throttle valve lever.
3 The idling speed should be adjusted as in paragraph 1. With engines up to No.WO105248 adjust the clearance 'a' to 0.020 in. to 0.040 in. (0.5 to 1.0 mm) with the engine idling. With the handbrake hard on and the gear lever in 'drive' the engine speed should be 700 - 750 rpm. If it is not, adjust 'a' until it is.

With engines WO 105249 onward adjust the idling speed as in paragraph 1, apply the handbrake, select the drive range and the engine speed 650 ± 50 rpm should coincide with a gap 'a' 0.020 to 0.040 in. If it is not adjust the gap to give the correct speed.

11 Modifications

1 The advent of stringent exhaust emission laws have brought modification to the F.I. system. Modified control units pressure sensors, and throttle valve switches to give closer emission control, and an earth (ground) connection to the temperature sensors to cut out induction effects caused by the ignition system.
2 In models exported to California from 1972 onward the fuel system has been further modified. A pneumatic (manual shift vehicles) or electro magnetic (automatic transmission) valve provides extra air on the engine overun to weaken the mixture. The hose connections are shown in Fig 3.2., and the wiring diagram in Fig.3.8.

10.1 The screwdriver is in the slot of the slow running adjusting screw

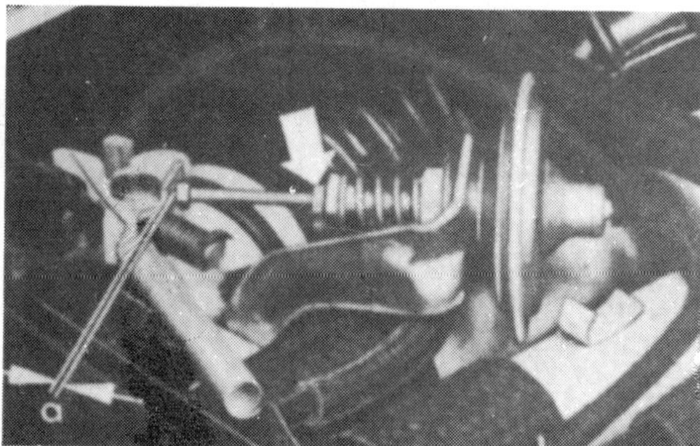

10.2 The idling speed limiter fitted to automatic transmission models in 1971. Gap "a" is adjusted by undoing the locknut (arrow) and turning the rod

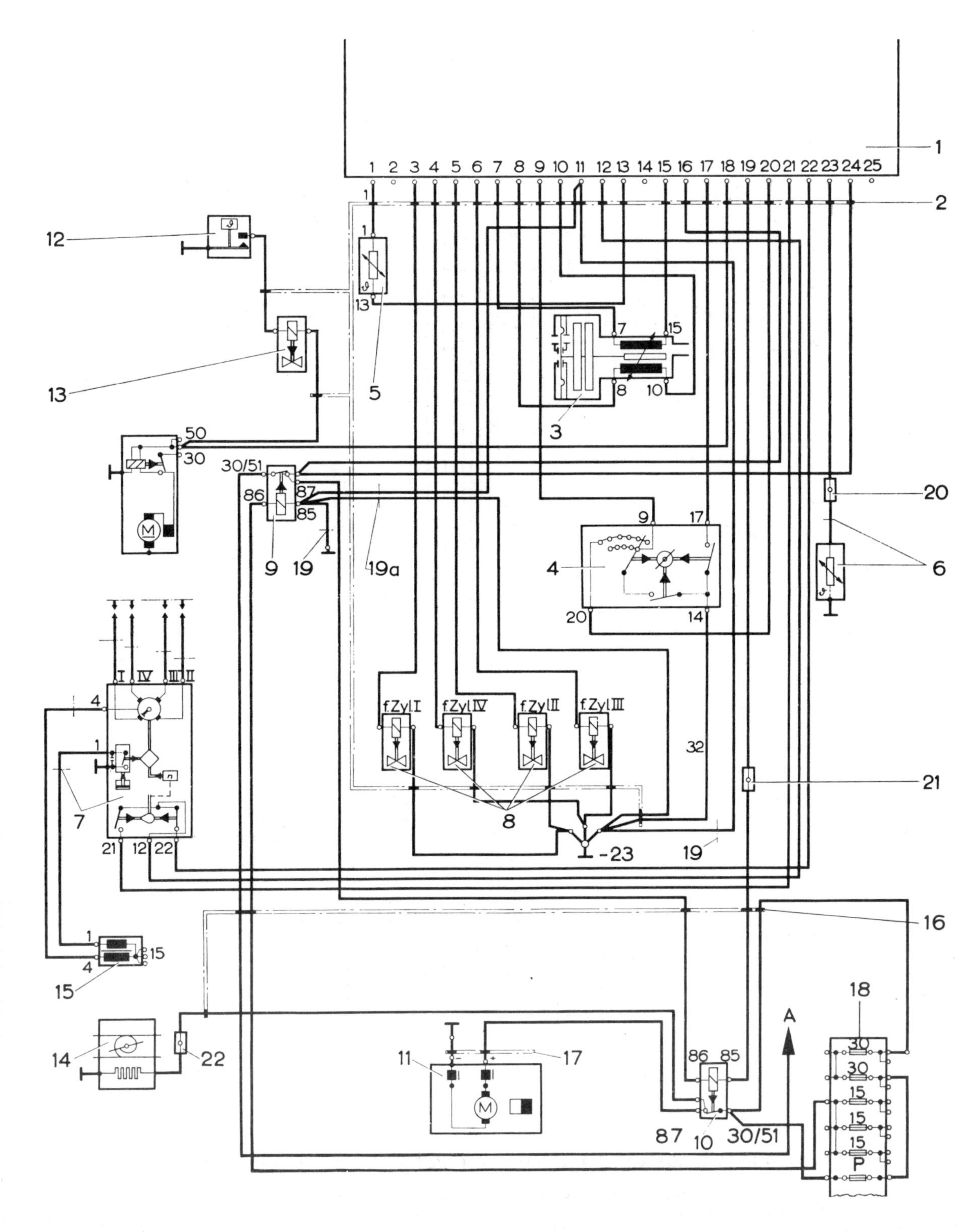

FIG. 3.6. WIRING DIAGRAM – FUEL INJECTION SYSTEM UP TO AUGUST 1971 (SEC. 9)

1 *Control unit*
2 *Wiring harness (electronic)*
3 *Pressure sensor*
4 *Throttle valve switch*
5 *Temperature sensor I (air intake)*
6 *Temperature sensor II (cylinder head)*
7 *Distributor trigger mechanism*
8 *Injectors*
9 *Relay (voltage)*
10 *Relay (pump)*
11 *Fuel pump*
12 *Thermo switch (cold start)*
13 *Cold start valve*
14 *Aux. air valve*
15 *Coil*
16 *Cable harness*
17 *Fuel pump cables*
18 *Fuse box*
19 *Earth wire Sedan*
19a *Earth wire Variant*
20 *Cable connectors (single)*
21 *Cable connectors (single)*
22 *Cable connectors (single)*
23 *Earth to engine housing*
A *Positive battery cable*

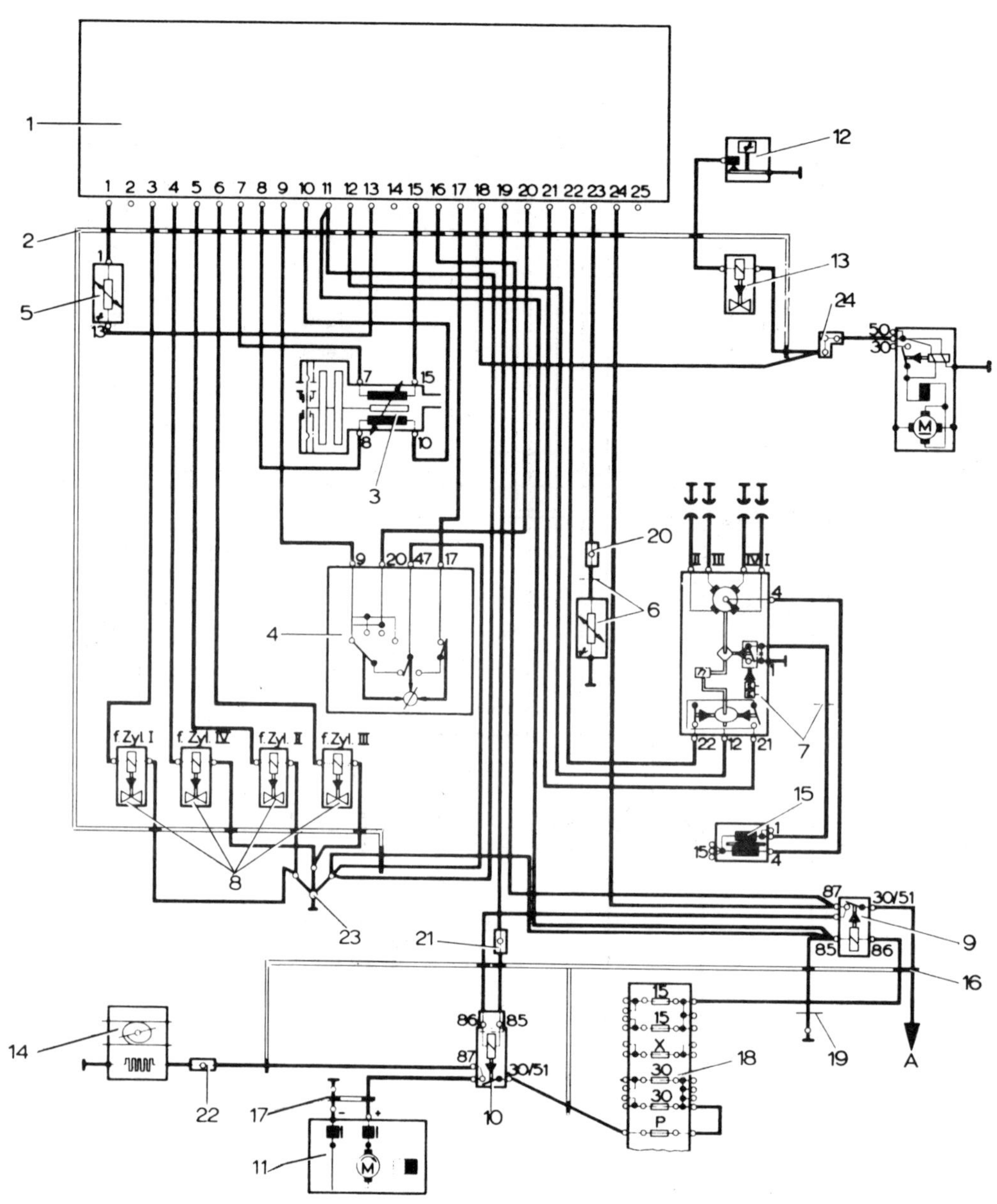

FIG. 3.7. WIRING DIAGRAM – FUEL INJECTION SYSTEM FROM AUGUST 1971 (SEC. 9)

1 *Control unit*
2 *Wiring harness electronics*
3 *Pressure sensor*
4 *Throttle valve switch*
5 *Temperature sensor I*
6 *Temperature sensor II*
7 *Distributor trigger mechanism*
8 *Injector*
9 *Relay (supply volts)*
10 *Relay (pump)*
11 *Fuel pump*
12 *Thermo switch*
13 *Cold start valve*
14 *Aux. air valve*
15 *Coil*
16 *Cable harness*
17 *Fuel pump cables*
18 *Fuse box*
19 *Wiring harness voltage supply relay*
20,21,22 *Flat connectors (single)*
23 *Earth connection*
24 *Cable distributor*
A *Battery +*

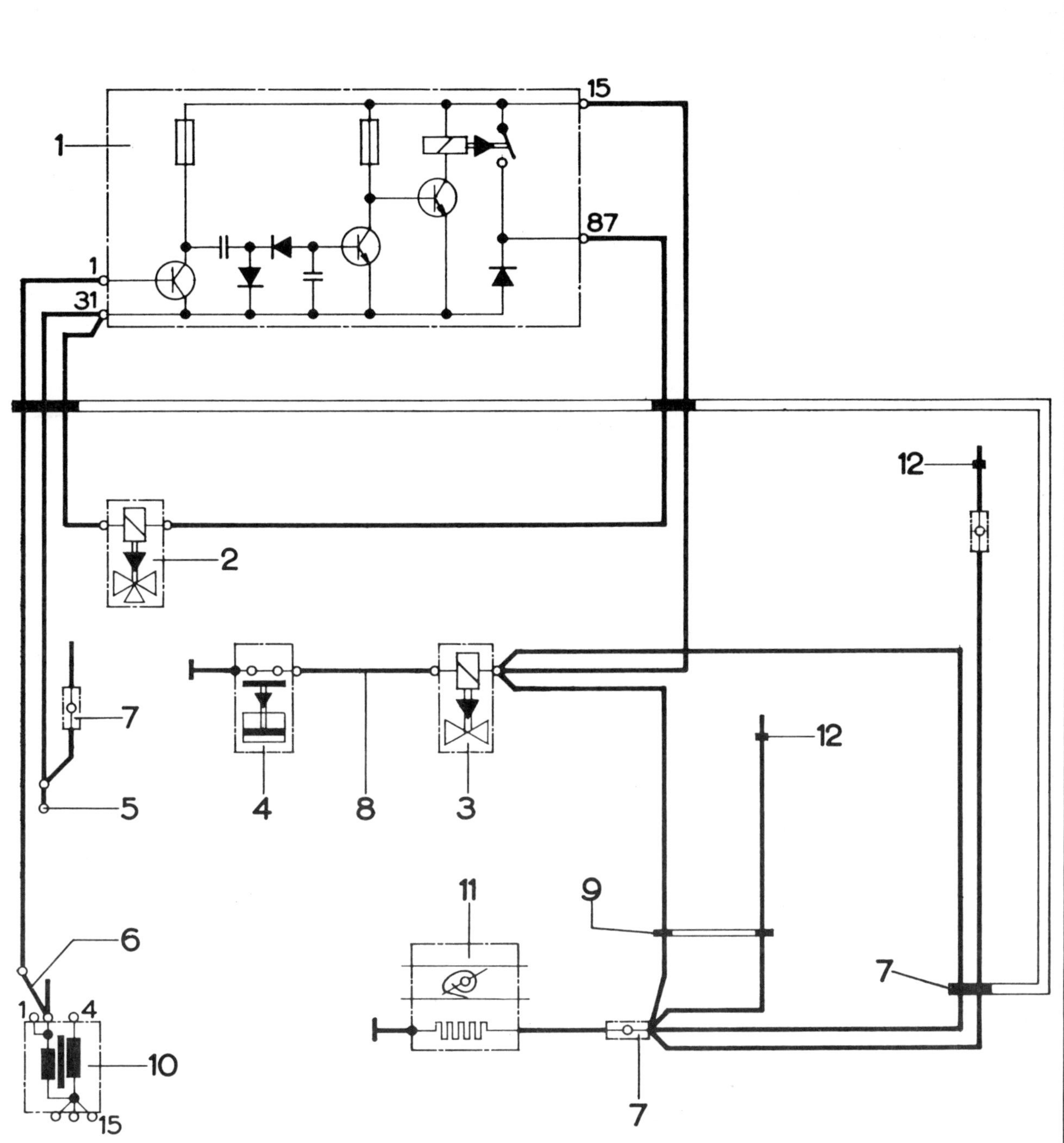

FIG. 3.8. ADDITIONAL WIRING DIAGRAM – US VERSION AUGUST 1971 ONWARDS (SECS. 9 AND 11)

1 Engine speed relay
2 2 way valve
3 Deceleration valve
4 Transmission oil pressure switch
5 Plug
6 Plug
7 Wiring harness
8 Wiring harness
9 Flat connector
10 Coil
11 Auxiliary air regulator
12 Main wiring harness

32 FAULT DIAGNOSIS

It is assumed that before looking seriously for faults in the fuel injection system that the battery is charged, the ignition circuit working and there is petrol in the tank.

Symptom	Reason/s	Remedy
Engine will not start. Electric pump not working	Cables to pump or relay defective. No voltage at terminal 86	Check cables and replace as necessary.
	No earth at terminal 85, but 12 volts at terminal 86	Check for open circuit. Check main relay.
	Fuse 8A (relay terminal 35/51) blown	Check for fault and replace fuse.
Engine will not start. Electric pump operative	Engine floods with petrol	Check pressure sensor plug and wiring. Replace if necessary. Check temperature sensor in cylinder head. Replace if necessary.
	No pressure in the fuel ring main	Check fuel filter. Check fuel lines for damage.
	It may be that the lack of fuel pressure is due to a defective pressure regulator. This requires a gauge to check it (VW Agent).	
Engine starts when cold but then stalls	Ignition trigger mechanism not working correctly	Check cables and trigger contacts. Replace if necessary.
	It may be that the pressure sensor is defective, but this requires test gear to check it (VW Agent).	
Engine misfires on one, or more cylinders	Sticking injector	See Section 8 of this Chapter.
White smoke from exhaust	Wiring to injector not correct	Check wiring and remedy.
Engine "hunts" excessively at idling speed	Faulty hose between auxiliary air regulator and air intake distributor (1)	Replace.
	Leaking throttle valve support (2)	Check seals and renew if needed.
	4/1700 automatic. Speed limiter incorrectly adjusted (3)	Readjust.
	Vacuum hose loose (4)	Tighten.

If all the cables are correct, the hoses in good order, and the points enumerated above checked, and there is still trouble. The only sensible remedy is to head for the VW Agent who has all the gauges and testers.

Chapter 4 Ignition system

Contents

Specifications

Spark plugs ... M 14 x 1.25 x 19 Long reach
- Normal conditions - carburettor engines ... Bosch W 145 T I
- - fuel injection ... Bosch W 175 T 2
- Continued high speed in temperatures above 80° F:
  - carburettor engines ... Bosch W 175 T 2
  - fuel injection ... Bosch W 225 T 2
- Spark plug electrode gap ... 0.028 in - 0.032 in (0.8 mm)
- Firing order ... 1 4 3 2

Coil ... 12 v 021 905 115 (Bosch)

Distributor ... One of two types is fitted, each with many variations according to the type of engine and date of manufacture.

SERIES	SUFFIX LETTER	ENGINE CODE	DATE
Bosch 021 905 205	—	V	12.8.68 - 11.8.69
	A *	V	12.8.69 - 11.8.72
	B	V automatic	12.8.68 - 11.8.69
	C *	Z automatic	12.8.69 - 11.8.72
	L	Z automatic	12.8.72 on
	K	Z	12.8.72 on
Bosch 022 905 205	A *	W	12.8.69 - 11.8.72
	P.Q *	EA. EB	12.8.72 on

* fitted with double acting vacuum control.
All fitted with both centrifugal and vacuum advance.

Breaker points - dwell angle ... 50° ± 3°
- gap ... 0.016 - 0.020 inch

Ignition timing, (vacuum hoses off, engine running):
- Carburettor engines ... 32° BTDC at 3500 rpm
- F.I. engines ... 27° BTDC at 3500 rpm

Timing marks: ... A notch and line indicates 32° or 27° BTDC according to engine (see Section 7).

1 General description

A conventional 12 volt system is used, having both mechanical and vacuum advance and retard mechanism in the distributor. The LT circuit goes via the ignition switch to terminal 15 of the coil, through the primary winding to terminal 1 and thence to the moving arm of the contact breaker. Current should flow in the LT circuit only when the points are closed. The condenser is connected in parallel with the points.

One end of the HT winding of the coil is earthed to the casing and the other led out of the top of the coil to the centre of the distributor cap and thence via the carbon brush to the spring leaf on the rotor arm. As the rotor arm rotates the high voltage crosses from the tip of the rotor arm to each segment in turn and via the distributor cap and plug lead to the plug where it produces a spark at the plug points

All this is elementary but it is necessary to keep this in mind when ignition problems arise. For instance the plug should spark only on the compression stroke, so only one spark is required for every two revolutions of the engine, so the distributor shaft runs at half the speed of the crankshaft and could be set 180° out of phase on assembly if care is not taken. Generally the problems of ignition are initial setting, maintenance of that setting, and checking that each unit is functioning correctly.

Its main enemies are moisture, loose connections and overheating.

2 Contact breaker

1 If the vehicle is taken to a VW agent the points will be set to give the correct cam dwell characteristics using special electrical equipment. The dwell angle should be $50^{o} \pm 3^{o}$.
2 However, providing there is no significant wear in the distributor shaft, it is possible to set the points using a feeler gauge. The correct setting in 0.016 to 0.020 in (0.4 mm). If there is significant wear in the shaft or bearings this state of affairs must be rectified before the points can be set satisfactorily.
3 Remove the distributor cap and the rotor arm. The wear can be checked by rocking the top of the shaft. If there is play turn to Sections 3 and 4 for rectification. If the play is negligible then all is well. Check the gap in the points. Consult photopraphs 2.3 (a) to (f) and adjust the points to the correct setting. Replace the rotor arm and cap.
4 The examination of the points is instructive. Normal wear gives pitting and small high points with tight surfaces. The high points should be removed with a fine oil stone. Leave the pitted surface alone so long as it is clean. If the surface is grey then either the gap was too small or the spring is weak. New points are quite cheap. A blue surface means that probably the coil or condenser is defective (see Sections 5 and 6). Yellow or black surfaces are due to oil or grease. Clean them off and do not over lubricate on reassembly.
6 Getting the cam follower on the high portion of the cam can be a problem. If the car has a manual gearbox put it in top gear and move the car a small amount. This will not work on a car fitted with an automatic gearbox. In this case remove the grommet from the fan housing and turn the engine with the alternator drive belt. It may be necessary to remove the spark plugs to do this easily.

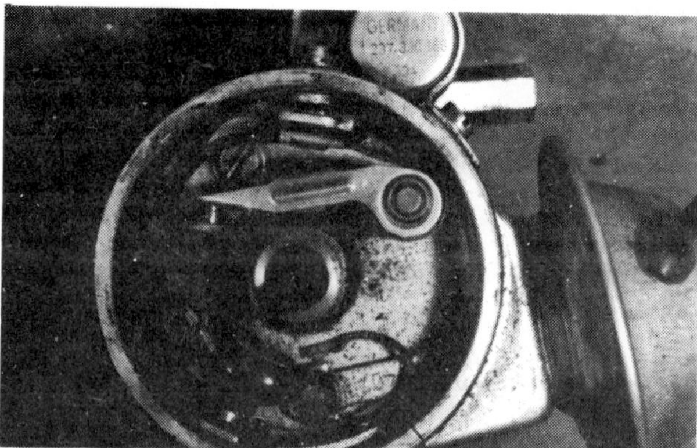

2.3a Contact breaker viewed from the top, cam follower on the low part of the cam, points closed

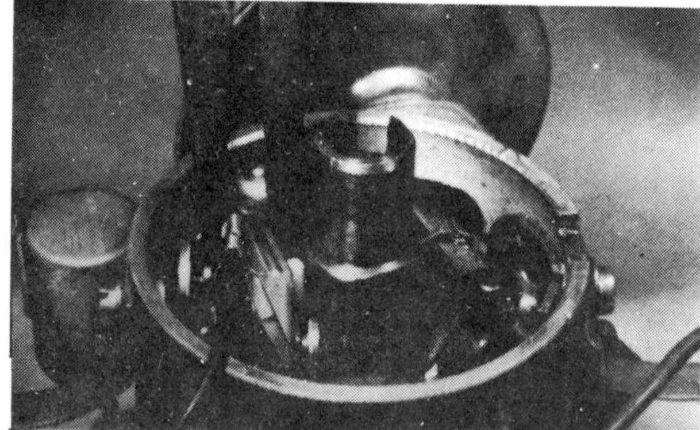

2.3b Lead pulled off the terminal. Grip the spring with pliers and pull off the spring, moving point and lead from the pivot **port**

2.3c Take out the securing screw and remove the fixed point for cleaning (see para. 2.4)

2.3d Clean off old oil and grease and lubricate the cam pivot with one drop of engine oil. Put a small amount of multipurpose grease on the cam.

2.3e Reassemble the clean (or new) points with the securing screw just holding the plate gently

2.3f With the cam followers on the high portion of the cam (see para. 6) move the fixed point (move the plate) until the gap is 0.020". Tighten the securing screw and check the gap again on all four high points of the cam.

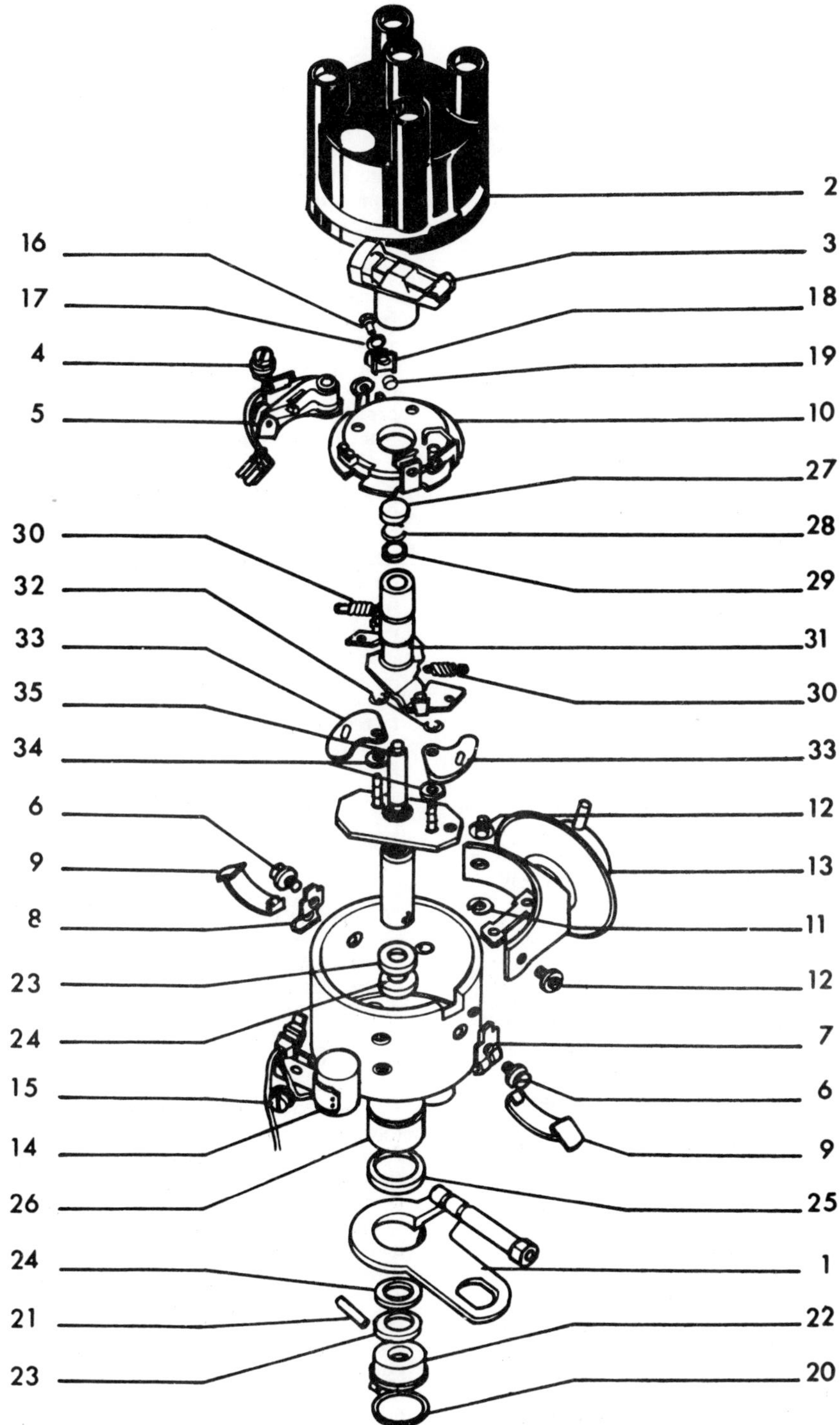

FIG. 4.1. DISTRIBUTOR WITH CENTRIFUGAL AND VACUUM ADVANCE – EXPLODED VIEW (CARBURETTOR ENGINES) (SEC. 4)

1 Mounting clamp bracket	*10 Contact points mounting plate*	*18 Retaining spring*	*27 Felt washer*
2 Cap	*11 'E' clip for pull rod*	*19 Ball*	*28 Circlip*
3 Rotor	*12 Screw*	*20 Circlip*	*29 Thrust ring*
4 Contacts securing screw	*13 Vacuum unit*	*21 Pin*	*30 Return spring*
5 Contact points	*14 Condenser*	*22 Driving dog*	*31 Cam*
6 Clip screw	*15 Screw*	*23 Shim*	*32 Circlip*
7 Clip retainer	*16 Screw*	*24 Fibre washer*	*33 Bob weights*
8 Clip retainer	*17 Spring washer*	*25 'O' sealing ring*	*34 Washer*
9 Cap clip		*26 Distributor body*	*35 Drive shaft*

Note: See Chapter 3 for distributor fitted to F.I. engines.

3 Distributor - removal and replacement

1 Remove the cap, release the LT lead from the coil (pull it off the coil), and pull off the vacuum hose. Do NOT SLACKEN THE DISTRIBUTOR CLAMP.
2 Undo the nut from the stud holding the distributor clamp to the crankcase and pull the distributor out (photo).
3 While the distributor is out do not move the engine, and check the position of the distributor rotor arm with reference to the body of the distributor.
4 Look down the hole and note when the dogs of the shaft engage the groove in the drive shaft. There is an offset. Cover the hole while the distributor is being examined.
5 Replacement is the reverse of removal. If the clamp bolt has not been slackened and the shaft is correctly positioned the engine timing will not have been altered.
6 Check the oil seal ring on the shaft and renew if necessary.

4 Distributor - dismantling, inspection and reassembly

1 If a dwell test has been done then the condition of the shaft and bushes will be known. If not try rocking the shaft in its bearing. There should be no appreciable play. If there is then it must be remedied.
2 The shaft can be replaced (if one is obtainable) but the bushes in the housing cannot. Axial play may be adjusted with shims (if you can get them).
3 The distributor may be dismantled by removing the driving dog from the bottom. Knock out the pin with a punch; note the position and number of washers. The breaker unit and vacuum unit are fastened with screws. Mark the position of the driving dog relative to the shaft, and the location of the centrifugal weights (Fig.4.1) (See Chapter 3 for distributor fitted to FI engines).
4 Assembly is the reverse of dismantling. Remember to fit a new sealing ring.
5 Generally speaking when there is radial play in the shaft there will be wear in the bushes. If the bob weights have broken adrift or the plate is rocking then the distributor has had its day. In the author's experience it is better to fit a genuine replacement. Beware of breakers yards, there are several different kinds of distributor, all of which may fit in your engine, but only one of them will make it go properly.

This is even more important if the car is fitted with fuel injection.

5 Condenser - testing and replacement

1 Although the condenser rarely goes wrong, if it does it will cause a lot of trouble. Not only does the condenser prevent arcing at the points but its correct functioning also affects the build up of voltage in the HT circuit. This will affect starting and power output at high torque and low revolutions.
2 Fortunately the symptoms are easily recognised, the points will be badly pitted. To confirm the diagnosis pull off cable 1 of the coil connect a test lamp between terminal 15 of the coil and cable 1 (in other words put a 12v bulb in place of the coil), switch on the ignition and open the points. The lamp must not light. If it does there is a short circuit in the condenser. If there is a short circuit then replace the condenser, clean up the points and all will be well.
3 It is unlikely but just possible to have an open circuit condenser. This would not show in the test but the effect would be similar, so if the burning of the points continues replace the condenser with a new one, or take the condenser for testing. The fault would most certainly be in the lead connection.
4 When replacing the condenser get the right one. One of the wrong capacity will not function properly, and one the wrong size will not fit. Get a new one to fit from the VW agent.

6 Coil - testing, removal and replacement

1 When the engine compartment lid is opened the coil is under the left hand rear edge. To remove it, undo the strap, (photo) pull off the connections and lift it out. A wise man labels the connections for easy reconnection. The others look for a wiring diagram.
2 There is a lot of wire in the case; if it is faulty nothing can be done about it, so the only task with the coil is to test it, and if necessary replace it. However it is easily tested while in the car.
3 First examine the cap. It will be dirty and probably oily. Wipe this off and look for evidence of shorting or tracking, thin black lines of carbon running from the case across the cap.
4 Now pull the HT cable out of the centre of the distributor cap. With it still in the coil hold the free end about 3/8 inch from the fan housing and turn the engine over with the starter.

There should be a spark from the cable end. As the voltage is several KV use a rubber glove or a pair of insulated pliers to hold the wire or the spark may not be the only thing that jumps.
5 If there is no spark check the voltage at terminal 15. (ignition on) It should be at least 9 volts. If it is higher then a further test is necessary.
6 Take the cap off the distributor so that with a pencil the points may be opened (turn the engine so that they are closed). Check the voltage from Coil terminal 1 to earth. There should be no reading at this terminal with the distributor points closed. Now open the points and there should be a reading on the volt meter. If there is no reading then the coil has an open circuit and must be replaced.
7 Be sure that the connections to the coil are firmly made. A small drop in voltage in the LT circuit will mean a big one in the HT circuit and possibly hard startingor misfiring under heavy load.

7 Ignition timing

The type 4 is very simple to time. At the front edge of the engine compartment on top of the fan housing is a plastic cap screwed into the housing. Remove this and the top of the fan is visible. It runs closely in the housing and directly under the cap a Vee is cut in the housing. Turn the engine and the fan periphery can be seen moving under the Vee. A clearly scribed line on the fan periphery just fits into the Vee and this is the timing mark. (See photo 8.7).
2 The next thing to discover is whether the piston of No 1 cylinder is on the exhaust stroke or the compression stroke. Both valves for No 1 cylinder should be closed (tappets slack). Check either by removing the valve cover or by removing the plug and holding something over the plug hole to see whether there is compression or not. Be careful nothing drops inside. With the piston on the compression stroke and the mark on the fan in the Vee push home the distributor so that the dog on the bottom of the shaft engages in the driven shaft and rotor arm points to the contact for No 1 cylinder plug lead. Tighten the nut holding the clamp to the cylinder block. If the clamp ring has not been loosened from the distributor shaft the job is done. If it has been loosened the distributor body should be turned (with the clamp ring slack) until the centre line of the rotor matches with the mark made on the top edge of the distributor body.
3 With the correct setting of the points already done the points should now be just opening. This can be checked electrically by connecting at 6 watt 12 volt bulb in parallel with them. With the ignition switched on and all LT circuit connections correctly made the lamp will light at the exact moment the points open, which can be fixed by turning the distributor body a few degrees either way. When this point is determined tighten the clamp ring, assemble the distributor cap and the job is complete.
4 No two engines are exactly the same. If it is thought that the engine is running hotter than usual and lacks power then advance the ignition slightly (slacken the clamp and turn the distributor

3.2 Removing the distributor. DO NOT UNDO THE CLAMP BOLT

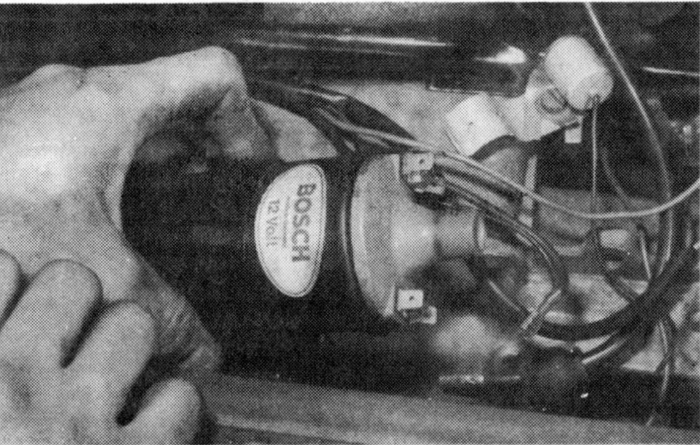

6.1 Removing the coil. Label the leads

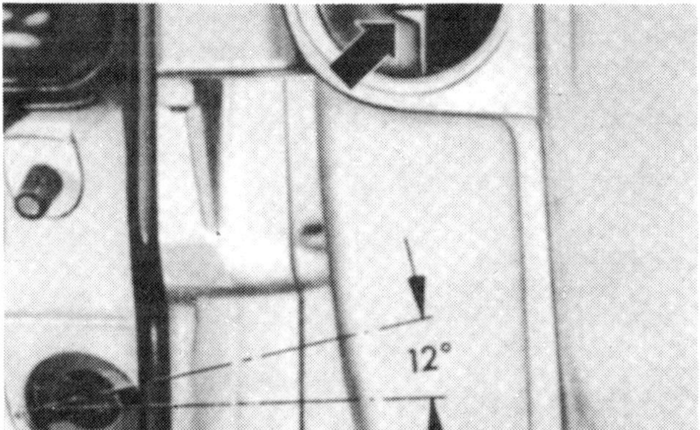

8.7a A view of the timing notch and distributor drive shaft. Note the smaller segment of the drive shaft is on the outside

8.7b Drive shaft ready to go in. Allow for the turn of the shaft on engagement of the helical gear

body in an anti-clockwise direction). If the engine "pinks" and is rough at low revolutions then it needs retarding a little (clockwise).

8 Distributor drive shaft - removal, reassembly and inspection

1 This will normally only be removed on dismantling and reassembling the engine. However it can be removed with the engine installed.

2 For carburettor type engines remove the fuel pump and flange. On fuel injection types this is obviously not necessary.

3 Set No. 1 cylinder to the firing point (Section 7).

4 Remove the distributor and the anti-rattle spring.

5 Withdraw the drive shaft turning it anti-clockwise as it comes out. It needs a special extractor but it is possible to use a tapered wooden plug or even long nosed circlip pliers.

6 There may be a shim under the shaft. A magnet will be required to lift this out. **If it is dropped inside, then the engine will have to be dismantled to recover it.**

7 To reinstall is the reverse of dismantling. Make sure the crankshaft has not moved (i.e. still on No. 1 cylinder firing point). When installed the offset slot in the top of the drive shaft is at an angle approximately 12° to the crankcase joint and points roughly to the rear securing screw of the air cleaner. The smaller segment is on the left (photo). Insert the shaft so that it turns clockwise when engaging the skew gear on the crankshaft, make allowance for this when judging the angle of assembly (photo). Do not forget the shim. Guide the shim into position on a piece of rod and **do not drop it inside the engine.**

8 Replace the anti-rattle spring in place and then assemble the distributor and fuel pump.

9 There is no point in fitting a new shaft if the gear teeth are worn, for there will be equal wear on the crankshaft gear and that also must be renewed. It may be necessary to renew the shim, if there is one. On the engine dismantled by the author there was not a shim.

Altogether there seems little point in taking out the shaft for curiosity and a grave danger of dropping the shim inside. Unless there has been a mishap between the drive dog of the distributor and the slot of the shaft it is thought better to leave the shaft in position until a complete engine overhaul is done.

9 Spark plugs and leads

1 Spark plugs should be renewed every 12000 miles. If it is not intended to fit new ones then the old ones should be taken to an agent who has the proper shot blast equipment and pressure tester, and cleaned and tested before reassembly. There is no other sensible method so do not mess about with wire bushes and sharp knives. A new set of plugs costs less than an oil change. The correct plug gap is 0.03 in (0.7 mm).

2 Always fit the correct grade (see specifications) and fit them with a proper VW plug spanner, (this has an insert to hold the plug and a universal joint). Check that the washers are not flattened. Before the old plugs are taken out blow out any grit or loose dirt which may fall inside.

Be careful not to cross the threads and do not overtighten. The torque required is 25 ft lbs (3.5 mkg). This is the equivalent of a "sharp nip" with the plug spanner. The cylinder head is aluminium and if the thread is stripped or overtightened causing cracks between the plug threads and the valve seat the engine will have to come out and a new head be fitted.

3 Leads should be inspected for wear and insulation cracks. The resistance of an HT lead should be between 5 and 10 thousand ohms. Terminals must be correctly fitted with proper crimping tools and the lead should be free from oil or moisture. Insulation tape is no use at all on HT leads. Again the cost of a new set of leads and caps is less than the cost of an oil change

PLUG ELECTRODES

White deposits and damaged porcelain insulation indicating over heating

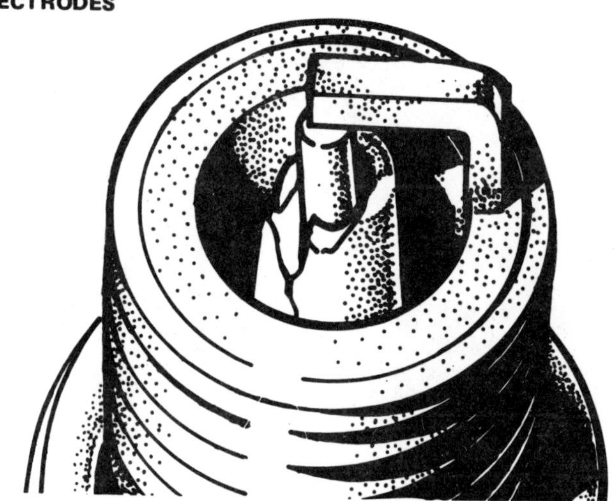

Broken porcelain insulation due to bent central electrode

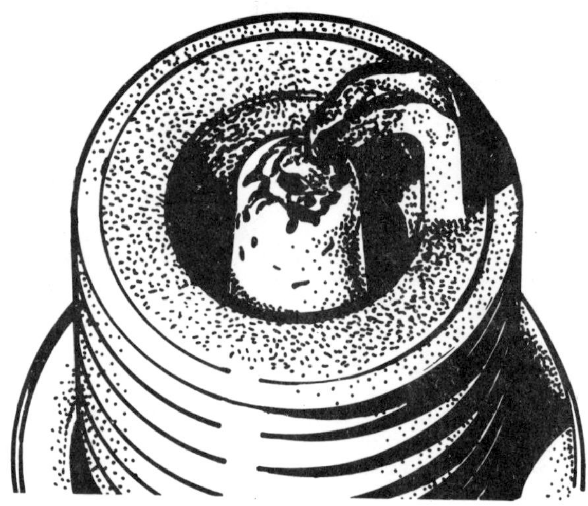

Electrodes burnt away due to wrong heat valve or chronic pre ignition (pinking)

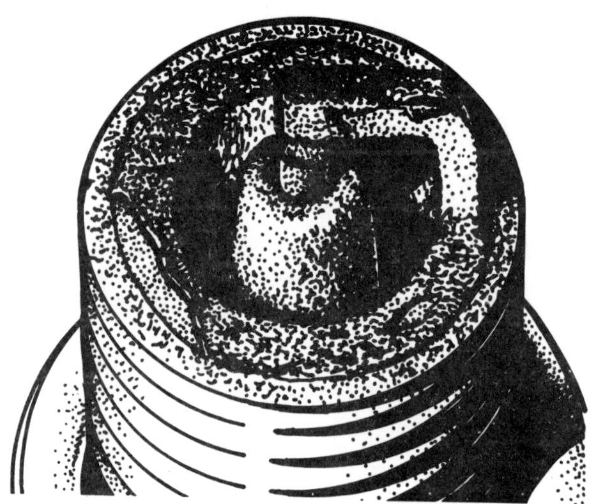

Excessive black deposits caused by over rich mixture or wrong heat value

Mild white deposits and electrode burnt indicating to weak or fuel mixture

Plug in sound condition with light greyish brown deposits

and the trouble that can stem from worn and faulty leads makes it a false economy not to renew them regularly.

4 The condition of the plugs will give an interesting side light on the state of tune of the engine. A diagram (Fig.4.2) showing plug point conditions is included in this chapter.

10 Fault diagnosis

1 Engine will not start.

a) The Type 4 engine is so enclosed that the normal wet condition after leaving the car in the open over night is not so prevalent. However before running down the battery when the car will not start after being left in the open have a look to see that everything is dry. If mist has penetrated then dry the moisture off, either with a cloth or with a proprietary type spray.

b) If the engine will not start when everything is dry, pull off a plug lead, turn back the plug cover and hold the metal end of the plug lead about 1/8" from the crankcase. With the ignition switched on spin the engine with the starter. If there is a spark, a good fat one, then the ignition system is working. Check that the distributor body is held tight in the clamp ring, then check the timing setting. Take off the distributor cap. Set the ignition timing mark on the fan periphery in the Vee (see Section 7) and check that the rotor arm is pointing to No 1 cylinder plug lead. If the spark is correct and the timing has not altered then the fault is not in the ignition system.

c) If there is not a fat spark then the ignition system is at fault. Begin by checking the LT circuit in the following order:-

(i) Are the points opening correctly? Are they clean?

(ii) Check the voltage at coil terminal 15. It should be at least 9 volts (ignition on). If no voltage then the wiring or the switch is at fault.

(iii) Check the voltage at coil terminal 1, points closed - no volts, points open - reading on the meter. If no reading on the meter with points open the coil has an open circuit.

(iv) With the ignition switched on check the voltage across the contact breaker points; points closed - no volts, points open - meter reads. Points open - no reading, then the condenser is faulty.

d) Check all the LT wiring and connections carefully and if the LT circuit is functioning correctly then proceed to the HT circuit. Check the following in the order given (ignition switched on).

(i) Pull the HT lead from the centre of the distributor and hold the end 1/8" from the crankcase. Spin the engine. There should be a spark. No spark means a faulty HT winding in the coil.

(ii) Turn off the ignition switch, put the lead back in the centre of the distributor cap and examine the carbon brush carefully. Is it making contact with the rotor arm spring? Examine the cap for cracks and tracking. Check that the segments are clean and that the rotor arm leading edge is not corroded. Clean these points if they are.

(iii) Replace the rotor arm; check the drive by turning the rotor gently. There should be a slight movement. Anything more than a slight movement means that the drive is suspect or the automatic advance and retard has disintegrated. The latter is rare but it has happened.

e) Finally remove a plug and check its condition. If it is oily, wet with petrol, or corroded, then clean it, and the other three. Check the gap (0.030"). Oily or corroded plugs mean an engine overhaul or at least a checking of the exhaust gas composition by an expert. Wet plugs may be flooding during starting.

2 Engine runs sluggishly but does not misfire.

a) Check the contact breaker points and the plug gaps.

b) Check the ignition timing.

c) Check the octane rating of the fuel.

3 Engine misfires, runs unevenly and cuts out at low revolutions.

a) Check contact breaker and plug gaps. (CB gap too large?)

b) Check the distributor shaft for wear.

c) Check the fuel system.

4 Engine misfires at high revolutions.

a) Check contact breaker and plug gaps (CB gap too small?)

b) Check the distributor shaft for wear.

c) Check the fuel system.

5 Ignition faults are quite often exasperating. Work steadily through the system checking all leads and connections methodically. Test the components, check the battery, and if finally the fault cannot be located then go to the expert. He has instruments specially designed to locate faults. But if his respect is to be obtained do not go about testing in a haphazard manner, that will only result in more faults being installed and the original one may never be located.

Castrol GRADES

Castrol Engine Oils

Castrol GTX

An ultra high performance SAE 20W/50 motor oil which exceeds the latest API MS requirements and manufacturers' specifications. Castrol GTX with liquid tungsten† generously protects engines at the extreme limits of performance, and combines both good cold starting with oil consumption control. Approved by leading car makers.

Castrol XL 20/50

Contains liquid tungsten†; well suited to the majority of conditions giving good oil consumption control in both new and old cars.

Castrolite (Multi-grade)

This is the lightest multi-grade oil of the Castrol motor oil family containing liquid tungsten†. It is best suited to ensure easy winter starting and for those car models whose manufacturers specify lighter weight oils.

Castrol Grand Prix

An SAE 50 engine oil for use where a heavy, full-bodied lubricant is required.

Castrol Two-Stroke-Four

A premium SAE 30 motor oil possessing good detergency characteristics and corrosion inhibitors, coupled with low ash forming tendency and excellent anti-scuff properties. It is suitable for all two-stroke motor-cycles, and for two-stroke and small four-stroke horticultural machines.

Castrol CR (Multi-grade)

A high quality engine oil of the SAE-20W/30 multi-grade type, suited to mixed fleet operations.

Castrol CRI 10, 20, 30

Primarily for diesel engines, a range of heavily fortified, fully detergent oils, covering the requirements of DEF 2101-D and Supplement 1 specifications.

Castrol CRB 20, 30

Primarily for diesel engines, heavily fortified, fully detergent oils, covering the requirements of MIL-L-2104B.

Castrol R 40

Primarily designed and developed for highly stressed racing engines. Castrol 'R' should not be mixed with any other oil nor with any grade of Castrol.

†Liquid Tungsten is an oil soluble long chain tertiary alkyl primary amine tungstate covered by British Patent No. 882,295.

Castrol Gear Oils

Castrol Hypoy (90 EP)

A light-bodied powerful extreme pressure gear oil for use in hypoid rear axles and in some gearboxes.

Castrol Gear Oils (continued)

Castrol Hypoy Light (80 EP)

A very light-bodied powerful extreme pressure gear oil for use in hypoid rear axles in cold climates and in some gearboxes.

Castrol Hypoy B (90 EP)

A light-bodied powerful extreme pressure gear oil that complies with the requirements of the MIL-L-2105B specification, for use in certain gearboxes and rear axles.

Castrol Hi-Press (140 EP)

A heavy-bodied extreme pressure gear oil for use in spiral bevel rear axles and some gearboxes.

Castrol ST (90)

A light-bodied gear oil with fortifying additives

Castrol D (140)

A heavy full-bodied gear oil with fortifying additives.

Castrol Thio-Hypoy FD (90 EP)

A light-bodied powerful extreme pressure gear oil. This is a special oil for running-in certain hypoid gears.

Automatic Transmission Fluids

Castrol TQF (Automatic Transmission Fluid)

Approved for use in all Borg-Warner Automatic Transmission Units. Castrol TQF also meets Ford specification M2C 33F.

Castrol TQ Dexron® (Automatic Transmission Fluid)

Complies with the requirements of Dexron® Automatic Transmission Fluids as laid down by General Motors Corporation.

Castrol Greases

Castrol LM

A multi-purpose high melting point lithium based grease approved for most automotive applications including chassis and wheel bearing lubrication.

Castrol MS3

A high melting point lithium based grease containing molybdenum disulphide.

Castrol BNS

A high melting point grease for use where recommended by certain manufacturers in front wheel bearings when disc brakes are fitted.

Castrol Greases (continued)

Castrol CL

A semi-fluid calcium based grease, which is both waterproof and adhesive, intended for chassis lubrication.

Castrol Medium

A medium consistency calcium based grease.

Castrol Heavy

A heavy consistency calcium based grease.

Castrol PH

A white grease for plunger housings and other moving parts on brake mechanisms. *It must NOT be allowed to come into contact with brake fluid when applied to the moving parts of hydraulic brakes.*

Castrol Graphited Grease

A graphited grease for the lubrication of transmission chains.

Castrol Under-Water Grease

A grease for the under-water gears of outboard motors.

Anti-Freeze

Castrol Anti-Freeze

Contains anti-corrosion additives with ethylene glycol. Recommended for the cooling systems of all petrol and diesel engines.

Speciality Products

Castrol Girling Damper Oil Thin

The oil for Girling piston type hydraulic dampers.

Castrol Shockol

A light viscosity oil for use in some piston type shock absorbers and in some hydraulic systems employing synthetic rubber seals. It must not be used in braking systems.

Castrol Penetrating Oil

A leaf spring lubricant possessing a high degree of penetration and providing protection against rust.

Castrol Solvent Flushing Oil

A light-bodied solvent oil, designed for flushing engines, rear axles, gearboxes and gearcasings.

Castrollo

An upper cylinder lubricant for use in the proportion of 1 fluid ounce to two gallons of fuel.

Everyman Oil

A light-bodied machine oil containing anti-corrosion additives for both general use and cycle lubrication.

Chapter 5 Clutch and actuating mechanism

Contents

Specifications

Type ...	F & S single plate diaphragm spring	
Operation ...	Hydraulic	
Diameter ...	200 mm (to August 1969)	215 mm (after August 1969)
Pressure ...	420 - 480 kgs.	
Area of lining ...	335 cm^2 (to August 1969)	375 cm^2 (after August 1969)
Master cylinder		
Bore ...	19.05 mm Note: In model year 1970 about 6000 cars were made with bore size 17.46 mm	
Stroke ...	30.00 mm	
Piston/pushrod clearance ...	0.020 in	(0.5 mm)
Clutch pedal free travel ...	0.12 - 0.16 in	(3 - 4 mm)
Stop screw adjustment - LHD ...	0.9 in	
- RHD ...	0.9 in up to chassis 4102030158 0.85 in after chassis 4102030158	

Torque wrench settings:	**lbs ft**	**mkg**
Clutch/flywheel screws M8 (to September 1969) ...	18	2.5
M7 (October 1969 onwards) ...	14	2.0
Master cylinder securing screws ...	29 - 33	4 - 4.5
Master cylinder support bracket screws ...	14	2.0
Slave cylinder securing bolts (later models) ...	14	2.0

1 General description

1 A single plate, diaphragm spring, friction clutch, operated by a hydraulic system. The design departs from usual VW practice in that the clutch cover, pressure plate and diaphragm are built as a unit and bolted to the flywheel. The unit must be replaced as an assembly as it is not possible to dismantle the diaphragm from the cover should it require renewal.
2 The master cylinder is located on the right of the steering column just below the facia board, and bolted to the side of the pedal support bracket. Access is from the interior of the car after the parcel shelf and steering column trim are removed.
3 The master cylinder is topped up from the same header tank (reservoir) as the brake master cylinder, the header tank is located in the front luggage compartment.
4 The clutch withdrawal lever and slave cylinder of earlier models differ considerably from those of later models. The different types are not interchangable. Up to August 1969 the slave cylinder was 22.2 mm diameter. After this date it was increased to 44.5 mm diameter. This is discussed later. To complicate matters further the later types are made by one of two manufacturers, and although they seem identical on the exterior, they are different inside.
5 A modification to the pivot plate in the transmission casing has strengthened the withdrawal lever pivot. A replacement plate should be obtained and fitted during overhaul.

2 Clutch operation and maintenance

1 When the pedal is depressed the piston is moved in the master cylinder actuating that in the slave cylinder which moves out the push rod against the release lever. The release lever moves on its pivot and the release bearing is pressed against the diaphragm and separates the clutch pressure plate from the clutch disc. When the pressure is released the diaphragm spring reverses the motion via the release lever and push rod returning the pistons in the slave and master cylinder to their original positions. A residual pressure valve between the master cylinder and the

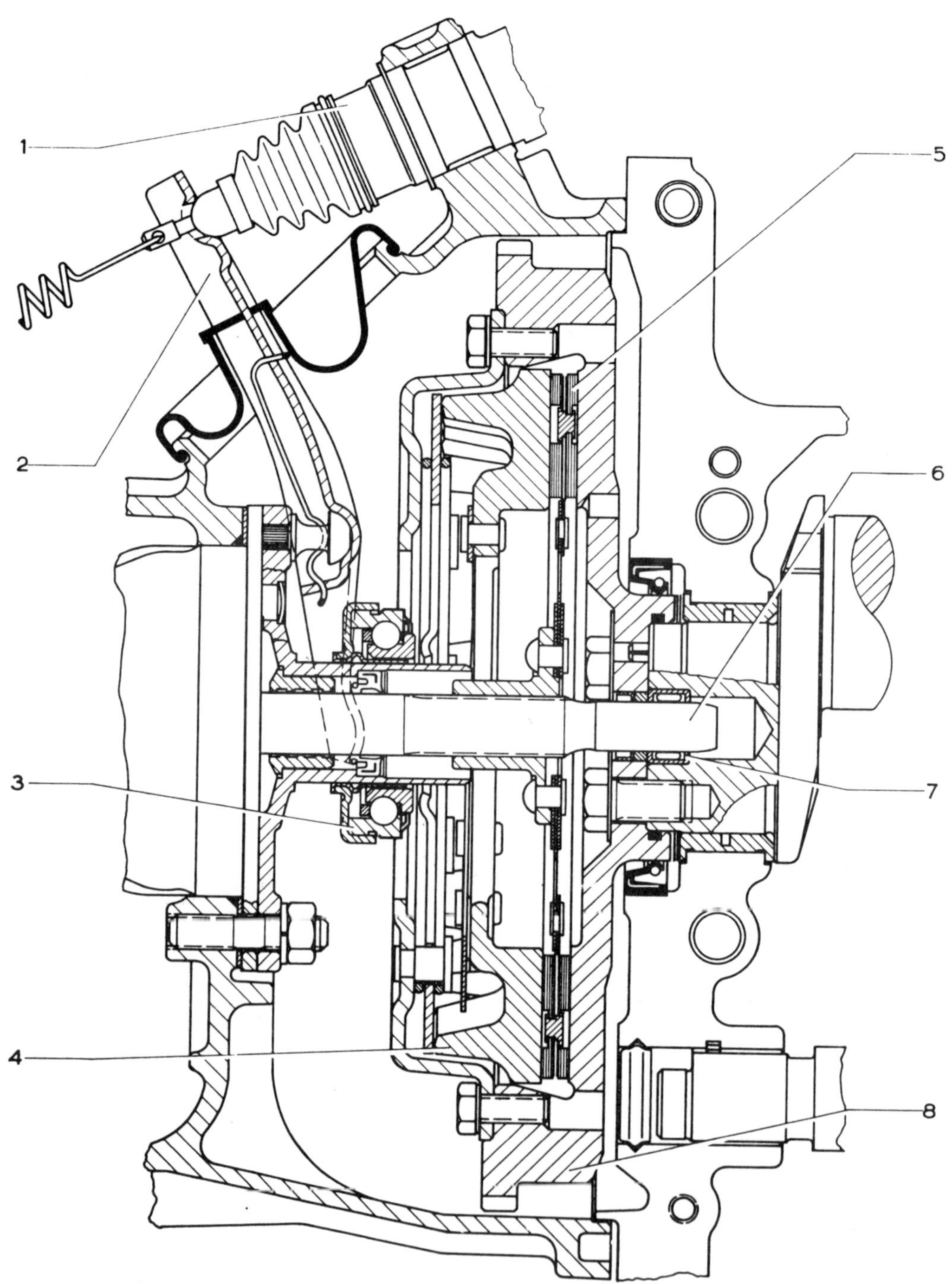

FIG. 5.1. CROSS SECTION OF THE CLUTCH (EARLIER TYPE OF SLAVE CYLINDER)

1 Operating cylinder	*3 Release bearing*	*5 Clutch plate*	*7 Needle bearing*
2 Clutch lever	*4 Diaphragm spring*	*6 Drive shaft*	*8 Flywheel*

Fig. 5.2. Modified clutch (after August 1969) showing diagram assembly, friction plate and flywheel. (old dimensions in brackets)

Clutch diameter *215 mm (200)*
Lining area *375 cm² (335)*
Pressure 420 - 480 kg (unchanged)

hydraulic line to the slave cylinder ensure that there is always a slight pressure in the slave cylinder so that the release bearing is always in contact with the release ring of the diaphragm spring. This is further intensified by a spring in the slave cylinder. Thus there is no clutch pedal free movement in the usual sense, but the play between the push rod and the piston in the clutch master cylinder must be adjusted.

2 To adjust the push rod access must be gained to the clutch master cylinder which is mounted on the right of the steering column on RHD vehicles and the left of the column on LHD vehicles. Referring to Fig.5.3 it will be seen that it is impossible to measure the necessary 0.5 mm between the push rod and piston as required by design specification. It is set in fact between the clutch pedal and the stop which limits the travel of the pedal, the latter being located on the pedal support, an M6 screw covered with a rubber cap.

3 Again refer to Fig.5.3, back off the push rod locknut and shorten the push rod a little. Remove the rubber cap from the stop screw and set the distance S_2 to 0.9" (22.5 mm) for LHD vehicles or 0.9" for RHD vehicles up to chassis 4102030 158 or 0.85" for later vehicles. Reinstall the rubber cap and increase the length of the push rod until the free play at the pedal is reduced to between 0.12 to 0.16 in (3-4 mm). Measure this horizontally at the tip of the clutch pedal (shown in the sketch as S_1). Lock the push rod and refit the rubber boot.

4 As the system is kept topped up by the communal brake fluid reservoir there is no other maintenance other than bleeding the system if necessary (discussed in Section 9 of this chapter) and keeping the pipe lines free from damage and corrosion. A long metal pipe runs from the master cylinder the length of the tunnel emerging into the transmission/engine area with a flexible piece and then another metal tube to the slave cylinder.

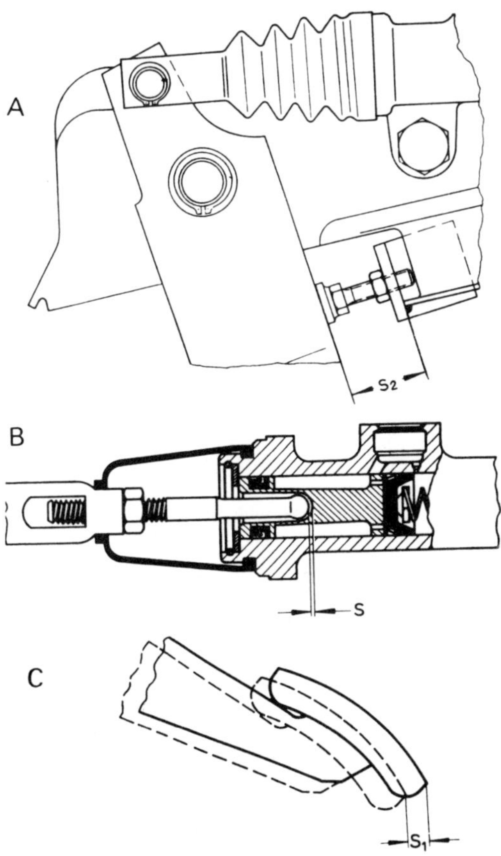

FIG. 5.3. CLUTCH MASTER CYLINDER – PUSH ROD ADJUSTMENT (SEC. 2)

(a) Layout of clutch pedal and stop (S_2 to be set at 0.9" or 0.85")
(b) Cross section of master cylinder (S = 0.5 mm)
(c) Clutch pedal free play S_1 = 3 to 4 mm

3 Removal inspection and replacement of the clutch

1 It is necessary to remove the engine from the chassis before the clutch can be dismantled. It is wiser to remove the engine and gearbox together and then split them to get at the clutch.

2 Once the gearbox has been removed from the clutch housing the diaphragm/pressure plate may be unbolted from the

flywheel.

3 However, if the hydraulic system is working properly and the engine is removed leaving the transmission in place, the slave cylinder can be left behind still connected to the master cylinder. It is a bit of a fiddle to get it out of the casing of the later types. It can be done as well before removing the combined engine transmission but this is ever more difficult. However it is worth a try as not only does it obviate bleeding the hydraulic system after assembly but it avoids a pool of brake fluid just when you do not want it. To do this, just remove the boot and retaining ring in the case of the older model or two nuts on the later ones. See Figures 5.4 and 5.5.

4 Mark the position of the cover relative to the flywheel with a centre punch, undo the six bolts and draw off the diaphragm spring/clutch pressure plate. The friction plate may now be removed as well.

5 Check the ends of the diaphragm springs where they make contact with the release bearing ring. Scoring up to 0.012 in (0.3 mm) can be ignored, but deeper marking means a new assembly. The one examined here had a fine coppery deposit but no scoring, even though the clutch had been abused.

6 Check the pressure plate friction surface for overheating, cracks or distortion. Put a straight edge over the pressure plate and check for warping. Taper of up to 0.012 in. over the width of the pressure plate can be ignored but beyond this it is best to consult the VW agent.

7 Now examine the straps between the cover and the pressure plate for cracks. Check the rivets for tightness. The diaphragm spring is held to the clutch cover by rivets between two wire rings. If the rivets are loose or the rivet heads or wire rings show signs of wear a new clutch should be fitted. See Fig.5.6.

8 The friction plate should be examined for wear. If the lining has worn so that the rivet heads are less than 0.025 in (0.6 mm) below the surface then the lining requires renewal. There should be no scoring. If there is then the flywheel face on the pressure plate will most certainly have corresponding marks. The flywheel will have to be removed and serviced or replaced (See Chapter 1). The pressure plate similarly, if the scoring is deep then a new cover plate/diaphragm assembly will be required.

9 Overheating due to a slipping clutch will show as discolouration on the pressure plate and flywheel. This may have affected the springs of the diaphragm plate.

10 If oil or grease has penetrated to the friction lining the friction face will be black and shiny. The friction plate must be replaced. Equally important the source of the contamination should be found and the fault rectified. It will be due to a leaking seal either from the front of the engine crankshaft or the transmission input shaft. (See Chapter 1 and Chapter 6).

11 The release bearing should have a smooth face and should spin easily in its hub. Do not wash this bearing in cleaning fluid. Check the fork pivots for wear and correct fastening (photo), and check the clutch lever pivot. There are two types of clutch lever depending on the type of slave cylinder fitted. For details see Sections 7 and 8 of this Chapter.

12 Do not be mean about replacements. If anything is suspect it will be a very false economy to use it again.

13 Once the various parts are passed as satisfactory the re-assembly is simple. Place the friction plate (right way round) (photo) on the flywheel centering it carefully so that the main drive shaft will pass through it into the flywheel centre bearing. If the gearbox is out of the car you can use the mainshaft itself to do this, or else make up a suitable wooden spigot. Unless this is done there will be trouble when the gear is joined to the engine.

Replace the diaphragm cover plate (with the markings made during dismantling, or you may get an imbalance), replace the six bolts and lock washer and working diagonally tighten to a torque of 18 lb ft (2.5 mkg).

14 Slide the clutch lever into place (photo) and check the pivot seat. The clutch is now assembled. Replace the slave cylinder in its housing as the engine is assembled to the vehicle, unless it was removed with the housing, in which case install it with the clutch lever, and then reconnect and bleed the system after assembly.

4 Master cylinder - removal and replacement

1 Take up the floor covering from the front floor and replace it with a sheet of polythene.

2 Syphon the brake fluid from the reservoir using a syphon that has been used only with brake fluid, and remembering that the fluid is poisonous and will spoil paint work.

3 Remove the parcel shelf and trim from the steering column and pedal support. The clutch master cylinder is on the left of the column on LH drive vehicles and the right on RH drive vehicles. As a further identification it is the one which does **NOT** have any electrical leads attached to it.

4 Pull the elbow from the sealing plug and remove the pressure line. Have a small bowl ready to catch any fluid which may escape.

5 Take out the two securing screws and remove the cylinder towards the front seat.

6 Replacement is the reverse process, tighten the bolts to 30 ft lb (4 mkg). Check and adjust the clutch pedal free travel (see Section 2.1) fill the header tank and bleed the system.

7 It will help assembly if the sealing plug, elbow and pipe flare are moistened with brake fluid.

8 Check that the push rod boot is correctly seated, re-install the trim and replace the floor mats.

5 Master cylinder - dismantling, overhaul and reassembly

1 Refer to Figs.5.7 and 5.8.

2 Remove the boot, spring ring and internal parts. Do **NOT** poke about inside the cylinder if the piston is stiff or the bore may be scratched and the cylinder scrapped. Plug up the inlet, or hold a finger over it and blow compressed air in the outlet union, holding a rag to catch the seals and spring. Remove the residual pressure valve before applying compressed air.

3 Clean the parts in methylated spirits and then immerse in clean brake fluid. Obtain a new secondary cup, cup washer, primary cup and stop ring.

4 Check that the compensating port is not blocked. This is the small hole by which excess returns from the cylinder to the reservoir (as opposed to the inlet port).

5 If either piston or cylinder are worn the complete master cylinder must be replaced. Take advice at the VW agent if there is any doubt.

6 Difficulty may be experienced in fitting a new secondary cup to the piston, there is a special tool supplied by TEVES to do this, it is merely a piece of pipe tapered to expand the cup sufficiently to slip it on to the piston. If in doubt take the secondary cup and piston to the agent from which the new parts were obtained and ask them for help.

7 Hold the piston vertically and place the cup washer primary cup spring plate and spring on the piston and push the piston into the cylinder. If the cylinder is not held vertically with the open end downwards the parts will fall off the piston.

8 Fit the stop washer and spring ring. Replace the boot.

9 Examine the sealing plug for the elbow and replace if necessary, remember any leaks will come to rest on your trouser bottoms.

10 Check the residual pressure valve and replace the seal if necessary. Any leak here will be a pressurised leak. All that can be done to check the valve is to see that the ball does move against the two springs. Press it down with a piece of wood to check without scratching it. It should be screwed into the cylinder with a torque of 14 lbs ft.

11 Finally try not to handle the piston and bore with bare hands, and see that they are liberally coated with brake fluid on assembly. If you have some VW brake cylinder paste apply a little to the new cups before assembly.

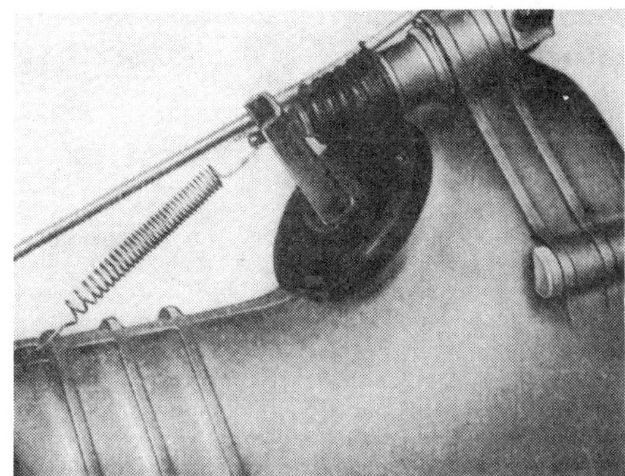

Fig. 5.4. Clutch slave cylinder (pre August 1969) (Sec. 3)

Fig. 5.5. Clutch slave cylinder (arrowed) (after August 1969) (Sec. 3.3)

3.11. Check the fastenings of the clutch lever bearing ring. Do not wash this bearing in cleaning fluid

3.13. Replacing the diaphragm plate/pressure plate and friction disc, note which way round the friction plate goes

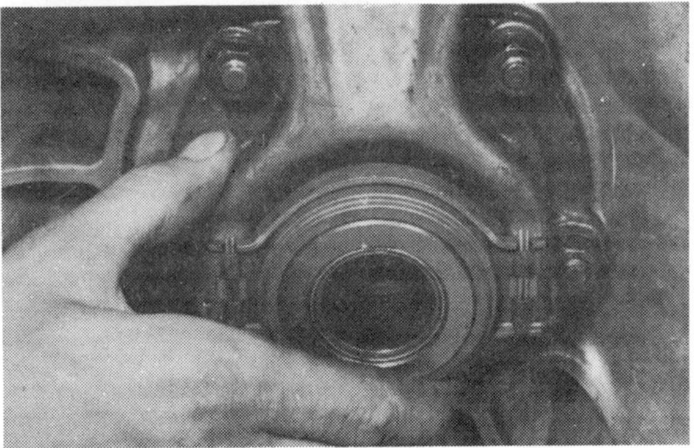

3.14. Replacing the clutch lever (this is a post 1969 type)

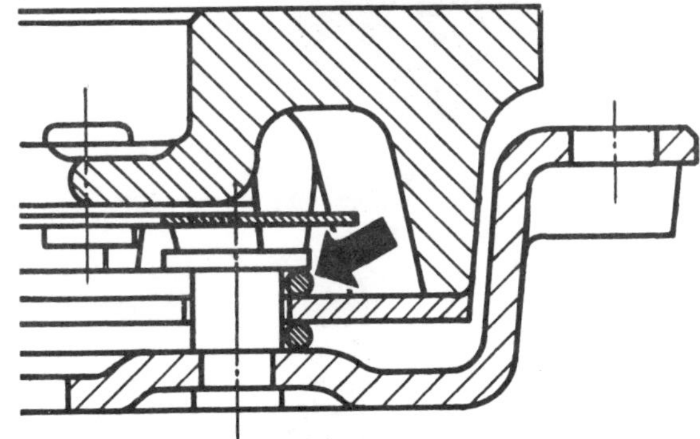

Fig. 5.6. Section through diaphragm/pressure plate assembly showing rivet heads and wire rings which must be examined for wear (Sec. 3.8)

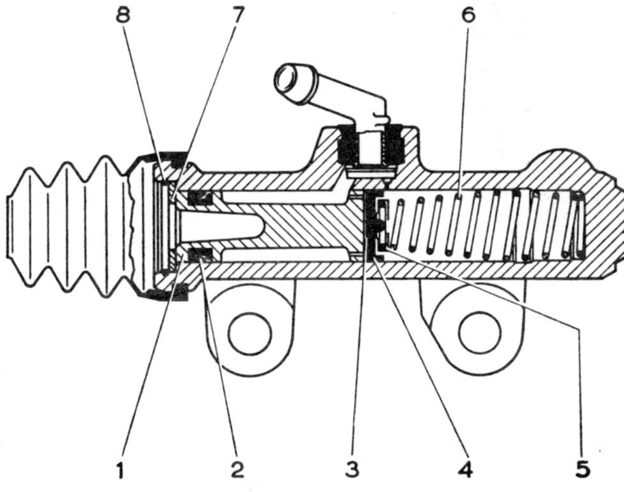

FIG. 5.7. CLUTCH MASTER CYLINDER – SECTION (SEC. 5)

1 Piston
2 Secondary cup
3 Cup washer
4 Primary cup
5 Support washer
6 Spring
7 Washer
8 Spring ring

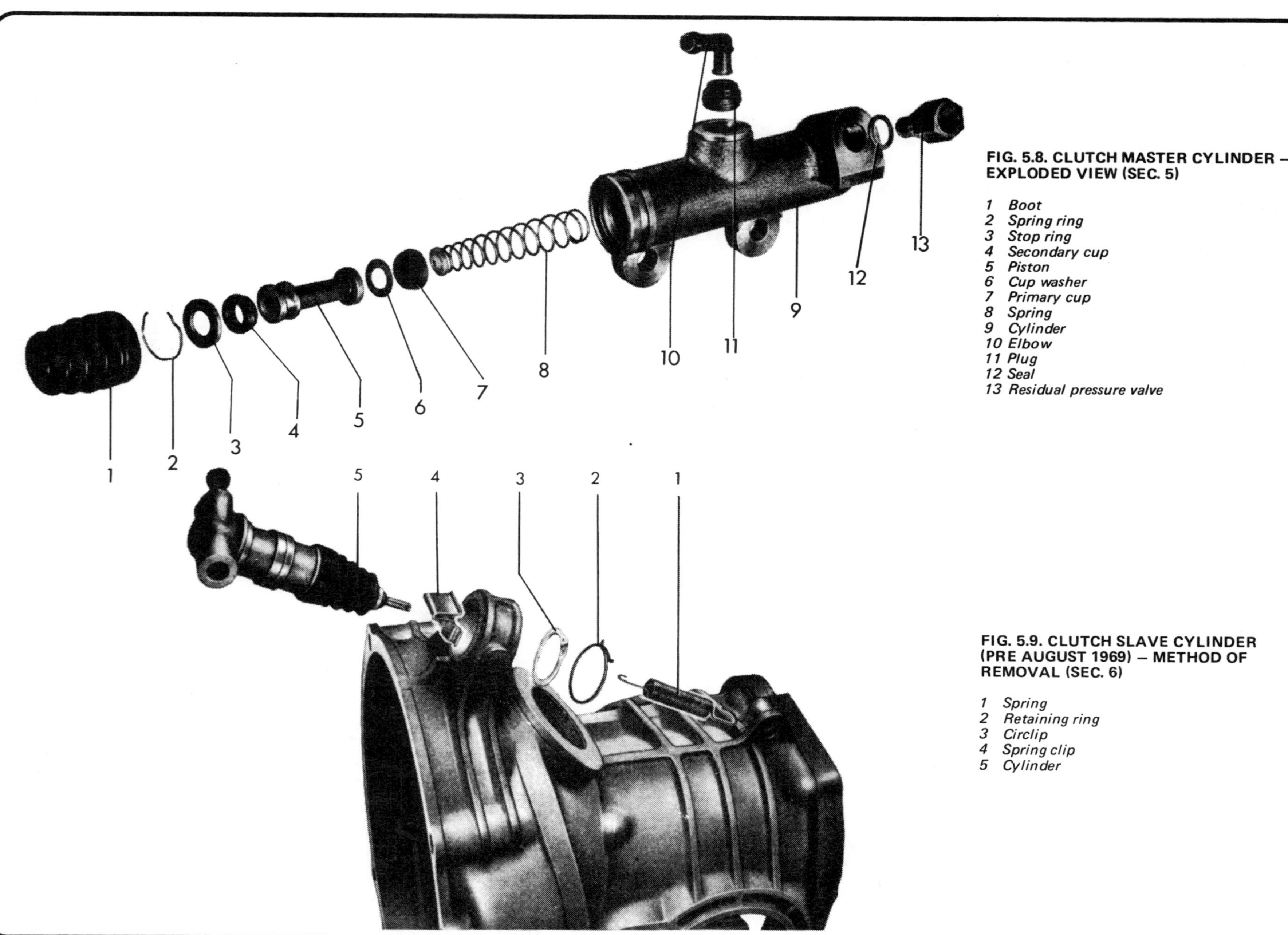

FIG. 5.8. CLUTCH MASTER CYLINDER – EXPLODED VIEW (SEC. 5)

1 Boot
2 Spring ring
3 Stop ring
4 Secondary cup
5 Piston
6 Cup washer
7 Primary cup
8 Spring
9 Cylinder
10 Elbow
11 Plug
12 Seal
13 Residual pressure valve

FIG. 5.9. CLUTCH SLAVE CYLINDER (PRE AUGUST 1969) – METHOD OF REMOVAL (SEC. 6)

1 Spring
2 Retaining ring
3 Circlip
4 Spring clip
5 Cylinder

6 Slave cylinder and operating lever (pre August 1969)

1 Refer to Figs.5.4, 5.9 and 5.10.

2 The slave cylinder (22.2 mm) is mounted in a boss cast on the transmission casing, held axially by a spring ring and prevented from turning by a sheet metal clamp. The push rod of the clutch slave cylinder presses against the top of the clutch lever which pivots on a special head pin in the clutch housing.

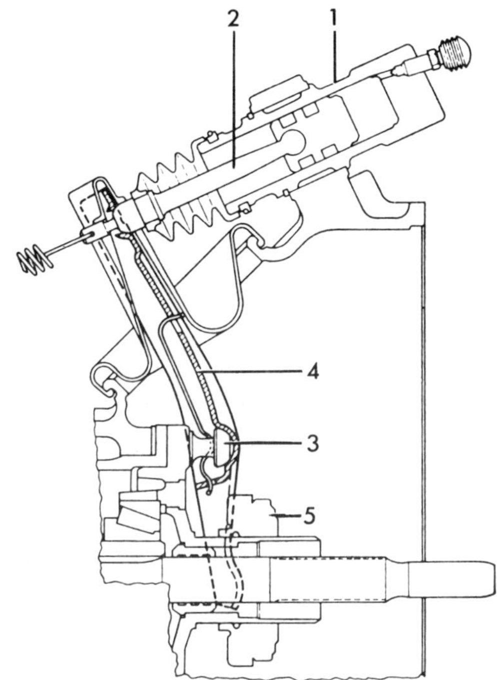

FIG. 5.10. CLUTCH SLAVE CYLINDER AND CLUTCH LEVER (PRE AUGUST 1969) (SEC. 6)

1 Slave cylinder
2 Push rod
3 Spherical head pin
4 Clutch lever
5 Release bearing

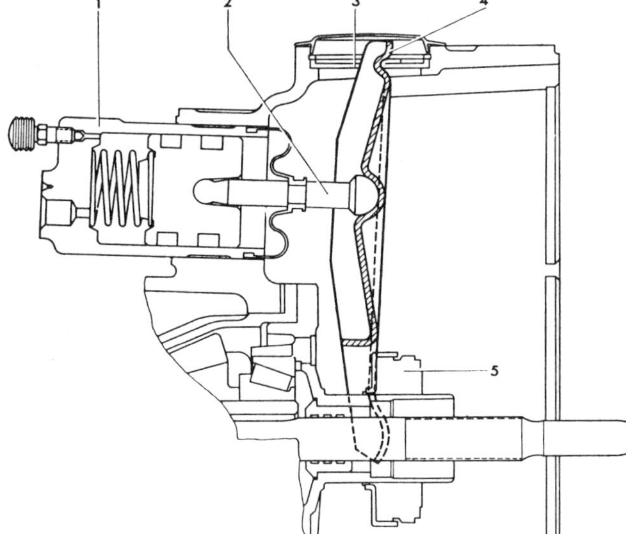

FIG. 5.11. CLUTCH SLAVE CYLINDER AND CLUTCH LEVER (AFTER AUGUST 1969) (SEC. 7)

1 Slave cylinder
2 Push rod
3 Thrust disc
4 Clutch lever
5 Release bearing

3 To remove the slave cylinder, disconnect the pressure line and block it to keep out the dirt, catch excess fluid as the union is undone.

4 Detach the spring from the push rod, remove the retaining ring from the boot and pull off the boot; take the circlip off the cylinder and press the cylinder out of the boss.

5 Installation is the reverse procedure, remember to bleed the system after refitting.

6 To dismantle the cylinder pull the piston and push rod out of the cylinder. Next detach the push rod from the piston. There is a small retaining ring on the push rod and a cup seal either side of the piston. Check all the parts for wear and replace as necessary. If either the piston or cylinder is worn a new assembly is required. Clean the parts in methylated spirits and coat with clean brake fluid.

7 To assemble the cylinder set the cup seals either side of the piston and push in the push rod. Fit the spring ring, and push the assembly into the cylinder.

7 Slave cylinder and operating lever (August 1969 onwards)

1 Refer to Figs.5.5, 5.11 and 5.12.

2 From chassis No 410 2000 001 the modified transmission mounting is fitted with a 44.5 mm diameter clutch slave cylinder. It is held into the casing by two studs only. The release lever is located in a bracket in the top of the clutch housing and the rod of the clutch slave cylinder presses on the release lever below the pivot point.

3 To remove the slave cylinder from the casing undo the two nuts on the studs, disconnect the pressure line and pull the cylinder out from the housing.

4 To reinstall it, push the cylinder into the housing, tighten the nuts evenly, reconnect the pressure line and bleed the system.

5 To dismantle the cylinder pull off the end cap with the push rod, and remove the piston and spring. Check for wear. If the piston or cylinder is worn the whole assembly must be changed.

6 There are two types which although they look identical externally differ internally. The first version has one seal only on the spring end of the piston. The other version has two seals and a modified piston. Regrettably it will be necessary to take the slave cylinder to the agent in order to obtain the correct replacement seals - which is what comes of having the same part made by different manufacturers who apparantly cannot agree.

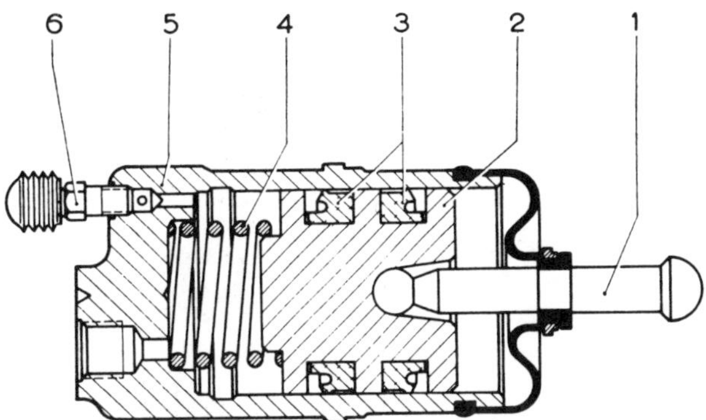

FIG. 5.12. CLUTCH SLAVE CYLINDER (AFTER AUGUST 1969) (SEC. 7)

1 Push rod
2 Piston
3 Seals
4 Spring
5 Housing
6 Bleed point

8 Bleeding the system

1 Basically the rules for bleeding brakes apply (see Chapter 9).
2 On the earlier versions (up to chassis 419 050 931) the bleed nipple is on the side of the slave cylinder and accessible from the engine compartment hatch.
3 On the later versions the bleed nipple is located on top of the slave cylinder facing forwards. It is necessary to raise the vehicle and get at the bleed nipple from underneath.
4 Because the pressure line is 6 mm diameter if no pneumatic bleeding machine is available and air is to be expelled by pumping the clutch pedal, it is essential to open the bleed valve to its full extent.

9 Pedal arrangements

1 These vary between LH drive and RH drive.
2 On LH vehicles the brake pedal is on the right and the clutch on the left of the pedal support.
3 On RH drive vehicles both pedals are on the left of the pedal support and the positions of the master cylinders are reversed.
4 Full details of the layout with fitting instructions are contained in Chapter 9. Fig.9.10 and Section 15.

10 Clutch faults

1 Clutch judder when taking up the drive is usually due to loose engine/gearbox mountings. Check that these are all in good condition and tightened correctly. If this does not cure the fault then the clutch must be dismantled and inspected for wear as in Section 3.
2 Clutch 'Spin' (failure to disengage) is probably due to a fault in the hydraulic system. Check through to find leaks, test the pedal free play. Pull off the rubber end caps of the slave and master cylinders to see whether fluid is seeping through past the piston seals. If the vehicle has been standing idle for some time this condition may be due to rust on the splines and regrettably the clutch must be dismantled to cure this condition. We do not recommend the old fashioned idea of depressing the pedal and tow starting in top gear with a clutch which may not disengage or even starting on the starter when in top gear. Even if you survive the experience the clutch has to come down and it was not designed to start on the battery in top gear with the brakes on.
3 Clutch slip means quite simply that the friction plate is not fully locked between the pressure plate and the flywheel so that the engine will increase speed without increase in speed of the road wheels. If the pedal and push rod clearances are correct then regrettably the clutch is worn out or soaked in oil. Either way it must be dismantled and rebuilt.
4 Clutch squeal is due usually to a worn clutch release bearing and again the remedy is dismantle and rebuild. This is usually brought about by using the clutch pedal as a foot rest and being too idle to take the car out of gear at the traffic lights, resulting in the bearing being given too much to do.
5 Finally, the pedal may go down to the floor suddenly, which means a burst pipe, or it may become "hard" quite suddenly which means an obstruction in the hydraulic system or a seized withdrawal race (most unlikely). The pedal may become 'spongy' and feel uncertain in operation which will be due to air in the system.
6 Bleed the system, check that the reservoir is full and check that the hydraulic pressure is going through the system by slackening a small amount the unions one at a time starting at the master cylinder. Pressure will be indicated when the pedal is pressed.

Chapter 6 Manual transmission

Contents

Specifications

Type	3 piece divided casting containing final drive, transmission case and gear shift mechanism. 4 forward speeds, 1 reverse Baulk ring type synchromesh on all forward gears. From 1972 (Nov) second gear synchro hub has 3 baulk rings instead of one.	
Oil capacity - SAE 90	3.5 Imp. pints/2 litres	
Ratios:		
1st gear	3.81 : 1	
2nd gear	2.11 : 1	
3rd gear	1.4 : 1	
4th gear	1 : 1	
Reverse	4.31 : 1	
Final drive ratios:		
Saloon - up to August 1970	3.73 : 1	
- August 1970 - June 1972	3.91 : 1	
- from June 1972	3.73 : 1	
Variant	3.91 : 1	
Torque wrench settings:	**lbs ft**	**mkg**
Gearbox casing to final drive casing cap nuts	14	2
Shift lever casing to gearbox casing nuts	14	2
Drive shaft to drive gear nut	14	2
Selector fork to rail clamp screw	14	2
Selector shaft bearing pin	10	1.5
Bearing carrier cover nuts	32	4.5
Oil filler and drain plugs	14	2

1 General description

1 The four speed gearbox and differential are combined together in a three part housing which is bolted to the engine at the rear and supported also by a cross beam which is attached to the body frame and fits over the clutch housing.

In effect the gearbox and differential are outboard to the power unit, the gear change mechanism passing through a hole in the centre of the rear axle carrier. Fig. 6.1 refers.

At the front is the shift housing, in the centre the gearbox proper, which has a sheet metal pan on the base, and the rear portion contains the differential.

At the top of the transmission a hollow mainshaft carries the drive gear for the counter shaft, the gears and synchroniser units for the forward speeds and the reverse gear. Third speed gear runs on a steel bush, the remainder on needle bearings. The synchro units for 1st/2nd gear and 3rd/4th gear are identical. From November 1972 the 2nd gear synchromesh unit has 3 rings instead of one.

The mainshaft runs on taper rollers in the bearing carrier at the rear and needle bearings in the drive gear for the counter-shaft at the front. The drive gear runs in ball bearings in the front end of the transmission casing.

The drive shaft runs the full length of the transmission box inside the hollow main shaft. It is splined into the clutch and at the front end into the gear which drives the countershaft, so that clutch, and the drive gear for the counter shaft are in effect a solid unit.

The drive shaft is located axially by a nut and washer and can

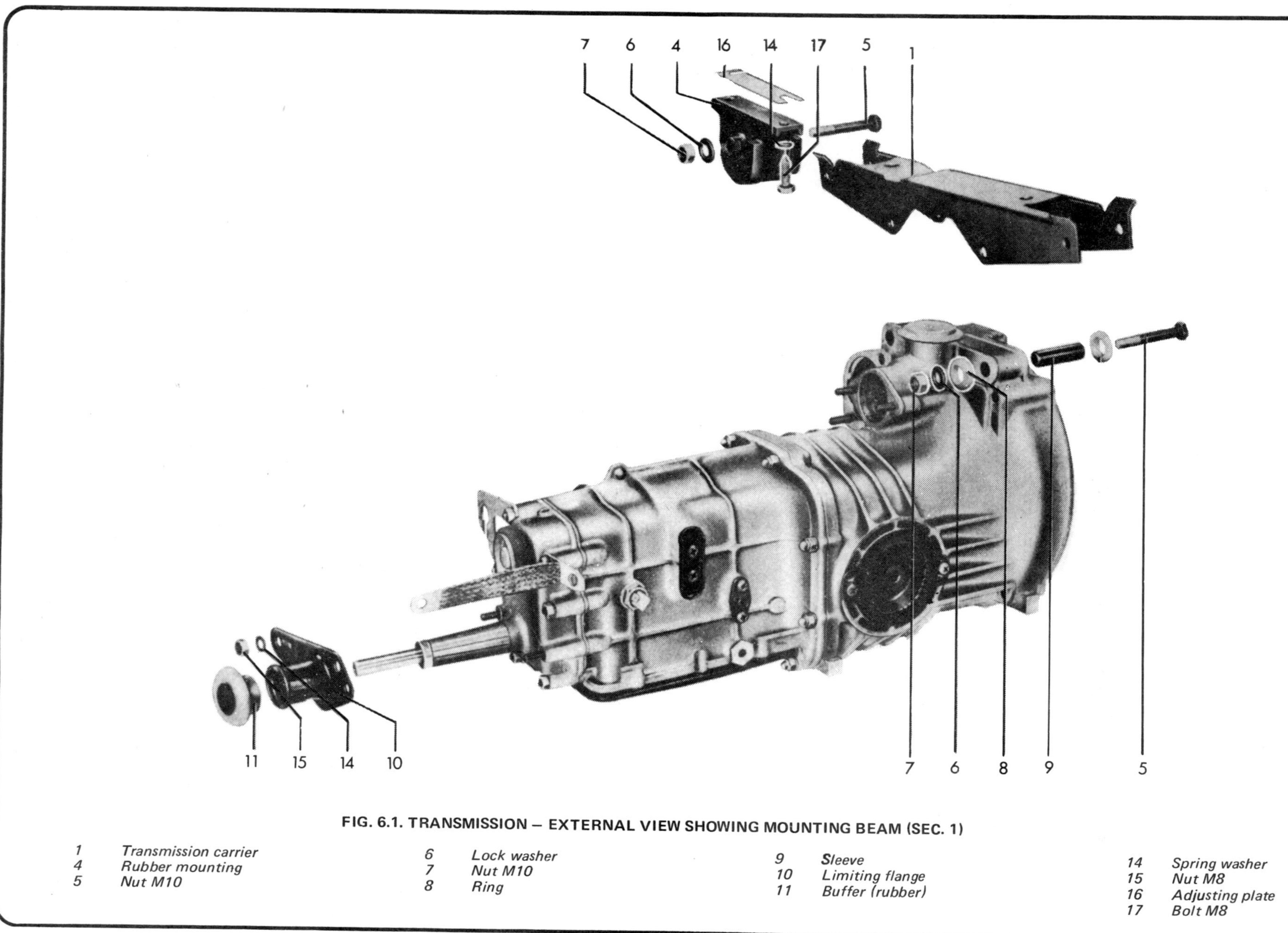

FIG. 6.1. TRANSMISSION – EXTERNAL VIEW SHOWING MOUNTING BEAM (SEC. 1)

1 Transmission carrier
4 Rubber mounting
5 Nut M10
6 Lock washer
7 Nut M10
8 Ring
9 Sleeve
10 Limiting flange
11 Buffer (rubber)
14 Spring washer
15 Nut M8
16 Adjusting plate
17 Bolt M8

be pulled forward out of the clutch, thus avoiding damage to the clutch if the engine is removed without the gearbox.
2 From the above it will be realized that the unit is a very complicated gear train and not one for learners to practice upon.
3 A few words of warning: The possession of a long extractor with a spread of four inches and a reach of ten inches is desirable. Some form of heating bushes and gears up to 100°C, a set of metric spanners and sockets, and a torque wrench are also necessary.

Add the cost of these to the estimated cost of a gearbox requiring a lot of spares, and then check the price of the replacement box.

Finally, the use of a press is essential, and a selection of mandrels.
4 Check the availability of spares. Gaskets, baulk rings and bearings, and possibly gears themselves. A set of gaskets is mandatory.
5 If this has not put you off then the rest of the chapter describes how a box was dismantled and reassembled by one person. Dismantling took roughly two hours, and reassembly the same. However this was by no means the first VW box the fitter had tackled.

2 Removal from the vehicle

1 Before starting work prepare a strong bench with a clean hard top. Assemble a collection of containers to put nuts, bolts and components safely inside. A number of wooden blocks and wedges to support the box during dismantling and assembly will be needed.
2 Drain the gearbox before removing it from the vehicle, but this will not extract all the oil from it, so have a suitable metal tray to catch the oil as and when required.
3 The gearbox cannot be removed unless the engine is removed, so either the two are removed together as in Chapter 1, or the engine has been removed and the problem is how to remove the box by itself. If the engine has been removed then the box will be left slung as in the photograph.
4 Working from underneath remove the boot clips from the drive shafts. Using an allan key remove the screws holding the drive shafts. An allan key is not the correct tool for this job, a special tool should be used, so be careful not to ruin the sockets, (see Chapter 8).
5 Watch out for oil when the C.V. joints are taken from the box, the joint should be packed with grease but if a seal has leaked a stream of oil will come out. This happened to us when about ½ pint ran up someone's sleeve.
6 With both joints removed (photo) next remove the gear shift rod joint. Pull back the boot (photo), remove the locking wire and take out the square headed screw. Pull the gearbox part of the shaft to the rear until it is clear of the joint. (photo).
7 Remove the battery wire and solenoid wire from the starter (Chapter 10).
8 Remove the slave cylinder from the clutch, it can be approached from the top (photo). It may need a little persuasion to come out, undo the pipe clip to ease it backward and it can be left in the car without disturbing the clutch hydraulic system.
9 Do not forget to remove the earth strap
10 The box is still supported by the sling. Take the weight of the box on a jack (photo) and undo the sling. Support the box on the jack and lower it down to the ground when it can be pulled clear of the car. (photo). Tie the C.V. joints up in polythene bags to prevent dust entering the joints.

3 Transmission - dismantling

1 The exterior of the body should now be cleaned. Use paraffin or GUNK, but clean it until it shines and then put it up on the bench, clean, dry and ready to be dismantled.
2 Remove the starter and solenoid (photo).
3 Now stand the box on the flange and remove the bottom

2.3. The engine has been removed and the transmission left slung from a baulk of wood placed across the top of the engine compartment. The slings are round the transmission carrier

2.6a. Both joints removed, the weight still on the sling makes it easy to move the box

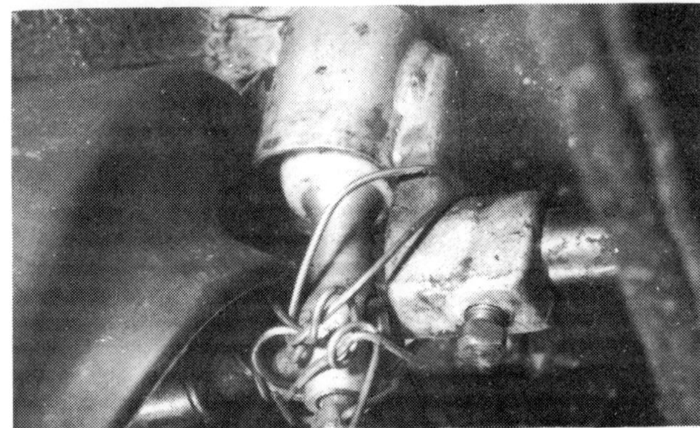

2.6b. Pull back the boot and remove the locking wire to undo the coupling on the gear change rod. Whoever had done this one up didn't intend it to come undone

2.6c. Pull the gearbox part of the shaft away until it is clear of the joint.

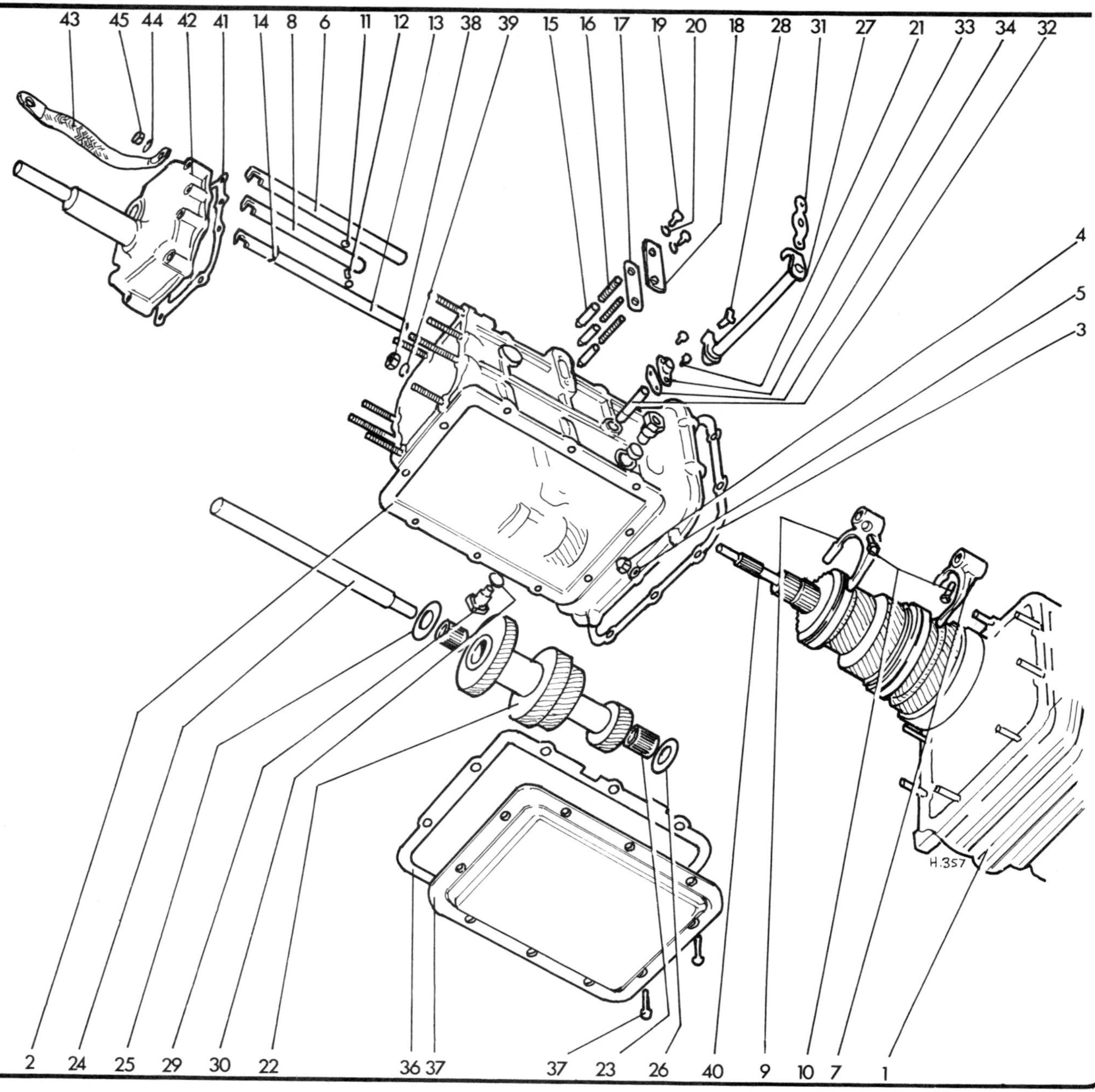

FIG. 6.2. TRANSMISSION CASE — EXPLODED VIEW

1 *Final drive complete (see Fig. 6.4)*
2 *Transmission case*
3 *Gasket*
4 *Cap nut*
5 *Washer*
6 *Shift rod 1st/2nd gear (medium length)*
7 *Shift fork 1st/2nd gear (wide)*
8 *Shift rod 3rd/4th gear (short)*
9 *Shift fork 3rd/4th gear (narrow)*
10 *Screw*
11 *Interlock pin*
12 *Interlock plunger*
13 *Shift rod reverse (long)*
14 *Circlip*
15 *Plunger*
16 *Spring*
17 *Gasket*
18 *Cover plate*
19 *Screw*
20 *Lockwasher*
21 *Screw*
22 *Counter shaft gear*
23 *Counter shaft needle bearing*
24 *Countershaft*
25 *Thrust washer (front)*
26 *Thrust washer (rear)*
27 *Selector shaft (reverse)*
28 *Shaft segment (reverse)*
29 *Bearing pin*
30 *Washer*
31 *Rocker lever*
32 *Eccentric pin*
33 *Cap*
34 *Gasket*
35 *Oil pan*
36 *Gasket*
37 *Screw M7*
38 *Nut M9*
39 *Lock washer*
40 *Drive shaft*
41 *Gasket*
42 *Shift housing*
43 *Earth strap*
44 *Spring washer*
45 *Nut M8*

2.8. The clutch master cylinder can be removed from on top. Hang it somewhere convenient

2.10a. Take the weight of the box on a jack, it would be better to have a wooden packing piece, ...

2.10b . . . . .lower it down and remove it to the rear

3.2. Remove the starter

3.3. Stand the box on end and remove the bottom plate

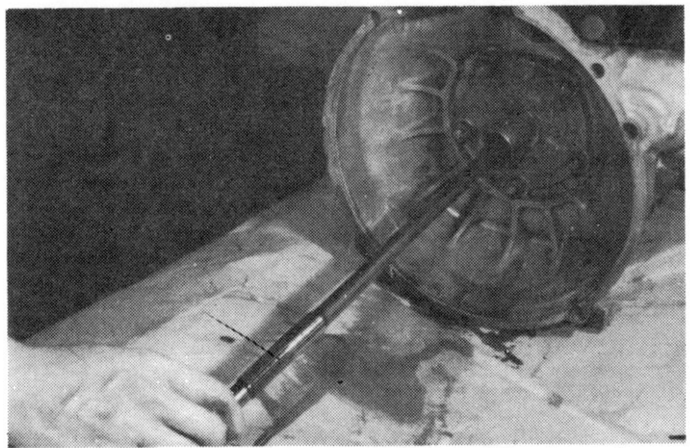
3.4a. Remove the torque shaft through the bellhousing and. . . . .

3.4b. . . . . .the gearbox mounting

3.5. Removing the shift housing

cover plate. Note the lockscrew painted green. (photo)

4 Remove the torque shaft from the bellhousing (photo), and take off the gearbox mounting plate (photo).

5 Now put the box in reverse gear, take off the shift housing screws and pull the housing back on the studs as far as possible (photo) then tilt it so that the end of the shaft relay lever is clear of the 1st/2nd gear shift rod by turning the shaft with a mole wrench and take off the shift housing and gasket.

6 Although the box taken to pieces for these pictures was drained the gear shaft housing was still full of oil and grease which ran out and rather ruined all the work of cleaning. This could be avoided by having the box on its side over a tray when the joint is broken.

7 Undo the reverse selector shaft bearing pins on the outside of the box (photo) and having pulled the reverse sliding gear forward take out the selector shaft and shift segment(photo).

8 Screw a M10 x 90 bolt into the end of the counter shaft gear shaft using a socket as a distance piece (photo) and pull out the shaft (photo). Take out the countershaft gear cluster with thrust washers. (Photo).

9 Remove the cover plate for the gear detent balls and springs and remove the springs and plungers (photo).

10 Pull the reverse shift rod out to the stop and turn it 90° and take out the rocker lever (photo).

11 Next take out the shift fork securing screws, use a 9 mm socket, pull the shift rods out of the forks and out of the case (photo) and fit the selector forks back on to the rods in the correct place to facilitate reassembly.

12 Remove the domed nuts from the studs holding the transmission case to the final drive case and tap the two apart, remove the gasket and set it on one side. (photo).

13 Swing the transmission round so that the mainshaft is vertical.

14 Remove the cap with a screwdriver (photo) and remove the circlip (photo).

15 The removal of the gears from the mainshaft is the next task. It is as well to layout and label the places where they are to be stored as they come off the shaft. If a long armed extractor with thin claws is available then all goes smoothly, but if it isn't then things become tricky.

16 Before starting to pull off any gear on models prior to August 1968 spread the ends of the circlip in the centering ring with outside circlip pliers; from August 1968 the circlip is in front of the ring.

17 Refer to Fig.6.3, which shows the layout of the mainshaft.

18 Place a suitable distance piece in the mainshaft and using a puller with long arms pull the centring ring against reverse gear. The claw of the puller must be right under the inner ring of the centering ring. Guide the reverse gear onto the splines for the synchromesh hub and pull the whole train off the shaft. (photo).

19 Because manufacturing tolerances and select fit assembly methods allow tight fits the bush for third speed gear may be

3.7a. Undoing the reverse selector shaft bearing pins

3.7b. Removing the reverse selector shaft and shift segment

3.8a. Use a M10 x 90 bolt and a socket to pull the countershaft gear shaft out of its bearings and . . . . .

3.8b . . . . .pull it right out of the box at the same time

3.8c . . . . .take out the countershaft gear cluster and thrust washers

3.9. Remove the detent springs and plungers

3.10. Removing the rocker lever

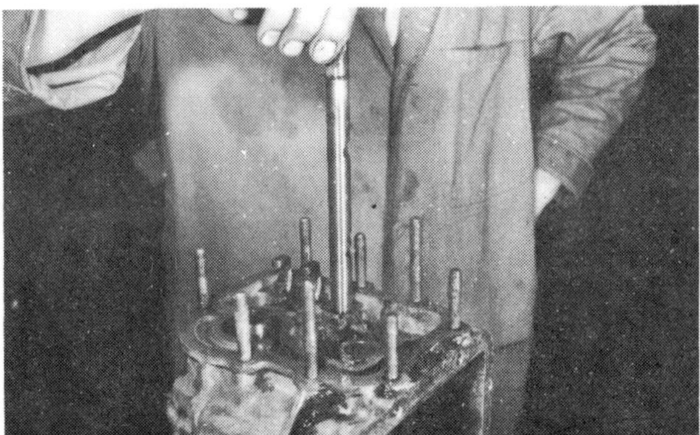
3.11. Pull the shaft rods out of the case

3.12. Separate the transmission case from the final drive case

3.14a. Remove the cap with a screwdriver. . . . .

13.14b . . . . .and the circlip

3.18. Using the special puller on the centring ring to pull off the whole gear train

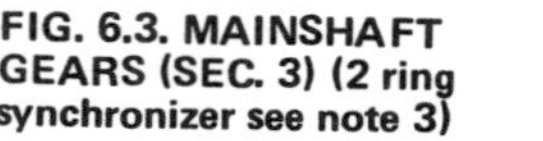
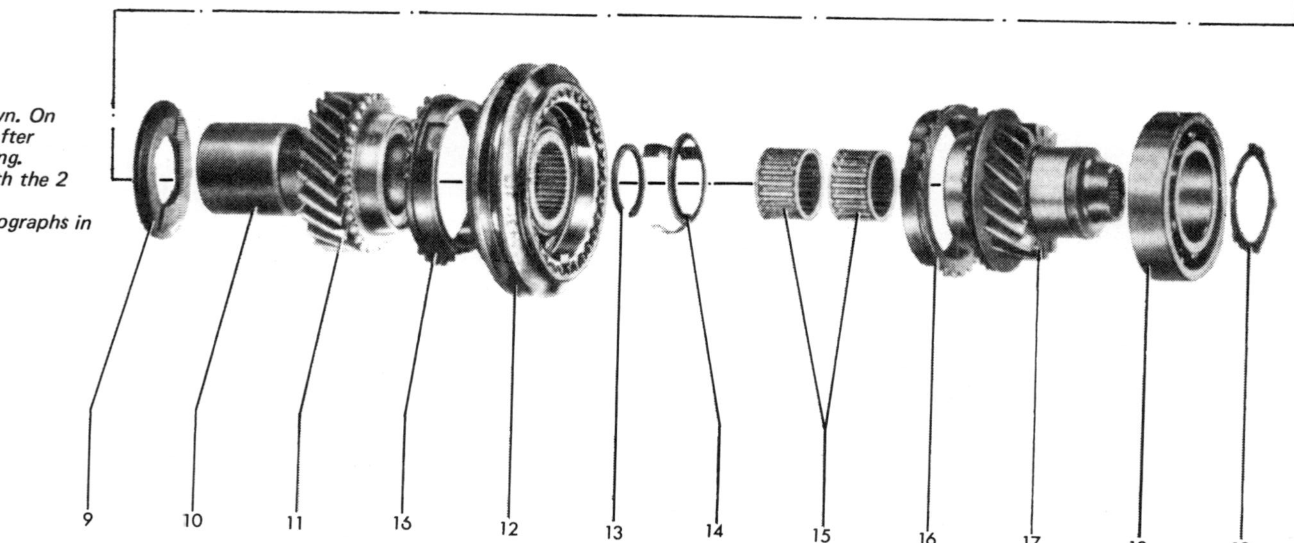
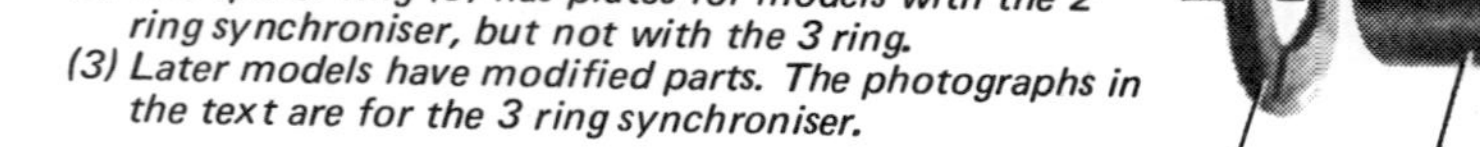

FIG. 6.3. MAINSHAFT GEARS (SEC. 3) (2 ring synchronizer see note 3)

1 *Centering ring*
2 *Reverse gear*
3 *1st speed gear*
4 *2nd speed gear*
5 *Needle bearing 1st/2nd gear*
6 *Synchroniser rings 1st/2nd gear*
7 *Synchroniser hub 1st/2nd gear*
8 *Plate for spacer ring*
9 *Spacer ring*
10 *Bush 3rd speed gear*
11 *3rd speed gear*
12 *Synchroniser hub 3rd/4th gear*
13 *Circlip*
14 *Locking cap*
15 *Needle bearing, drive gear*
16 *Synchroniser rings 3rd/4th gear*
17 *Countershaft drive gear*
18 *Ball bearing*
19 *Lock ring*
20 *Final drive (see Fig. 6.4)*

Notes (1) *The circlip for the centering ring is not shown. On early models it was at the back, on models after August 1968 at the front of the centering ring.*
(2) *The spacer ring (9) has plates for models with the 2 ring synchroniser, but not with the 3 ring.*
(3) *Later models have modified parts. The photographs in the text are for the 3 ring synchroniser.*

very tight indeed in which case pull off the 2nd speed gear with all above it first and then pull the remainder off separately.

20 However if no puller is available the job can still be done. The synchro hub for 3rd/4th gear is splined to the shaft and can be removed by patient gentle tapping with a soft drift (photo).

21 The spacer ring and second gear may be removed with the bush for 3rd gear again by gentle tapping but this is the bush which causes the trouble. On the box dismantled for this manual it was very tight indeed so a little heat was applied to the bush, very little indeed sufficed and two screwdrivers under the spacer ring (photo) moved the bush far enough to get an ordinary set of pullers under the spacer ring and pull the bush off. (photo)

22 Remove second gear, its bearing rings and synchro hub (photo).

23 Remove the synchro hub 1st/2nd gear, 1st gear and the roller bearing (photo).

24 Reverse gear may now be levered up from the splines and

3.20. The synchro hub for 3rd/4th gear and 3rd gear can be removed by patient tapping

3.21a. After warming 3rd gear bush use two screwdrivers under the spacer ring to ease it up enough to . . . . .

3.21b . . . . .pull it off with an extractor

3.22. . . . .second gear. . . . .

3.23. . . . .synchro hub, 1st/2nd gear, and first gear and rocker bearing . . . . .

3.24 . . . . .next reverse gear

3.25a. . . . . remove the circlip

taken off (photo)

25 Remove the circlip from the centering ring (photo) and using two wooden levers (hammer handles) ease the centering ring off the shaft (photos). It may be necessary to warm the ring to 100°C, but not beyond that and do not use too much force or the ring may buckle.

26 Now turn the casing onto its side, undo the nuts from the bearing cover and lever the cover out of its housing through the clutch slave cylinder hole (photo).

27 Refer to Fig.6.4. Remove the circlip from the end of the differentail shaft after removing the cap. The cap should be pierced with a screwdriver and a new cap will be needed. Now use two levers and press off the flange. Remove the screws holding the retaining plates for adjuster rings and take the plates off (photo).

28 The adjuster rings must now be removed. Before starting make centre punch marks on the ring and housing to facilitate reassembly. A special tool is really required to remove and install these rings but we didn't have one. A little judicious tapping with a very soft drift, the retainer used as a spanner, and a pair of tin snips opened out and fitted into the serrations were all employed. The number of turns on the side was 5. 2/3 turns, and the opposite side 5½ turns. It is very important to count the turns, if the same differential is to be reinstalled, as they give the correct pre-loading. If a new differential is to be fitted the assembly must go back to the agent for correct fitting and preloading with the appropriate jigs and tools. (Photo).

29 With the differential out of its bearings it is possible to move it to one side and withdraw the carrier with pinion and mainshaft complete. (photo)

30 The differential may now be lifted out of the casing and laid safely on one side (photo).

3.25b Lever out the centering ring

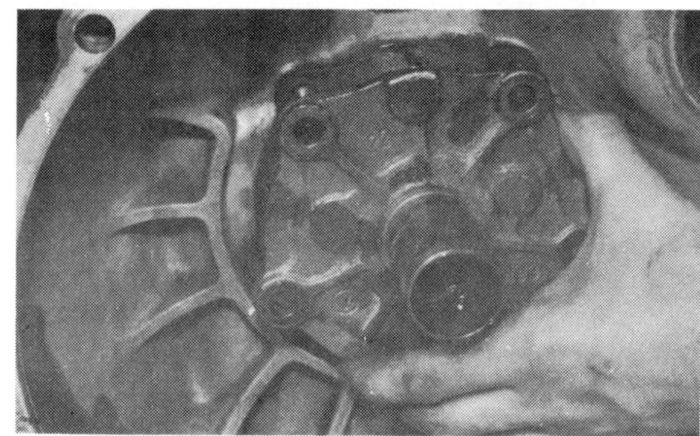

3.26. Remove the bearing cover . . . . .

3.27. The retaining plate for the adjuster ring removed (the cleaning seems to be of poor quality here)

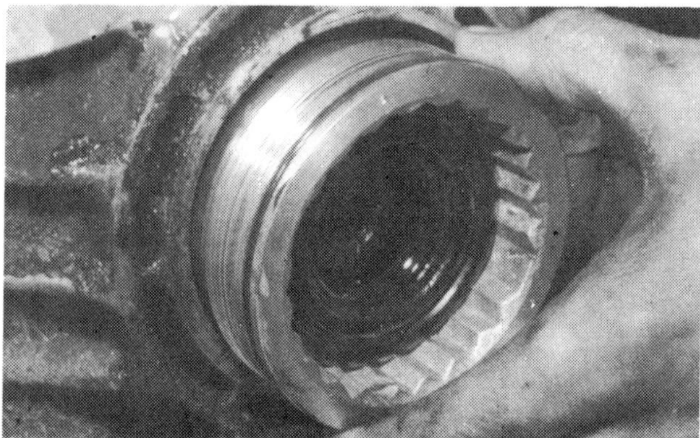

3.28. Removing the adjuster ring. Make centre punch marks and count the turns required to remove the ring

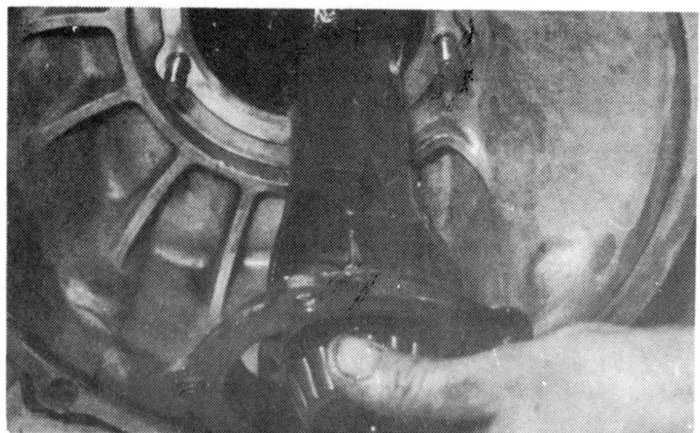

3.29. Removing the carrier with pinion and mainshaft . . . . .

3.30. . . . . and the differential assembly

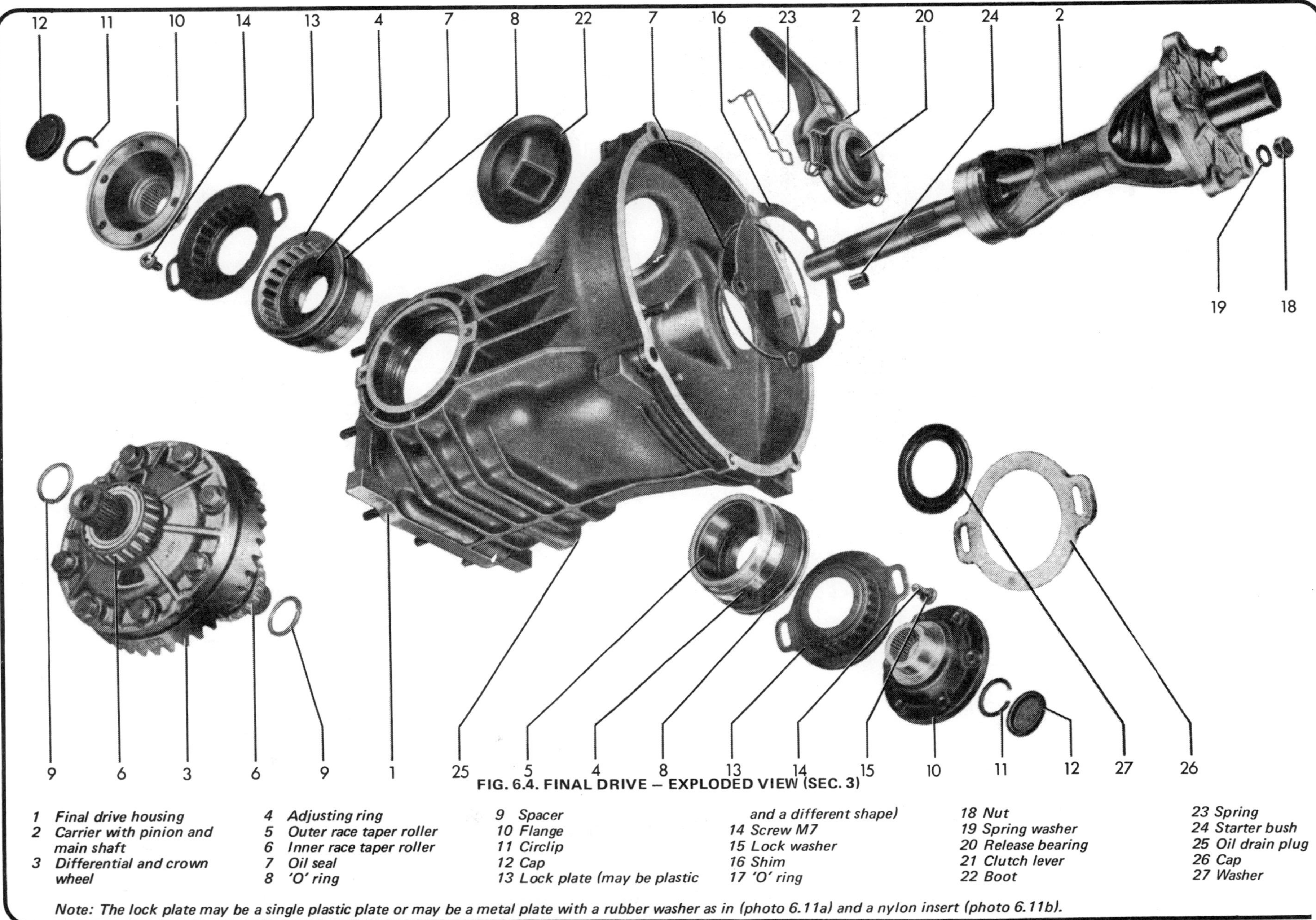

FIG. 6.4. FINAL DRIVE – EXPLODED VIEW (SEC. 3)

1 Final drive housing
2 Carrier with pinion and main shaft
3 Differential and crown wheel
4 Adjusting ring
5 Outer race taper roller
6 Inner race taper roller
7 Oil seal
8 'O' ring
9 Spacer
10 Flange
11 Circlip
12 Cap
13 Lock plate (may be plastic and a different shape)
14 Screw M7
15 Lock washer
16 Shim
17 'O' ring
18 Nut
19 Spring washer
20 Release bearing
21 Clutch lever
22 Boot
23 Spring
24 Starter bush
25 Oil drain plug
26 Cap
27 Washer

Note: The lock plate may be a single plastic plate or may be a metal plate with a rubber washer as in (photo 6.11a) and a nylon insert (photo 6.11b).

4 Inspection of transmission components

1 Each component should be cleaned carefully and wiped dry. Spend a little time on this and get rid of all the old oil and grease, clean the place up and start the inspection with a clean bench, clean hands and clean wiping rag.
2 The inside as well as the outside of the castings should be clean and dry. Examine them for cracks or superficial damage. Studs should be checked for tightness and nuts tried on the stud threads.
3 Examine all the gears for tooth wear, chipped teeth and spalling (cracks and scoring). Damaged gears should be regarded with suspicion. If there is doubt about them consult the VW agent. However it is better to put a slightly worn gear back then to mate a new one with an old one. If new gears are installed consideration should be given to replacing the gear with which the new gear is to mesh.
4 Needle and roller bearings should be washed in white spirit, lightly oiled and checked for axial and radial play. If they are alright then they should be greased lightly to retain the components in position. Not too much grease though or it may get in places it is not intended for, with disastrous results.
5 The synchromesh units should be checked for wear. Check the case with which the sleeve and hub slide on each other, and check for backlash. Check the coupling teeth and the wear of the selector forks in the grooves. This clearance should be between 0.040 ins, and 0.050 ins. (1 to 1.2 mm).
6 Check the shafts for signs of wear or scoring. Splines should not be in any way damaged. If they are remove the burrs or damaged portions carefully with a fine file.
7 Finally if all the parts are laid out in good order, and new parts acquired have been cleaned and put ready in order with the old ones have a good check round again. Lay out a set of gaskets in a safe place ready for installation (photo).

5 Differential and pinion assembly

1 Do NOT dismantle the differential or the carrier with pinion and mainshaft assembly. Doubt is not cast on the owner's ability for both of these units nave preloaded bearings which require not only special jigs to reassemble them, but a variety of spacers and shims and measuring instruments with again special fittings to enable tolerance to be calculated.
2 Furthermore unless the pinion is meshed correctly with the crownwheel, which again requires exact setting, a guaranteed built in whine will be produced and the whole job will have to be done again.
3 If either the differential or the pinion and mainshaft carrier assembly require rework then both of them complete with the final drive housing and its components should be taken to the agent for reassembly. This may be a little expensive but not nearly so expensive as a final drive which disintegrates while the car is going along at speed.
4 It may be argued why dismantle the final drive casing at all. If when the mainshaft gearing has been removed it is obvious that the crown wheel or the various gears require renewal then it would be better to take the whole casing to the agent right away. If the final drive is suspect but not obviously wrong then it can be dismantled for a closer look, but that is all.

6 Transmission - reassembly of final drive

1 As stated in Section 5, if no repair has been done to the main components then reassembly may go ahead, otherwise this job should be done by the agent.
2 Prise out the old oil seal from the bearing cover and replace it with a new one (photo). Press it in firmly with a suitable mandrel, preferably in a press.
3 Now place the final drive housing on the clean bench and insert the differential assembly into the housing (photo).

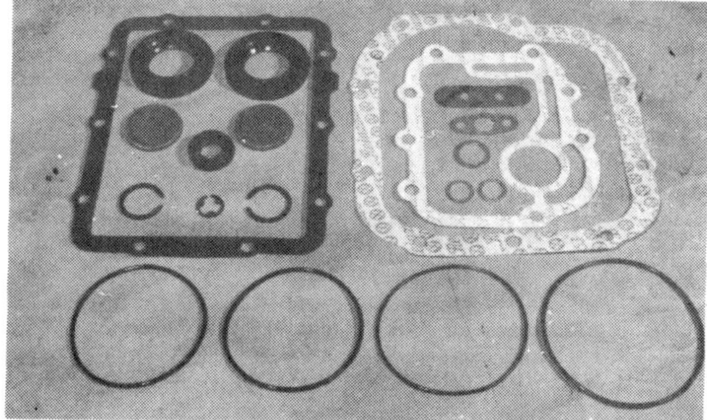

4.7. Lay out a new set of gaskets ready for installation. These come as a set and should all be used

6.2. Inserting a new seal to the bearing cover

6.3. Inserting the differential into the final drive housing

6.4. Fit a new oil seal into the bearing cover

4 Fit a new oil seal into the bearing cover (photo).
5 Fit a new oil ring and shim over the mainshaft carrier (photo) and fit the bearing cover to the mainshaft carrier (photo). Tap it gently into place.
6 Insert the mainshaft and cover into the final drive housing (photo), it will only go one way over the studs. Now fit the nuts and torque them to 32 lbs.ft. (4.5 mkg), (photo).
7 Turn the housing onto its broad face to assemble the differential flanges.
8 Prise the old oil seal from the adjusting ring and fit a new one (photo). Do not push this right down, the top of the seal should be flush with the inner surface of the adjusting ring.
9 Fit a new oil ring into the groove of the adjusting ring (photo) and screw the adjusting ring into the bearing housing (photo). It must be screwed in the exact number of turns that were required to move it (Sec. 3.28). (Remember that if the differential has been taken apart the whole assembly must go to the agent for correct reassembly). Use the lock plate as a spanner but be careful, it gets very tight at the end.

The adjusting ring will pick up the taper roller of the differential. Be sure both are clean and lubricated before assembly.
10 Now repeat the process for the adjusting ring, oil seal oil ring, and screw it in picking up the other bearing of the differential. It goes in quite easily at first using the locking ring as a spanner but it gets very tight as the pre-load becomes evident. However it MUST go in the same number of turns that it required to take it out, right until the centre punch marks coincide. It **can** be tapped round but it is far better to devise a tool to fit the locking ring. We used the nose of a pair of tin snips opened out into the serrations and turned with a mole wrench.
11 Fit the rubber washer and the spacer ring (photo), fit the nylon piece and the locking plate (photo) and secure the locking plate with the screw (photo).
12 Now fit the flange (photo) and the circlip (photo) and finally the cap (photo).
13 Repeat the process for the opposite flange.

7 Assembly of the mainshaft gearing

1 The mainshaft is now held firmly in the final drive housing and the pinion is mated with the crownwheel. There may be a little backlash but if you have screwed back the adjusting rings correctly there is no need to worry. Stand the final drive housing on the clutch housing face so that the mainshaft sticks up vertically.

Check that all is clean and no odd bits of dirt or rag have crept in while the struggle with the adjusting rings was going on.
2 Warm the centering ring to 100°C in boiling water and slide it onto the mainshaft carrier so that the two lugs engage in the recesses in the carrier (photo). The circlip must be spread while doing this; the opening in the centering ring for the ends of the circlip must point to the rear. The two lugs are arranged so that the ring can be fitted only one way. (Photo).

It is a good idea to rehearse this betore heating the ring for it cools quickly and you should be sure of what you are going to do before fitting the hot ring.
3 Heat the reverse gear to 100°C and slide it onto the mainshaft with the narrow shoulder downwards, drive it on firmly (photo).
4 Now fit on the synchroniser hub 1st/2nd gear and the operating sleeve the synchronising 2nd gear, the needle bearing 1st/2nd gear and 1st/2nd speed gears onto the mainshaft. Support 1st gear while this is being done (photos).
5 Now fit the spacer ring (photo). If new gears have been fitted then the the advice of the agent must be sought as to whether a different size spacer ring is required. The axial play of the whole shaft must be 0.003 to 0.006in. (0.09 to 0.16 mm). This requires a special tool for resetting so once again the good services of the agent must be sought. There is a choice of 8 different sizes for the spacer ring, and if new gears have been fitted only one size of the spacer ring is correct.
6 Heat the 3rd speed gear bush to 100°C and slide it on the

6.5a. Fit the shim and oil ring onto the mainshaft carrier . . . . .

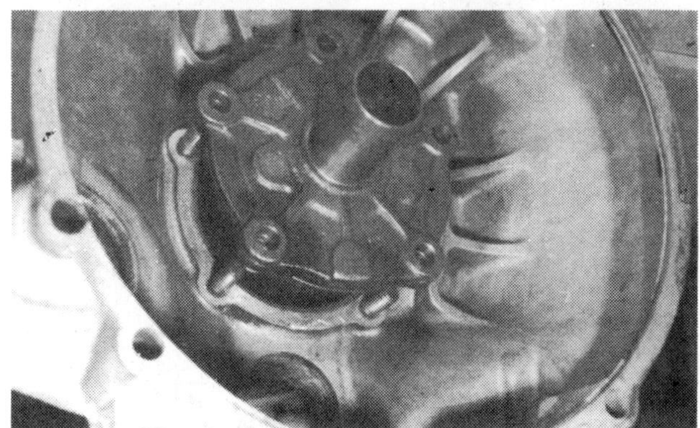
6.5b. . . . . and fit them together

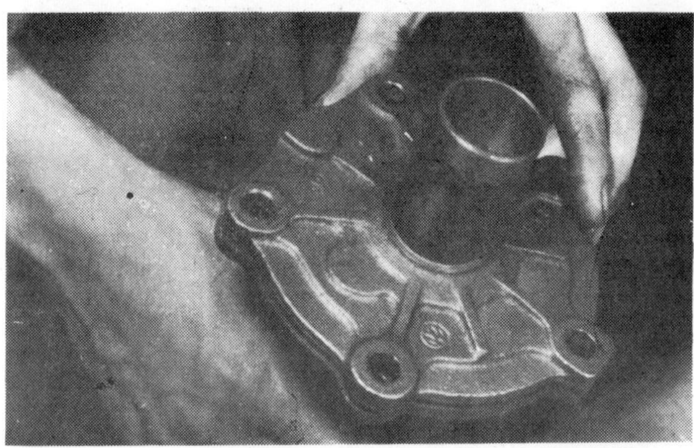
6.6a. Insert the mainshaft and cover into the final drive housing. . .

6.6b. . . . . and torque to 32 lbs ft.

6.8. Fit the oil seal to the adjusting ring......

6.9a. . . . . and the oil ring . . . . .

6.9b.. . . and screw it in to the housing

6.11a. Fit the rubber washer . . . . .

6.11b. . . . .the nylon piece and the locking flange. . . . .

6.11c. . . . . and the locking bolt . . . ..

6.12a. Fit the flange . . . . .

6.12b . . . . . and the circlip. . . . .

6.12c. . . . . and the cover plate

7.2a. Heat the centering ring and fit it over the mainshaft

7.2b. Now fit the circlip

7.3. Fitting the reverse gear to the mainshaft (hot)

7.4a. Fitting 1st gear bottom half synchroniser rings 1st/2nd gear, needle bearings 1st/2nd gear synchroniser hub 1st/2nd gear

7.4b. Fitting second gear and the top half of the synchroniser rings 1st/2nd gear

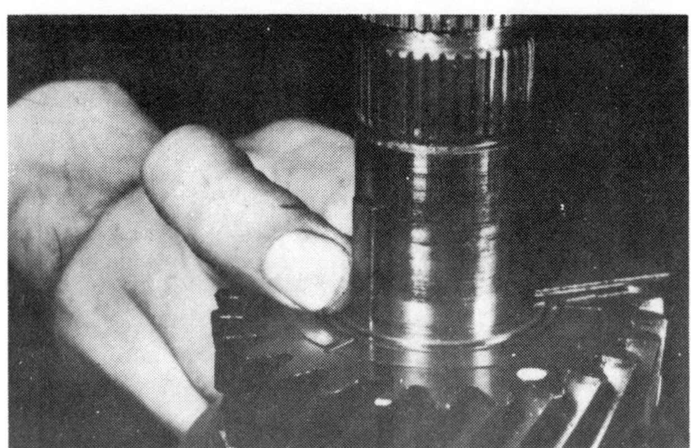
7.4c. Second gear firmly in place

7.5. Fitting the spacer ring

shaft (photo).
7 Now install 3rd speed synchroniser ring and drive the 3rd/4th speed synchroniser hub into position. The annular groove in the operating sleeve MUST be towards 4th speed gear (photos).
8 Install the circlip and the cap (photos). The open side of the circlip must be towards one of the recesses for the synchroniser keys so that the lugs on the cap can engage.
9 Now install the needle bearing (photo).
10 This is as far as we go with the final drive housing/mainshaft assembly for the moment. Now get the transmission casing off the rack.

8 Transmission casing assembly with gears

1 Fit the reverse idler gear into the transmission casing and insert the shaft (photo), be careful to line up the hole in the shaft with the hole in the casing or the locking pin will not go in when the bottom cover is assembled (see Section 8.12).
2 Install 4th gear into the casing complete with its bearing (photo) and fit the large circlip (photo).
3 Fit a new gasket to the final drive housing (photo).
4 Now drive the transmission casing onto the centering ring lining the studs of the final drive housing with the holes in the transmission case (photo).It may help if the transmission case is warmed a little round the bore in which the centering fits.
5 Fit the domed nuts and torque to 14 lbs ft (2 mkg) (Photo).
6 Swing the casing round so that the opening is at the top. Fit the 1st/2nd gear shift rod and the large shift fork and tighten the locking screw. (photos)
7 Insert the interlocking pin between the lower and centre shift rods. This goes down through the holes for the other shift rods and can be a tricky operation. Now fit 3rd/4th gear shift rod and the small fork (photos). Tighten the screw to 14 lbs ft., install the interlock plunger and the second interlock pin.
8 Install the top shift rod and rocker lever for reverse. The rocker lever should be positioned so that the long end is toward the opening (photo). The rocker lever is mounted on an eccentric pin (photo). If the pinion, mainshaft carrier, final drive shaft or transmission casing have been replaced then the position of the sliding reverse gear must be adjusted. Engage reverse gear and take the knurled cap off the eccentric pin, turn the pin until the sliding gear and the reverse gear on the mainshaft are flush, disengage reverse gear and check that at least 0.020" clearance exists between the sliding gear and the mainshaft gear when the the gear is pushed toward the casing. When this is done fit the knurled cap and tighten the screws.
9 Now install the countershaft. There are two thrust washers, one at each end. Installation is a little difficult. Stick the large washer in place with grease (photo), install the countershaft with the needle rollers and align it with the shaft to hold the needle bearing and washer in place (photo). Now fit the small washer (photo) lubricate the shaft and drive it right home.
10 Install the detent plungers and springs (photo). Fit the cover plate (photo) and secure with the phillips screws.
11 Now install the reverse gear selector shaft. Fit the bearing pins (photo) from outside. The shaft when installed looks like photo 8.11b. Press the gear towards the shift housing and tighten the bearing pins so that a flat or a point is towards the oil pan. This will lock the pin safely. (photo).

9 Transmission - fitting the shift housing

1 Stand the transmission casing and final drive housing on the bellhousing flange and clean carefully the top flange. Fit a new gasket (photo).
2 The shift housing mechanism is still in the casing as it was when the box was dismantled. Check round it for play or wear and renew the parts if necessary. (photo).
3 Install the shift housing onto the transmission case. This should be done with reverse gear engaged (photos). If necessary pull the reverse shaft lever out a bit to engage the relay lever.

7.6. Fitting 3rd speed gear bush (hot)

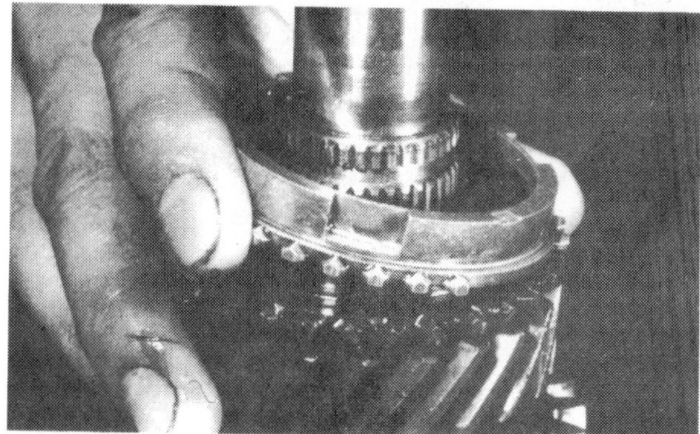
7.7a. Install 3rd speed synchroniser ring . . . . .

7.7b. . . . . and the 3rd speed synchroniser hub

7.8a. Fit the circlip . . . . .

7.8b . . . . . and the cap

7.9. Install the needle bearing

8.1. Fitting reverse gear and shaft into the transmission casing

8.2a. Fit 4th gear and bearing into the transmission casing. . . . .

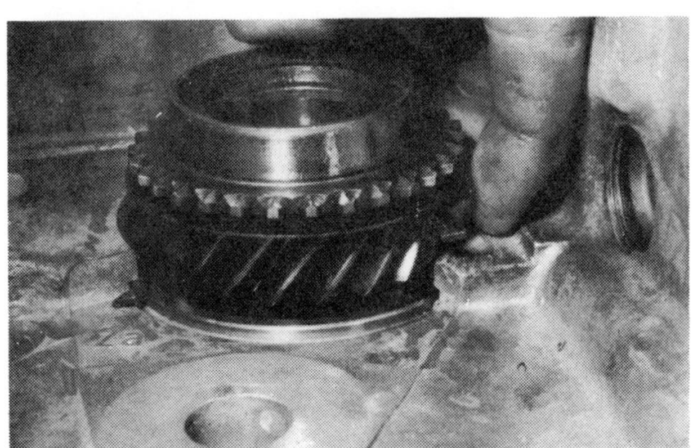
8.2b. . . . . and install the large circlip

8.3. Fit a new gasket to the final drive housing

8.4. Fit the transmission case to the final drive housing

8.5. Torque the nuts to 14 lbs ft (2 mkg). The initial fitting can be done with a ring spanner

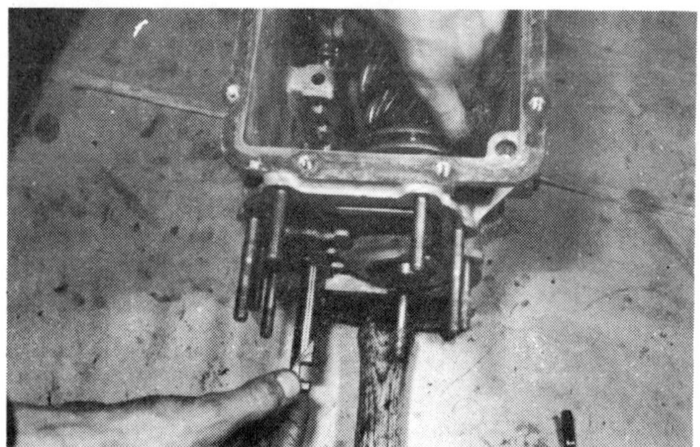
8.6a. Insert 1st/2nd shift rod

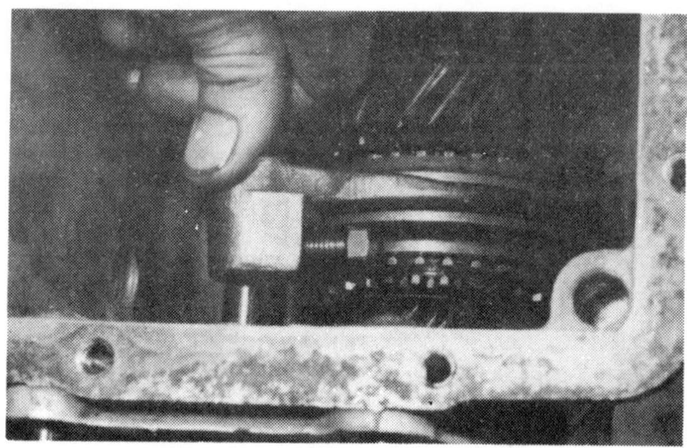
8.6b. The large shift fork goes here

8.7a. Insert the interlocking pin

8.7b. 3rd/4th gear shift rod

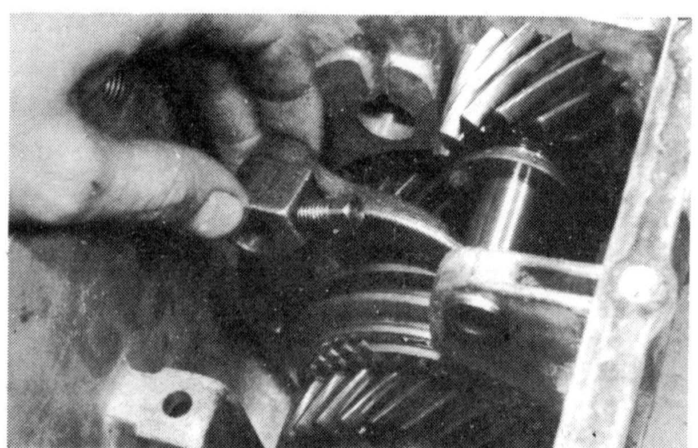
8.7c. The small fork goes here

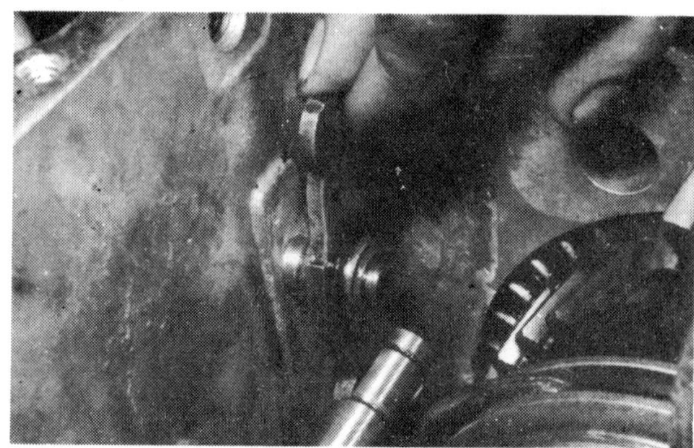
8.8a. Installing reverse gear rocker arm

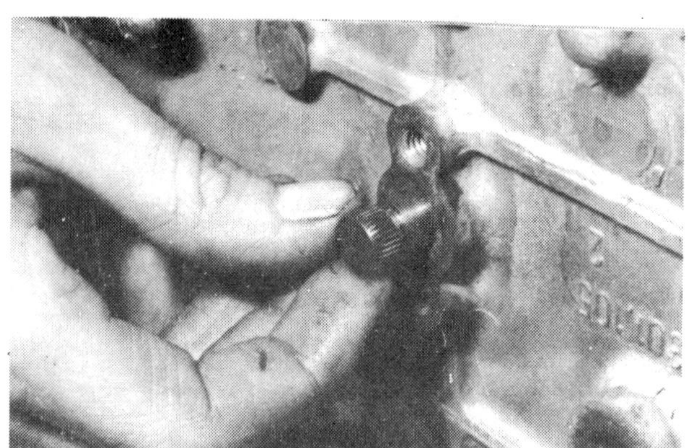
8.8b. The knurled knob of the eccentric pin on which the rocker arm is mounted

8.9a. Stick the large thrust washer in place

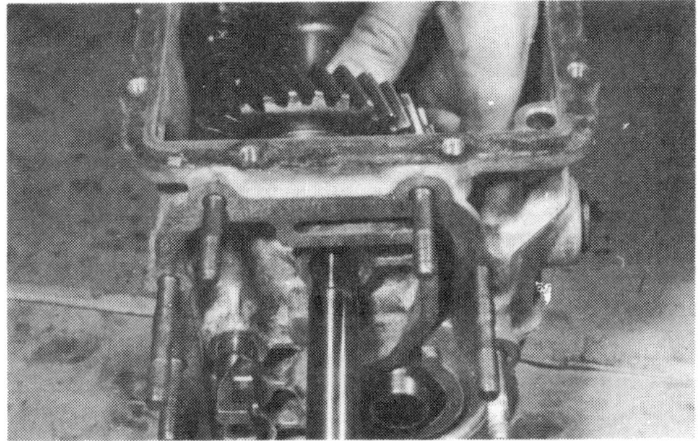
8.9b. Align the larger washer, countershaft and needle rollers with the shaft

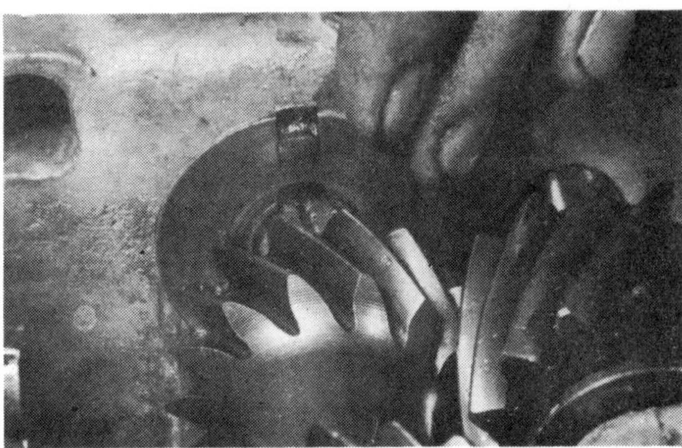
8.9c. Insert the small washer and drive the shaft home

8.10a. Fit the detent plungers and springs . . . . .

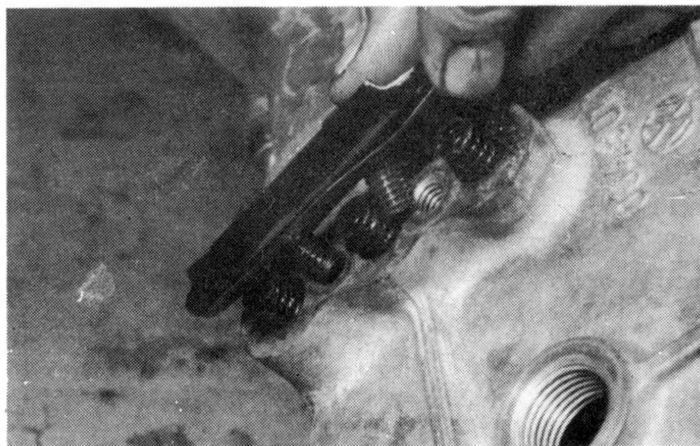
8.10b. . . . . and fit the cover plate

8.11a. Fit the reverse shaft bearing pins

8.11b. The shaft should look like this

8.11c. Press the gear toward the shift housing when tightening the bearing pins

9.1. Fit a new gasket to the top of the transmission case

9.2. The shift housing mechanism

9.3a. Fit the shift housing to the transmission case

9.3b. Engage the reverse gear, if necessary pull out the selector rod

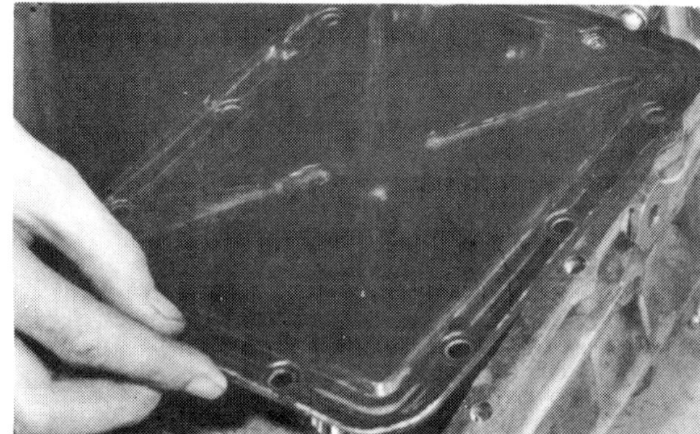
10.1a. Refit the oil pan to the transmission case

10.1b. The long bolt locks the reverse idler shaft

10.2. Refit the bracket for the brake fluid pipe

10.3. Install the bonded rubber mounting (new nuts)

10.4. Refit the starter

Torque down the nuts of the casing to 14 lbs ft. (2 mkg).
4 Check that all gears engage. If necessary adjust reverse gear (Section 8.8).

10 Gearbox - final assembly

1 All the gears engage and the box is nearly complete, now fit a new gasket to the transmission case and install the oil pan. (photo). Torque the bolts to 7lb ft (1 mkg). Note that the long bolt goes down to lock the idler gear shaft which is why it was necessary to line up the holes so carefully (photo) (Sec.8.1).
2 Fit the bracket for the brake fluid pipe to the slave cylinder (photo).
3 Install the bonded rubber mounting using new self-locking nuts (photo).
4 Refit the starter motor and solenoid (photo).
5 Now install the drive shaft (photo) and tighten the nut (photo). The retaining washer must seat properly in the groove (Fig.6.5). Lock the transmission to tighten the nut. Install the cap over the drive shaft (photo).
6 Fit the reverse light switch, tighten it carefully (photo).
7 Refit the clutch withdrawal fork and bearing (Chapter 5).
8 The box is now ready to be bolted to the power unit for installation to the vehicle.

11 Shift Linkage

1 The shift linkage is shown in Figure 6.6.
2 The gear lever pivots on a spherical ball held in a mounting screwed to the floor. The lower half protudes below the floor and terminates in a ball which transmits axial and radial motion to the gear shift rod, which in turn passes this to the gearbox

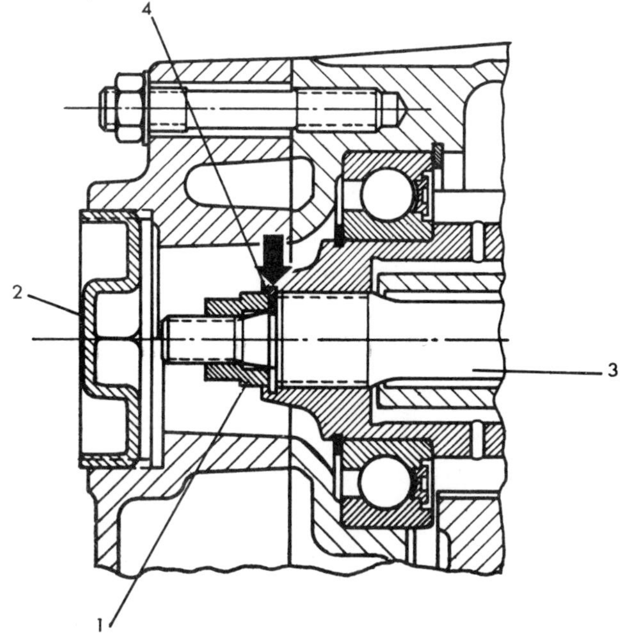

FIG. 6.5. DRIVE SHAFT SECURING ARRANGEMENTS IN THE TRANSMISSION CASING

1 Nut
2 Cap
3 Shaft
4 Circlip

10.5a. Install the drive shaft . . . . .

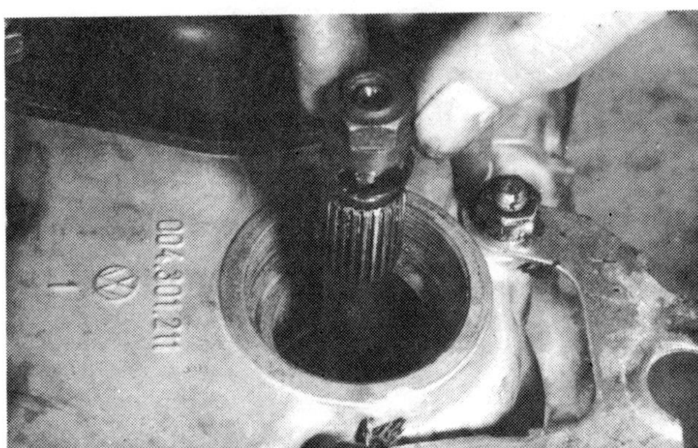

10.5b . . . . . and the retaining nut

10.5c. Fit the cap over the drive shaft nut

10.6. Fit the reverse light switch

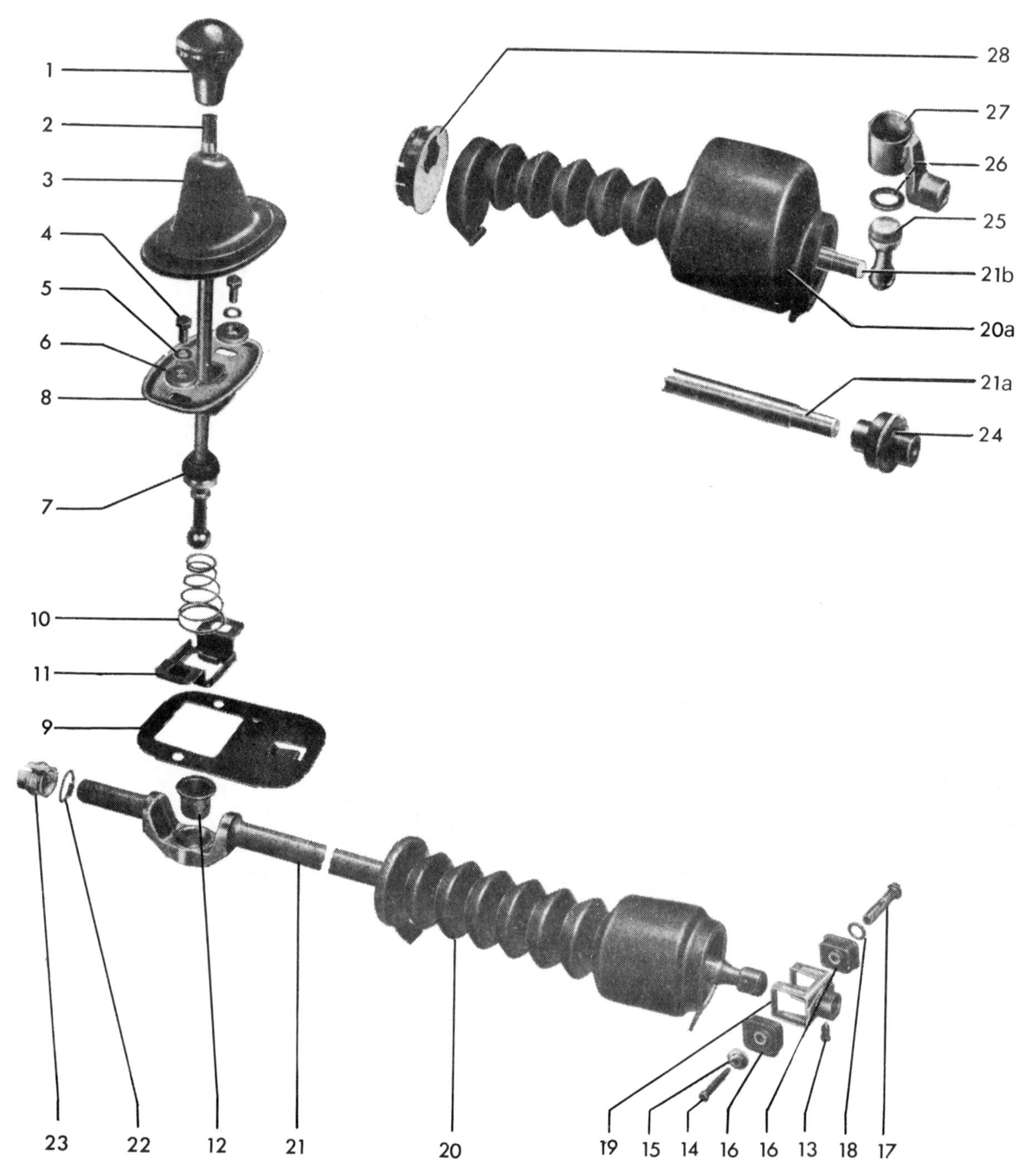

FIG. 6.6. SHIFT LINKAGE (INSET FOR MODELS AFTER APRIL 1970) (SEC. 11)

1 Knob
2 Lever
3 Boot
4 Bolt M8
5 Spring washer
6 Washer
7 Friction cap
8 Mounting
9 Cover plate
10 Spring
11 Stop plate
12 Guide bush
13 Screw
14 Tapping screw
15 Locking cap
16 Insert
17 Clamp sleeve
18 Washer
19 Housing
20 Bellows
20a Bellows (later models)
21 Shift rod (early models)
21a Shift rod (from August 1969)
21b Shift rod (from April 1970)
22 Ring
23 Guide bush
24 Coupling (with part 21a)
25 Shift finger (with part 21b)
26 'O' ring (with part 21b)
27 Relay lever (with part 21b)
28 Guide ring (with part 21b)

selector mechanism.

3 The shift rod and mechanism may be removed from the vehicle only when the engine and gearbox have been removed. It is suggested that this should be done on that occasion as the work involved is small compared with the removal of the power unit specially for the linkage overhaul.

4 To adjust the linkage engage 2nd gear and loosen the bolts which hold the mounting to the floor. Depress the clutch and move the lever in second gear. It must be exactly at right angles to the transverse plane and sloping back at about 8°. Tighten the bolts. The lever should now have about ½ inch transverse movement measured at the knob.

5 Engage all gears in turn using the H pattern. Check that the reverse catch works correctly.

See next page for Fault diagnosis

12 FAULT DIAGNOSIS

It is sometimes difficult to decide whether it is worthwhile removing and dismantling the gearbox for a fault which may be nothing more than a minor irritant. Gearboxes which howl, or where the synchromesh can be 'beaten' by a quick gear change, may continue to perform for a long time in this state. A worn gearbox usually needs a complete rebuild to eliminate noise because the various gears, if re-aligned on new bearings, will continue to howl when different wearing surfaces are presented to each other.

The decision to overhaul therefore, must be considered with regard to time and money available, relative to the degree of noise or malfunction that the driver has to suffer.

Symptom	Reason/s	Remedy
Ineffective synchromesh	Worn baulk rings or synchro hubs	Dismantle and renew.
Jumps out of one or more gears (on drive or over-run)	Weak detent springs or worn selector forks or worn gears or all three	Dismantle and renew.
Noisy, rough, whining and vibration	Worn bearings, (initially resulting in extended wear generally due to play and backlash	Dismantle and renew.
Noisy and difficult engagement of gear	Clutch fault	Examine clutch operation.

Chapter 7 Automatic transmission

Contents

Specifications

Gear ratios:

1st speed	2.65 : 1
2nd speed	1.59 : 1
3rd speed	1 : 1
Reverse	1.8 : 1

Final drive ratio - engine fitted with twin carburettors ... 3.67 : 1 (3.91 from August 1970)
- engine fitted with fuel injection ... 3.91 : 1

Torque convertor

Maximum torque multiplication	2.5
Stall speed (rpm)	1900 - 2100

Oil capacities:

		Litres	Imperial pints
Torque converter and gearbox (ATF)	- initial amount	6	10.5
	- refill (oil change)	3	5.25
Final drive (SAE 90)		1	1.75

Gear shift speeds mph (kph in brackets):

Gear change	Throttle shut	Full throttle	Kick down
1 – 2	10 – 13 (17 – 21)	18 – 20 (29 – 33)	34 – 41 (55 – 66)
2 – 3	15 – 18 (24 – 29)	47 – 52 (75 – 84)	57 – 62 (92 – 100)
3 – 2	14 – 10 (22 – 16)	38 – 32 (61 – 52)	58 – 53 (93 – 86)
2 – 1	9 – 5 (14 – 9)	14 – 12 (23 – 19)	37 – 30 (60 – 48)

Note: The downshift **can** occur below the la rger figure but it **must** occur below the smaller one.

Torque wrench setting:	**lb ft**	**mkg**
Torque converter to drive plate bolts	14	2.0

1 General description and operation

1 The unit consists of a torque converter and a three speed epicyclic gearbox, the torque converter taking the place of a conventional clutch. The system is fully automatic changing gear at the speeds shown in the specification.

2 The torque converter is a form of oil operated turbine, a multibladed motor (the pump) directly connected with the engine crankshaft directing oil into another multibladed motor (the turbine), which is connected to the input shaft of the gearbox.

At low engine revolutions the energy imparted to the oil is insufficient to turn the turbine but as the engine speeds up the pump generates more energy and the oil impinging on the blades of the turbine causes it to rotate thus driving the gearbox.

An intermediate multibladed rotor (the stator) directs and regulates the flow of oil back to the pump after it has passed through the turbine.

3 The gearbox consists of a planetary gear set in constant mesh and gear selection is made by applying a brake to hold the annulus gear stationary on one or more of the gear trains.

This braking is effected by one of the three servo operated multiplate clutches and a band brake which operates on the outer surface of the annulus gear.

4 The automatic operation of the three clutches and the low

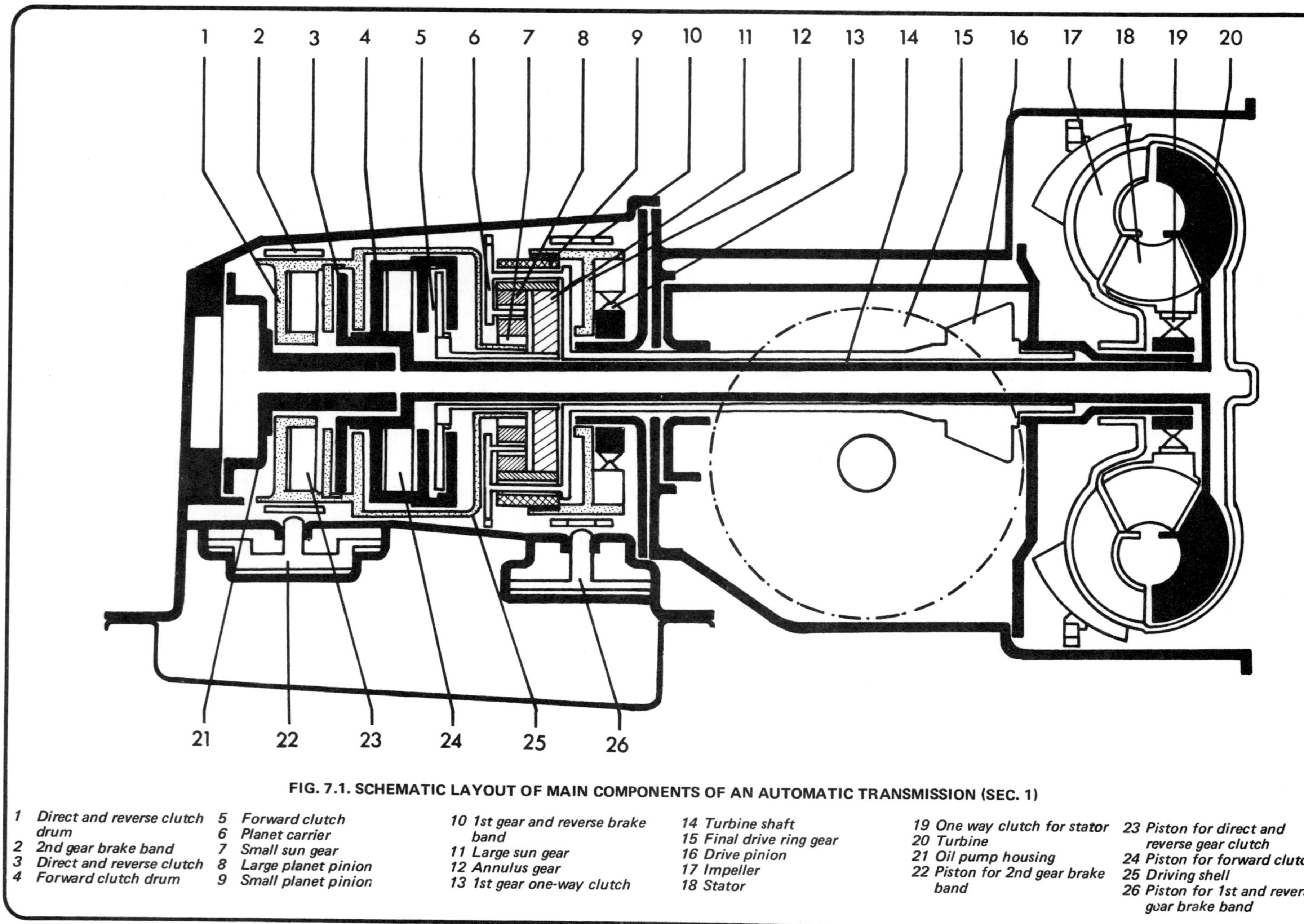

FIG. 7.1. SCHEMATIC LAYOUT OF MAIN COMPONENTS OF AN AUTOMATIC TRANSMISSION (SEC. 1)

1 Direct and reverse clutch drum
2 2nd gear brake band
3 Direct and reverse clutch
4 Forward clutch drum
5 Forward clutch
6 Planet carrier
7 Small sun gear
8 Large planet pinion
9 Small planet pinion
10 1st gear and reverse brake band
11 Large sun gear
12 Annulus gear
13 1st gear one-way clutch
14 Turbine shaft
15 Final drive ring gear
16 Drive pinion
17 Impeller
18 Stator
19 One way clutch for stator
20 Turbine
21 Oil pump housing
22 Piston for 2nd gear brake band
23 Piston for direct and reverse gear clutch
24 Piston for forward clutch
25 Driving shell
26 Piston for 1st and reverse gear brake band

speed band involves a servo/hydraulic pump system controlled by road speed, inlet manifold vacuum and the accelerator position. A cross section of the gearbox in diagrammatic form is given. (Fig.7.1).

2 Operation

The six positions of the selector are described below.

1 **'P' Park:** Engine running or stopped, no gears 'engaged' and the gearbox output shaft mechanically locked. This in turn locks the rear wheels and immobilises the car. To select 'P' the selector lever must be lifted. Do not select 'P' while the car is in motion, the resultant damage will be horribly expensive.

2 **'R' Reverse:** To go backwards lift the gear lever, while the car is stationary and move the lever to R. While the brakes are on the car will not move but when they are released and the engine accelerated the car will move in reverse. Lift the foot off the accelerator and the engine acts as a brake, but at low revolutions with the car brakes off the car may roll either way as the slope dictates. Again, do not engage reverse while the car is moving.

3 **N' Neutral:** Gearbox positions the same as 'P' parking except that the output shaft is not mechanically locked. This is the only position in which the engine can be started.

4 **'D' Drive:** The normal driving position. Engages low gear, as the engine accelerates the car moves and the gears change up at the stated speed, or down according to the throttle position. The engine acts as a brake in all three speeds.

5 **'2' Intermediate:** Used in traffic or hilly country to stop the gearbox selecting top. Will change the gear from top to second or even first when selected but should not be selected at speeds over 60 mph.

6 **'1' Low:** Used in heavy traffic, when climbing a long hill slowly or as a brake on steep downhill roads. Should not be selected when the speed is over 35 mph. Changes automatically up and down between 2nd and 1st gear.

7 There are six more points to be clear about.

a) It is not possible to push or tow start the car as the transmission oil pump works only when the engine is running.

b) If the car is towed the selector should be in 'N', and a limit of 30 miles of towing should not be exceeded as lubrication of the transmission is inadequate when the engine is not running and overheating and seizure may occur.

c) If there is a fault in the transmission the car must be towed with the driving wheels clear of the road; ie: a rear suspended tow.

d) If '2' or '1' are selected for overrun braking when on a slippery surface the gear will change and there may be a skid you did not expect. Do not change down at high speeds in these conditions.

e) The cooling fins and areas must be kept clean. The transmission fluid heats up and on long climbs can get very hot indeed.

f) There is a modification to be done to the converter if it is wished to tow a caravan; consult a VW agent before fitting a tow bar.

3 'Kickdown' position

1 When the accelerator pedal is pressed right down past the 'hard spot' to the kickdown position yet another control valve is brought into the system. Its effect is to move the gear shift points of first and second gears to correspond with maximum engine revolutions, thus 1st/2nd change moves to 34 mph (55 Kph) and 2/3rd to 59 mph (95 Kph).

2 So if you are in a hurry and stamp on the pedal when you are in top gear at 45 mph, the gearbox will change into second, the engine will move up to maximum revolutions, the car will accelerate up to 59 mph very quickly and then change back into top with the engine at maximum power with the speedometer needle climbing rapidly. Be careful where this is done for it can cause wheel spin and possibly skidding.

3 When the pedal is lifted back through the "hard spot" normal gear change points are resumed.

4 Maintenance and fluid level

1 Apart from keeping the cooling surfaces clean and seeing that nuts and bolts are tight, electrical connections correct and hydraulic joints in order there is no maintenance other than that of the correct fluid level in the transmission.

2 ATF (Automatic Transmission Fluid) is a special oil and although suitable grades are available from most mineral oil firms it is a wise thing to consult the VW agent as to the best one to use.

3 The torque convertor and the transmission are both operated and lubricated with the same ATF fluid.

4 The oil level should be checked every 6,000 miles (10,000 Km). To do this, warm up the transmission by running the engine with the selector lever at N and the handbrake applied, open up the engine compartment, and withdraw the transmission oil dipstick. This is at the forward edge of the engine compartment (photo). Wipe the dipstick and check the level. There are two marks and the level **MUST** be maintained between these marks. The capacity difference between the marks is only 0.7 pints (0.4 litres). Make sure the dipstick handle is vertical when

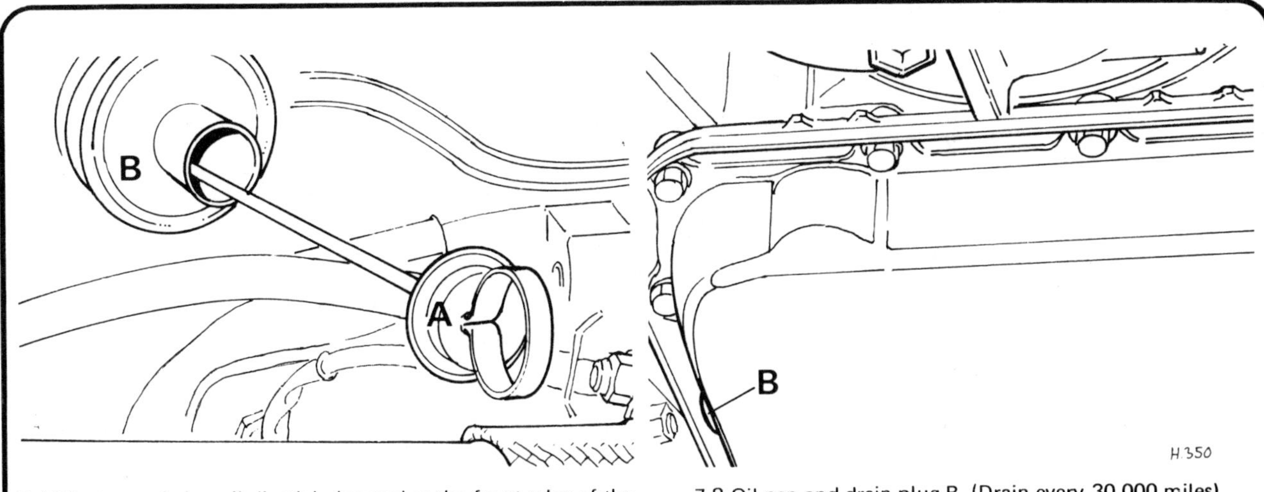

7.4 The transmission oil dipstick, located at the front edge of the engine compartment. Top up every 6000 miles. A is the dipstick, B the filler neck

7.8 Oil pan and drain plug B. (Drain every 30,000 miles) Remember to fit a new gasket.

checking and be careful not to overfill.
5 Use a plastic funnel with about 24" of plastic tubing and pour in a little at a time. If it is overfilled the excess must be drained off or trouble will ensue.
6 The level should be checked while the engine is idling.
7 The ATF should be changed every 30,000 miles (50,000 Km) under normal operating conditions. If the vehicle is used for towing, or other heavy load conditions the interval becomes 18,000 miles.
8 Take out the drain plug and allow the oil to run out. Remove the oil pan and the strainer and clean them thoroughly. Reinstall the oil pan and strainer using a new gasket. Tighten the screws to a torque of 7 lb ft (1 Mkg). Retighten after about 10 minutes to the same torque. (photo).
9 Fill with 5 to 7 pints (3 to 4 litres) of ATF and start the engine. Move the selector to each position in turn to allow the oil to circulate. Check the dipstick level with the selector at N. Top up if necessary until oil just shows on the tip of the dipstick. Drive the vehicle a short way to warm the transmission and then check the oil level and if necessary correct it.
10 Under no circumstances start the engine, or tow the vehicle, when there is no ATF in the transmission.

5 Tests and adjustments

1 To be very honest the skill required to test and adjust an automatic gearbox is beyond that of the very good mechanic who has not done the VW course, and the instruments required special tools and test gear are both complicated and not obtainable.

This means that if the automatic gearbox is not working properly then it **MUST** go to the VW agent for overhaul.

But this does not mean that it is not possible do a great deal to find out whether it is the box that is wrong or whether it is an external fault. That is what this section is about, if the gearbox is jerky or gets overheated carry out the tests given next.
2 Examine the casing for external damage, leaks, either ATF from the transmission or hypoid oil from the final drive. Look for loose nuts. Make sure the casing is secured properly to its mounting.
3 Check the oil level. If this is incorrect then correct it and maybe the trouble will disappear. Sample the ATF, if it is dirty replace it and retest. Again the trouble may go - but the dirt has come from somewhere. Sniff the oil sample, there may be a smell of burnt friction linings. If there is then the box must be overhauled.
4 The engine settings and performance should have been checked. If the power unit is not adjusted correctly the transmission will reflect its roughness.
5 Adjust the kickdown switch. To set it first depress the accelerator pedal as far as it will go and keep it there with a heavy weight. Now move the accelerator cable at the bell crank against the pressure of the spring until it touches the stop of the lever. The accelerator cable should be locked in this position. Switch on the ignition and connect one wire of a test lamp to the terminal on the switch which has the cable leading to the transmission. Then slowly allow the accelerator pedal to return until there is a gap of 0.020 - 0.040 ins between the accelerator cable lever and the stop on the end of the lever. At this point the switch should operate and the lamp will go out. Adjustment may be made by loosening the screws and moving the switch.

On 411/412 E models the accelerator cable spring can be disconnected and the lever moved without having to press the accelerator pedal. Adjustment is the same.
6 Check the adjustment of the selector cable lever (Section 7).
7 When all these points have been checked try another road test. Check the shift speeds against the specification.
8 The next test is a stall speed test. For this it is necessary to measure the engine speed accurately. With the engine warmed up, brakes hard on and the wheels chocked engage drive range 3 and press the accelerator to the floor. The engine speed should steady between 1900 and 2100 rpm. Allow only 10 seconds for this test or the ATF will overheat. If the engine rpm is too high then either the torque converter oil supply or the low band servo in the transmission are suspect. If the rpm are too low then the torque convertor unit is suspect. Either way the unit requires expert attention.
9 At this point the owner driver must accept that the box has a serious fault. The car should be taken to the VW agent for confirmation of the foregoing tests and for a pressure test. The VW test involves two gauges (one 0-350 psi and the other 0-140 psi) and a complicated routine to diagnose the nature of the problem.

6 Removal and replacement

1 If the expert diagnosis is that the gearbox must be dismantled then the owner driver can remove the gearbox and take it for exchange or overhaul, at the same time doing any necessary work on the clutch, engine, alteration, or other parts exposed when the engine/transmission is removed.
2 Full details of removal and replacement are given in Chapters 1 and 6.
3 The only other part of the automatic transmission within the capacity of the owner driver to overhaul is the gear shift.

7 Shift mechanism

1 See Fig . 7.2 The control consists of a bracket in which the selector lever and segment are mounted. On the left of the lever a pin projects into a slot in the bracket. Thus it is necessary to lift the lever to move to P or R. A contact plate with four contacts on the right of the bracket ensures that the engine can only be started in N. The two rear contacts are for the starter inhibitor switch and the front ones for the back up lights. (See Fig.7.3).

The Bowden cable runs through the tunnel emerging just in front of the rear axle. (See Fig.7.4).
2 To remove the shift mechanism first loosen the nut on the clamping pin or the transmission end. (See Fig.7.5).
3 Push back the bellows and undo the locknut. Ease the cable out of the bracket.
4 Remove the knob from the lever and take off the cover. Remove the floor mats, pull the cables of the contact plate, take the screws out of the bracket, lift the bracket up and disconnect the Bowden cable from the segment.
5 Press the seal and grommet out of the tunnel (underneath the car) and pull the cable out to the rear.
6 Installation is the reverse of removal. After attaching the cable to the transmission it is necessary to adjust the assembly.
7 The cable must be free from kinks, rust, or dirt and lightly greased.
8 Put the selector lever in Park.
9 Slide the cable into the clamp on the lever.
10 Press the lever on the transmission fully to the rear against the spring pressure. Hold the lever in this position and tighten the nut on the clamp. (See Fig.7.5).
11 Now chock the wheels and get into the driving seat. Start the engine with the selector in N and run it at a fast idle (1000 - 1200 rpm). Press on the footbrake and then move the lever to R.
12 There should be a drop in engine speed.
13 Move the lever to P. The speed should rise denoting reverse is disengaged. Pull the lever towards R against the stop. There should be no drop in speed.
14 Engage R once again then move to N. The engine speed should rise.
15 Move the lever to 3, there should be a drop in engine speed.
16 The lever should move to 1 without having to overcome any resistance.
17 Adjustment of the cable must be redone until these tests are satisfactory.
18 On later models the selector lever console is illuminated to facilitate gear changing in the dark. The illuminated console may be installed in earlier vehicles.

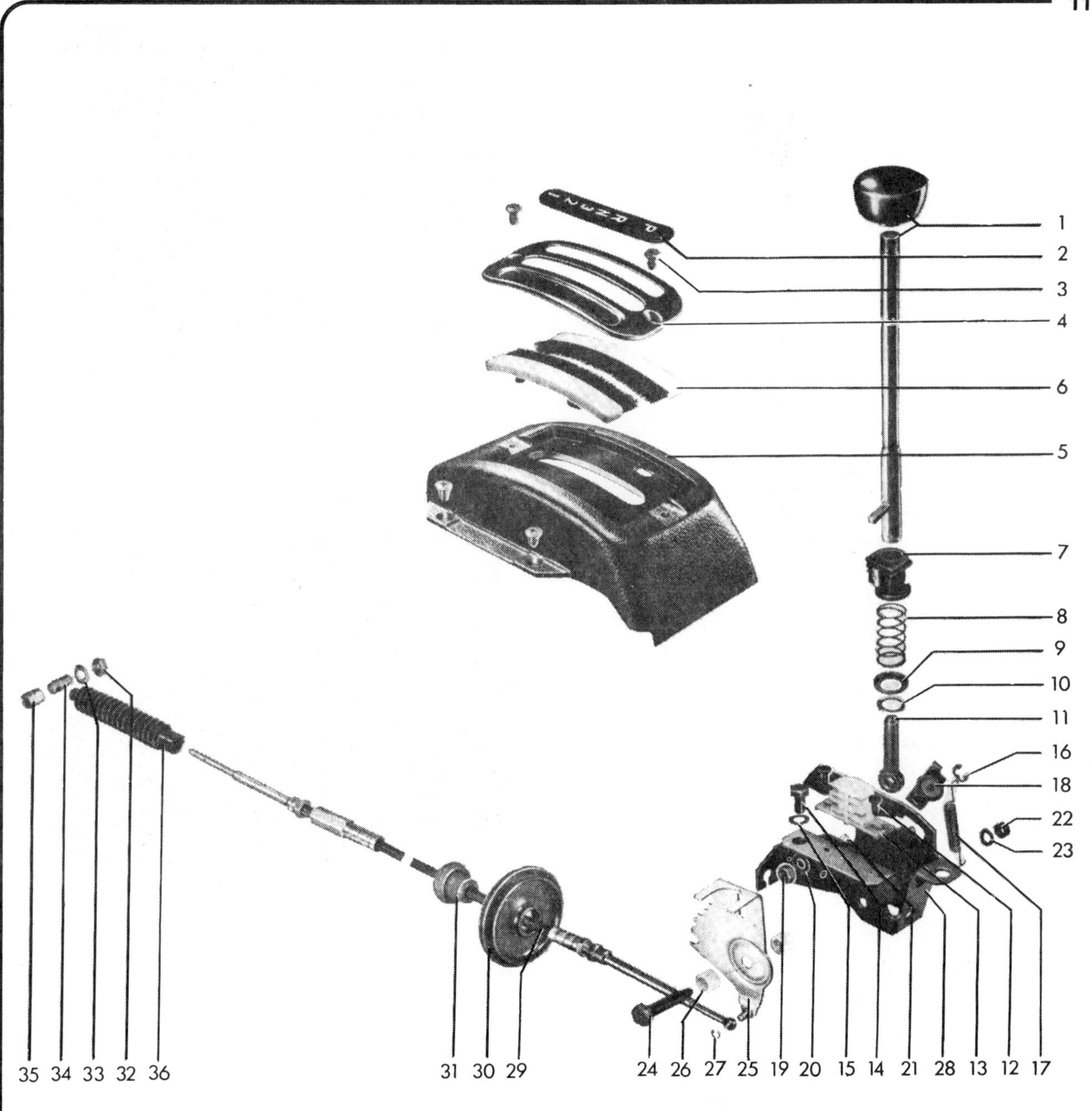

FIG. 7.2. SELECTOR LEVER ASSEMBLY – EXPLODED VIEW (SEC. 7)

1 Lever	*10 Circlip*	*19 Nut*	*28 Bracket*
2 Scale	*11 Pin*	*20 Spring ring*	*29 Cable*
3 Screw	*12 Screw*	*21 Pin*	*30 Tunnel seal*
4 Plate	*13 Contact plate*	*22 Nut*	*31 Grommet*
5 Cover	*14 Screw*	*23 Spring washer*	*32 Nut*
6 Brush	*15 Spring washer*	*24 Pin*	*33 Spring washer*
7 Contact	*16 Lock washer*	*25 Selector segment*	*34 Pin*
8 Spring	*17 Spring*	*26 Spacer*	*35 Sleeve*
9 Washer	*18 Stop lever*	*27 Circlip*	*36 Bellows*

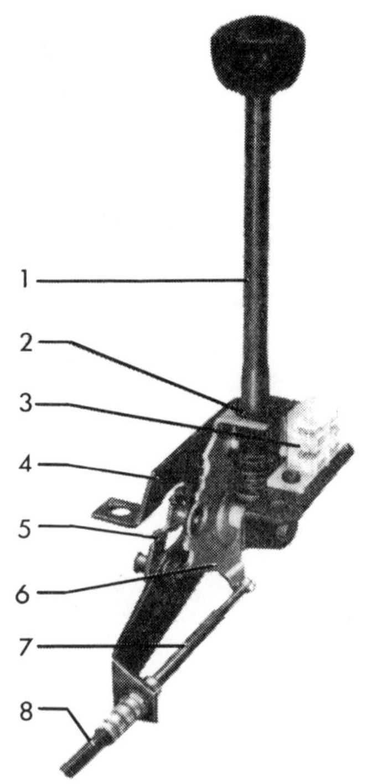

FIG. 7.3. GEAR SHIFT LEVER (SEC. 7)

1 Lever
2 Contact
3 Contact plate
4 Bracket
5 Stop lever
6 Selector segment
7 Cable
8 Cable sleeve

Fig. 7.4. Selector cable emerging from tunnel (Sec. 7)

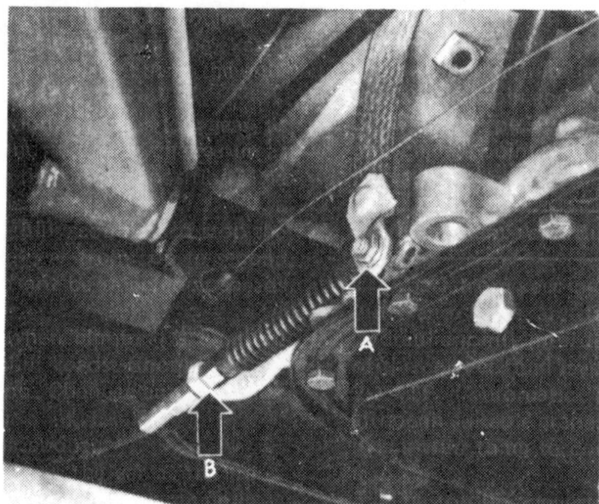

Fig. 7.5. Adjustment points on selector lever cable

A is the clamping pin
B is the lock nut

Chapter 8
Rear suspension - shock absorbers and drive shafts

Contents

Specifications

Rear suspension		
Type ...	Independant, trailing wishbones with coil springs and telescopic shock absorbers. Transverse stabilizer bar fitted from August 1969 to Sedans only	
Track ...	1342 mm 52.875 in	
Coil springs	Sedan	Variant
Effective coils ...	7	7.5
Mean coil diameter ...	135 mm	135 mm - 139 mm
Wire thickness ...	15.1 mm 0.59 in	16.6 mm 0.65 in
Rear wheel toe-in ...	5' ± 5' for each wheel	
Shock absorbers		
Sedan ...	Hydraulic with hydraulic bump stop	
Variant ...	Gas filled	
Torque wrench settings:	**lbs ft**	**mkg**
Shock absorber to body ...	14	2
Shock absorber to wishbone ...	42	6
Wishbone to bracket ...	60	8.5
Wheel bearing cover ...	43	6
Stabilizer to rear axle carrier ...	18	2.5
Stabilizer to wishbone ...	10	1.5

1 General description

1 The Type 4 finally breaks with VW tradition and goes away from the well known torsion bar system which has given such good service, to a straightforward trailing wishbone with a coil spring between the body and the wheel end of the wishbone. Fig 8.1 refers.

2 The wishbones are pivoted on th rear axle carrier in bonded rubber bushes in adjustable brackets. Thus the wishbone bears all the forces of drive and braking to the rear axle carrier.

Vertical movement is controlled by a combination of a coil spring mounted co-axially with the shock absorbers. It is terminated by a bump stop (photo) which is hollow. Fig.8.6 refers. A stabilizer bar is fitted to the Sedan from August 1969.

3 The wheel bearings are carried on the outer end of the wishbone. Castings are pressed into the wishbone and welded and the hub shaft is carried in this housing (Fig.8.4 refers). The rear wheel shaft is carried in two identical taper roller bearings and held in position splined to the inner flange by a clamp bolt (Fig.8.3 refers).

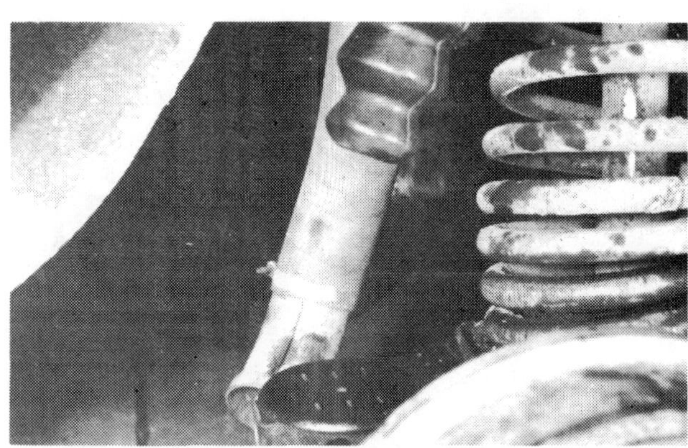

1.1. The hollow rubber bump stop and the rebound surface on the end of the wishbone. The vehicle is jacked up and the wheel is off. This photo was taken while the engine was out of the vehicle

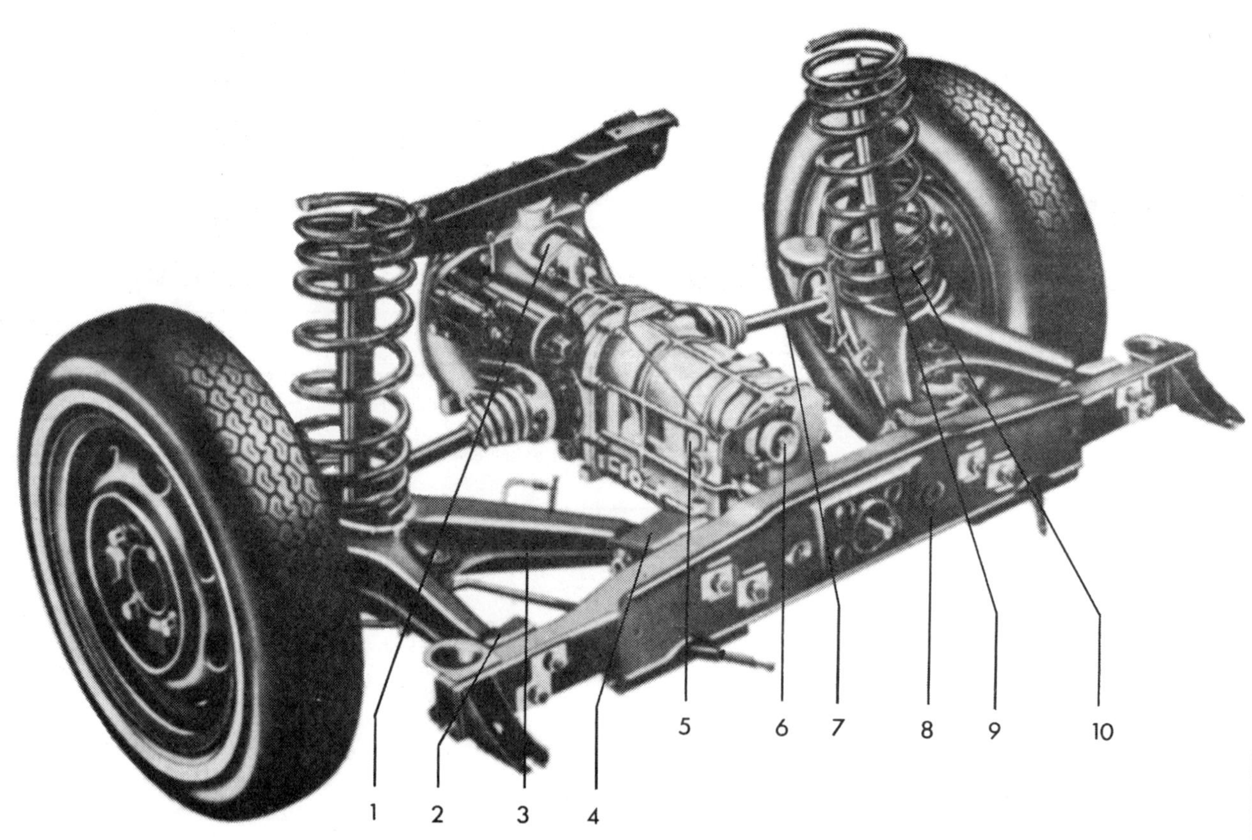

FIG. 8.1. REAR AXLE LAYOUT (SEC. 1)

1 *Clutch operating cylinder*
2 *Outer bracket*
3 *Wishbone*
4 *Inner bracket*
5 *Gearbox*
6 *Cover plate*
7 *Drive shaft*
8 *Rear axle carrier*
9 *Shock absorber*
10 *Coil spring*

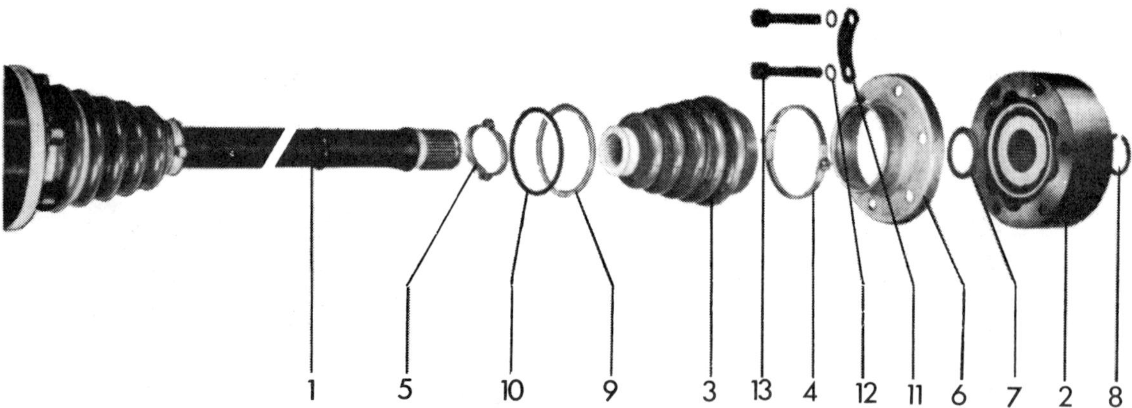

FIG. 8.2. DRIVE SHAFT AND CONSTANT VELOCITY JOINTS (SECS. 1 AND 2)

1 *Drive shaft*
2 *C.V. joint*
3 *Boot*
4 *Clip (clamp type)*
5 *Clip (pinch type)*
6 *Cap*
7 *Dished washer*
8 *Circlip*
9 *'O' ring (yellow)*
10 *'O' ring (black)*
11 *Plate*
12 *Lock washer*
13 *Socket head screw M8*

4 The drive is conveyed to the inner flange by a drive shaft carrying a constant velocity (C.V.) joint at either end. An exploded view is given in Fig.8.2.

5 Geometry, not steering geometry, but the essential adjustment to keep the rear wheels at the right geometrical plane to the road to give the best riding, braking and cornering angles, is a very important consideration in this suspension layout, which has provisions for adjustment.

2 Drive shafts and C.V. joints

1 Refer to Fig.8.2. To remove the drive shaft from the vehicle undo the socket head screws holding the C.V. joints to the flanges at either end. This is easier said than done. The screws are in very tightly (30 lb ft torque). If a special splined key has been obtained to undo the M.8 socket head screw all is well, but they seem to be difficult to obtain. However a straightforward allan key will do the job. Make sure it is a good fit and use plenty of easing oil (photo). Go gently, it is easy enough to grind a piece off the allan key, but if the serrations in the socket screw are damaged there is a long hard time ahead.

2 With all the screws removed, mark the C.V. joint and the flange so that they go back in the same relationship and take the drive shaft away. Although the screws are difficult it is better to take the shaft away form the vehicle if it is necessary to service the C.V joints.

3 Hang the shaft in a vice after easing the boot from the joint and prise out the end cap, (if one is fitted) (photo).

4 Remove the circlip (photo) and take the C.V. joint from the shaft (photo). Recover the concave washer from behind the joint. (photo).

5 It is possible to dismantle the joint but it is a futile exercise because spares are not forthcoming. VW replace the entire joint if it is faulty. Any harshness or lumpiness felt in the joint indicates damage or the presence of grit. In all cases where the boot has been damaged (photo) the joint must be flushed out and examined for malformation. If none is found repack with grease (photo). Replace the joint cap, the surface between the joint and the cap must be clean and free from grease.

It may be difficult to get 90 grams of grease into a C.V. joint, two thirds of it are packed in from the joint facing the boot and the remainder should be forced in from the front face of the joint. It will go into the boot so put this in after the boot has been reassembled.

6 Holding the shaft in a vice fit the inner clip (photo), next the boot (photo), the outer clip (photo) and the concave washer. Fit the C.V. joint onto the shaft and press it down.

7 Because of the spring of the concave washer the CV joint will not go far enough down for the circlip to be fitted. Put a new circlip over the shaft and using a suitable sized socket drive it down until it slips into the groove (photo). Now using the circlip pliers make sure it is seated in the groove.

8 Fasten the inner and outer hose clips (photo) making sure that the bolt holes in the joint cap and the joint line up and the

2.1. The socket head screws may be removed with an allen key if the correct tool is not obtainable. Care must be taken not to damage the sockets

2.3. Prise out the end cap

2.4a. Remove the circlip . . . . .

2.4b. . . . . ease the C.V. joint from the shaft.....

2.4c. . . . .and recover the concave washer from behind the joint

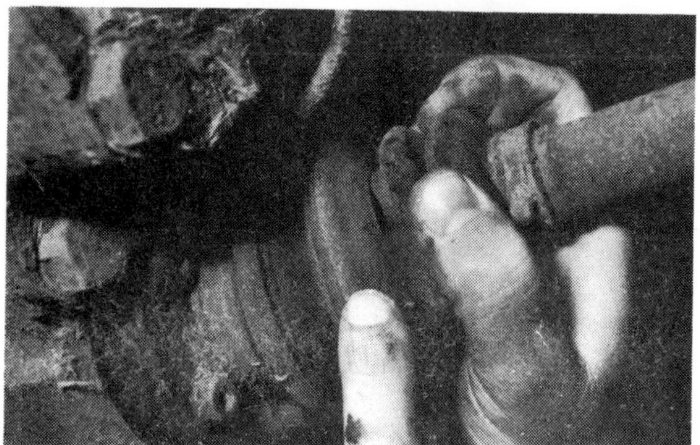

2.5a. If the boot has been damaged the joint must be flushed out. This boot has been split

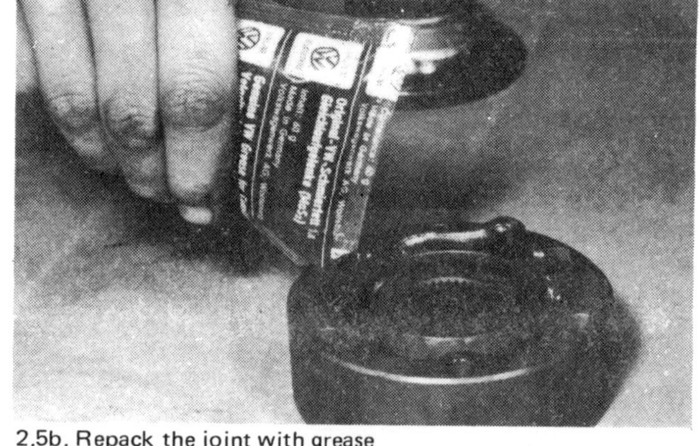

2.5b. Repack the joint with grease

2.6a. Fit the inner clip. . . . .

2.6b. . . . . the boot . . . . .

2.6c. . . . . the outer clip

2.7. Drive the circlip down until it fits into the groove

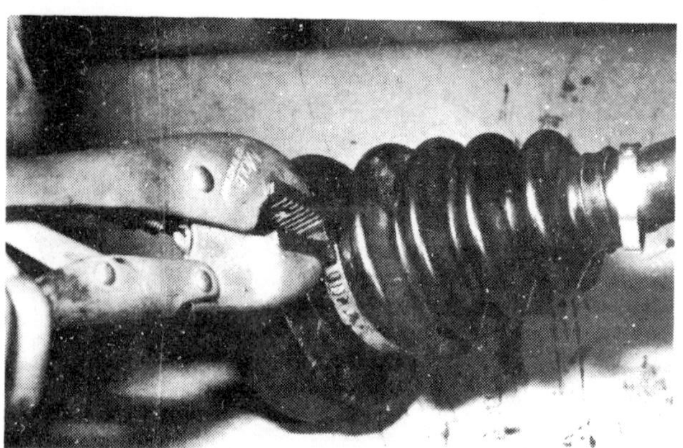

2.8a. Fasten the outer hose clip

2.8b. Tap the cap firmly onto the joint

hose clip fastening is between two bolt holes. Tap the cap firmly back onto the joint (photo) and make sure the boot fits snugly. Squeeze in any surplus grease from the front of the joint and replace the outer cap if applicable.
9 Refit the shaft to the vehicle. Do not forget the locking plates and spring washers. The socket head screws should be torqued to 30 lb ft. If it is not possible to use a torque wrench tighten them as hard as possible with the allan key and recheck after the vehicle has done 100 miles.

3 Rear wheel bearings and hubs

1 Refer to Fig.8.4. To remove the hub and rear wheel bearings first remove the wheel and the brake drum (Chapter 9) and unship the brake pipe from its clips on the wishbone.
2 Disconnect the drive shaft from the inner flange and tie it to one side (Section 2).
3 Remove the clamping bolt which screws into the flange nut on the inside and the wheel shaft may be pulled out. (Fig.8.3) Remove the bolts holding the bearing retainer on the wheel side of the hub and top off the bearing retainer and the backplate. It is not necessary to disconnect the brakes if you are careful. Drift the oil seal out of the retainer.
4 Remove the flange,the outer taper roller, and the spacer which separates the two bearings. It will be necessary to knock the outer race out with a drift.
5 Knock the inner race and the inner oil seal out together using a soft drift. Keep the races separate and identified.
6 Clean and examine the bushes, races and taper rollers. Examine the wheel shaft and nut for wear. Check the bearing retainer. Obtain new 'O' rings and oil seals.
7 To assemble the hub first install the outer race of the inner bearing, using a suitable drift and a plastic hammer. Then top the outer race of the outer bearing into the hub with a plastic hammer.
8 Grease the inner bearing with multi-purpose grease and install it in the outer race. Next fit the oil seal on the inner side. Tap it into place. Note dimension 'a' on Fig.8.3.
9 Pack approximately 30 grams (1.2 oz.) of grease into the housing. Lightly oil the spacer and insert it into the housing.
10 Press the outer oil seal into the bearing retainer. It is important that dimension (b) of Fig.8.3 is maintained. It can be checked by placing the retainer on a flat surface and measuring from the upper surface of the seal with a depth gauge or vernier.
NOTE: The measurements –

(a) = 8.2 ± 0.2 mm = 0.323" ± .008"
(b) = 24.5 ± 0.1 mm = 0.964" ± .004"

These measurements are set by VW by using special mandrels. Set your depth gauge as near as possible to the figure shown and move the seal to conform with the depth gauge, and don't worry too greatly. Make sure the lips of the seal are filled with grease before installation and oil the seals lightly to ease installation.
11 Fit the backplate and the bearing retainer with a new O ring. Tighten the bolts to 43 lbs ft. (6 mkg).
12 Fit the rear wheel shaft and flange, fit a new 'O' ring and lockplate on the clamping bolt and tighten it to 100 lb ft. (14 mkg).
13 The lockplate for the clamp bolt is in a groove under the washer and not under the bolt head. It may be found that the washer moves slightly but this does not matter as long as it does not turn and the bolt head is held between two flats.
14 The torque required to turn the shaft when assembled should not exceed 0.25 lb ft (30 cmkg). If it does, slacken the clamping nut a little (as far as 95 lb ft). If this does not have the required effect, then a new spacer or bearings are required.
15 Reassemble the drive shaft and the brake drum, secure the brake pipe to the wishbone and refit the rear wheel.

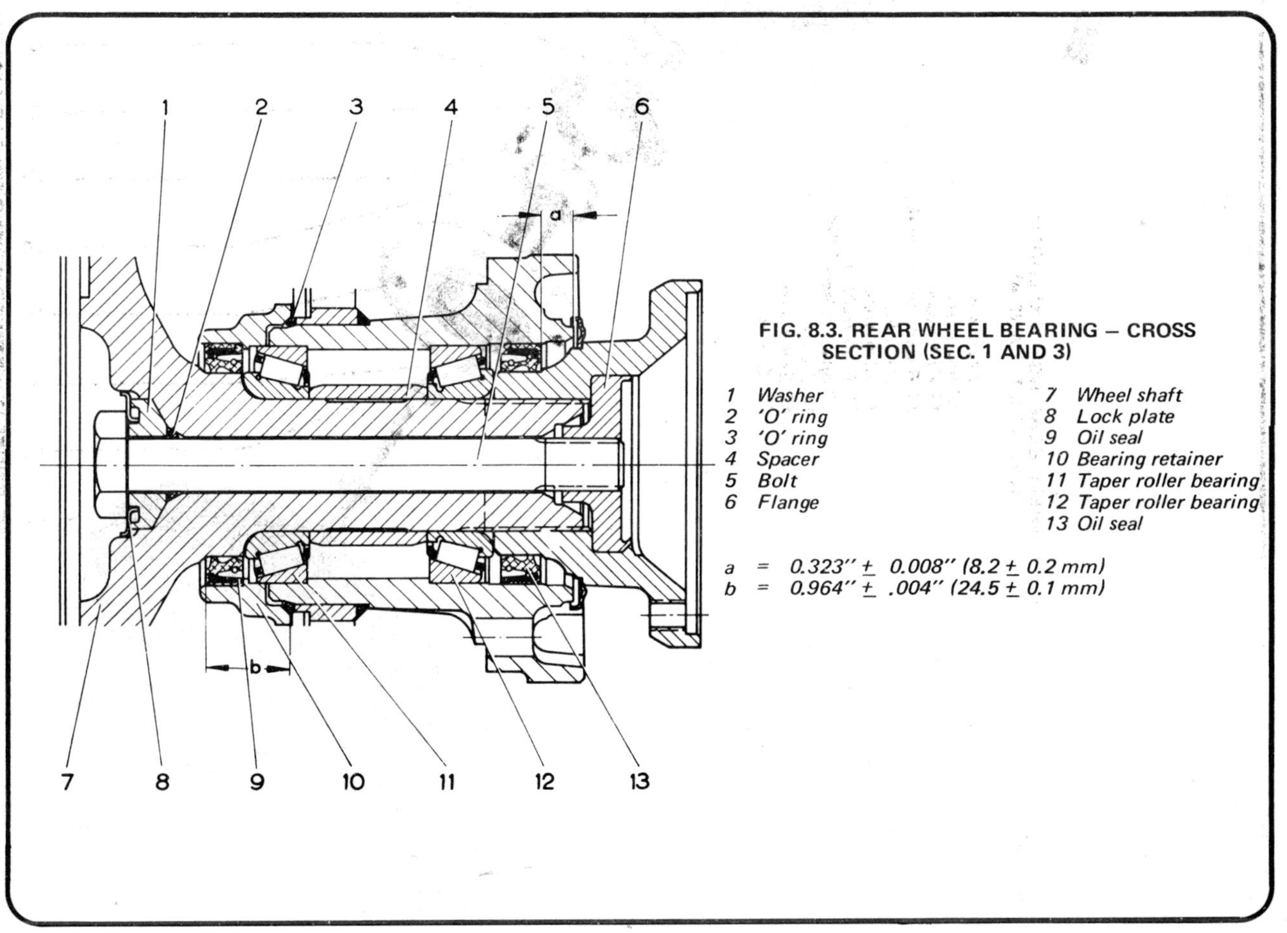

FIG. 8.3. REAR WHEEL BEARING – CROSS SECTION (SEC. 1 AND 3)

1 Washer
2 'O' ring
3 'O' ring
4 Spacer
5 Bolt
6 Flange
7 Wheel shaft
8 Lock plate
9 Oil seal
10 Bearing retainer
11 Taper roller bearing
12 Taper roller bearing
13 Oil seal

a = 0.323" ± 0.008" (8.2 ± 0.2 mm)
b = 0.964" ± .004" (24.5 ± 0.1 mm)

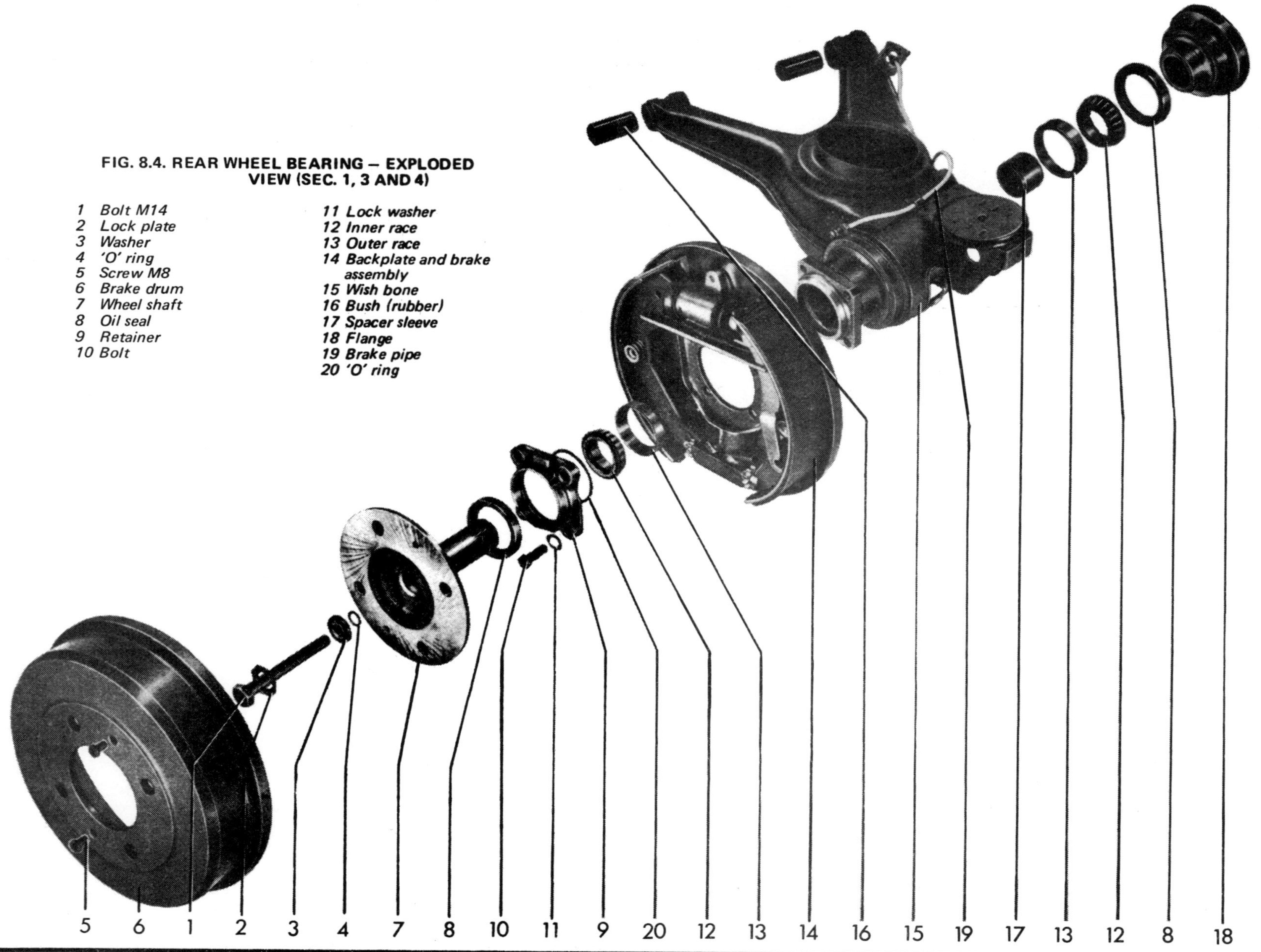

FIG. 8.4. REAR WHEEL BEARING – EXPLODED VIEW (SEC. 1, 3 AND 4)

1 *Bolt M14*
2 *Lock plate*
3 *Washer*
4 *'O' ring*
5 *Screw M8*
6 *Brake drum*
7 *Wheel shaft*
8 *Oil seal*
9 *Retainer*
10 *Bolt*
11 *Lock washer*
12 *Inner race*
13 *Outer race*
14 *Backplate and brake assembly*
15 *Wish bone*
16 *Bush (rubber)*
17 *Spacer sleeve*
18 *Flange*
19 *Brake pipe*
20 *'O' ring*

4 Wishbone and stabilizer bar - removal, replacement and overhaul

1 Refer to Fig.8.6. The wishbone is hinged on the rear axle carrier and can be removed without disturbing the carrier. The inner hinge bolt is an eccentric bolt. Before it is disturbed its exact position should be marked by centre punch dots on the head and the carrier arm so that the toe-in of the wheel will be approximately correct on reassembly.
2 Do not jack the vehicle up at this point. Disconnect the drive axle shaft from the wheel hub and cover it in a plastic bag. (Section 2). The wheels should be chocked to prevent the vehicle moving. Slacken the wheel nuts of the wheel on the wishbone to be removed.
3 Disconnect the brake pipe and the handbrake (Chapter 9).
4 Now with the weight of the vehicle still on the road wheel remove the bolt holding the shock absorber to the wishbone (photo). If the bolt is difficult to withdraw get someone to sit in the back of the car to compress the spring.

Now raise the body by jacking at the rear jacking point when the spring and shock absorber should come out of the wishbone.
5 If it is wished to remove the spring and shock absorber detach the floor covering from the rear luggage shelf and remove the plastic cover over the shock absorber (photo). Undo the self locking nut at the top of the shock absorber and withdraw the spring and shock absorber from below. The top of the piston rod can be held if necessary with an open mouth spanner to help undo the nut.
6 Check the arrangements for supporting the body and if possible replace the jack with a trestle or stand.
7 The wheel may now be removed, it will be easier if the nuts were slackened as suggested in paragraph 2.
8 Support the wishbone on blocks or with a trolley jack. Undo the nuts holding the pins in the bonded rubber bushes (remember to check the position of the inner one and mark it if not already done) and tap the pins away from the bushes. They may be stiff, use a soft drift or new pins will be necessary.

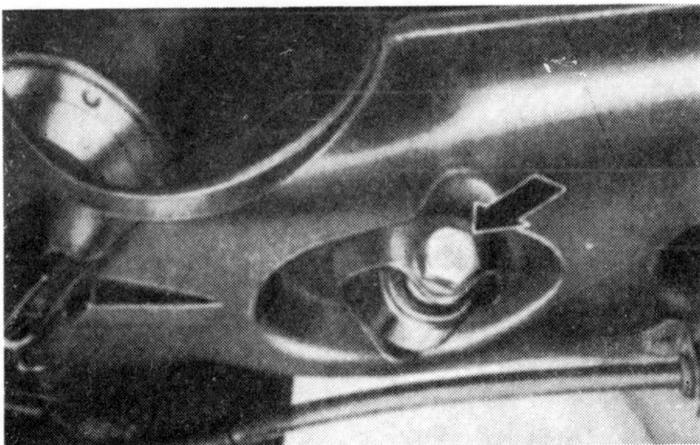

4.4. Remove the bolt holding the shock absorber to the wishbone. This must not be done when the vehicle is jacked up

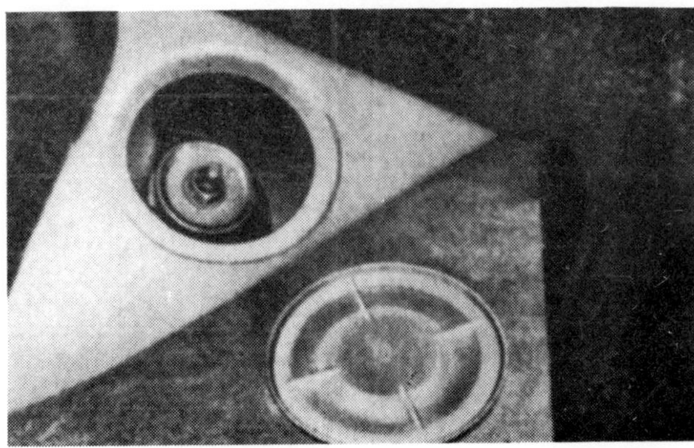

4.5. View of the aperture giving access to the top of the shock absorber

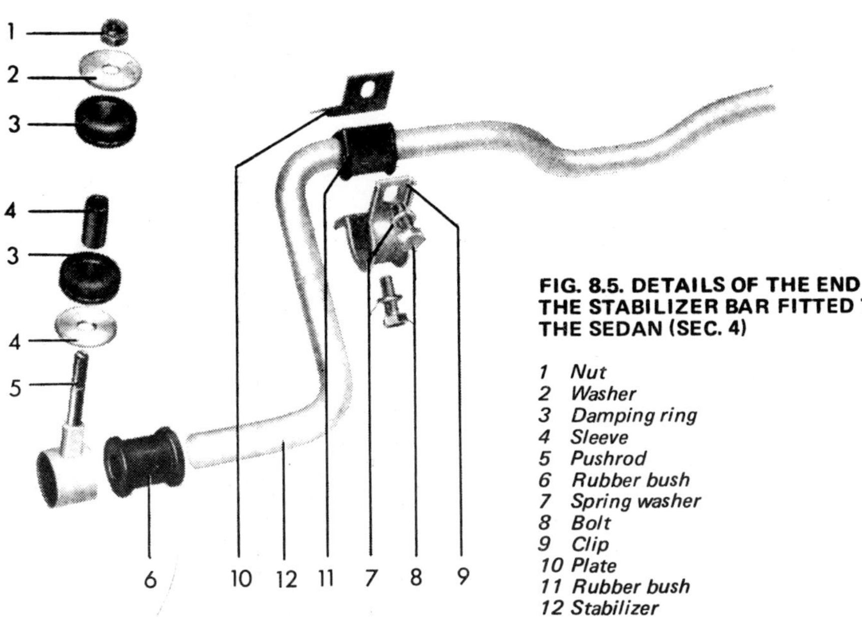

FIG. 8.5. DETAILS OF THE END OF THE STABILIZER BAR FITTED TO THE SEDAN (SEC. 4)

1 Nut
2 Washer
3 Damping ring
4 Sleeve
5 Pushrod
6 Rubber bush
7 Spring washer
8 Bolt
9 Clip
10 Plate
11 Rubber bush
12 Stabilizer

FIG. 8.6. REAR AXLE – WISHBONE – SPRING AND SHOCK ABSORBER (SECS. 1 AND 4)

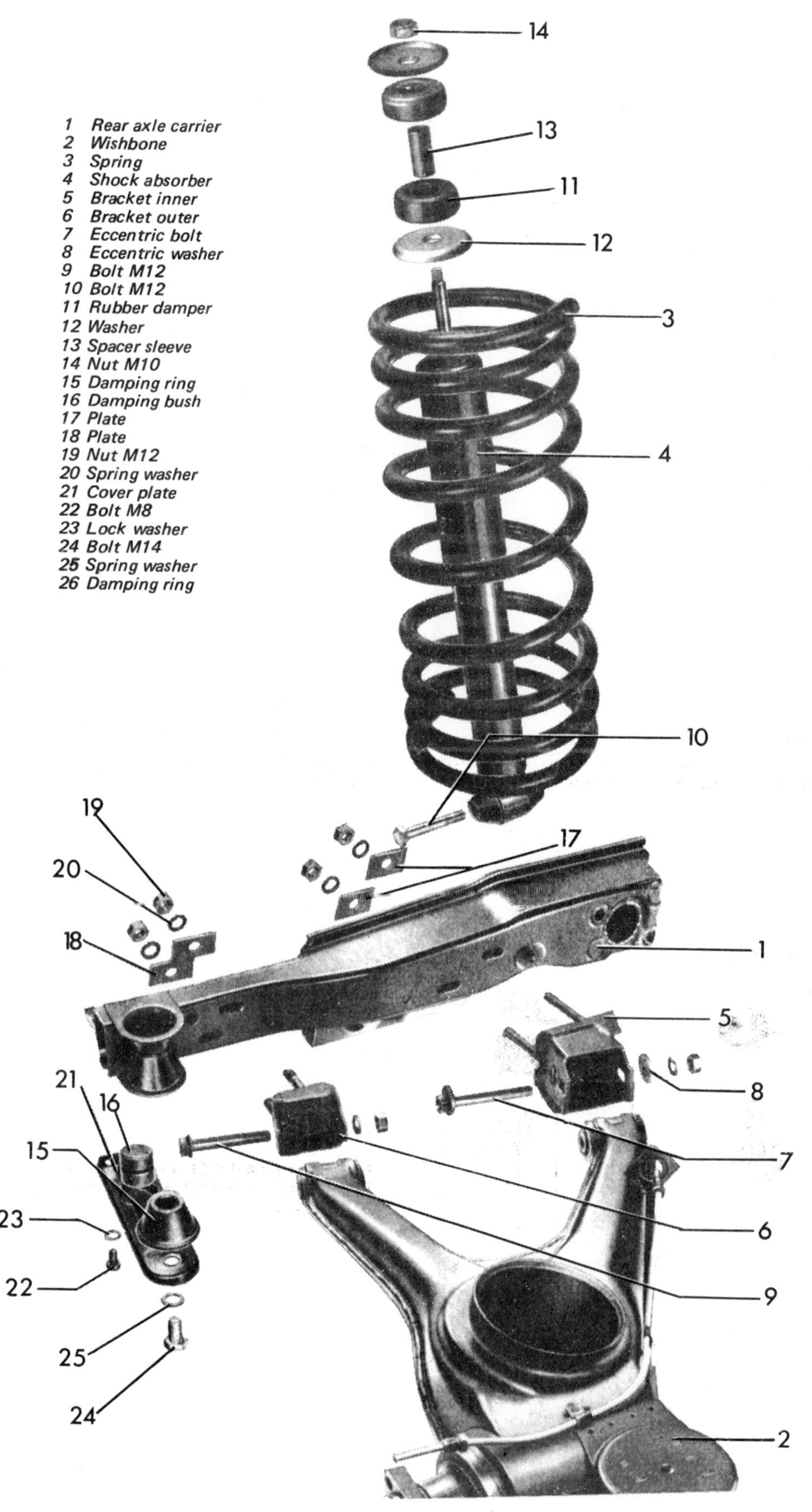

1 Rear axle carrier
2 Wishbone
3 Spring
4 Shock absorber
5 Bracket inner
6 Bracket outer
7 Eccentric bolt
8 Eccentric washer
9 Bolt M12
10 Bolt M12
11 Rubber damper
12 Washer
13 Spacer sleeve
14 Nut M10
15 Damping ring
16 Damping bush
17 Plate
18 Plate
19 Nut M12
20 Spring washer
21 Cover plate
22 Bolt M8
23 Lock washer
24 Bolt M14
25 Spring washer
26 Damping ring

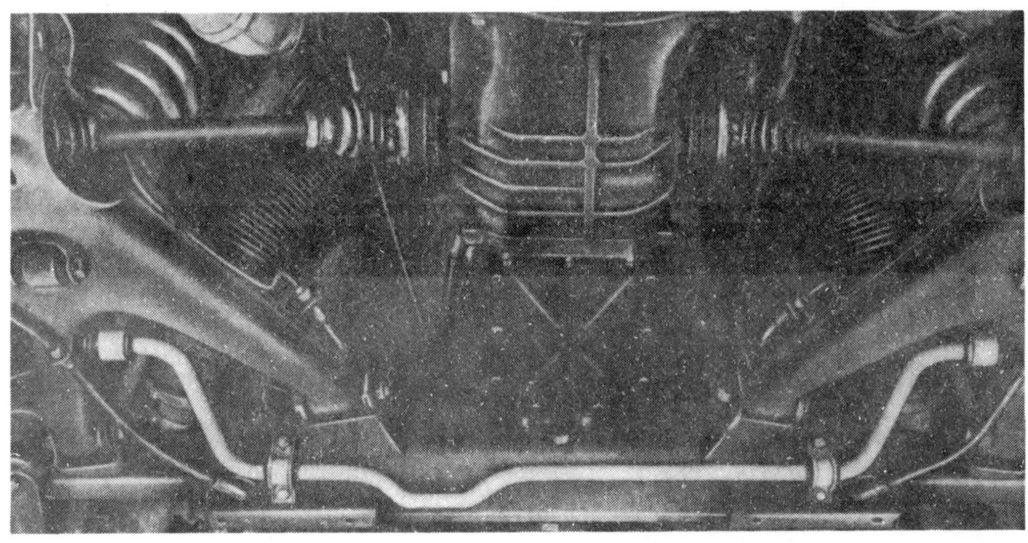

4.10. The stabilizer on the rear axle carrier of the Sedan. The early manual gearbox vehicles (August 1969) had straight bars. All stabilizer bars are cranked now as shown

9 The wishbone may now be removed from the vehicle complete with the wheel hub.

10 On the sedan there may be a stabilizer bar, clamped to the rear axle carrier and attached by tie rods to the wishbone. See Fig.8.5. This must be removed from **BOTH** wishbones and from the rear axle carrier or it will get in the way. It isn't a long job, (photo).

11 The only repairs possible on the wishbone are the renewal of the bushes which must be pressed out using suitable mandrels. The bushes are made of bonded rubber (Fig.8.4) and the installation of new ones may present problems. Unless proper tools are to hand it would be better to leave this to the VW agent who supplies the new bushes.

12 Distorted or cracked wishbones or stabilizer bars must be replaced with new ones.

13 Reassembly of the wishbone and coil spring/shock absorber is the reverse of removal. If the hub has been removed reassemble it before refitting the wishbones (Section3).

14 Refit the wishbone to the rear axle carrier. Make sure the eccentric bolt is replaced correctly. If a new one is fitted transfer the marking from the old bolt to the new one. Tighten the nuts to 60 lbs ft. (8.5 mkg).

15 Refit the wheel to the hub. Install the coil spring. Take care that the spring seats correctly in the wishbone and at the upper end in the body housing. Lower the vehicle so that the spring is in its housing. The spring has a plastic cover on the lower coils. To put this on a new spring requires patience and dexterity. It should be coated inside with vaseline and coaxed into position. Better by far ask for a new spring with the cover in place.

16 There are two types of spring, SYMMETRIC (old type) and ASYMMETRIC (new type). The important thing is that the new spring, if one is fitted, should be the same as the one on the other side of the vehicle.

17 The spring should be reasonably compressed by the weight of the vehicle. Now install the shock absorber in the centre of the spring. Tighten the shock absorber to body, using a new nut to 22 lb ft (3 mkg). The bottom connection may present a little problem. Make sure the bush is lined up before tightening the top nut finally. An assistant to use his weight to bear down a little on the vehicle may be necessary. Tighten the bottom bolt to 42 lb ft (6 mkg).

18 Refit the handbrake, connect the brake pipes, adjust the handbrake and bleed the brake hydraulic system (Chapter 9).

19 Refit the stabilizer bar. Use new locking nuts to the wishbone arms.

20 Add a little extra grease to the C.V. joint and reinstall it to the flange (Section 2).

5 Shock absorbers

1 To test the shock absorber away from the vehicle clamp the body in a vice and exercise the piston in a vertical plane. Resistance should be steady throughout the stroke both ways.

2 The shock absorber for the SEDAN is a hydraulic type incorporating a hydraulic lower stop. The one fitted to the VARIANT is gas filled.

3 Where there is reason to suspect a weak or faulty part the shock absorber should be taken to the agent for a replacement, which must be of the same specification.

6 Rear axle carrier

1 It is possible to remove the rear axle carrier from the body when the engine and gearbox are taken out. However, such a requirement can only be by accident damage or neglect to a severe degree. In this case the job is best left to the experts who have jigs and setting gauges, and who will ensure correct assembly.

Incorrect assembly will not only give incorrect road wheel geometry but will misalign the transmission.

For this reason the author considers the task beyond the ability of skilled mechanics who do not have access to VW instructions and gauges.

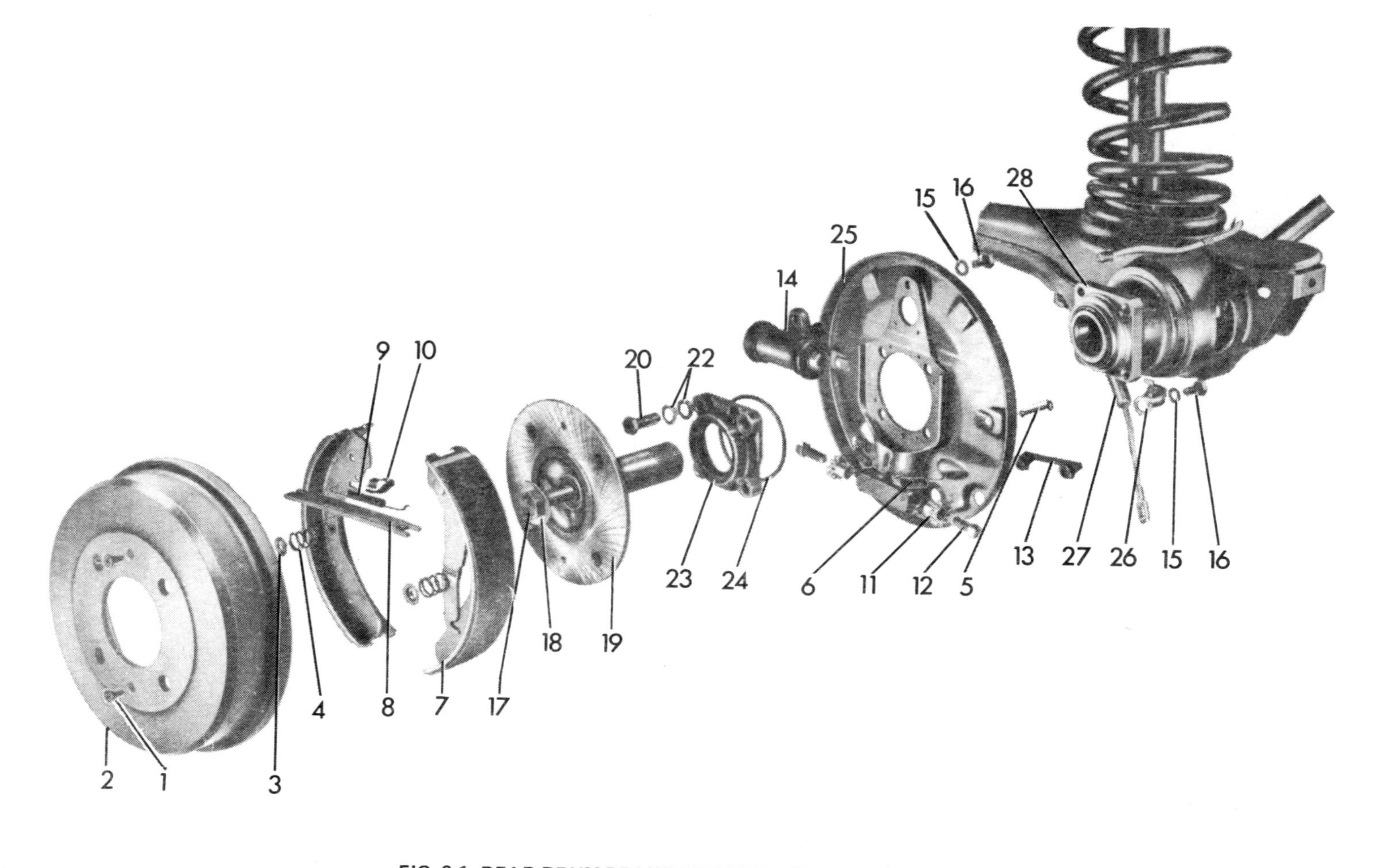

FIG. 9.1. REAR DRUM BRAKE AND HUB ASSEMBLY (SECS. 2 AND 4)

1 Philips screw
2 Brake drum
3 Spring plate
4 Spring
5 Pin
6 Return spring
7 Brake shoe
8 Connecting link
9 Return spring
10 Clip
11 Adjusting nut
12 Adjusting screw
13 Sealing plugs
14 Wheel cylinder
15 Lock washer
16 Bolt
17 Bolt
18 Lock plate
19 Wheel shaft
20 Bolt
21 Spring washer
22 Washer
23 Bearing cover
24 'O' ring
25 Back plate
26 Brake cable bracket
27 Brake cable
28 Wheel bearing housing

Note: From August 1970 (chassis 411 2 000 001) the brake drum is replaced with a steel back drum, the Philips screw by a socket head screw and a modified wheel shaft is used.

Chapter 9 Braking system

Contents

Specifications

Type ... ... Front disc brakes, fixed calipers
Rear drum brakes, later types self adjusting
Hydraulic operation, dual circuit, tandem master cylinder with optional servo assistance. Brake face limiting valve in rear circuit.

	ins	mm
Front brakes		
Discs - diameter ...	11.06	281
- thickness ...	0.433	11
- run out limit ...	0.0008	0.02
Calipers:		
Piston diameter ...	1.654	42
Friction pad thickness (to August 1972) ...	0.394	10
(from August 1972) ...	0.551	14
Minimum pad thickness ...	0.079	2
Total friction area (4 pads) ...	15.5 ins^2	100 cm^2
Master cylinder (tandem):		
Bore ...	0.748	19.05
Stroke (front circuit) ...	0.59	15
(rear circuit) ...	0.59	15
Master cylinder tandem with servo:		
Servo factor ...	2.15	
Cylinder diameter ...	0.805	20.64
Stroke (front circuit) ...	0.551	14
(rear circuit) ...	0.63	16
Wheel cylinders (rear) bore ...	0.89	22.2
Drums (rear)		
Diameter ...	9.7	248.1
Shoe lining thickness ...	0.1575	4.0
Shoe lining width ...	1.772	45
Shoe lining surface area (total) ...	69.8 in^2	450 cm^2
Brake pressure regulator:		
Piston diameter ...		18
Regulating commences at ...	525 lbs/sq in	37 kg cm
Hydraulic fluid capacity of system including clutch:		
Manual ...	400 cc	
Automatic ...	380 cc	

Torque wrench settings:

	lbs ft	mkg
Master cylinder mounting bolts	33	4.5
Master cylinder to servo	9.4	1.3
Caliper to steering knuckle (M12)	60	8
Hose and pipe unions	11 - 15	1.5 - 2
Bleed valves	3.6	0.5
Rear wheel cylinder to backplate	14 - 22	2 - 3
Pressure regulator securing nuts	14	2
Pressure regulator body plug	80	11
Regulator adjusting screw nut	18 - 25	2.5 - 3.5

1 General description

The braking system on the Type 4 is conventional. Hydraulically operated discs on the front and drum brakes on the rear.

The dual circuit, with a tandem master cylinder, has a warning light on the dash board (an optional extra). Should either circuit fail the car still has brakes on one axle.

The handbrake operates a mechanical linkage to the rear wheel brakes.

A balancing valve is fitted in the rear wheel hydraulic circuit to prevent the wheels locking when braking fiercely. (photo).

The heater tank, which also provides for the clutch cylinder is in the luggage compartment. (photo).

A servo assistance is provided, again as an optional extra, and is located in the front luggage compartment (photo).

A welcome innovation is the installation of the master cylinder inside the car on the side of the pedal cluster bracket, thus removing this important piece of machinery from the mud and obscurity of its conventional mounting and dispensing with a long mechanical linkage. (photo).

In August 1972 larger calipers have been installed to the front discs, with 14 mm thick friction pads (as opposed to 10mm) longer caliper pistons, with modified brake discs, steering knuckles and splash shields.

2 Brake adjustment - rear wheels

1 The rear brakes may be adjusted without taking off the wheels. Jack up the rear axle on both sides. Chock the front wheels .

2 Back off the adjustment on the handbrake (Section 3).

3 In the backplate there are four holes covered by rubber plugs. The holes are in pairs and give access to the adjusting nut (photo) and the lining (photo).

The state and thickness of the lining may thus be seen without taking off the drum.

4 Adjustment can be carried out by moving the adjusting nut round with a screwdriver used as a lever.

The adjusting nut should be turned until a slight drag is felt when the wheel is turned, and then it should be backed off by four teeth to allow the wheel to turn freely.

5 The other shoe is adjusted in the same way but note the adjusting nut is effective in the opposite direction.

6 When the shoes on one wheel have been adjusted apply the foot brake sharply and recheck. This action will make sure the shoes are centralized.

7 Repeat the operation for the other wheel.

3 Brake adjustment - handbrake

1 Jack up the rear wheel having chocked the front wheel.

2 Adjust the rear brakes as described in Section 2.

3 Tension the handbrake cables so that the road wheels can just be turned by hand at this setting. The adjusting nuts are shown in Fig.9.2. It is necessary to pull back the rubber shroud in order to get at them.

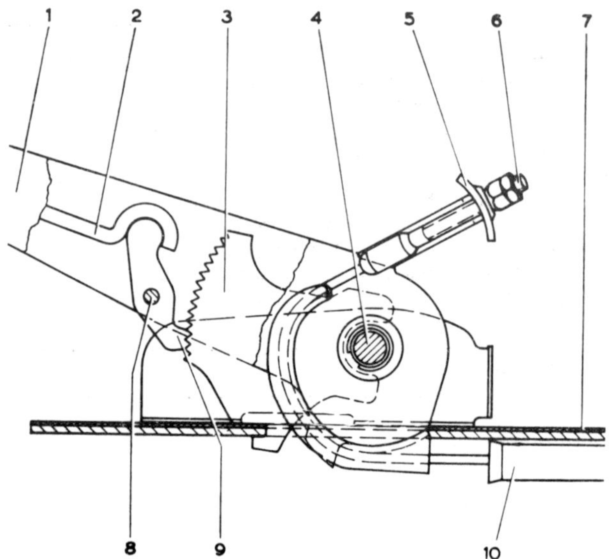

FIG. 9.2. HANDBRAKE CROSS SECTION (SEC. 3)

1 Lever
2 Pawl rod
3 Ratchet segment
4 Lever pivot pin
5 Cable compensator
6 Adjusting nuts on cable
7 Floor pan
8 Pawl pin
9 Pawl
10 Cable guide tube

Slacken off the locknut on the threaded end of each cable, and then holding the cable with a screwdriver in the slotted end tighten the adjusting nut the required amount. Retighten the locknut and replace the sleeve. The drag on each wheel should be equal.

4 Rear brake - dismantling, overhaul and reassembly

1 Refer to Fig.9.1. Jack up the car and remove the road wheel. Slacken the nuts before lifting the wheel from the ground.

2 Prior to August 1970 the drum was secured to the hub by Philips screws. These were replaced by socket head screws. (photo). Remove the screws and draw the drum away from the lining. It may be necessary to slacken off the adjusters to free the drum from the hub.

3 The inside surface of the drum on which the lining bears should be smooth, bright and free from oil or grease. If it is scored or deeply grooved, it should be skimmed on a lathe or ground out on a grinding machine. Ovality should be treated in a similar manner, but before doing this consult the VW agent. Brake shoes for reconditioned drums must be fitted with special oversize linings, and to be strictly correct the drum on the other side should be machined as well, although that may be too pedantic. It could be better to acquire a serviceable brake drum and stick to standard size linings.

4 With the drum removed the linings and wheel cylinder can be serviced (photo). To remove the shoes turn the spring plate on

1.a. The warning light on the dashboard shines only when one system has failed

1.b. The balancing valve which prevents the rear wheels from locking when braking fiercely

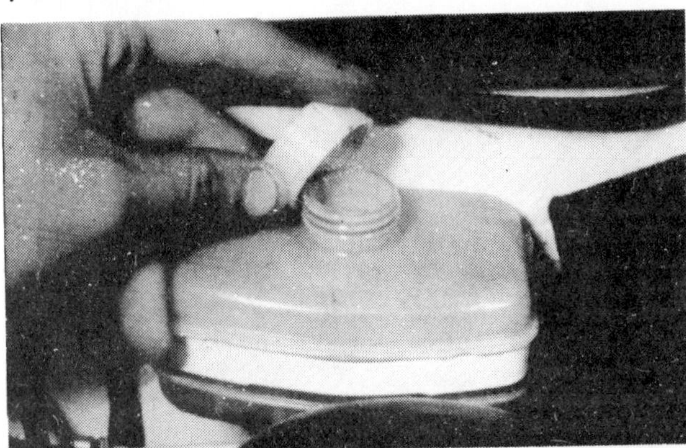

1.c. The header tank in the luggage compartment also services the hydraulic clutch master cylinder

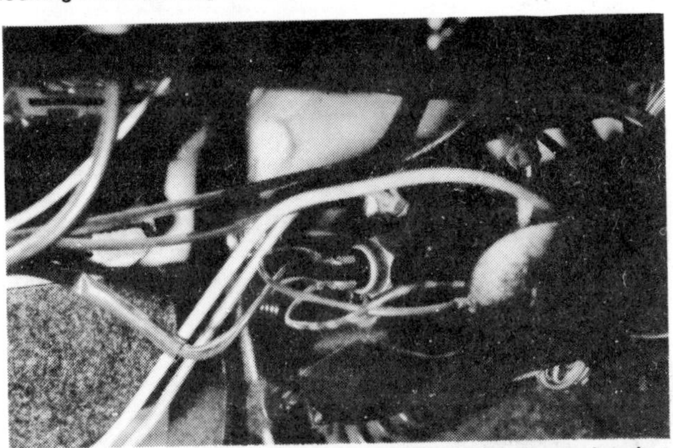

1.d. The master cylinder mounted on the pedal cluster bracket inside the car away from mud and water

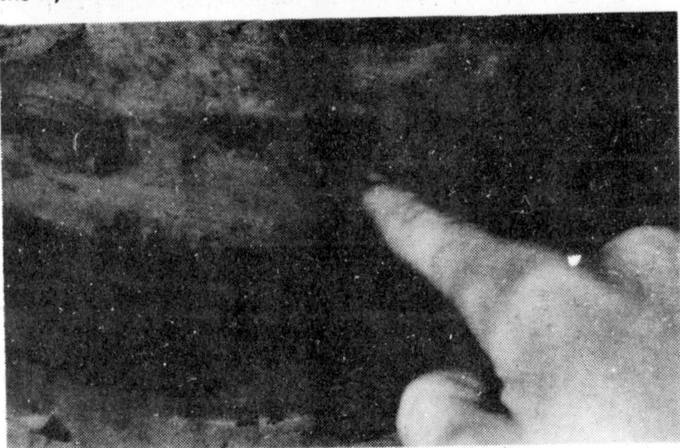

2.3a. The hole giving access to the adjusting nut, note the second pair of holes are still covered with the rubber plugs

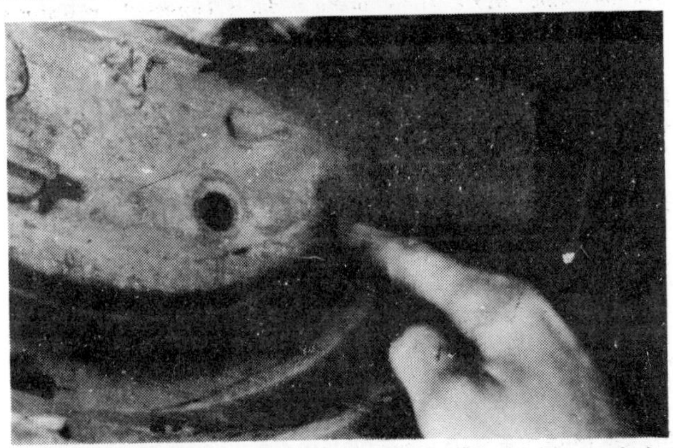

2.3b. The inspection hole through which the thickness of the lining can be seen

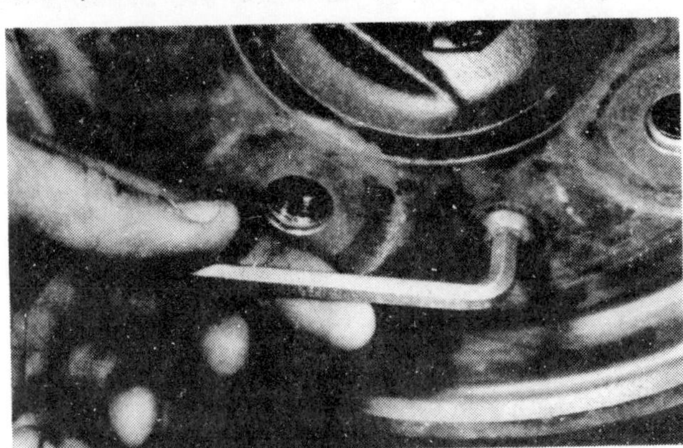

4.2. Remove the two socket head screws

4.4. Rear brake, drum removed

the steady pin through 90° and remove the spring and plate. Remove the return spring and the handbrake cable and the shoes may be withdrawn.

5 Brake linings must be smooth and free from grease or signs of overheating. There should be at least 0.020 in. of lining above the rivet heads (0.4 mm). If the lining does not come up to this specification it must be renewed. Linings must be renewed in sets and both sets on one axle are mandatory. It will probably be better to do all four wheels at the same time.

6 A great deal is said about the way to bed in linings and most of it is nonsense. Relined shoes should be obtained from the VW agent. These will have been riveted properly and the outside face correctly set. They must be handled with clean hands. Put the shoes back in the housing, assemble the rest of the brake and leave it alone. If it is correctly adjusted it will bed itself down. It is good practice to recheck the adjustment after 1000 miles from the time of replacement.

7 When reassembling the shoes, make sure the one with the lever is on the correct side and that the angled end of the shoe fits correctly in the adjusting screw.

8 The adjusting screw and nut should be cleaned and greased lightly with 'white' grease. It is not generally realised that temperatures in the region of 500°C are reached in the braking mechanism on long down-hill descents, and at this temperature ordinary grease runs like oil. A lithium based grease is ideal.

9 The only other item to require attention is the wheel cylinder which is discussed in the next Section.

10 Reassembly is the reverse of dismantling. Put the lever back on the brake shoe, first the pin then the spring washer followed by the lever, shoe and clip. Assemble the shoes to the backplate, fit the return spring and the handbrake cable, check all round for correct operation and assemble the drum and wheel.

11 One final word of warning; If the shoes are removed from the wheel cylinder, tie the wheel cylinder in such a way that the pistons cannot move. If the brake pedal is depressed the pistons will come out and a lot of extra work will be required.

5 Hydraulic wheel cylinders (drum brakes) - renewal of seals and cylinders

1 If the wheel cylinders show signs of leakage, or of pistons being seized up then it will be necessary to dismantle them and fit new seals. Refer to Fig.9.3.

2 Remove the brake drum and the brake shoes and seal the cap of the fluid reservoir with a piece of plastic film to minimise loss of fluid from the system when the cylinder is dismantled.

3 Pull off the rubber boots from the ends of the cylinder, bringing the pistons and slotted ends with them. Behind the pistons are the seal cups and in the centre there is a spring with two 'cup expanders' which fit inside each seal and as their name implies force the seals outwards into the cylinder bore under the pressure of the spring.

4 With the cylinder clear examine the bore surfaces for signs of ridging or scoring. Any residue stuck in the bore should be cleaned out with brake fluid or meths - if very stubborn a gentle rub with some No.400 wet and dry paper will clean it up. Any noticeable scores or ridges indicate that a new cylinder should be fitted. No attempt should be made to smooth them out as this will be unsuccessful.

5 To remove the cylinder undo the brake pipe union from behind the backplate. Cover the end of the pipe with the dust cap from the bleed nipple pro tem. Undo the securing screws from the backplate and the cylinder may be lifted out. If a new cylinder is fitted the diameter of the bore must be exactly the same as the diameter of the one being replaced, otherwise the balance of the brakes will be upset.

6 With the cylinder perfectly clean lubricate the bore with brake fluid and insert the spring complete with seal cup expanders at each end.

7 Lubricate the new seals with fluid and put one in at each end of the cylinder with the lips facing inwards. Take great care not to turn the lip back whilst doing this.

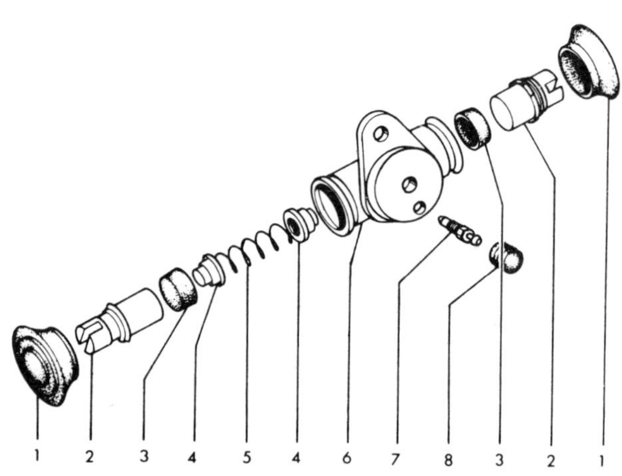

FIG. 9.3. REAR WHEEL BRAKE CYLINDER – COMPONENTS (SEC. 5)

1 Boot
2 Piston
3 Cup
4 Cup expander
5 Spring
6 Housing
7 Bleeder valve
8 Dust cap

8 Put a piston into the bore of the cylinder behind each seal and then fit the rubber boot over the cylinder and piston so that it engages in the grooves.

9 Absolute cleanliness of hands and parts is essential during reassembly.

10 If a new wheel cylinder is being fitted reconnect the brake pipe union taking care not to cross the thread, kink the pipe or overtighten the union.

11 Installation is the reverse of removal.

12 It is necessary to bleed the brake on completion of the job.

6 Self adjusting drum brakes

1 On certain export models the rear drum brakes are self adjusting, the adjustment being carried out as the footbrake is operated.

2 Refer to Fig.9.4. An adjusting lever is mounted on the secondary brake shoe, so that as the lining wears the adjusting lever return spring pulls on the adjusing lever and moves the adjusting wheel on the connection link when the brakes are operated. The length of the connection link is thereby increased and the brake shoes are automatically adjusted.

3 To adjust the footbrake when installing new linings screw the connecting link into the sleeve as far as it will go.

4 To adjust the handbrake first adjust the footbrake as in paragraph 3. Set the handbrake lever in the off position and tension the cables until the brake lever in the rear brake just starts to move off the stop on the secondary shoe. Watch the brake lever for movement through the inspection hole in the back plate. This job needs two people. It should only be necessary when installing new lines or cables. When the brake is satisfactorily adjusted lock the cable with the lock nut.

5 It may be that the drums will not come off easily. If so slacken off the handbrake. Then push back the brake lever past the stop on the brake shoe. This can be done with a screwdriver through the inspection hole and allows the shoes to move closer together, facilitating the removal of the drum.

6 The handbrake lever has a different curved section when

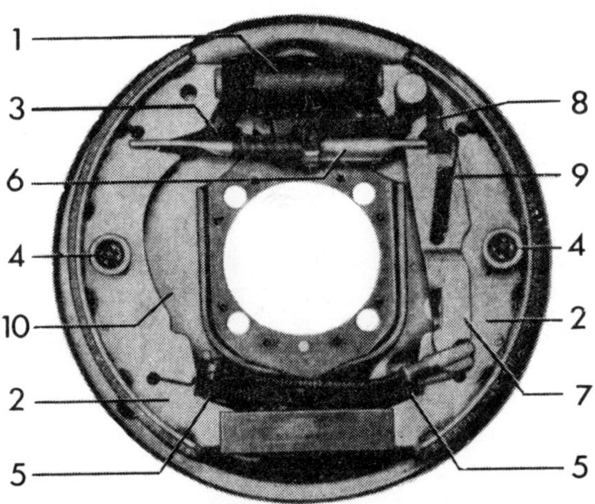

FIG. 9.4. SELF ADJUSTING DRUM BRAKES (SEC. 6)

1 *Wheel cylinder*
2 *Brake shoe*
3 *Upper return spring*
4 *Spring with cup and pin with wheel and sleeve*
5 *Lower return spring*
6 *Adjustable connecting link with wheel and sleeve*
7 *Brake lever*
8 *Adjusting lever*
9 *Return spring for adjusting lever*
10 *Back plate*

compared with those fitted to non adjusting rear brake systems.

In addition the bearing cover is modified to ensure sufficient clearance for the adjusting wheel. If new bearing covers are not available and for some reason an old type one must be fitted it will work well enough provided it is installed 90° from its normal position.

7 Front disc brakes - method of operation

1 Refer to Fig.9.5. The disc which is part of the hub runs between friction plates contained in a caliper which is bolted to the steering knuckle. The inner surface of the disc is protected by a circular splash plate similar to the rear wheel brake back-plate. The outer surface is protected by the road wheel.

2 The caliper contains pistons operated hydraulically from the master cylinder which bear on the friction plates and force them against the disc when the brake pedal is depressed. The caliper is so arranged that the friction pads are opposite one another on each side of the disc, thus when the brake is operated the disc is pinched by the caliper equally on either side and the resultant side thrust is nil. Running clearance between the friction pads and the disc is very small (0.002 - 0.008 ins) (0.05 - 0.2mm).

3 As the pistons are forced forward by hydraulic pressure they distort rubber seals, and when the pressure is released the action of the seal withdraws the piston. The friction pads which are pressed against the pistons by spreader springs move away from the disc and allow it to rotate freely again.

4 Adjustment is not necessary as when the friction pads wear so that the piston moves further than the lateral deflection of the rubber seal the piston slides through the seal and is retracted on release of the brake pedal by the seal gripping it in a new

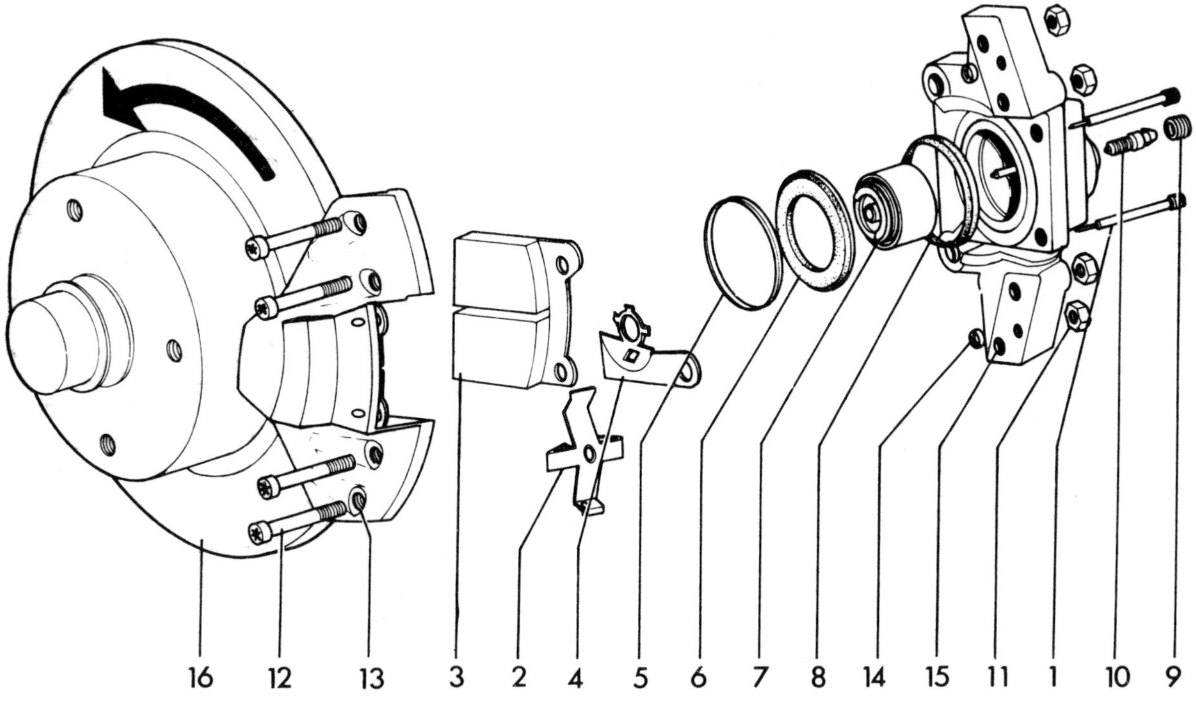

FIG. 9.5. DISC AND CALIPER – COMPONENTS (SEC. 7 AND 11)

1 *Pad retaining pin (see note)*
2 *Spreader spring (see note)*
3 *Friction pad*
4 *Piston retaining plate*
5 *Clamp ring*
6 *Seal*
7 *Piston*
8 *Rubber seal*
9 *Dust cap*
10 *Bleeder valve*
11 *Hexagon nut*
12 *Cheese head screw*
13 *Caliper outer housing*
14 *Seal*
15 *Caliper inner housing*
16 *Brake disc*

place, the withdrawal being effected as before. The friction pads adjust themselves automatically according to wear.
5 The main advantages the discs have are better resistance to fade and less unsprung weight. The main reason for using drums on the rear instead of discs is connected with the complication of fitting a handbrake to the disc.

8 Front disc brakes - inspection and maintenance

1 Jack up the vehicle and remove the wheel. The disc will now be exposed (photo). The surface of the disc should be free from scoring or signs of overheating. Look carefully for cracks and check that the face of the disc is flat.
2 If the disc is rusty or only slightly scored the VW agent can service it in situ using special polishing pads in place of the friction pads.
3 The run out of the disc should not exceed 0.008 inch (0.2 mm). This may only be checked with a clock gauge.
4 Discs with heavy scoring, cracks or runout above the permitted limit must be replaced.
5 The front wheel hub adjustment should be checked before measuring disc run out.
6 Check the clearance between the disc and the friction pads. This should be between 0.002 and 0.008 ins (0.05 - 0.20 mm). Measure this with a feeler gauge.
7 If the gap is greater it is probably due to a sticking piston. The remedy for this is described later in Section 9.9 of this Chapter.
8 The thickness of the lining on the pads must not be less than 0.080 in. (2mm). This may be difficult to measure so if there is any doubt knock out the retaining pins with a thin punch, (photo) remove the pad spreader plate and ease the pad out sufficiently to get a good look at it. (photos). Do not pull the pad right out, it will slide back quite easily and the spreader plates and pins can be reassembled without disturbing the piston . If the vehicle is later than August 1972 the larger caliper and pads are fitted.
9 If all is well replace the wheel and repeat on the other side.

9 Front disc brakes - friction pad removal, inspection and replacement

1 To remove the friction pads jack up the vehicle and remove the wheel.
2 Use a thin punch and knock out the retaining pins from the caliper and remove the pad spreader plate (photo 8.8a).
3 Pull the pads out from the caliper. If it is intended to use them again mark them so that they go back in the same place. If they are interchanged it will affect the braking efficiency. Before pulling the pads out force them away from the disc with a flat lever to push the pistons back.

This may cause the fluid in the header tank in the luggage compartment to overflow so remove a quantity of fluid from the tank before moving the pistons. An empty plastic bottle will act as a syphon but be sure it is clean.
4 Once the pistons are pushed back and the pads are out remove the piston retaining plate. Note that there is a cutaway portion on one side of the piston. Provided the piston is not rotated after the retaining plate is taken out there will be no difficulty in replacing the plate. If by chance the piston does move it must be adjusted so that the cut out portion of the piston will allow the piston retaining plate to be reassembled flush, and with the lugs engaged in the piston recesses.
5 Blow out the aperature of the caliper and examine the seal. It should be supple and show no signs of cracking. If it does it must be renewed. (Section 10).
6 Clean off the piston retaining plates with methylated spirits. If they are rusted or damaged get new ones. Replace the piston retaining plates so that the circular part fits firmly into the piston crown, and the plate must lie below the relieved part of the piston. Turn the piston with a pair of pliers if the plate does

8.1. Disc and caliper with wheel removed

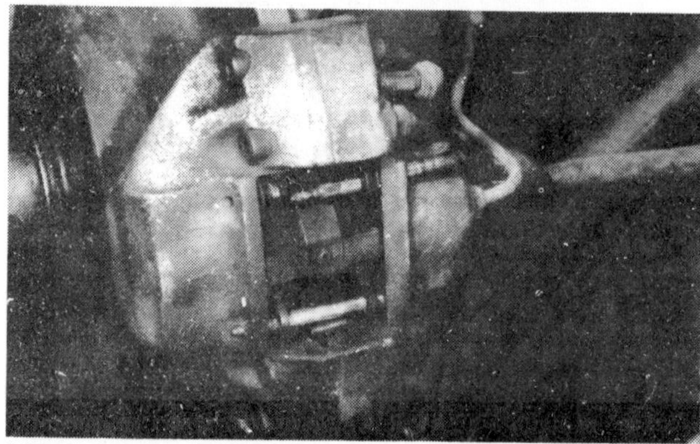
8.8a. Knock the pins out with a thin punch. . . . .

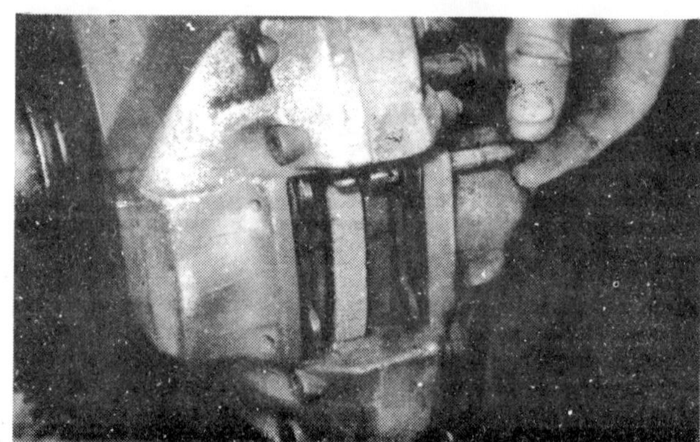
8.8b. . . . . remove the spreader plate . . . . .

8.8c. . . . . and pull the friction pad out far enough to get a look at it. Do not disturb the piston or piston retaining plate

not fit snugly until such time as it does. Take care not to scratch the piston.

7 Replace the pads (new ones if necessary). Replace the pad spreader plate (a new one should come with new pads) and tap home the retaining pins from the inside. Do not use a punch as there is a possibility of shearing the front shoulder of the pin by the split clamping bush.

8 Pump the brake pedal to bring the pads up to the disc and check the level of the fluid in the header tank.

9 If the clearance between the pad and the disc is too great then there is a probability that the inner seal on the piston is sticking and distorting more than usual, thus pulling the piston back too much. This can usually be cured by removing the friction pad and replacing it with a piece of wood 6mm thick. Pump the brake to force the piston further out and then push the piston back. Do this several times and the problem may disappear. If not, proceed to the next Section.

10 Front disc brakes calipers, pistons and seals overhaul

1 Before assuming that anything is wrong with the pistons make sure that the checks in Sections 8 and 9 have been done.

2 The caliper assembly must be taken off. Jack up the car, remove the wheel, disconnect the hydraulic line and plug it, and remove the two bolts holding the caliper to the steering knuckle.

3 The caliper must not be removed when it is hot.

4 If the pistons are to be removed from the caliper thought must first be given as to how pressure can be applied to force them out. Only one piston can be worked on at a time as the other piston must be installed and clamped in position so as to maintain pressure to force the other out. Air pressure can be applied from a foot pump if you rig up a spare hydraulic pipe union and short length of pipe to which the pump connector will fit. One piston will have to be clamped in such a way that there will still be room enough for the other to come right out. Here again a tong-like clamp may have to be made up from some 1½ x 1/8 inch flat steel bar if you are unable to obtain a suitable tool.

5 Mount the caliper assembly in the vice padding the jaws suitably so that the flange of the caliper will not be scored or marked. The friction pads and retaining plates should be removed (see Section 9).

6 Prise out the spring ring from the outer seal using a screw-driver. Then, with a blunt plastic or wooden tool prise out the seal itself. Do not use sharp tools for fear of scoring the piston or cylinder.

7 Using a clamp to hold one piston force the other out under pressure as described in paragraph 4. To prevent damage in case the piston should come out with force put some cloth in the caliper to prevent it striking the piston and clamp opposite.

8 With the piston out the rubber sealing ring can be taken out of its groove in the cylinder; once again use only a blunt article to get it out.

9 With methylated spirits or hydraulic fluid, clean the piston and cylinder thoroughly. If there are any signs of severe scoring or pitting then renewal will be necessary. With the cylinder this involves renewing the whole caliper unit.

10 When renewing seals the spring ring and piston retaining plate must also be renewed. The VW service kit includes all items needed. Use them. Before reassembly it is advantageous to coat the piston and new rubber seal with VW cylinder paste specially formulated for the job. Otherwise make sure they are thoroughly lubricated with clean hydraulic fluid. On no account use anything else.

11 Fit the rubber seal in the cylinder groove and then fit the piston into the seal. Great care must be taken to avoid mis-aligning the seal when doing this and the piston must be kept square while it is pushed in. The cut-out portion of the piston should lie at an angle of 20° from a line across the disc diameter facing in to the centre of the disc and against the direction of forward rotation.

12 Fit the new outer seal and spring ring.

13 Repeat the process for the other piston.

14 Refit the caliper to the knuckle tightening the securing bolts to 60 ft lbs (8mkg). Replace the piston retainer plates and pads as described in Section 9. The brake must be bled as described in Section 19.

15 Replace the wheel and the job is complete.

16 Always replace the caliper to the wheel from which it has come, never use any cleaning fluid other than methylated spirits or hydraulic brake fluid, and keep the operation clinically clean. Try not to handle the pistons and cylinder with dirty hands at any time.

17 It is rare that the caliper housing has to be split, and this should not be done unless it it obviously leaking. Undo the four socket head screws (after the pads and pistons have been removed) and split the caliper. Install two new seals ('O' rings) align the halves of the caliper together and replace the bolts. Tighten them from the centre outwards to a torque of 7 lbs ft. and then in sequence to 15 lbs ft. (2 mkg).

11 Front disc brakes - removal and replacement of disc

1 Refer to Fig.11.4 and Fig.9.5.

2 Jack up the car and remove the wheel. Remove the caliper, this must not be done if the caliper is hot. There is no need to disconnect the hydraulic system but the caliper must be supported in such a way as to avoid strain on the hydraulic line.

3 Remove the C washer (left side only) and remove the hub cap. Unscrew the clamp nut and remove the hub assembly. See Chapter 11, section 3.

4 Reinstallation is the reverse of removal. Assemble the hub as directed in Chapter 11 section 3. Replace the calipers.Tighten the caliper holding bolts to 60 lbs ft.

5 Check the new disc for run-out before installing the wheel and check the gap between the disc and pads (Section 8).

12 Tandem master cylinder - removal and replacement

1 The master cylinder is located on the pedal cluster support bracket by the side of the steering column. Remove the interior trim and take up the carpet from the floor of the car. Protect the metal work, remembering that brake fluid is not only poisonous but excellent paint remover.

2 The master cylinder may be indentified as opposed to the clutch master cylinder as it is the one with the electric cables going to it (photo). For this reason disconnect the battery, before going any further.

3 Carefully pull off the electric connections noting which goes where and labelling them. Fasten them out of the way.

4 Now pull the elbows from the sealing plugs and then detach the brake lines. Catch any escaping fluid.

5 Undo the securing screws and remove the cylinder.

6 To reinstall refit the cylinder to the pedal bracket, tighten the screws to 18 lbs ft. (2.5 mkg).

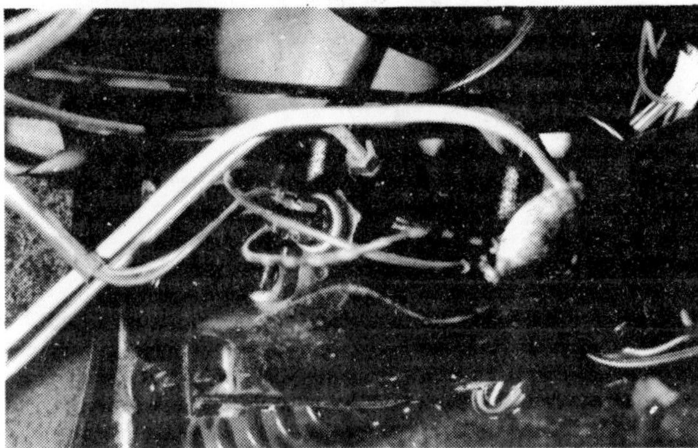

12.2. The master cylinder mounted on the pedal support bracket. This is on a R.H.D car. It is identified by the electric cables going to it for the stop lights

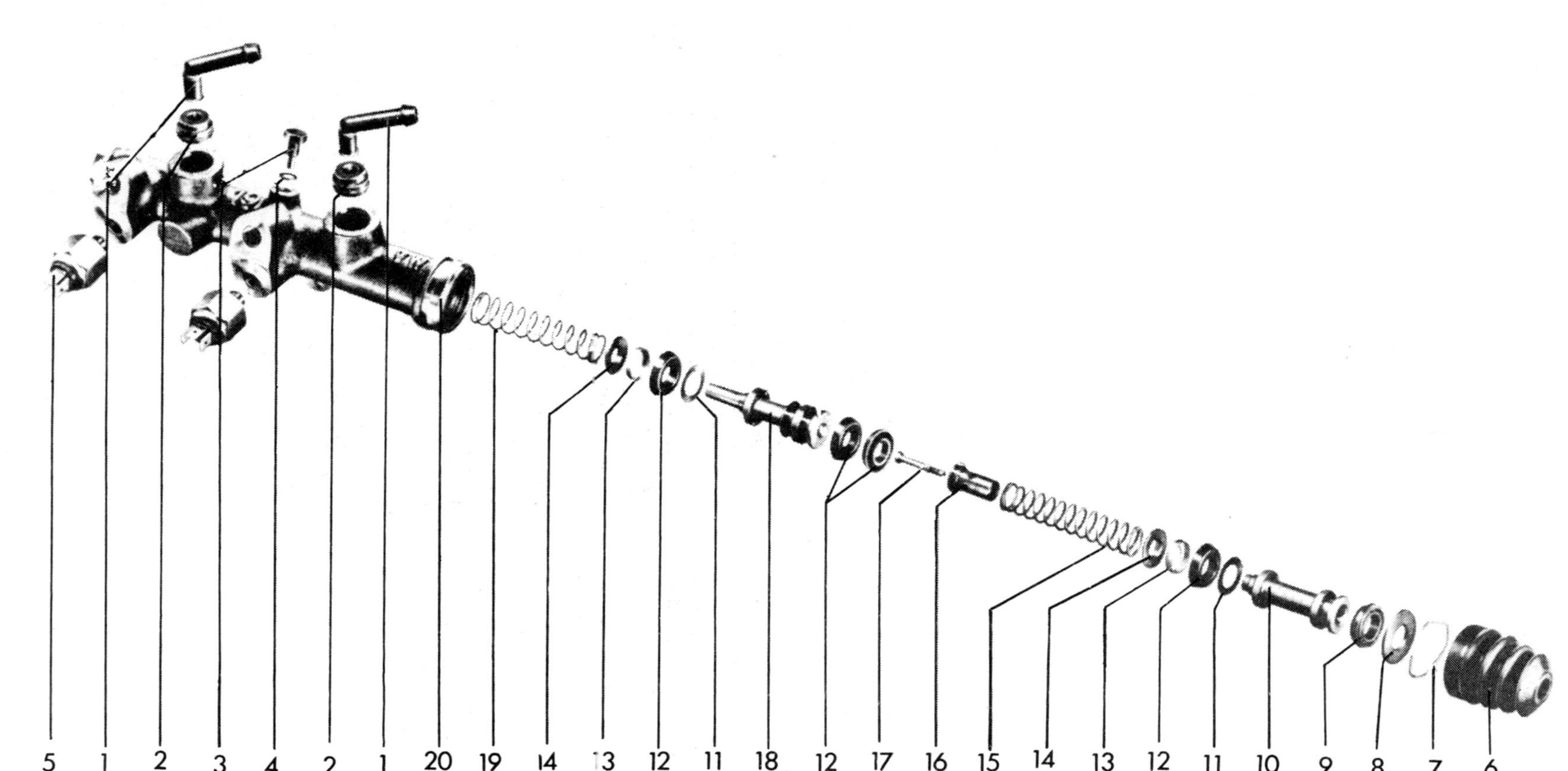

FIG. 9.6. TANDEM MASTER BRAKE CYLINDER – EXPLODED VIEW (SEC. 13)

1 Elbow
2 Sealing plug
3 Stop screw
4 Seal
5 Brake light switch (2)
6 Boot
7 Spring ring
8 Stop ring
9 Secondary cup
10 Push rod piston
11 Cup washer
12 Primary cup
13 Support washer
14 Spring plate
15 Push rod piston
16 Stop sleeve
17 Stroke limiting screw
18 Intermediate piston
19 Intermediate piston spring
20 Master cylinder housing

Note: Master cylinders are supplied either by Teves (Ate) or Schafer ('S'). The complete master cylinders are interchangeable but the individual parts are NOT. A repair kit must be matched with the master cylinder.

7 Adjust the brake pedal free travel. To do this refer to Fig.9.7 Slacken the locknut on the push rod and shorten the push rod slightly.
8 Remove the rubber cap from the screw stop of the brake pedal and set the distance 'S' to be:
a) for LHD and RHD up to chassis 410 2 030 158 – 0.96 in. (24.5 mm)
b) for RHD from chassis 410 2 030 159 – 0.93 in. (23.5 mm)
9 **Reinstall** the rubber cap. Increase the length of the push rod until the horizontal free play of the brake pedal is 0.24 ins. (6.5mm)
10 Lock the push rod and push the boot over the hexagon. The vent hole in the boot must always face downwards.
11 Moisten the sealing plugs with brake fluid and install the elbows. Reconnect the brake lines and electric wires.
12 Bleed the brakes (see Section 19).
13 Reinstall the trim and refit the carpet
14 For removal and installation of master cylinder with Servo see Section 14.

13 Tandem master cylinder - overhaul

1 Refer to Fig.9.6. Thoroughly clean the exterior of the unit before starting to dismantle. Then remove the piston stop screw located between the two fluid inlet ports.
2 Remove the boot from the rear of the cylinder and take out the internal circlip.
3 The two pistons and all their component parts may then be drawn out. Do this carefully taking note of the order and position in which they come out.
4 All internal seals are fitted to the grooves in the pistons. They can be pulled off and fitted without special tools but care must be taken not to overstretch them. The primary piston is fitted with three seals all the same size and shape. The front two face forward and the third to the rear. The secondary piston has two seals, both facing forwards. The front seal is the same as those on the primary piston but the rear one is the odd one out so do not confuse it with the others.

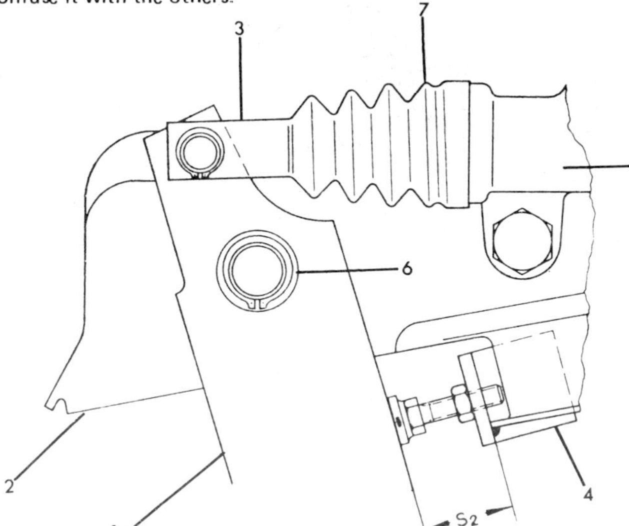

FIG. 9.7. DIAGRAM SHOWING PUSH ROD ADJUSTMENT FOR BRAKE PEDAL (SEC. 12)

1 Brake pedal
2 Pedal support bracket
3 Push rod stirrup
4 Pedal stop
5 Master cylinder casting
6 Pedal pivot
7 Boot

Note: When the boot is pulled back it will be seen that the push rod screws into the stirrup. Undo the locknut and the push rod length can be adjusted by screwing it in or out of the stirrup.

5 When reassembling the pistons into the cylinder first place the cup washer, cup seal, support washer, spring plate and spring, in that order over the nose of the primary piston (to which the new secondary cup and rear seal should have been already fitted). Hold the cylinder vertical with the open end downwards and feed the assortment back in so that the loose items do not fall off the piston.
6 The secondary piston primary cup is held in location by a support washer and spring plate also. These in turn are held firm by the stop sleeve and stroke limiting screw. By undoing the stroke limiting screw inside the stop sleeve all these component parts may be released. The new seal is then easily placed in position.
7 When replacing the secondary piston it should be pushed far enough forward to enable the stop screw to be put in so that it fits behind the rear end of the primary piston. This is most important. It must not be fitted so that it engages the recessed part in the shank of the primary piston.
8 Refit the stop ring, circlip and rubber boot over the end of the cylinder.
9 The cylinders are supplied by either TEVES (ATE) or Schafer ('S'). Repair kits match the cylinder and are NOT interchangeable, but the complete cylinders are interchangeable.

14 Servo assisted brakes

1 The Servo assisted brake cylinder is fitted to some vehicles after August 1971. Although the pedal arrangements seem the same the layout is completely changed. The master cylinder is now situated in the forward luggage compartment (photo) and the pedal arrangements are as shown in Fig.9.8.
The tandem master cylinder operates in exactly the same way but the servo mechanism is interposed between the brake pedal and the push rod. The servo unit is operated by a connecting rod from the brake pedal lever via a relay lever. The vacuum is taken from between the intake air distributor and the auxiliary air regulator via a non return valve. The vacuum lines go through the interior of the vehicle.
2 The Boosting factor is 2.15. In order to adjust the push rod back off the push rod locknut and shorten the push rod. Remove the rubber cap from the stop screw of the brake pedal to:-
For LHD 24.5 mm (0.96 ins).
RHD up to Chassis 410 2.030.158 – 24.5 mm (0.96 ins).
RHD after Chassis 410 2.030.159 – 23.5 mm (0.93 ins).
Refer to Fig.9.8; remove the connecting rod pin at the relay lever and the securing clip. Turn the brake servo unit operating rod so that the lower hole in the relay lever lines up with the forked end of the connecting rod and push the pin home. Refit the circlip.
3 The master cylinder is modified at the end to permit the

14.1. When the vehicle has a servo assisted brake system the master cylinder, servo, and header tanks are situated on the floor of the front luggage compartment

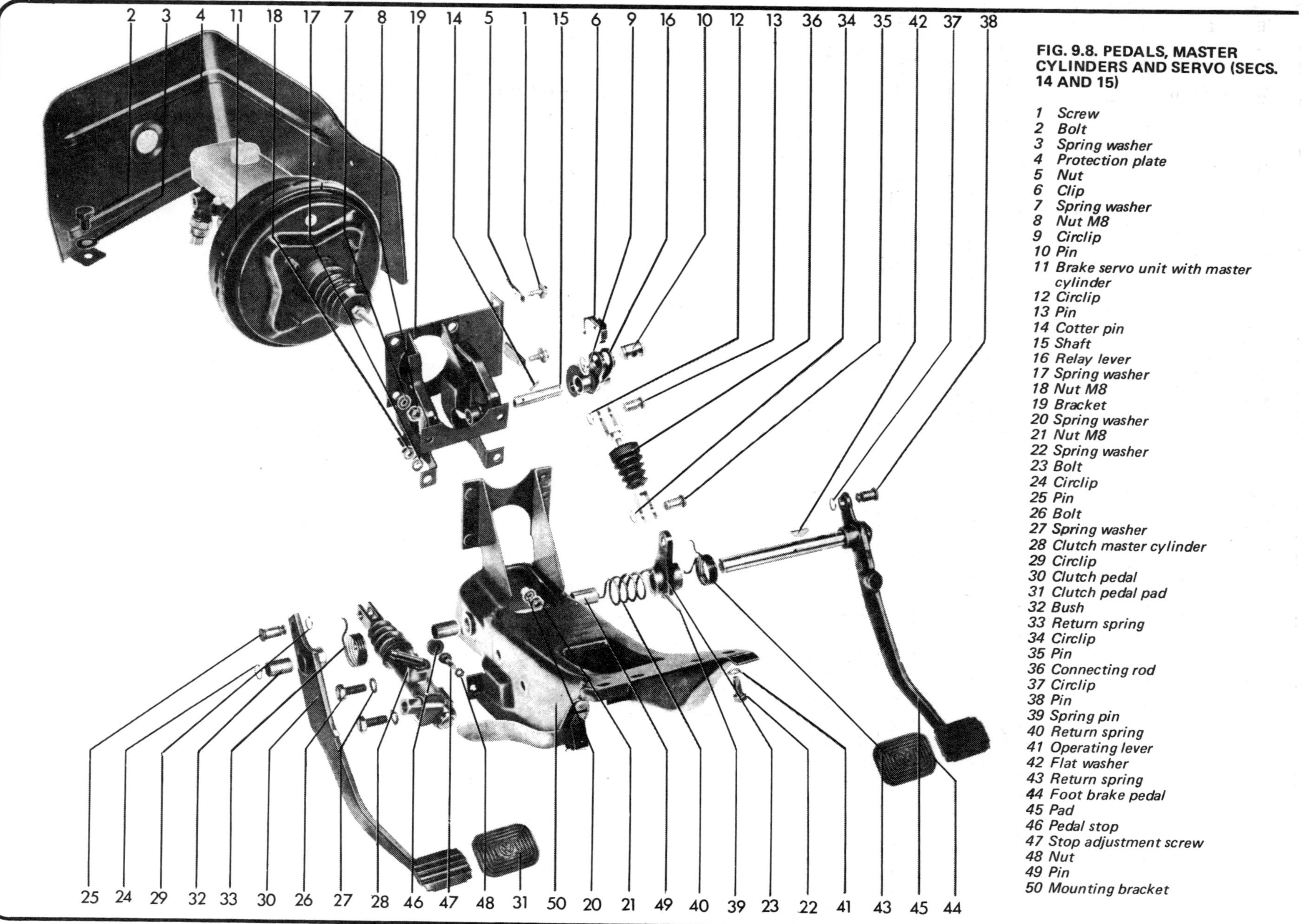

FIG. 9.8. PEDALS, MASTER CYLINDERS AND SERVO (SECS. 14 AND 15)

1 *Screw*
2 *Bolt*
3 *Spring washer*
4 *Protection plate*
5 *Nut*
6 *Clip*
7 *Spring washer*
8 *Nut M8*
9 *Circlip*
10 *Pin*
11 *Brake servo unit with master cylinder*
12 *Circlip*
13 *Pin*
14 *Cotter pin*
15 *Shaft*
16 *Relay lever*
17 *Spring washer*
18 *Nut M8*
19 *Bracket*
20 *Spring washer*
21 *Nut M8*
22 *Spring washer*
23 *Bolt*
24 *Circlip*
25 *Pin*
26 *Bolt*
27 *Spring washer*
28 *Clutch master cylinder*
29 *Circlip*
30 *Clutch pedal*
31 *Clutch pedal pad*
32 *Bush*
33 *Return spring*
34 *Circlip*
35 *Pin*
36 *Connecting rod*
37 *Circlip*
38 *Pin*
39 *Spring pin*
40 *Return spring*
41 *Operating lever*
42 *Flat washer*
43 *Return spring*
44 *Foot brake pedal*
45 *Pad*
46 *Pedal stop*
47 *Stop adjustment screw*
48 *Nut*
49 *Pin*
50 *Mounting bracket*

fitting of the servo. The header tank for brake fluid has also been moved (see Fig.9.8).

4 To remove the servo first remove the header tank from the master cylinder. It will assist matters if the guard is removed and steps taken to protect the inside of the luggage compartment against contamination by brake fluid. The tank should be emptied before removal, an empty plastic bottle makes a good syphon, but make sure the bottle is clean. Pull the tank upwards and catch any brake fluid that spills.

5 Disconnect the brake fluid lines from the master cylinder and plug them. Catch any fluid that spills.

6 Remove the master cylinder from the servo. There are two nuts to undo and an 'O' ring to take out. See Fig.9.9. Be careful with the pressure piston shaft.

7 Disconnect the vacuum servo hose from the brake servo.

8 Remove the connecting pin from the stirrup (Fig.9.8), undo the servo nuts and pull the servo out to the front.

9 Reassembly is the reverse of removal, torque the servo nuts to 1.3 mkg (9.5 ft lbs), and do not forget to bleed the system right through.

10 Unfortunately little can be done to repair a faulty servo. The filter damping washer and boot are the only replaceable items. Refer to Fig.9.9. Pull the boot off its seating, lever the cap of the valve housing and pull the damping washer and filter out of the valve housing. When refitting the new filter and damping washer make sure the slits are at 180° to one another.

15 Pedal arrangement

1 The Type 4 has different pedal arrangements to suit L.H. and R.H. drive, Manual and Automatic transmission and Servo assisted braking. The latter arrangement is shown at Fig.9.8. For the L.H. drive manual transmission the pedal arrangements are similar to Fig.9.8, but the brake master cylinder is brought back onto the right side of the bracket.

Right hand drive manual gearbox pedal arrangements are shown at Fig.9.10.

For the automatic gearbox the clutch pedal is obviously not fitted and the brake pedal plus cylinder are on the right hand side of the bracket for both R.H. and L.H. drive cars.

2 In order to remove the pedals or push rods the complete pedal support must first be removed. This involves removal of the steering column (Chapter 11). The clutch and brake master cylinders must be removed, but it is not necessary to disconnect the fluid lines or electric cables. The pedal support bracket may then be removed.

3 Reinstallation is the reverse. The push rods for the clutch and brake master cylinders must be inserted correctly, the bracket positioned correctly and the bolts tightened to 15 lbs ft. (2 mkg). The master cylinders are then refitted and the steering column.

4 Unless something is broken it hardly seems worth while doing all this just to renew the bushes which is all that can be done in the way of repair.

5 Dismantling and reassembling the pedals from the support is a straightforward business but watch how the springs are fitted.

16 Brake pressure regulation (pressure sensitive)

1 This device (photo 1b) fitted in the rear brake circuit ensures that the pressure to the rear wheels increases at a lower rate than that to the front wheels. It is not fitted to all vehicles.

2 The first problem is to find it. It is situated at the rear of the vehicle under the parcel section floor. Get someone to press the brake pedal sharply and listen for the 'knock' as it functions. If no knock can be heard or felt then the valve is not functioning. This means that the valve must be taken out of the circuit and either overhauled or replaced. It is advisable to consult the VW dealer as to whether he is willing to adjust the valve after you have installed it at this juncture.

3 Disconnect the hydraulic pipes and plug them. Catch the fluid which spills. Undo the securing screws and remove the valve complete with bracket. Future policy will be to replace faulty regulators when the present stocks of repair kits are used. Until then the following method of repair can be used.

4 Refer to Fig.9.11. Place the regulator in a vice and undo the socket head cap screws. The regulator should be held in such a way as to keep the spring compressed, (photo) until the screws are removed. Undo the vice slowly releasing the spring and remove the parts from the cylinder.

5 If repair kit is available ALL parts should be used.

6 Apply a very thin layer of brake cylinder paste to the piston cap and seal and install them. Put the seal over the threads of the plug and screw the plug into the regulator body. Tighten to 80 lb ft (11 mkg). Lubricate the thrust cap interior with the silicone grease provided in the repair kit. DO NOT use any other type of grease. Push the cap on to the regulator body shoulder. The space between the shoulder and the cap must be full of grease.

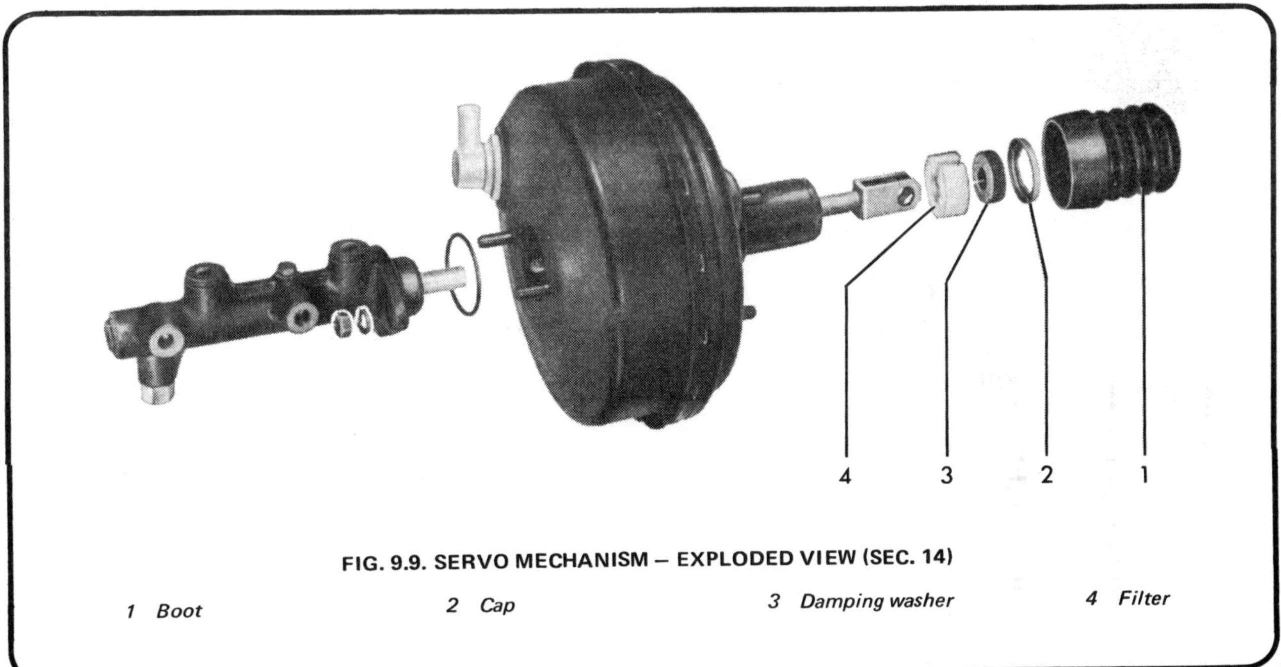

FIG. 9.9. SERVO MECHANISM – EXPLODED VIEW (SEC. 14)

1 Boot *2 Cap* *3 Damping washer* *4 Filter*

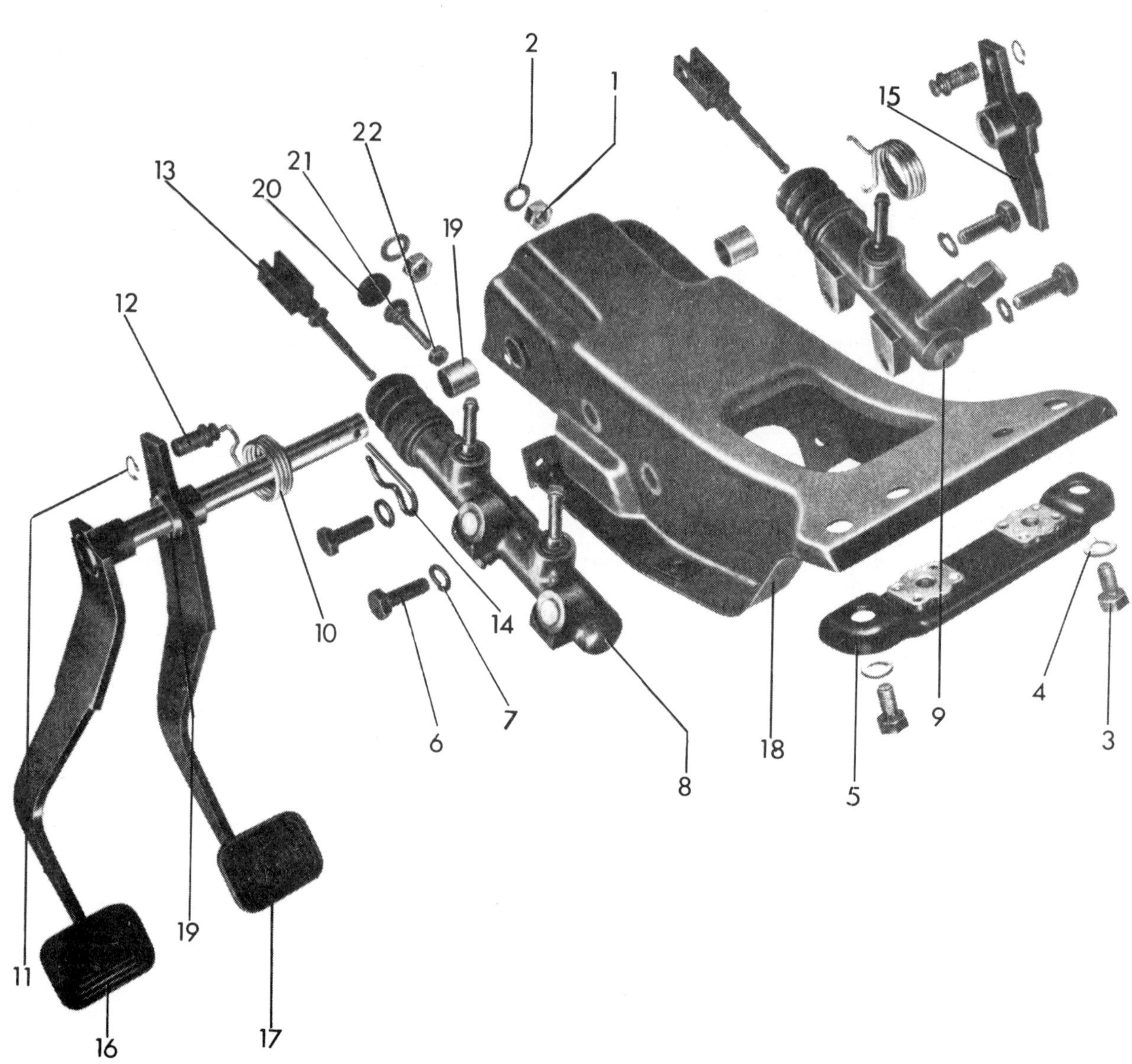

FIG. 9.10. PEDAL ARRANGEMENT – MANUAL TRANSMISSION R.H.D. (SEC. 15)

1 Nut
2 Spring washer
3 Bolt
4 Lock washer
5 Bracket for steering column tube
6 Bolt
7 Lock washer
8 Brake master cylinder
9 Clutch master cylinder
10 Return spring
11 Circlip
12 Pin
13 Pushrod
14 Clip
15 Operating lever
16 Clutch pedal
17 Brake pedal
18 Pedal support
19 Bush
20 Stop screw rubber cap
21 Stop screw M6
22 Nut M6

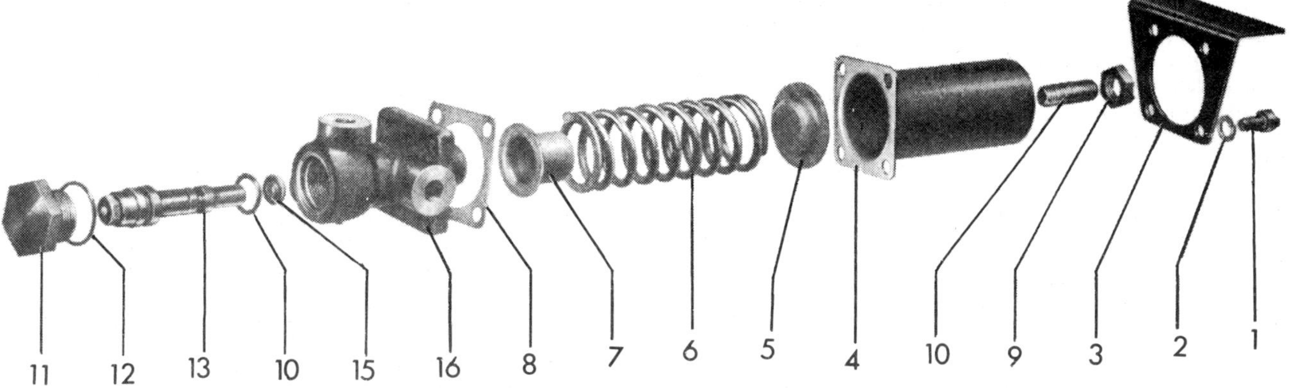

FIG. 9.11. BRAKE PRESSURE REGULATOR (PRESSURE SENSITIVE) (SEC. 16)

1 Cap screw	*5 Spring plate*	*9 Nut*	*13 Piston*
2 Spring washer	*6 Spring*	*10 Adjusting screw*	*14 Seal*
3 Bracket	*7 Thrust cap*	*11 Plug*	*15 Cup*
4 Spring housing	*8 Gasket*	*12 Seal*	*16 Regulator body*

16.4. Grip the regulator in a vice, undo the screws with an allen key and then open the vice slowly to decompress the spring

7 Reinstall the rest of the parts, put the regulator back in the vice and compress the spring, tightening the socket screws to 7 lb ft. (1 mkg).

8 Refit the valve and bleed the system. Check the working of the valve by listening to the 'knock' as in paragraph 2.

9 Now comes the difficult bit. The valve can only be set correctly with high pressure gauges. This is a job for the VW agent and it MUST be done. Incorrect setting may lead to a rear wheel skid of memorable proportions. So come to a sensible arrangement with the dealer before you start the job. One further piece of warning, if there is any sign of corrosion in the valve, scrap it and fit a new one. When present stocks of repair kits are used up it will be necessary to fit a new one anyway.

10 When the regulator has been set the locking screw should be tightened to 24 lb ft (3 mkg) and sealed with a mastic compound to make it waterproof. VW compound D 14 should be used.

17 Handbrake - removal and refitting of lever and cable

1 Slacken off the locknuts at the lever end of both handbrake cables and remove them together with the adjusting nuts.

2 Remove the rear brake drums and unhook the cable for the operating lever on the shoe.

3 Undo the bolt which holds the outer sleeve clip to the brake backplate where the cable passes through. Disengage the clip from behind the washer and spring on the cable and draw the cable out from the backplate. Then pull the cables out of the tube from the other direction.

4 Before fitting a new cable make sure that at the brake end the spring and washer are properly fitted between the eye of the cable and the outer sleeve.

5 It is necessary to remove the handbrake lever before the threaded ends of the cable can be reconnected to it. Remove one of the circlips from the end of the lever pivot pin and withdraw the pin. Keep the hands well clear of the ratchet button and then move the whole lever assembly forward so that it disengages from the floor plate. If the ratchet button is inadvertently pressed the ratchet will fall down. It must be put back before replacing the lever.

6 Put the cable through the backplate and then work the sleeve clamp through the hole in the backplate so that the spring and washer are on the inside of the slotted bracket of the clamp. Replace the bolt into the back of the backplate and tighten it. Then hook the cable onto the lever.

7 Feed the threaded end of the cable into the tubes in the frame fork and finally see that the outer sleeve fits into position in the end of the tube. The threaded ends should appear inside the car under the handbrake lever mounting position. It may be necessary to hook them up with a piece of wire.

8 Making sure that they are not crossed, insert the cables into the two eyes in the base of the lever and then put the lever in position checking that the rear section engages properly in the floor section. Once again be careful not to press the ratchet release button. Replace the pivot pin and circlip and screw on the adjuster and locknuts.

9 Adjust the handbrake as described in Section 3.

18 Hydraulic lines - inspection and renewal

1 Large scale research in the U.S.A. has shown that brake pipe line corrosion may be expected in cars only four years old. Laboratory tests show that new pipes can be corroded to the point of leaking by only 90 days of exposure to salt spray such as is thrown up when salt is used to melt snow. A copper alloy

called Kunifer 10 is being used to make replacement tubes, which is resistant to salt but not as yet fitted to new vehicles. It is worth asking about if you have pipes to renew. Inspect the pipe lines in the autumn and spring as a routine task.

2 Trace the routes of all the rigid pipes and wash or brush away accumulated dirt. If the pipes are obviously covered with some sort of underseal compound do not disturb it. Examine for signs of kinks or dents which could have been caused by flying stones. Any instances of this mean that the pipe section should be renewed but before actually taking it out read the rest of this section. Any unprotected sections of pipe which show signs of corrosion or pitting on the outer surfaces must also be considered for renewal.

3 Flexible hoses, should show no signs of external chafing or cracking. Move them about and see if surface cracks appear. Also, if they feel stiff and inflexible or are twisted they are nearing the end of thei r useful life. If in any doubt renew the hoses. Make sure also that they are not rubbing against the bodywork.

4 Before attempting to remove any pipe for renewal it is important to be sure that you have a replacement source of supply within reach if you do not wish to be kept off the road for too long. Pipes are often damaged on removal. If a Volkswagen agency is near, you may be reasonably sure that the correct pipes and unions are available. If not, check first that your local garage has the necessary equipment for making up the pipes and has the correct metric thread pipe unions available. The same goes for flexible hoses.

5 Where couplings from rigid to flexible pipes are made there are support brackets and the flexible pipe is held in place by a 'U' clip which engages in a groove in the union. The male union screws into it. Before getting the spanners on, soak the unions in penetrating fluid as there is always some rust or corrosion binding the threads. Whilst this is soaking in, place a piece of plastic film under the fluid reservoir cap to minimise loss of fluid from the disconnected pipes. Hold the hexagon on the flexible pipe coupling whilst the union on the rigid pipe is undone. Then pull out the clip to release both pipes from the bracket. For flexible hose removal this procedure will be needed at both ends. When you are renewing a flexible hose, take care not to damage the unions of the pipes that connect into it. If a union is particularly stubborn be prepared to renew the rigid pipe as well. This is quite often the case if you are forced to use open ended spanners. It may be worth spending a little money on a special pipe union spanner which is like a ring spanner with a piece cut out to enable it to go round the tube.

6 If you are having the new pipe made up, take the old one along to check that the unions and pipe flaring at the ends are identical.

7 Replacement of the hoses or pipes is a reversal of the removal procedure. Precautions and care are needed to make sure that the unions are correctly lined up to prevent cross threading. This may mean bending the pipe a little where a rigid pipe goes into a fixture. Such bending must not, under any circumstances, be too acute, otherwise the pipe will kink and weaken.

8 When fitting flexible hoses take care not to twist them. This can happen when the unions are finally tightened unless a spanner is used to to hold the end of the flexible hose and prevent twisting.

9 After removal or slackening of a brake pipe union the hydraulic system must be bled.

19 Hydraulic system - bleeding to remove air

1 The purpose of the process known as bleeding the brakes is to remove air bubbles from the hydraulic system. Air is compressible - hydraulic fluid is not. Bleeding should be necessary only after work on the hydraulic system has allowed air into the system. If it is found necessary to bleed brakes frequently then there is something worse and the whole system should be checked through to find where the air is getting into it. Cars left unused for a long time may also require brake bleeding before full efficiency is restored.

In any case VW recommend that all hydraulic fluid be drained and renewed every two years. This is a very sound practice and if you can summon up the energy it is a good thing to renew all the seals as well.

2 Normally, if work has been carried out at the extremities of the system - e.g. at wheel cylinders of adjacent pipes, then it should only be necessary to bleed that particular section. Work on the master cylinder, however, would call for all four wheels to be bled.

3 Before starting, make sure you have an adequate supply of the proper fluid, a clean receptacle and a tube which will fit over the bleed nipple securely and which is conveniently long enough. A useful device is the tube which is fitted with a non-return valve. This avoids the necessity of keeping the outer end of the tube submerged in liquid whilst bleeding is in progress.

4 Clean off the bleed nipple (or pull off the protective cap). Put about 1 inch depth of fluid in the receptacle (a salad cream jar is ideal and needs less fluid!). Connect the pipe to the nipple and put the other end in the jar and undo the nipple about half a turn - no more is necessary.

5 A second person is needed to operate the brake pedal at your instruction. The pedal should be depressed smartly one full stroke to the floor and allowed to return slowly. This should be repeated until no more bubbles emerge from the tube in the jar. Smart operation of the pedal ensures that the air is forced along the pipe rather than by-passed. Keep a watch on the level of fluid in the reservoir. If it gets too low it will let air into the master cylinder and then you will have to bleed all four wheels.

6 Once all the air is expelled, the best moment to tighten the bleed nipple is during the return stroke of the pedal.

7 Repeat the procedure for each wheel as necessary. Do not put fluid bled out of the system back in. Always use fresh.

8 Later models have two bleed nipples fitted to each caliper. The top one is for normal bleeding operations. The lower one is used when the system is being drained. After draining close the lower screw and bleed from the upper one.

20 FAULT DIAGNOSIS

Before diagnosing faults in the brake system check that any irregularities are not caused by:

1 Uneven and incorrect tyre pressures
2 Incorrect 'mix' of radial and cross-ply tyres
3 Wear in the steering mechanism
4 Defects in the suspension and dampers
5 Misalignment of the bodyframe

Symptom	Reason/s	Remedy
Pedal travels a long way before the brakes operate	Siezed adjuster on rear shoes or shoes require adjustment	Check, repair, and adjust.
	Disc pads or linings worn past limit	Inspect and renew as necessary.
Stopping ability poor pedal pressure firm	Linings, pads, discs or drums worn	Renew pads, linings, discs and drums as necessary.
	One or more caliper piston or rear wheel hydraulic cylinder seized	Inspect and repair as necessary.
Car veers to one side when brakes are applied	Brake pads on one side contaminated with oil	Remove and renew. Repair source of oil leakage.
	Hydraulic pistons in calipers siezed or sticking	Overhaul caliper.
	Wrong pads fitted	Install correct pads.
Pedal feels springy when brakes are applied	Rear linings not bedded into drums (after fitting new ones)	Check adjustment.
	Severe wear in rear brake drums	Renew drums and shoes.
	Master cylinder, brake caliper, or drum backplate loose	Tighten bolts as necessary. Fit new bolts.
Pedal feels spongy when brakes are applied	Air in the hydraulic system	Bleed brakes and check for signs of leakage. Top up header tank.
Pedal travels right down with no resistance and brakes do not operate	Fluid reservoir empty	Check refill and bleed all brakes.
	Hydraulic lines fractured	Trace through and replace as necessary.
	Seals in master cylinder have failed	Dismantle cylinder and rebuild with new seals.
Binding, juddering, overheating	Check all the above faults	Inspect and overhaul the complete system.
	Reservoir air vent blocked	Clean vent with probe. Clean filter.
Servo mechanism: (a) pedal pressure high no servo assistance	Vacuum line leaking	Tighten clips.
	Diaphragm leaking	Fit new servo.
	Master cylinder leaking	Dismantle and overhaul.
(b) pedal pressure increases from a certain position	Master cylinder piston shaft damaged	Repair master cylinder.
Brake pressure regulator: Rear wheel brakes too fierce	Pressure regulating point too high	Ask dealer to set regulator correctly.
	Piston corroded, check valve will not close	Fit new regulator.

Chapter 10 Electrical system

Contents

Specifications

Battery ... 12v 45 amp hour capacity, negative earth

Alternator			
Part number	021 903023	021 903023B	021 903023A
Maximum current amps	35	45	55
Mean regulating voltage	14	14	14
Nominal output speed rpm	2000/2200	2200/2400	2200

Regulator ... Mechanical, single contact
Alternator cut in speed ... 1000 rpm
drive pulley ratio ... 2.26 : 1

Starter motor ... Pre engaged 12v 0.7 hp
Earlier models VW or Bosch, later models Bosch. Automatics 12v 0.8 hp

Windscreen wiper current - Normal speed ... 2.5 amps
- High speed ... 3.5 amps

Lamps

Headlamp bulb	45/50 watt
Headlamp sealed beam	50/40 watt (12.8v)
Headlamp Halogen	
Turn signal	21 watt
Brake/tail lamp	21/5 watt
Rear number plate	10 watt
Reverse lamp	25 watt
Interior light (festoon)	10 watt
Parking lights/side markers	4 watt
Warning lamps	1.2 watt

Rear window heater current load ... 80 watt (6.6 amps)

Fresh air fan - low speed ... 2 amps
- high speed ... 3 amps

Fuse boxes

There are 12 fuses rated 8 amps or 16 amps. At least two types of fuse layout have been fitted. The owner is advised to check his own box against one of the lists underneath. There are four other fuses besides the main box (see Section 26).

Fuse No.	Size amps	Carburettor type engine model 411/	Size amps	Fuel injection engine model 411E
1	8	L & R parking lights, right tail light, number plate (license plate)	8	Temperature regulating switch (warning lamp) left tail lamp, selector lever console light, left parking light.
2	8	Left tail light	8	Right parking light, right tail light.
3	8	Left low beam	8	Right low beam
4	8	Right low beam	8	Left low beam
5	8	Right high beam	8	Right high beam
6	8	Left high beam high beam warning light	8	Left high beam High beam warning light
7	8	Side parking lights	8	License plate light
8	8	L & R back up lights, turn signals, fuel gauge warning lamps, fresh air fan	8	Interior light Emergency flasher
9	16	Windscreen wipers	16	Cigarette lighter, fuel pump
10	8	L & R brake lights Horn	16	Temperature regulating switch, fresh air fan, wipers, rear window heater
11	8	Hazard warning lights, interior light	8	Back up lights, warning lamps, turn signals, fuel gauge
12	16	Heating incl. rear window	8	Horn brake warning lights, stop lights

1 General description

The electrical system works at 12 volts. A 45 ampere hour battery, installed under the front seat (photo) is charged by an alternator which is fitted with rectifier diodes installed in the housing, and supplies DC direct to the battery. Under this arrangement no cut-out is required because the rectifier diodes prevent the passage of current from the battery to the alternator. A Bosch voltage regulator is installed in the engine compartment adjacent to the alternator (photo). It is a mechanical single contact type. The earlier types of vehicle were fitted with an alternator with an output of 35 or 45 amps. From chassis no 410205245 this was increased to 55 amps.

The starter motor on early models was either VW or BOSCH manufacture, but from March 1970 Bosch only; solenoid operated over running clutch type in design throughout. It is mounted on the clutch housing in the engine compartment.

The lighting arrangements have varied considerably, from the early 411 models with single headlamps on either side, to twin sealed beam of circular appearance on either side, and from chassis 41020000001 to halogen dual headlamps.

The revision of the body style in August 1972 bringing in the 412 also rearranged the ancillary lighting. The steering column arrangements have also varied.

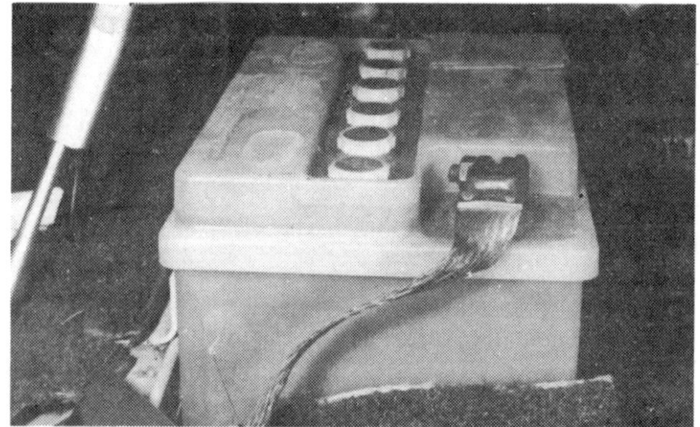

1.a. The battery as seen from the side when the seat is tipped this is the earth strap

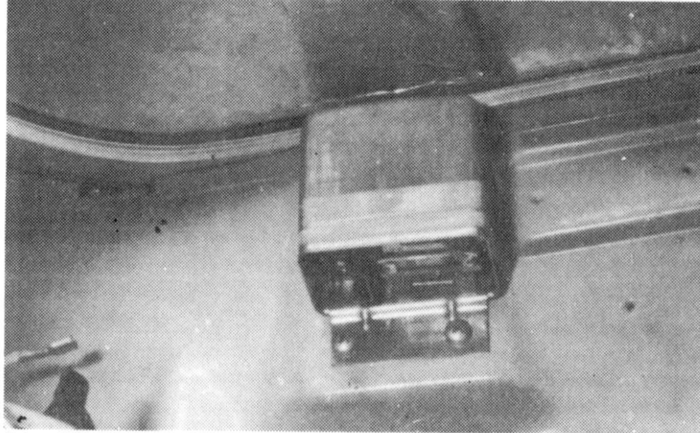

1.b. A view of the voltage regulator, plug removed taken from below when the engine had been removed. The securing screws are visible. Be careful when re-installing not to damage the plug and cable. It may be necessary to use a mirror to re-install the plug

2 Battery - removal and reinstallation

1 Tilt the driver's seat backrest in a forward direction on the 412. On the 411 push the seat as far forward as possible, pull the release lever and tilt the seat backwards.

2 The battery is thus exposed. Remove the earth cable and the positive terminal with its three cables (one to the fuse box terminal 30, one to the control unit of the F.I. system and the battery charging cable. (photo).

3 Remove the strap and lift out the battery.

4 Wipe off any deposit from the battery tray. Clean the battery case.

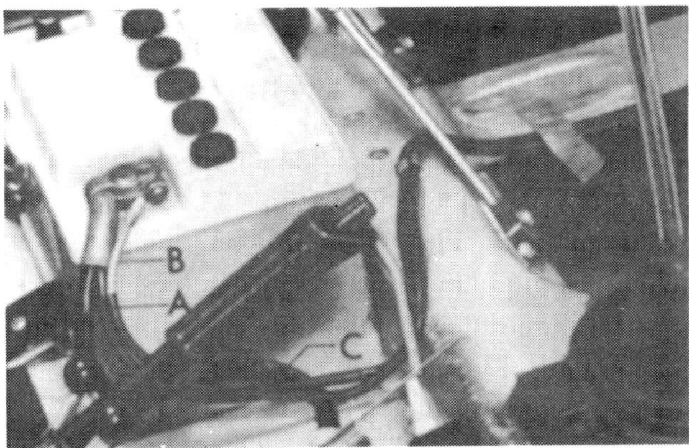

2.2. The other end of the battery. The positive terminal may have three cables. A to fuse box terminal 30, B to the control box on fuel injection systems (not on carburettor ends) and C, the battery charging cable (via starter terminal 30)

5 When replacing the battery make sure that the terminals bed correctly on the battery posts. Cover the terminals lightly with a film of petroleum jelly (not grease).

3 Battery - maintenance and inspection

1 Normal weekly battery maintenance consists of checking the electrolyte level of each cell to ensure that the separators are covered by ¼ inch of electrolyte. If the level has fallen, top up the battery using distilled water only. Do not overfill. If a battery is overfilled or any electrolyte spilled, immediately wipe away the excess as electrolyte attacks and corrodes any metal it comes into contact with very rapidly.

2 As well as keeping the terminals clean and covered with petroleum jelly, the top of the battery, and especially the top of the cells, should be kept clean and dry. This helps prevent corrosion and ensures that the battery does not become partially discharged by leakage through dampness and dirt. If topping up the battery becomes excessive and the case has been inspected for cracks that could cause leakage, but none are found, the battery is being over-charged and the regulator should be checked.

3 With the battery on the bench at the three monthly interval check, measure its specific gravity with a hydrometer to determine the state of charge and condition of electrolyte. There should be very little variation between the different cells and if a variation in excess of 0.025 is present it will be due to either;

a) Loss of electrolyte from the battery at some time caused by spillage or a leak, resulting in a drop in the specific gravity of electrolyte when the deficiency was replaced with distilled water instead of fresh electrolyte.

b) An internal short circuit caused by buckling of the plates or a similar malady pointing to the likelihood of total battery failure in the near future.

4 The correct readings for the electrolyte specific gravity at various states of charge and conditions are:

	Temperate	Tropical
Fully charged	1.285	1.23
Half charged	1.20	1.14
Discharged	1.12	1.08

4 Electrolyte replenishment

1 If the battery is in a fully charged state and one of the cells maintains a specific gravity reading which is 0.025 or more lower than the others, and a check of each cell has been made with a battery tester to check for short circuits (a four to seven second test should give a steady reading of between 1.2 to 1.8 volts), then it is likely that electrolyte has been lost from the cell with the low reading at some time.

2 Top the cell up with a solution of 1 part sulphuric acid to 2.5 parts of water. If the cell is already fully topped up draw some electrolyte out with a pipette.

3 When mixing the sulphuric acid and water NEVER ADD WATER TO SULPHURIC ACID - always pour the acid slowly onto the water in a glass container. IF WATER IS ADDED TO SULPHURIC ACID IT WILL EXPLODE.

4 Continue to top up the cell with the freshly made electrolyte and then re-charge the battery and check the hydrometer readings.

5 Battery - charging

1 In winter time when heavy demand is placed upon the battery such as when the starting from cold and much electrical equipment is continually in use, it is a good idea occasionally to have the battery fully charged from an external source at the rate of 3.5 to 4 amps. Always disconnect it from the car electrical circuit when charging.

2 Continue to charge the battery at this rate until no further rise in specific gravity is noted over a four hour period.

3 Alternatively, a trickle charger, charging at the rate of 1.5 amps, can be safely used overnight. Disconnect it before charging or you will damage the alternator.

4 Specially rapid 'boost' charges which are claimed to restore the power of the battery in 1 to 2 hours can cause damage to the battery plates through over-heating.

5 While charging the battery note that the temperature of the electrolyte should never exceed 100°F.

6 Make sure that your charging set and battery are set to the same voltage.

6 Vehicles fitted with a second battery

1 As an optional extra (M558) a second battery may be fitted, located under the right hand front seat. It may be used to provide extra power for the petrol-electric heater in cold climates, or for a two-way radio.

2 The installation is a major job which must be tackled by the VW agent, who has the drawings and parts.

3 When the engine is running, both batteries are charged at the same time. When the engine is switched off the second battery is automatically cut out of the main electrical system and is available for the heater or two-way radio. In this way the main vehicle battery is not run down.

4 Tests and adjustments of this system consist of checking the continuity of the wiring and the replacement of components. This task is best left to the VW agent.

7 Alternators - safety precautions

1 ALL alternator systems use a negative earth. Care must be taken not to reverse the battery connection or damage to the diodes will be extensive. Never run the alternator with the output wire disconnected.

2 ALWAYS disconnect the battery completely if an outsdide charging operation is contemplated (e.g. trickle charge). Disconnect the battery and the alternator output wire if welding is being done to the car.

3 DO NOT use test connections which can 'short' accidentally. The fuses will not blow, the diodes will burn out.

4 WHEN replacing a faulty alternator clear external faults first, or yet another alternator may be required.

8 Alternator - belt drive adjustment

1 The alternator is driven by a belt from the fan at the extreme rear of the engine (photo). The tension device is enclosed in the sheet metal covering of the engine. A small aperture is closed by a plastic seal. This is on the right side of the engine.
2 Remove this seal and the adjusting screw of the alternator drive belt is visible. This screw which is a socket head may be undone by use of a suitable key (photo). The alternator may now be moved about in the vertical plane, move it to the right or left until the belt can be depressed 9/16 ins. (15 mm), when pressed down with the thumb. Tighten the socket screw and replace the grommet.
3 A word of warning; the splined key necessary to undo this nut is not always available. A metric allan key may undo it, but do not twist too hard. If the splines are sheared off the alternator is in such a position that it may be necessary to take the engine out to undo this nut. So much depends upon the belt driving the alternator efficiently, and the job can be done so quickly with the proper tools, that it seems a false economy not to go to the VW agent if the proper tools are unobtainable. (photo).

9 Alternator - testing in situ

1 PRECAUTION – NEVER RUN THE ALTERNATOR WITH THE BATTERY DISCONNECTED.
2 The official method of testing involves the possession of a voltmeter (0-20v), ammeter (0-60 amps), a battery switch (recommended type SUN No. 7052 -003), and adjustable electric load and a tachometer (0 - 2,500 rpm). If you are in possession of this kit then all that is needed is the following table. A circuit diagram is given with operating instructions.

Alternator VW part no.	Max current amps.	Mean regulating volts.	Nominal output speed rpm.
021903023	35	14	2000-2200
021903023B	45	14	2200-2400
021903023A	55	14	2200

3 If the correct readings are not given, replace the voltage control. If that does not solve the problem the alternator must be removed and serviced. Do not prolong the test more that 30 seconds or the voltage regulator will overheat.
4 This state of affairs can be avoided by the purchase and installation of an ammeter permanently in the charging circuit. One can be had in kit form quite inexpensively with fitting instructions, and enables the driver to take action before the battery is flat.

10 Alternator - removal and replacement

1 On the earlier models before August 1971 it is not possible to remove the alternator without taking the engine from the chassis.
2 In August 1971 the rear engine cover plate was redesigned so that it is now fitted in two sections.
3 When working on the Variant, remove the silencer and the right lower warm air deflector (see Fig.1.5). Then remove the air cleaner and the hose between the heat exchanger and the heater blower. Remove the hoses for the dipstick and the bellows between the intake duct and the body.
4 Slacken off the fan belt and remove it (Section 7).
5 Remove the righthand engine cover plate, the muffler cover plate and the alternator cover plate (this is bolted to the fan housing).
6 Detach the cooling air elbow from the intake cover of the alternator, disconnect the alternator harness from the starter and voltage regulator and remove the alternator downwards.
7 On the Sedan it it not necessary to remove the muffler; the

8.1. The generator drive belt. This picture was taken with the engine removed

8.2. Removing the plug from the sheet metal housing to get at the alternator drive belt adjusting screw

8.3. Undoing the adjusting screw. Be careful (see text)

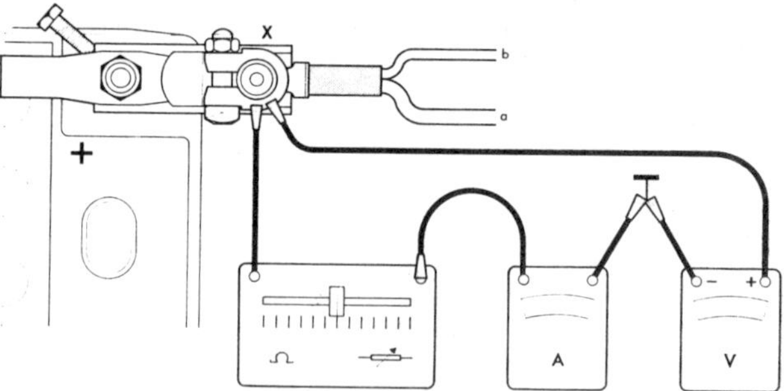

FIG. 10.1. CIRCUIT LAYOUT FOR TESTING CHARGING CIRCUIT IN SITU.

x is the battery switch (SUN electric No. 7052-003
a to starter
b to lighting switch terminal 30
Run up to 2000 rpm (with switch on) adjust load to 25 amps, operate switch to cut battery out and adjust to readings in the text 8.1.

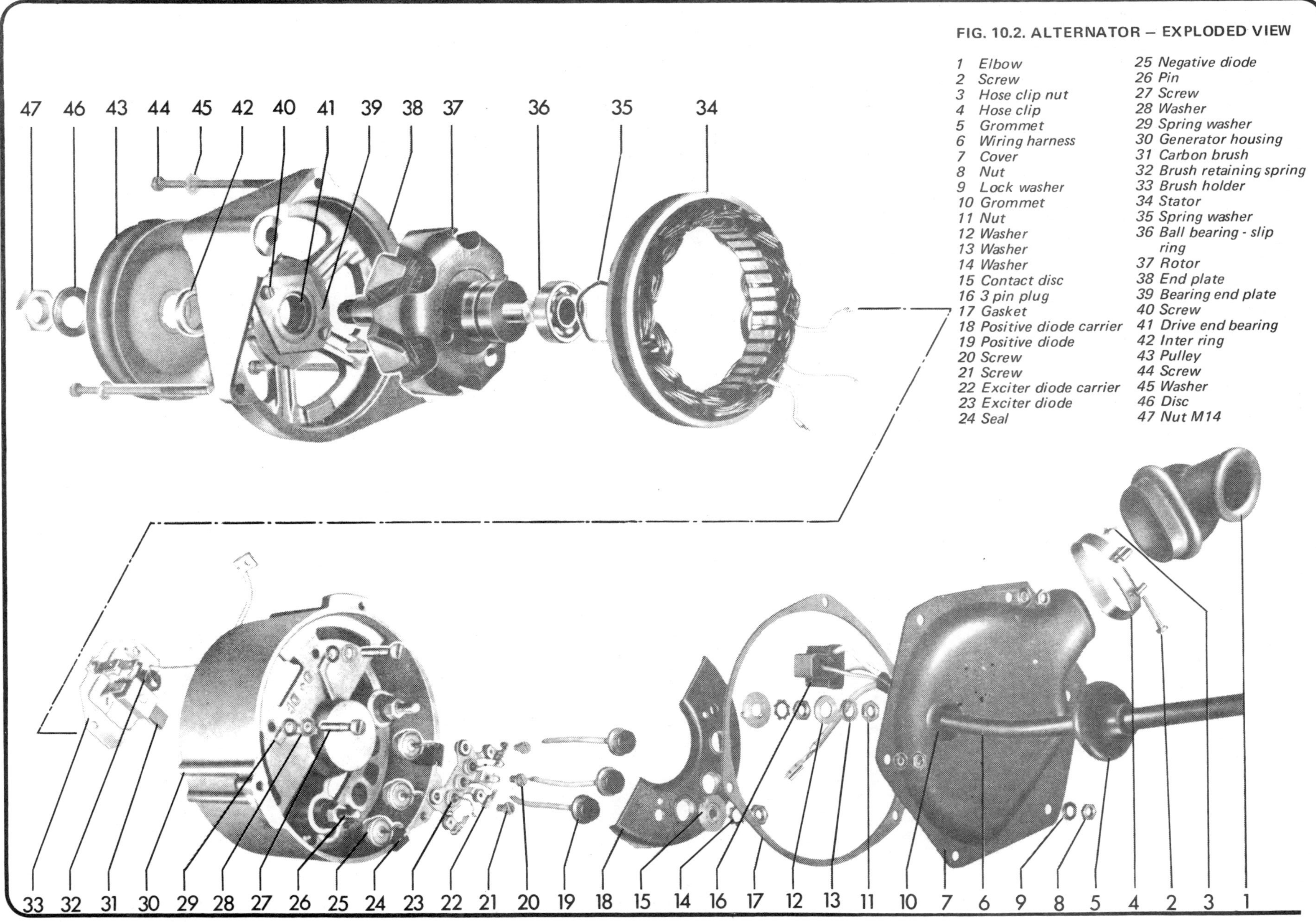

FIG. 10.2. ALTERNATOR – EXPLODED VIEW

1 *Elbow*
2 *Screw*
3 *Hose clip nut*
4 *Hose clip*
5 *Grommet*
6 *Wiring harness*
7 *Cover*
8 *Nut*
9 *Lock washer*
10 *Grommet*
11 *Nut*
12 *Washer*
13 *Washer*
14 *Washer*
15 *Contact disc*
16 *3 pin plug*
17 *Gasket*
18 *Positive diode carrier*
19 *Positive diode*
20 *Screw*
21 *Screw*
22 *Exciter diode carrier*
23 *Exciter diode*
24 *Seal*
25 *Negative diode*
26 *Pin*
27 *Screw*
28 *Washer*
29 *Spring washer*
30 *Generator housing*
31 *Carbon brush*
32 *Brush retaining spring*
33 *Brush holder*
34 *Stator*
35 *Spring washer*
36 *Ball bearing - slip ring*
37 *Rotor*
38 *End plate*
39 *Bearing end plate*
40 *Screw*
41 *Drive end bearing*
42 *Inter ring*
43 *Pulley*
44 *Screw*
45 *Washer*
46 *Disc*
47 *Nut M14*

same process is followed but the alternator comes out from above.
8 The removal of the alternator from the engine after the engine has been taken out of the vehicle is discussed in Chapter 1.

11 Alternator - repair

1 Refer to Fig.102. R=ad the whole section before starting work, as the job may become unnecessary.
2 The pulley is removed after the nut has been taken off. It may be necessary to use an extractor. Mark the position of the tensioning arm to the housing before removing it. (photo).
3 Pull the carbon brushes out with a wire hook. If they are pulled out far enough they can be held by the retaining spring.
4 Undo the housing screws (through bolts) ease the rubber grommet along the wiring harness and the sections of the alternator may be eased apart. The motor will remain in the end plate. Catch the nuts and washers off the housing screws and put them in a safe place.
5 Having got so far, clean away any dust with a new paint brush and a soft cloth, and have a good look round. Burnt out windings are usually obvious by the distinctive smell and charred wires, open circuits are hot. Wear on the slip rings is obvious, the diameter should not be less than 1.24 ins. (31.5 mm) and the ovality should not exceed 0.001 ins. (0.03 mm).

The minimum length of the carbon brushes is 0.5 in. (14 mm). These unfortunately are not obtainable separately and if renewal is required the complete brush holder must be purchased with brush installed.
6 At this stage a decision as to whether to go further must be made. The connections to the diodes must be unsoldered, unless this is done by an experienced electrician, who knows how to use long nosed pliers as a heat sink while unsoldering the wires, damage will be done to the diodes and they will have to be replaced.
7 When the positive and negative diodes and the stator windings have been disconnected from the connecting strip of the exciter diode carrier it will be possible to test the windings and diodes.
8 Further cleaning may now be done. Use only trichlorethylene or benzine and use it sparingly.
9 Check the diodes with a test lamp or meter and maximum voltage of 24 volts. Current should flow only one way, if it flows both ways the diode must be replaced. Keep the test current down to 0.8 mA and do not allow the diode to heat up.
10 Check the stator and rotor windings for earth shorts and open circuits. The rotor winding should have resistance 4 ohms $\pm$ 0.4 ohms. This is between slip rings. The stator windings between phases is 0.2 ohms $\pm$ 0.02 ohms for 021903023 and 021903023B, and 0.13 ohms $\pm$ 0.013 ohms for 021903023A.
11 Bearings may be renewed if a press is available. The rotor must be pressed out of the end plate to get at the end plate bearing, and the slip ring end bearing pulled off with a puller. New bearings should be installed
12 The diodes may be pressed out of the diode ring and new ones pressed in if required. Coat the diodes with silicon oil before pressing in, and be careful not to overheat them when reconnecting. Make a suitable tubular tool to press the diodes in and out.
13 You were asked to read the whole section before starting the job. The only thing to watch on reassembly is to re-route the brush connections the same way as they were installed when dismantled. The pulley nut is tightened to 29 lbs ft. (4 mkg). The alternator must now be tested. The figures are given in Section 9 but a more detailed test should be done on an oscilloscope if the alternator is to be absolutely checked. This must be done by an auto-electrical firm.
14 There is a lot of work entailed in removing and replacing the alternator. If this is not to be wasted then the component must be 100%, before reinstallation. The experienced electrical engineer will no doubt be able to overhaul the alternator if he has the time and the equipment AND the spares available. The author's advice to the average owner is to settle for a repair either by the VW agent or a reputable auto-electrical firm. It will save a lot of time.

11.2. The alternator being removed from the engine

12 Starter motor - testing, removal and replacement

1 On the Volkswagen the starter is an inaccessible article and short of checking that the mounting bolts are tight and the electrical connections properly made to the solenoid, there is nothing else to be done except take it out if it malfunctions. If the starter fails to kick at all ascertain that current is being fed from the starter switch to the solenoid. This can be done by connecting a suitably long lead to test each of the terminals on the solenoid in turn. Connect the other end via a voltmeter or bulb to earth. When connected to the smaller terminal (the lead from the ignition switch), there should be an indication on the bulb or voltmeter when the starter switch is operated. If there is not then check the other end of the wire at the starter switch terminal in the same way. If there is no voltage then the fault is not with the starter. Then connect the lead to the larger terminal on the solenoid.

Normally the solenoid can be heard to move but this does not necessarily mean that it is switching the main current to the starter. If the solenoid plunger can be heard to move yet no voltage is recorded at the large terminal then the solenoid is defective.
2 The starter is held by a bolt at the top and a stud and nut at the bottom. The bolt head is not hexagonal. It is circular with a flat which engages in a recess in the starter mounting flange. To remove it. The lower stud nut is accessible under the car (photo).
3 From underneath the car, pull off the small lead at the connection and then undo the nut securing the large cable. All this must be done mainly by feel. Do not confuse the two large terminal nuts on the solenoid. The lower one connects the strap between solenoid and starter. (photo).
4 Remove the lower nut and the starter can be lifted out.
5 Replacement is a reversal of the removal procedure. Before fitting, grease the end of the pinion shaft. It runs in a plain bush in the engine crankcase casting.

13 Starter motor - dismantling and reassembly

1 Five types of starter motor have been fitted to the Type 4 since its inception. The early models had either a VW product (VW 111911023A) or a BOSCH (311911023B). These both worked at 12v consuming 0.7 HP. The Automatic gearbox vehicle had a slightly heavier starter again BOSCH (311911023A) which consumed 0.8 HP. Later models 311911023 C and D have aluminium field coils, the latter with a short housing.

Figures 10.3 and 10.4 show exploded views of the VW and BOSCH starters which are similar in construction.

The text which follows refers to the BOSCH but applies

equally to the VW.
2 Clean the exterior of the starter carefully and arrange to hold it in a vice. Remove the cover plate to give access to the brushes. If these do not protude beyond their holders renewal is necessary which calls for further dismantling.

Undo the nut connecting the strap between the solenoid and the starter and then the two screws holding the solenoid to the end frame, (photos).
3 The solenoid can now be unhooked from the operating lever inside the end frame. (photo).
4 If the solenoid only is faulty this is as far as it is necessary to go. A new solenoid unit can be fitted now.
5 Remove the two screws holding the end cover cap, (photo).
6 Slide out the 'U' clip and remove the shims from the end of the shaft. These shims control the endfloat, (photos).
7 Remove the two through bolts from the end cover and the end cover may then be taken off giving access to the commutator brushes, (photos).
8 Hook up the springs holding the carbon brushes in the holders and push them to one side so that the pressure is relieved. The yoke complete with the brush holder mounting plate may then be drawn off with the armature. Watch out for the washers on the end of the shaft, (photo).
9 To renew the brushes, two may be detached by simply removing the screws whilst the other two need to be cut off and new ones soldered to the braided leads. Leave sufficient length to solder the new ones onto easily.

10 To remove the end frame from the drive end of the shaft first push back the stop ring with a suitable tube so that the jump ring underneath can be released from its groove. The end cover assembly complete with the pinion may then be drawn off.

11 The pinion drive should turn one-way only inside the clutch easily. If it does not the whole unit needs renewing. The pinion teeth should not be badly worn or chipped. The yoke of the pinion operating lever should be a good fit in the groove of the pinion sleeve.

12 Reassembly is a reversal of the dismantling procedure. Thoroughly grease the moving parts of the pinion operating lever first. When replacing the yoke engage the cut-out and tongue correctly (photo).

13 The carbon brushes should all be held up in their holders and this can be achieved if the springs are jammed against the sides of the brushes. The armature has two washers, on the end of these, which must be fitted so that the thrust washer goes on first and the insulating washer after that.
14 When the pinion stop ring is refitted stake it into position over the jump ring after the latter has been fitted in its groove.

15 When refitting the solenoid ensure the plunger hooked end is securely placed over the operating lever.

16 The screw heads and joint faces of the commutator end cover, the solenoid and end frame should all be treated with sealing compound to keep water out. Use the Volkswagen product specially for this if possible. It is important that it is not applied too thickly, otherwise clearance distances may be upset. If, after reassembly, the endfloat of the shaft exceeds 0.012 inch it should be reduced by adding shim washers under the U retaining clip on the end of the armature shaft under the small cover.

17 Before reinstalling the motor it is well worthwhile checking that it works first. Clamp the starter body firmly in a vice and take the battery out of the car. Connect a heavy cable from the large solenoid terminal to the '+' terminal of the battery and an equally heavy one from the body of the starter to the negative terminal on the battery. Then use a piece of smaller wire to connect the '+' terminal of the battery to the small blade terminal on the solenoid. When this is done the pinion should shoot forward and the motor revolve. Note: Although the wires in this test do not need to be as heavy as those used in the car, if they are too small they will heat up.

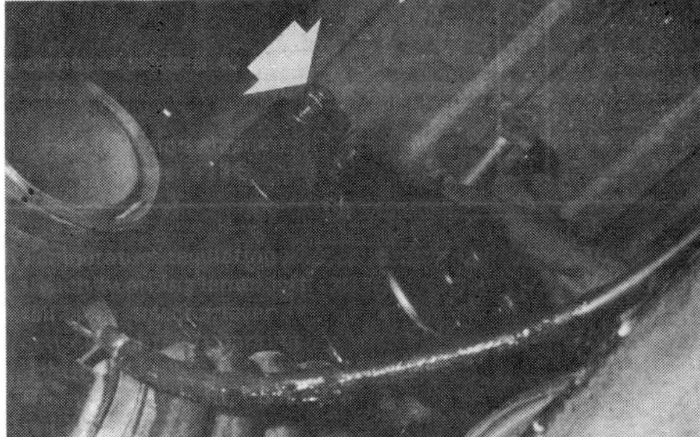

12.2. Removing the starter top bolt, note the top bolt head and the terminal for the main cable connection (arrowed)

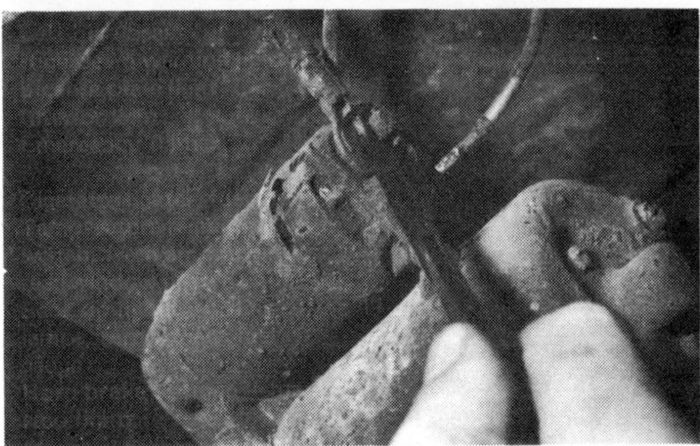

12.3. Do not confuse the two nuts on the solenoid

13.2a. Undoing the connection strap terminal nut

13.2b. Removing the solenoid retaining screws

13.3. Unhook the solenoid from the operating lever

13.5. Remove the end cover cap screws

13.6a. Remove the U clip from the end of the shaft. . . . .

13.6b. . . . .. and the shim washers

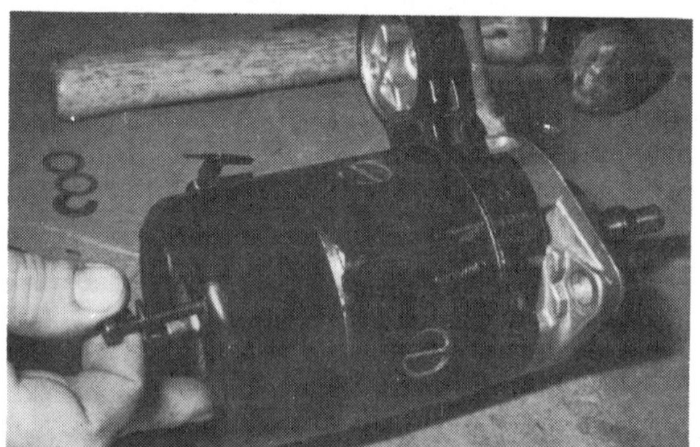

13.7a. Remove the through bolts (housing screws)

13.7b. Take off the end cover

13.8. Lift the yoke and brush holder off the armature

13.12. Refit the yoke so that the tongue and cut-out fit together

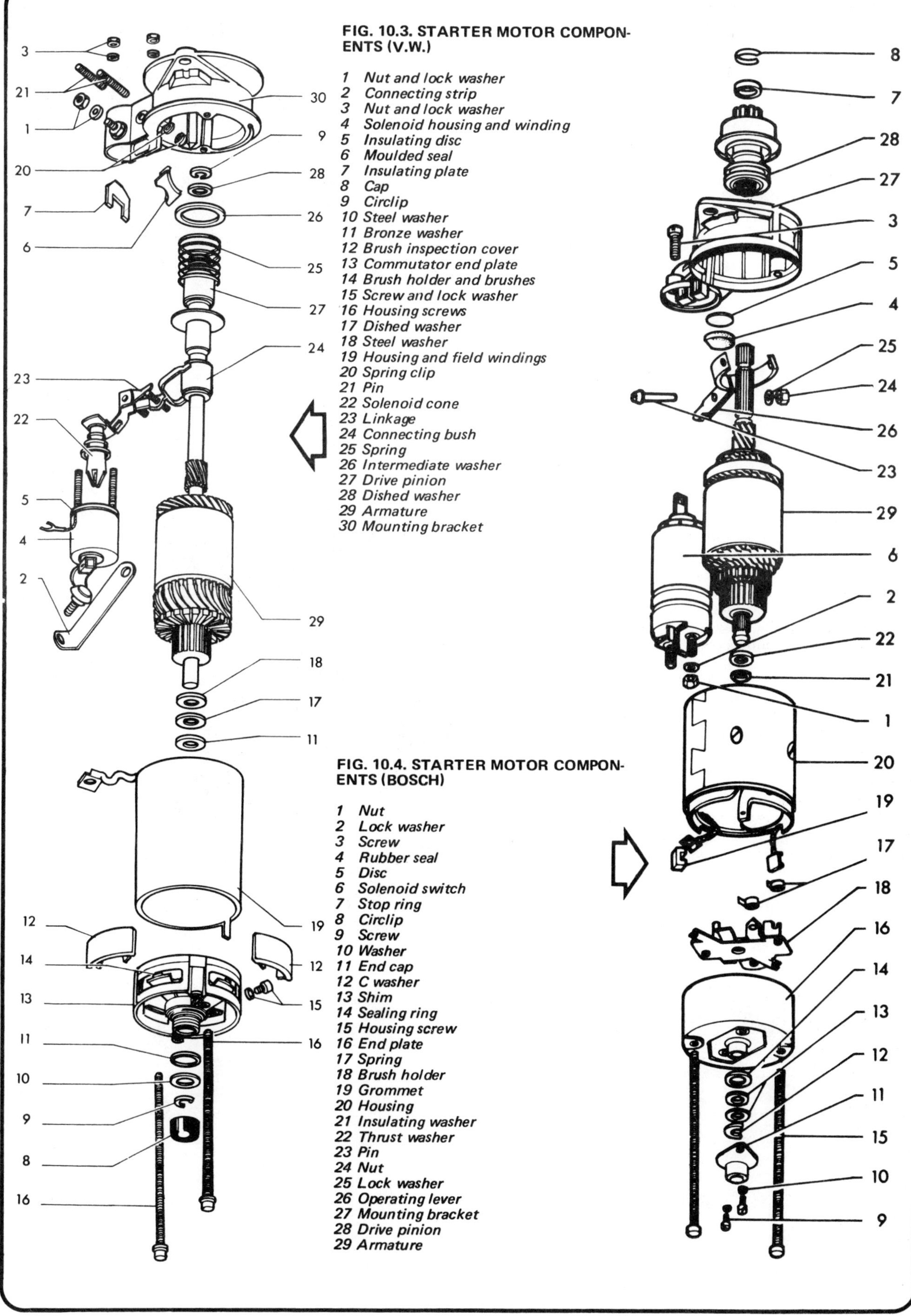

FIG. 10.3. STARTER MOTOR COMPONENTS (V.W.)

1 Nut and lock washer
2 Connecting strip
3 Nut and lock washer
4 Solenoid housing and winding
5 Insulating disc
6 Moulded seal
7 Insulating plate
8 Cap
9 Circlip
10 Steel washer
11 Bronze washer
12 Brush inspection cover
13 Commutator end plate
14 Brush holder and brushes
15 Screw and lock washer
16 Housing screws
17 Dished washer
18 Steel washer
19 Housing and field windings
20 Spring clip
21 Pin
22 Solenoid cone
23 Linkage
24 Connecting bush
25 Spring
26 Intermediate washer
27 Drive pinion
28 Dished washer
29 Armature
30 Mounting bracket

FIG. 10.4. STARTER MOTOR COMPONENTS (BOSCH)

1 Nut
2 Lock washer
3 Screw
4 Rubber seal
5 Disc
6 Solenoid switch
7 Stop ring
8 Circlip
9 Screw
10 Washer
11 End cap
12 C washer
13 Shim
14 Sealing ring
15 Housing screw
16 End plate
17 Spring
18 Brush holder
19 Grommet
20 Housing
21 Insulating washer
22 Thrust washer
23 Pin
24 Nut
25 Lock washer
26 Operating lever
27 Mounting bracket
28 Drive pinion
29 Armature

14 Headlamps - dismantling and reassembling

1 Three patterns of headlamps have been used since the 411 first came onto the market.
2 The earliest type (Fig.10.5) had an elongated reflector held in position with springs and adjusting screws. To get at the bulb and adjusting screws the cover is pulled off at the two bottom lugs. The bulb is twisted out in the normal way. Do not handle the bolt with bare fingers. It is not necessary to remove the whole lamp to renew the lens. The front rim is held on by two fillister headed screws.
3 The second type consists of sealed beam dual headlamps. The outer sealed beam has a low beam and a high beam filament. The inner lamp has a high beam filament only. The general arrangement is shown in Fig. 10.6.

When removing, the front surround is held in place by the two fillister headed screws. The back cover is held in place by knurled knob. As the name indicates the units are sealed and must be replaced complete. The aiming adjusters are knurled knobs and the inner beam is carried in an aiming ring.

When dismantling first disconnect the low beam guide for the flat terminal. The springs for the locators should be removed and installed with long nosed pliers. The only difference between the left and right locators is the position of the aiming screws. The aiming screws in the aiming ring are at the top right when looking at the headlamp from the rear. The spring for the locator is at the bottom left.
4 The third type of headlamp installed in Type 4 from chassis No. 4102000001 has halogen dual headlamps. The outer beam is the dipped beam and the inner one the main beam. The parking light is installed in the dipped beam insert, the lens, reflector, and bulb holder are sealed in one unit but it is possible to renew the bulb. Fig.10.7 gives the general arrangement. The surround may be removed by taking away the two screws. The rear cover comes away when the knurled screw is removed from it (photo).
5 The view at the rear now discloses a number of springs. Grip these with a pair of pliers and ease them away from the casing (photo).
6 When they are all cleared the whole headlamp assembly will come forward for examination and servicing (photo).
7 There is no need to remove the assembly to renew bulbs. Pull off the cap (photo) unship the clip and the bulb may be withdrawn. (photo).
8 The headlamps, whichever kind, should be dismantled once a year and inspected for rust. Faulty seals and rusty parts should be replaced before the corrosion spreads. Bulbs should be replaced at yearly intervals. The more expensive sealed beam and QH units should be tested at the local agent for efficiency. It is surprising how quickly the efficiency of lights deteriorates.
9 A check of the actual voltage received at the bulb holder may startle the owner of an elderly model. The voltage has been known to fall 12% due to corroded switches and faulty connections.

14.4. Undo the knurled screw and pull off the back

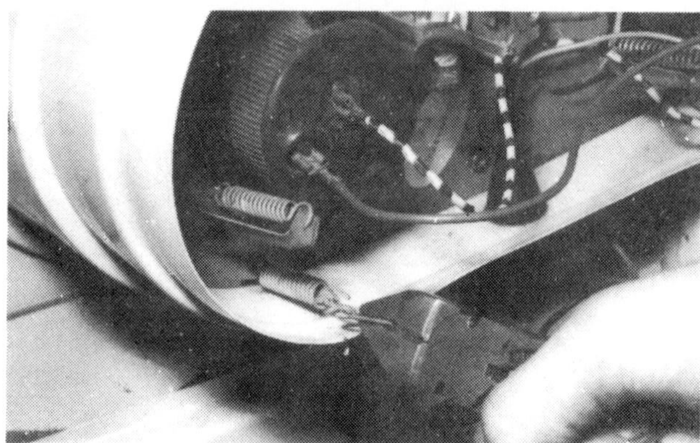
14.5. Grip the spring firmly and ease it away from the case

14.6. The assembly removed to the front

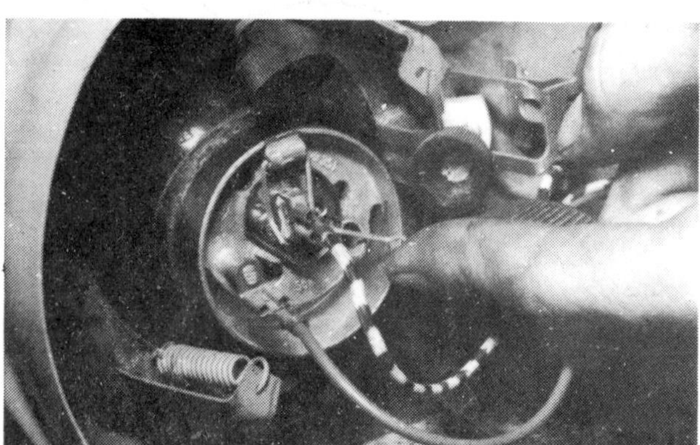
14.7a. Undo the cap and remove the clip. . . . .

14.7b. . . . . the bulb may now be withdrawn

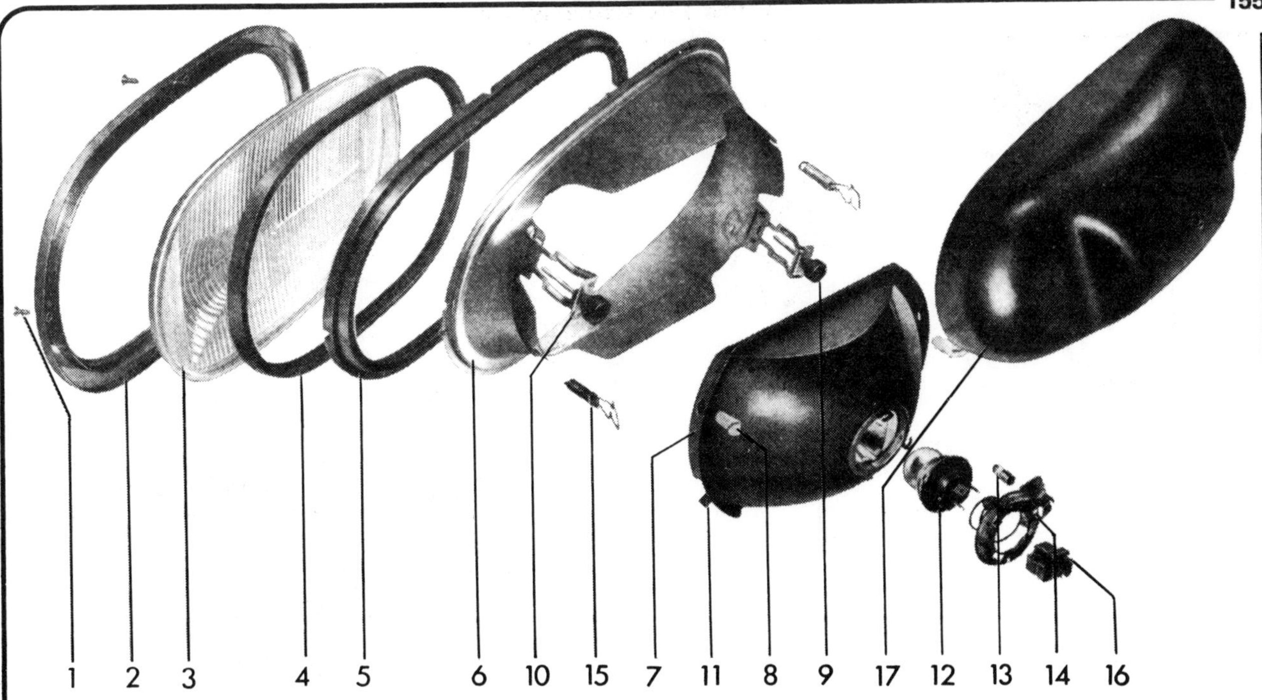

FIG. 10.5. HEADLAMPS – EARLY TYPES – CONVENTIONAL DOUBLE FILAMENT SINGLE BULB (12 v. 45/40w) AND PARKING LIGHT

1 Screw
2 Rim
3 Lens
4 Seal
5 Seal
6 Reflector housing
7 Reflector
8 Adjusting screw support
9 Adjusting screw lateral
10 Adjusting screw vertical
11 Rubber bush
12 Bulb 45/40w
13 Bulb 4w
14 Cap
15 Spring
16 Flat terminal guide
17 Cover

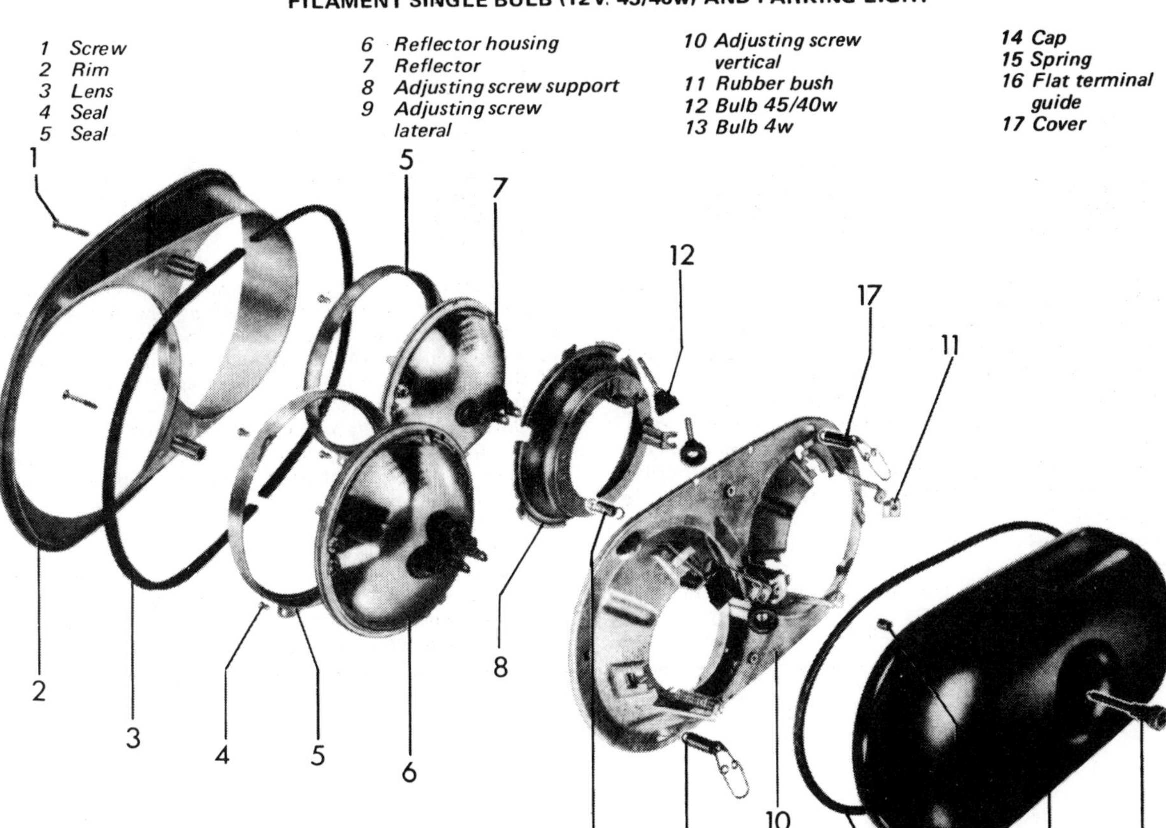

FIG. 10.6. HEADLAMPS – SEALED BEAM DUAL HEADLAMPS

1 M4 screw
2 Surround
3 Seal
4 Screw M4
5 Retainer
6 Low beam sealed unit
7 High beam sealed unit
8 Aiming ring
9 Spring
10 Locator
11 Screw M5
12 Aiming screw
13 Seal
14 Cover
15 Cover holding screw
16 Seal
17 Spring

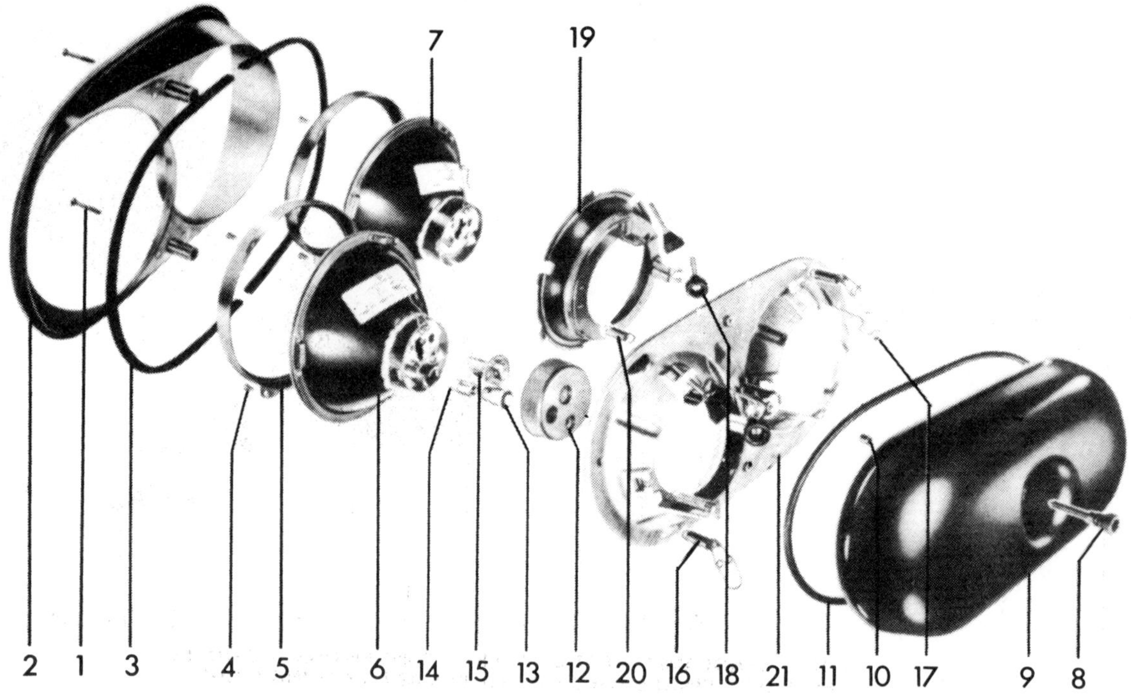

FIG.10.7. HEADLAMPS - HALOGEN DUAL TYPE
(Fitted to Type 4 from chassis 4102 000 001)

1 *Screw*
2 *Surround*
3 *Seal*
4 *Screw*
5 *Retainer*
6 *Low beam insert*
7 *High beam insert*
8 *Screw*
9 *Cap*
10 *Sealing ring*
11 *Seal for cap*
12 *Cap*
13 *Parking light bulb holder*
14 *Parking light bulb 12v 4w*
15 *Halogen bulb 12v/55watt type A.1*
16 *Spring*
17 *Plate*
18 *Adjusting screw*
19 *Adjusting ring*
20 *Spring*
21 *Support*

15 Headlamps - beam aiming

1 Regulations vary from country to country so no attempt is made in this manual to lay down hard and fast rules.

2 By far the best way to have the lights adjusted is at the VW agent, who will do the job properly with the correct equipment.

3 However, if this is not possible, a rough and ready way of doing the job is shining the lights on a wall after dark and adjusting them one by one to fit the local regulations. The car should be on level ground and loaded as it normally is, i.e. driver only, or some seats occupied. Bounce it up and down to settle the springs.

4 For the single bulb early type lights 5 metres from the wall, for the later types 7 to 10 metres.

5 Mark a vertical line on the wall to correspond with the vertical centre line of the car. Measure the distance between the centre line of the car and the centre lines of the lights being adjusted and transfer these distances to the wall so that there are now two more vertical lines representing the vertical centre lines of the lights. Mark a horizontal line representing the horizontal centre line of the lights.

6 Cover up the lights not being adjusted and switch on the light to be adjusted. By using the vertical and horizontal adjusters the beam of light may be adjusted to the area defined as correct. It will be given in relation to the lines you have drawn.

7 Where the same lamp has main and dip filaments in the same frame adjust the main beam only.

8 A diagram for the single and sealed beam type as used in UK is given at Fig.10.8. A diagram similar to this should be constructed. Failing this trial and error on a straight deserted road after dark is the only answer.

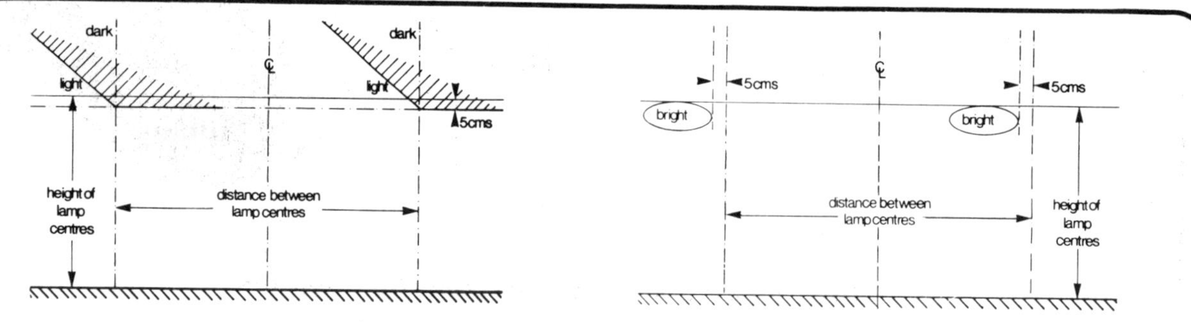

Fig.10.8. Diagram to show the light pattern for adjusting headlamps in U.K. for R.H drive. Similar diagrams should be made to suit local regulations
Left - Single bulb unit — main beam
Right - Sealed beam unit — main beam

16 Side, parking, interior, brake and indicator lights

1 The bulb table is given in the specifications to this chapter.
2 The method of removing these lights is shown in the photos below.
3 Wiring and switching arrangements are straightforward except for the back-up light. The cable for this light joins the reversing light fuse box in the engine compartment.
4 The photographs are for a 411 Variant. The number-plate light on the Sedan is even simpler still. Remove the two screws and the bulb is accessible.
5 The positions of the lights have been altered on the 412 but the method of access is the same.
6 The front turn signal lights on vehicles destined for USA have slightly larger lens and there may be a parking light filament in the turn signal bulb.
7 On USA vehicles there is also a bulb for the rear side marking light. It is in the same compartment as the back-up light. There may also be a front side marker light on the fender. Remove the two screws and the bulb is accessible.
8 The lamps should be checked regularly to be sure that they operate properly. Do not handle bulbs or reflectors with the bare hand, use a clean cloth. If the weather seals are hard or distorted, renew them. Check the points where cables enter the holder to ensure that the rubber seals are keeping the water out. Replace cracked lens as soon as possible, cover up broken lens with polythene and tape in an emergency to keep water from the reflector.
9 For countries where regulations state that the license plate light must go on when the headlight flasher is operated e.g. USA, a special relay is fitted, this is located beneath the fuse box at the right hand in models up to July 1970 and on the left (the others are turn signal/emergency relay and combined relay) for vehicles after July 1970.

16.2a. The rear number plate light is dismantled by undoing the three screws and pulling the light from the body

16.2b. The bulbs are then easily removed

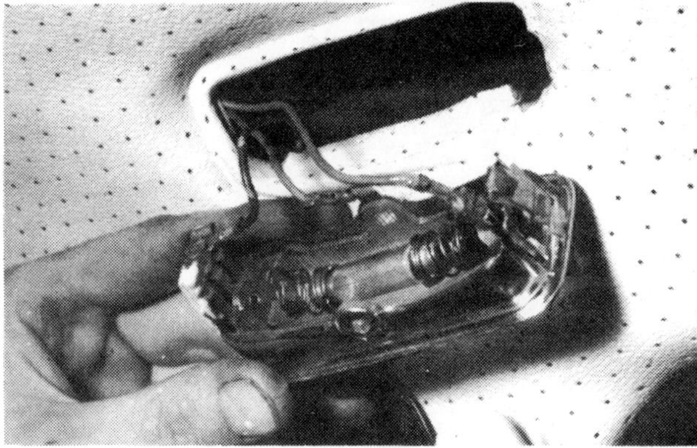
16.2c. The interior light is prised from the ceiling trim to give access to the festoon type bulb

16.2d. The double unit at the rear has two covers. This one is removed by undoing two screws and gives access to the (inner) back up light and (outer) brake light and rear light

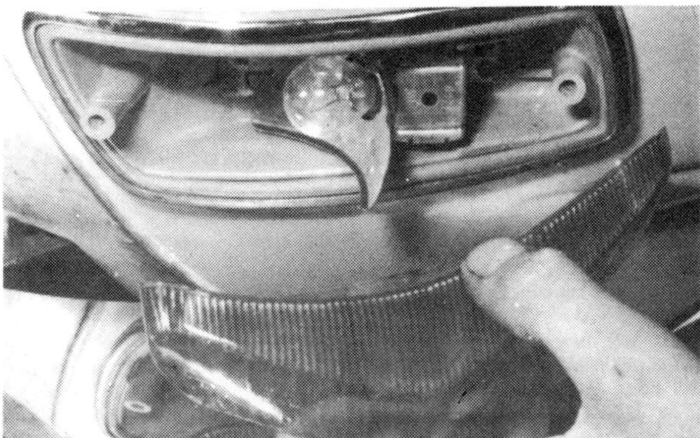
16.2e. The other cover (two more screws) gives access to the turn signal light

16.2f. The front turn signal (two screws) light. When coupled with sealed beam equipment this has also the parking light and side marker bulb

17 Steering column - turn signal and wiper switch

1 The Type 4 has had three different arrangements in three years. From its introduction to Chassis No. 4112000000 it used the column identical with the Type 3. In August, 1969 at Chassis No. 4112000001 the column illustrated at Fig.10.9 was installed. The two types vary in minor details only.

In August, 1971 the assembly shown in Fig.10.10 was installed, this incorporates the wiper and washer controls which were formerly on the dashboard. A different pattern was installed in August 1970. Altogether there are several combinations of switch gear on the column but they are all straightforward enough.

2 The horn pad at the top does not seem to have any fastening. It is pulled off by hand from the three dowels underneath. The battery should be disconnected before working on the column.

3 The steering wheel is removed by undoing the nut at the top. In the later version a rubber plug must be removed from the nut before undoing it. The gap between the wheel and the column switch must be between 2 and 4 mm.(0.08 to 0.16").

4 When dismantling the earlier version remove the steering wheel, pull the plug for the turn signal switch out at the bottom of the column switch, remove the screws for the turn signal switch and pull the switch out upwards with guide rail for wires.

5 When reinstalling the older type ensure that the spacer sleeves for the securing screws are put in correctly. Locate the wires in the guide rail and fix the terminal tabs in the retainers. The switch lever must be in a central position or the cancelling tongue will foul the cam in the switch.

6 On the later types the guide channel is in two pieces, held together by plastic hooks. These must be taken out very carefully.

The guide channels may then be taken from the locating slots in the wiper switch. When assembling be careful not to crush the turn signal cables with the wiper switch.

The washer control valve may have its hose secured by a clip, or it may be just pushed on. If the hose clip is removed during overhaul it must not be replaced. A special piece of 'double hose' should be obtained from the dealer and fitted over the washer hose. The washer hose should then be pushed hard up to the enlarged section of the washer valve pipe, and the 'double hose' then pushed over this enlarged section. Use a drop of water as a lubricant, but nothing else.

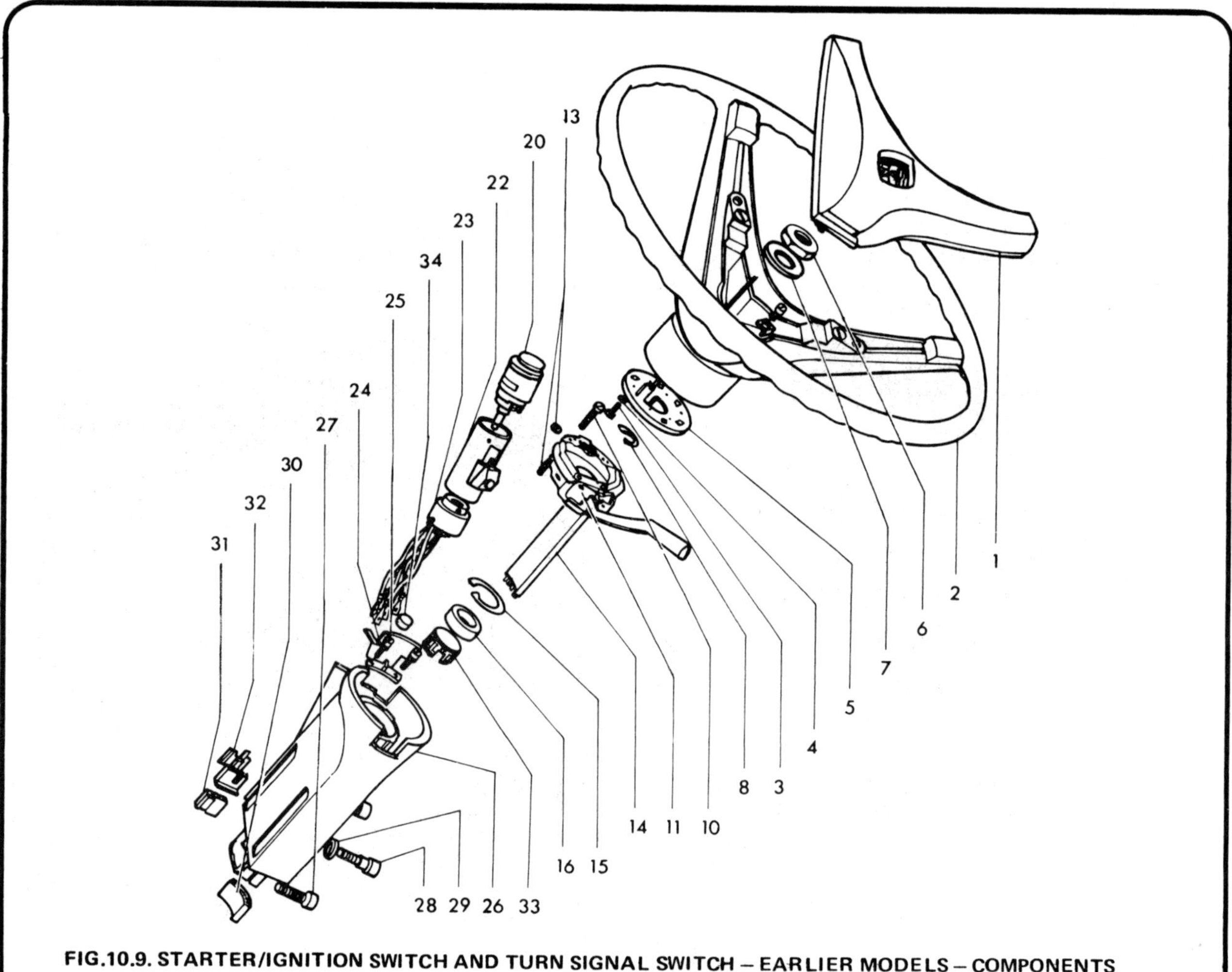

FIG.10.9. STARTER/IGNITION SWITCH AND TURN SIGNAL SWITCH – EARLIER MODELS – COMPONENTS

1 Padded cover
2 Steering wheel
3 Screw
4 Lock washer
5 Cancelling ring
6 Nut
7 Spring washer
8 Column circlip
9 Spring for turn signal switch
10 Screw for turn signal switch
11 Turn signal switch
12 Dimmett contact
13 Spacer sleeve and washer
14 Guide rail for wires
15 Circlip for bearing
16 Bearing
20 Lock cylinder
22 Steering lock
23 Ignition/starter switch
24 Screw and washer
25 Retainer
26 Column siwtch cover
27 Clamp bolt
28 Socket head screw
29 Spring washer
30 Plug for turn signal switch
31 Plug for starter switch
32 Guide for wires
33 Contact ring
34 Insulating caps for screws

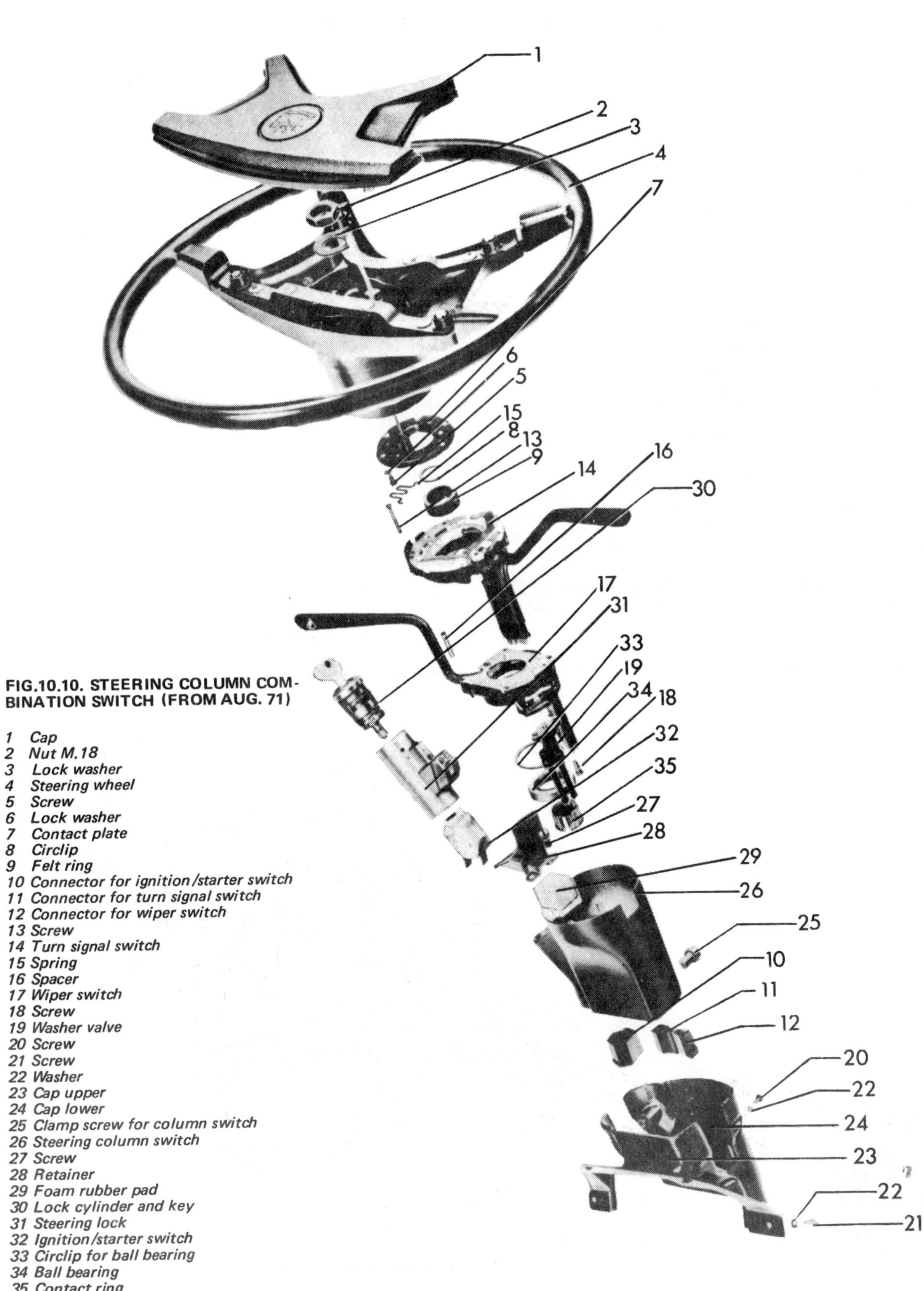

FIG.10.10. STEERING COLUMN COMBINATION SWITCH (FROM AUG. 71)

1 Cap
2 Nut M.18
3 Lock washer
4 Steering wheel
5 Screw
6 Lock washer
7 Contact plate
8 Circlip
9 Felt ring
10 Connector for ignition/starter switch
11 Connector for turn signal switch
12 Connector for wiper switch
13 Screw
14 Turn signal switch
15 Spring
16 Spacer
17 Wiper switch
18 Screw
19 Washer valve
20 Screw
21 Screw
22 Washer
23 Cap upper
24 Cap lower
25 Clamp screw for column switch
26 Steering column switch
27 Screw
28 Retainer
29 Foam rubber pad
30 Lock cylinder and key
31 Steering lock
32 Ignition/starter switch
33 Circlip for ball bearing
34 Ball bearing
35 Contact ring

18 Steering column - steering lock and ignition switch

1 On models prior to August 1971 it is necessary to remove the steering wheel and take the column switch off (see Section 17) before the ignition starter switch can be serviced.
2 Remove the retainer, press the starter switch out of the guide and disconnect the cables (photo). After pulling out the lock cylinder and the steering starter lock, remove the retaining screw and pull the starter switch out the the rear.
3 When replacing put the switch in the lock so that the screw can be fitted and the rest is the reverse of dismantling.
4 On models after August 1970 there is an extra problem. An additional contact in the starter switch ensures that the head-lamps will not work when the ignition is not switched off.
5 Models after August 1971 are easier to service. It is not necessary to remove the steering column switch. Remove the turn signal and wiper switches and the steering column ignition lock and switch may be removed. This type has a plug type connection to the cable harness , which enable it to be removed separately.

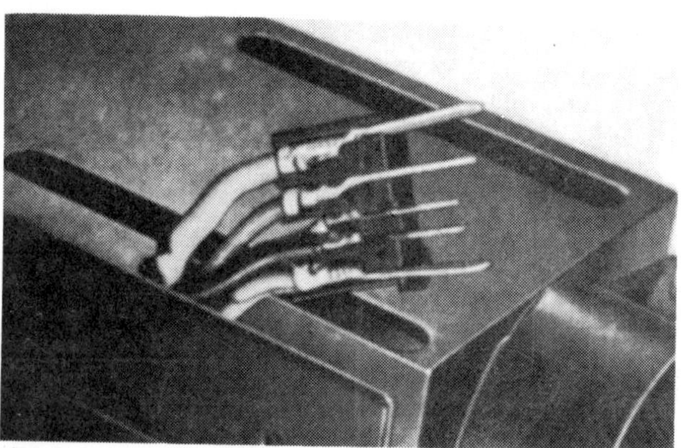

18.2. Press the plug out of the guide and take the cables out of the plug

19 Electric horn circuit

1 The horn is mounted behind the front bumper. It must be secure on its bracket but must not touch the bodywork.
2 The electrical circuit is shown at Fig. 10.11.
3 If the horn does not work first check the fuse, then with the ignition switched on check with a voltmeter that the correct voltage is reaching the horn terminals.

If this is not so check the wire back to fuse 12 on the fuse box. Next check that the earth return wire from the horn to the steering wheel switch is maintaining continuity. This is a problem as the circuit has to reach the steering column, pass through the horn switch and contact the moving steering shaft to earth, thus requiring an earth wire to bridge the flexible coupling which is also an insulator. The best way to check this is to pull off the horn pad on the steering wheel and using a long lead and a voltmeter, test the circuit from the horn terminal to the contact on the steering wheel, then test the other side of the horn switch to earth.
4 If the circuit is found to be faulty then there is no short cut. The column must be dismantled and the wiring checked. However check the wiring external to the column first.
5 The horn itself may be faulty. It can be tested by supplying 12V across its terminals direct. As a last resort the adjusting screw at the back may be turned, but it rarely does any good. Take the horn to an agent or a reputable electrical auto repair shop.

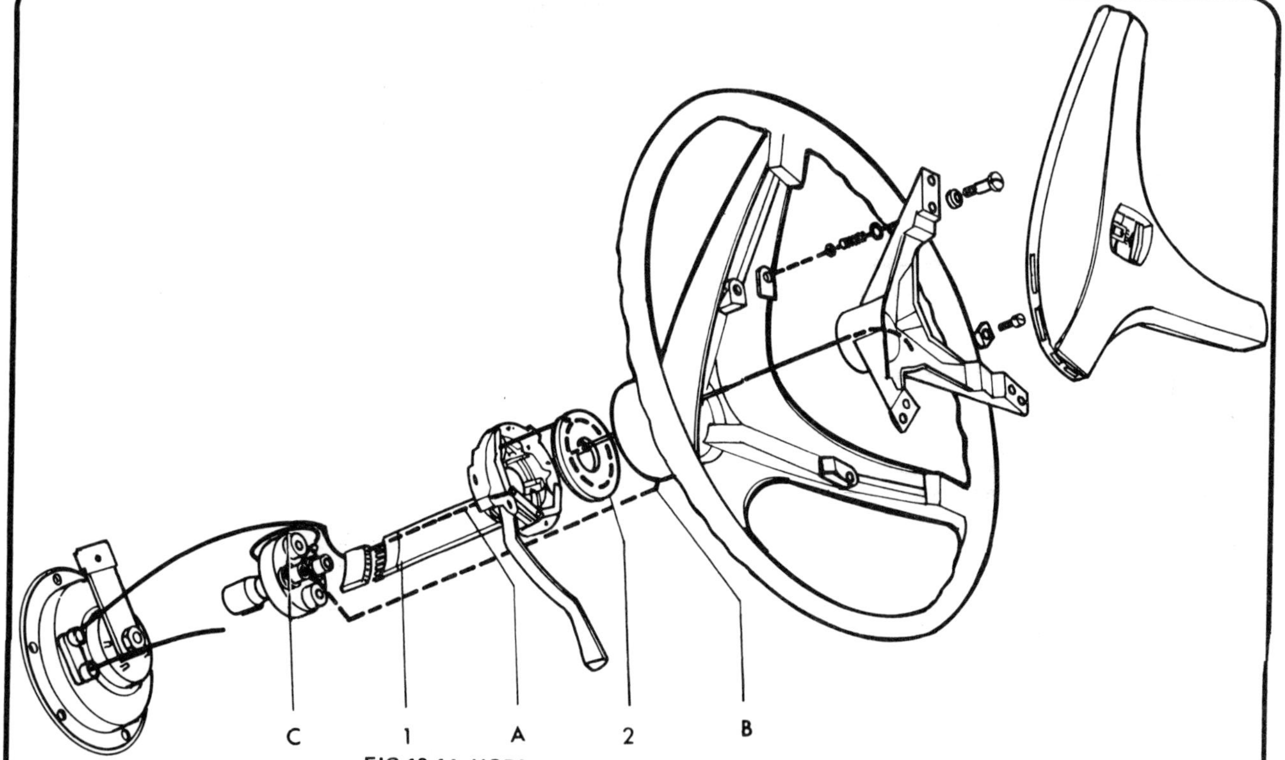

C 1 A 2 B

FIG.10.11. HORN – EARTH WIRE CIRCUIT (SEE 19)

A *Earth wire from horn*
C *Earth wire through shaft coupling*
B *Steering column*
1 *Part of turn signal switch with horn contact*
2 *Slip ring*

20 Stop lamp circuit - fault finding

1 The stop lamps light up when the brakes are applied. To achieve this two hydraulically operated switches are connected in parallel to the stop lamps at the rear and when the pressure in the master cylinder rises sufficiently high the lamp is lit by the pressure switch being closed. Even if one system fails the other will still illuminate the stop light.
2 Whilst both brake circuits are functioning correctly the diaphragms of both brake light switches are under equal pressure when the brake pedal is pressed, both switches are closed and there is no circuit to contact 81a. The warning light stays unlit.
3 However if one circuit is not functioning the pressure on the switch in that circuit will drop and the contact pin will not be depressed by the diaphragm. Thus the circuit will be completed via contact 82a - 81 of the effective brake circuit and via contact 81 - 81a of the ineffective circuit and the warning lamp will light up. Fig. 10.12 refers.
4 If the light does not work at the rear check the fuse, the bulbs and the connections. Switch on the ignition and pull the leads off the hydraulic switch and touch them together. If the light comes on then the hydraulic switch is at fault. Repeat for the other switch.
5 To replace a switch, screw it out, catching any brake fluid that may spill. Screw in the new switch (torque 18 lbs ft), reconnect the wires and then bleed the system right through.

21 Windscreen wipers - fault finding

1 If the wipers do not work when they are switched on, first check the fuse. If this is sound then there is either an open circuit in the wiring or switch, the wiper motor is faulty, or the pivot spindles or linkages may be binding.
2 If the wipers work intermittently then suspect a short circuit in the motor or a poor contact to earth. The earth is connected at the main mounting screw. Alternatively, the armature shaft endfloat adjustment may be too tight or the wiper linkage may be binding.
3 Should the wipers not stop when they are turned off there must be a short circuit in the switch or wiring.
4 Two circuit diagrams are given, the second one for 'flick wipers' at Figs. 10.13 and 10.14.

22 Windscreen wipers - removal of frame and motor

1 Disconnect the battery earth cable, unscrew the cap nuts on both wiper arms and take the arms off.
2 Remove the bearing cover and unscrew the hegagon nut. Now take off the steering column cover trim and the hoses between the fresh air control box and the vents. Take out the clock, there is no need to disconnect the clock cables.
3 Remove the left fresh air and defroster vent and take the

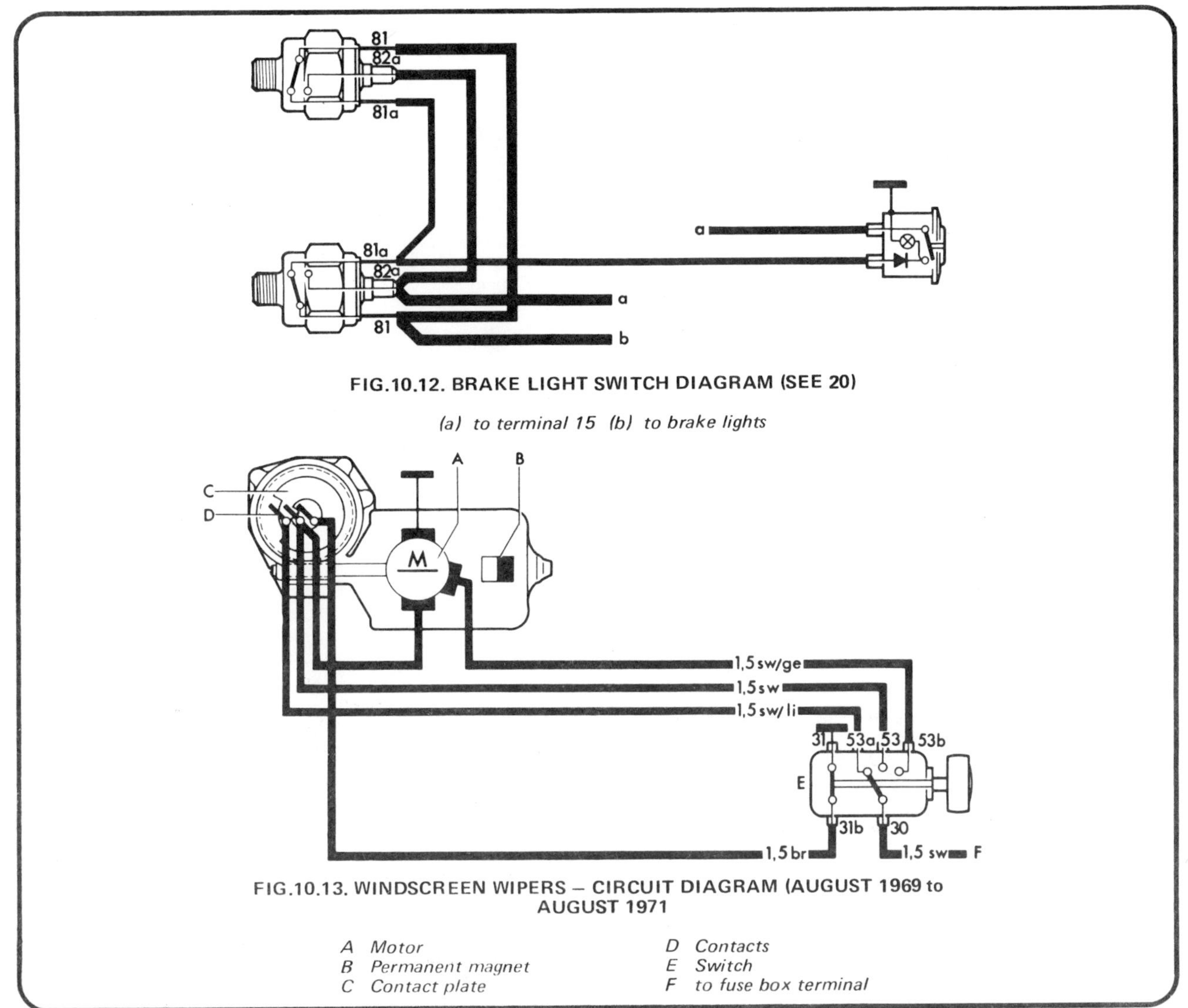

FIG.10.12. BRAKE LIGHT SWITCH DIAGRAM (SEE 20)

(a) to terminal 15 (b) to brake lights

FIG.10.13. WINDSCREEN WIPERS – CIRCUIT DIAGRAM (AUGUST 1969 to AUGUST 1971

A Motor
B Permanent magnet
C Contact plate
D Contacts
E Switch
F to fuse box terminal

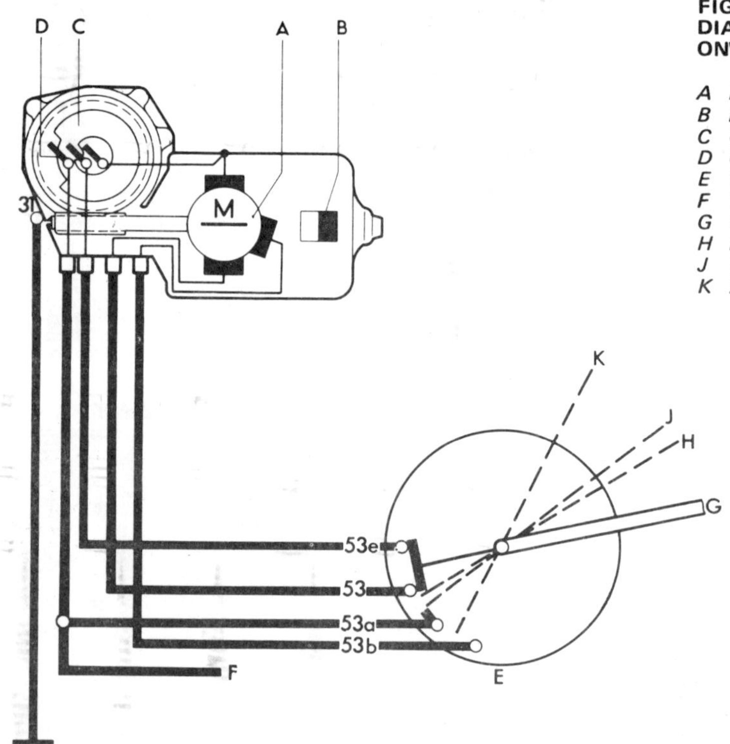

FIG.10.14. WINDSCREEN WIPER – CIRCUIT DIAGRAM – FLICK WIPING AUGUST 1971 ONWARDS

A Motor
B Permanent magnet
C Contact plate
D Contacts
E Wiper switch
F To fuse box terminal F
G Wiper switch lever
H Flick wiping position
J 1st speed
K 2nd speed

hose off the vent. It is now possible to see the screw securing the wiper motor. Undo and remove it and the wiper frame and motor can be removed downwards towards the right.
4 Replacement is the reverse of removal. Make sure the wiper shafts are perpendicular to the windscreen.
5 To remove the motor from the frame press the connecting rods of the ball pin on the drive crank. Mark the position of the motor before removing the screws. When assembling grease the ball pin and spherical seat.

23 Windscreen wiper motor - dismantling and reassembly

1 Other than for renewal of the carbon brushes, dismantling for further repair is not economical.
2 To renew the carbon brushes the wiper motor and frame assembly must be removed from the car as described in the previous section and the motor separated from the frame.
3 Remove the armature end cover by undoing the clip.
4 The brush holders are held in tension against the commutator by a common spring. Unhook this and swing the holders outwards.
5 On motors fitted with a self-parking device check that the points gap is 0.8 mm (0.031 inch) and that the points are clean.
6 Renewal of the brushes entails replacing the complete brush plate assembly.

24 Windscreen wiper spindle bearings - renewal

1 One of the causes of jamming could be due to wear in the spindle bearings and these can be renewed after the assembly has been removed from the car.
2 Having disconnected the driving link and connecting rod by means of removing the spring clips and washer, take off the seal and washer and undo the locknut securing the bearings to the frame.
3 Replace any of the smaller bushes that may be worn also.
4 Fig.10.15 refers.

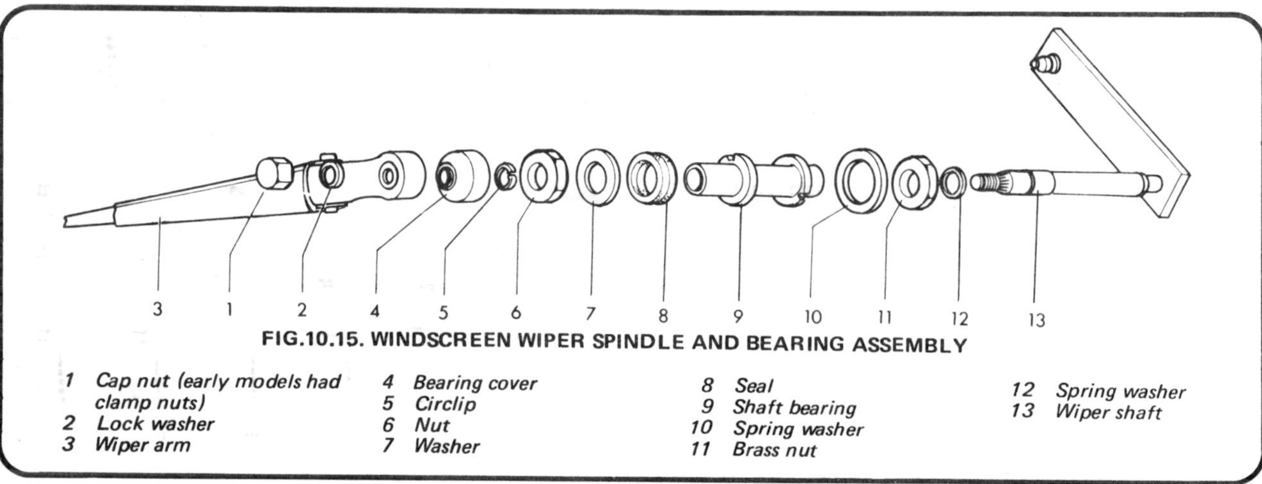

FIG.10.15. WINDSCREEN WIPER SPINDLE AND BEARING ASSEMBLY

1 Cap nut (early models had clamp nuts)
2 Lock washer
3 Wiper arm
4 Bearing cover
5 Circlip
6 Nut
7 Washer
8 Seal
9 Shaft bearing
10 Spring washer
11 Brass nut
12 Spring washer
13 Wiper shaft

25 Windscreen washer

1 Early models have the valve mounted on the dashboard. This may be removed by first disconnecting the battery earth strap and then unscrewing the knob from the switch. Then from behind the panel pull off the wires and washer pipes, unscrew the retaining ring and take off the switch.
2 The later models have the valve incorporated with the wiper switch on the steering column.
3 The tank is situated in the forward luggage compartment (photo).
4 It is pressurised from the spare wheel which must be kept at 42 p.s.i. (Sedan) and 56 pounds per square inch (Variant). The hoses are black for the Sedan and red for the Variant.
5 When adjusting the screen jets the jets should hit the screen at a point 6½ inches from the top of the screen and 17 inches from the outside of the screen if optimum wiping is to be obtained.

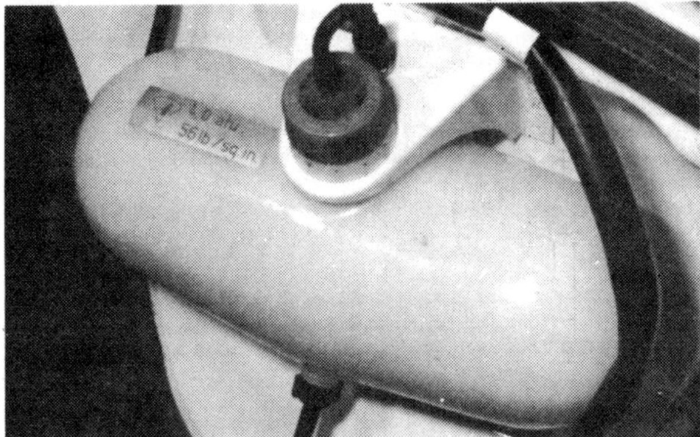

25.3. The washer tank is situated in the forward luggage compartment

26 Fuses and relays

1 The fuses are located under the dash panel. (photo). Their function is detailed in the specification. If any fuse should blow it is normally due to a short circuit in the circuit concerned. With the aid of the wiring diagram, therefore, first check visually at all the points in the circuit where such a fault is most likely to occur. The most likely places are where wires pass through individual holes into lamp units or through holes in the bodywork where grommets have been disturbed. In the ignition circuit check the connections at the coil and choke. Feel switches to see if they are hot, which they should not be.
2 If no obvious solutions occur disconnect all items on the particular circuit (e.g. the parking light bulbs if that is the circuit concerned). Fit another fuse of the proper rating. Then reconnect one item at a time, switching on each time until the fuse blows again. This will isolate the faulty part of the circuit and a closer examination can be made in that area. If you choose to fit a fuse of a much higher rating to try and overcome persistent blowing, the least that can happen is that the wiring will burn out somewhere. The worst result could be a fire.
3 Relays are in effect remote switches which avoid having to carry the full operating current to the apparatus through the actual operating switch (a starter solenoid is a relay).

On the latest models the fuse rack incorporates a relay console as well so that they may be simply plugged into it for renewal or additional wiring requirements. There are normally at least two relays fitted, one a combined relay for lights, flashers, horn etc, and another for the turn signal/emergency flasher circuit. Relays should be checked by substitution of a sound unit where malfunction of a circuit covered by them occurs.
4 In addition to the fuse box there are 4 more fuses. On the Sedan these are all in the engine compartment. On the Variant only the back up light fuse is in the engine compartment (photo) the other three are under the rear seat (photo). The back up light fuse is 8 amps., the others under the rear seat are the main fuse for the petrol heater (16 amps), overheating switch for the heater (8 amps) and the main fuse for the heated rear window.
5 The owner is strongly advised to check all the fuses in the peace and quiet of his garage at home. It is a simple job, take out the fuse and see what doesn't work. Make a list of what goes where and keep it with a box of spare fuses in the glove compartment. In the author's experience fuses either blow in a snow storm or in heavy traffic on a hot day. Mark well the one which when removed stops the horn from blowing continuously.

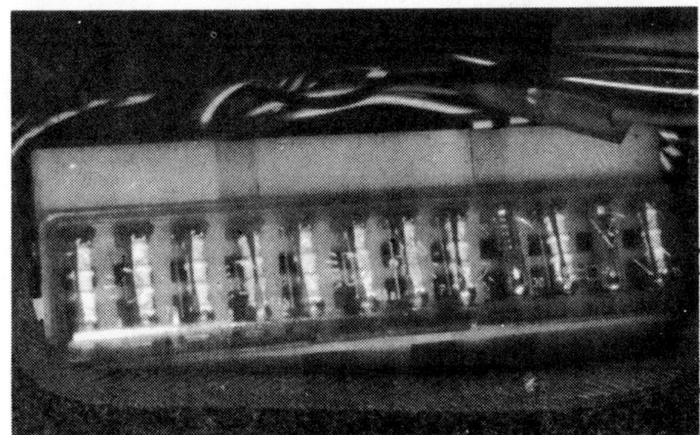

26.1. The fuse box is located under the dashboard on the left hand side

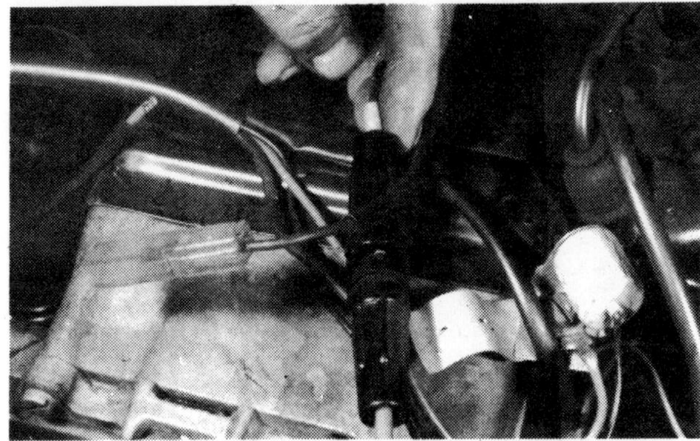

26.4a. The back up light fuse in the engine compartment

26.4b. The other three fuses under the rear seat (Variant)

27 Instruments, speedometer and warning lamps

1 The three instrument clusters are each held into the panel by leaf spring clips at each side. By reaching around under the panel the clips can be squeezed and the whole unit pushed out. To

remove them completely the various wires must be disconnected. In the case of the speedometer head the cable coupling knurled screw must be detached before the instrument can be pushed out. This can be reached through the aperture once the clock has been removed. The speedometer head can then be pulled clear and the wire connections detached.

2 The warning lamp bulbs may be withdrawn from the instrument clusters once they have been taken from the panel.

28 Lighting switch and emergency flasher switch

1 Both these switches are of the push pull type. The headlamp switch also has a rotary motion to control the brightness of the instrument illumination lamps.

2 To remove either of the switches first disconnect the battery and then pull the grip knob off the escutcheon. The escutcheon can then be unscrewed to release the switch from the facia panel. The wires should be disconnected only when it is possible to note to which terminal they are connected.

29 Computer diagnosis

Volkswagen has recently developed a maintenance check system linked into a recording and measuring apparatus.

The main purpose of the system is to reduce the human error, primarily one of omission, in the check list for their 6000 mile service.

A standard print-out sheet to cover all models lists 88 separate checks. 65 of these checks apply to all models.

It must be emphasised that the scheme is purely a diagnosis and that apart from ensuring that the tyre pressures are correct to start with (so that headlamp alignment may be measured correctly) the diagnosis service man does not do any rectification work.

All models from August 1971 onwards (1972 model year) are fitted with a multipin socket which is wired to all the necessary points for the computer which is plugged into it. For models prior to that time back as far as about 1966 (depending on the model in question) the diagnosis equipment can be hooked up on a special cable fitted with crocodile clips attached to the strategic terminals.

The model of car is first determined together with any of the standard options fitted. Since the introduction of the plug-in socket every car carries a sticker in the engine compartment showing its computer diagnosis code number. This number corresponds with a plastic card measuring about 12 x 6 inches which is punched full of holes corresponding to the specifications for that particular car. This card is fed into the computer. From then on everything measured on the vehicle is compared with the standard specifications on the punch card. The print-out indicated + (OK) or – (not OK) for those operations where the checking is done automatically.

The technician has a hand set connected to the computer and a window in this hand set shows each check requirement. At the time of writing only 24 of the 88 items are checked automatically. The rest are checked by the technician and where all is well he presses a button marked '+'. If not applicable there is another button and if unsatisfactory a third button marked '–' When any of these is pressed the mark is noted on the print-out sheet and the window in the hand set moves forward to the next item for checking.

The items which are measured by the equipment automatically are the steering geometry, ignition and charging systems and cylinder compression. Lights and battery condition are checked automatically only on those models fitted with the connection socket.

The steering geometry is checked by photo electric beams and mirrors as the steering wheel is turned through 180°, 90° each side of the straight ahead position. This is done within a 20 second period and measures toe and camber and prints out the answer in degrees and minutes. The ignition and charging systems are measured by the resistances of the various circuits. It is important that all connections are clean and that cable sizes are standard.

The cylinder compression is measured by calculating the load on the starter motor when the engine is turned over. The state of the battery and the temperature of the engine oil is measured and taken into account for this check.

There is no doubt that the system is quick, accurate and calculated to tell the unhappy customer all the awful things wrong with his vehicle in the shortest possible time. However, it is gratifying to be able to record that like all computer systems it is dependent on the information it is given and in this case the information is based on the experience and conscientiousness of the technician in control.

As far as the car owner is concerned there are a few words of warning to be given. The diagnosis can only be carried out accurately (as far as the automatic side of it is concerned) when the vehicle being processed conforms exactly to the types and options of the computer card which sets the standard. Additions and modifications in the electrical system can upset the measured resistances. Damage to the wiring system, or unusual resistances caused by faulty connections, corrosion or deteriorated insulation can also affect readings. It is perhaps for this reason that the automatic diagnosis is as yet not very extensive, depending as it does on electrical measurement within the vehicle circuitry.

To sum up therefore, it can be seen that the computer diagnosis system has the following positive advantages as part of any routine maintenance programme.

1 A complete check list which follows a logical sequence in the shortest possible time – thus saving time and money.

2 A reduction in the possibility of human error by omission.

3 A printed record of the decision made on each and every check by the diagnosis technician.

4 Provided the record is kept regularly the car's value is maintained at a much higher level than otherwise.

But the system is still only as good as the personnel using it.

30 Fresh air ventilation - electrical circuit

1 A two speed blower motor installed beneath the fresh air control box is controlled by the right hand lever Fig.10.16.

2 The blower draws fresh air from the louvres in the front cowl and delivers via hoses to the screens and fresh air outlets on the instrument panel.

3 The blower has two speeds consuming 2 amps at 3,500 rpm and 3 amps at 5,500 rpm.

4 To remove the blower take off the hoses from the fresh air control box and take off the fresh air control box. There is no need to remove the bowden cables. Disconnect the wires at the motor. Undo the nuts and washers from the bonded rubber mountings and take the motor out.

5 When reinstalling the motor make sure the rubber bushes are not under tension. The cables are connected to the numbered terminals, 31 - earth, 31 f 1st speed, 33 b second speed.

6 Refer to Fig.10.17. The blower motor may be dismantled partially. The fan should not be taken off as the fan and rotor are balanced as a unit. If the 1st speed does not operate when switched to that speed test the series resistance and replace if necessary. It should measure 2 ohms. Brushes may be renewed by unsoldering the copper pigtail.

If the rotor is damaged in any way it should be replaced as a unit. Remember it goes round at 5,500 rpm.

31 Wiring diagrams

These vary with the model and in total present a large number of diagrams. Two typical ones are given, 411 - 1971 and 411 - USA version 1971. Consult the agent if these diagrams do not solve the problem. His diagrams will be up to date for local regulations and the latest modifications.

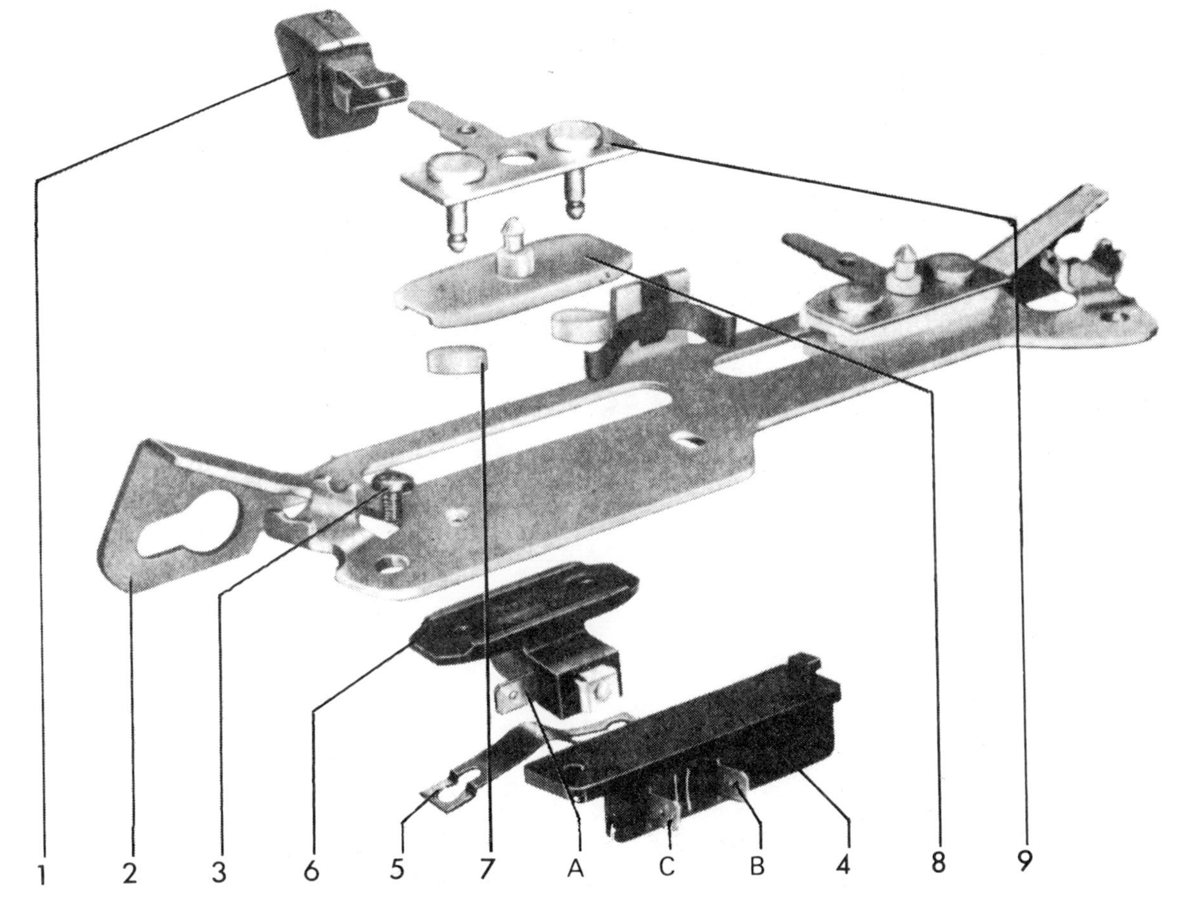

FIG.10.16. FRESH AIR VENTILATION SWITCH

1 *Regulating knob*
2 *Base plate*
3 *Screw*
4 *Contact plate*
5 *Leaf spring*
6 *Switch*
7 *Roller*
8 *Slide*
9 *Lever*
A *from terminal 15*
B *low speed 3,500 rpm*
C *high speed 5,500 rpm*

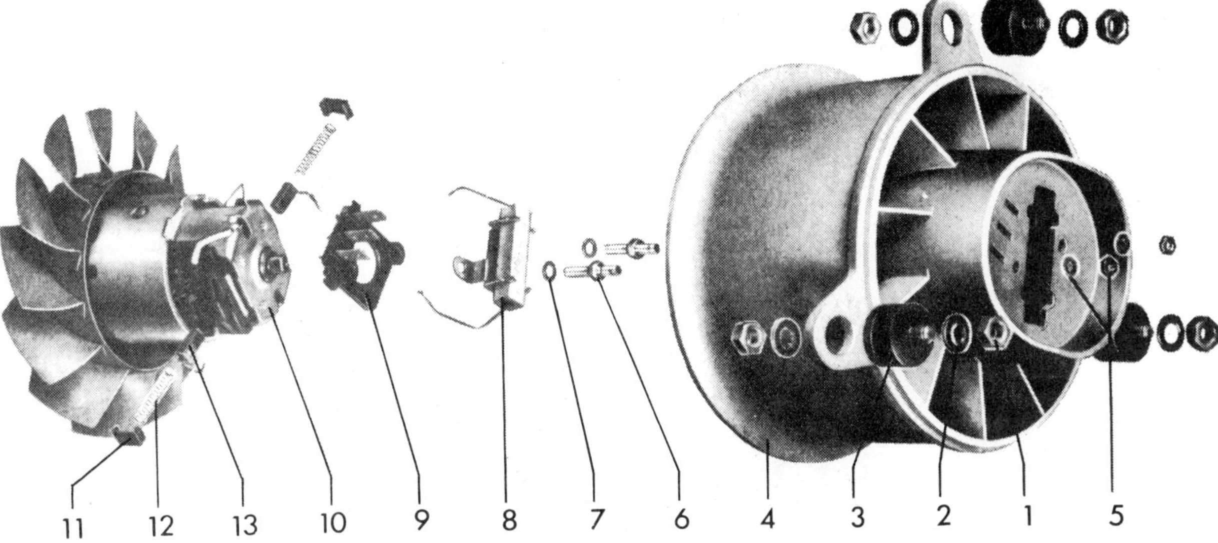

FIG.10.17. FRESH AIR VENTILATION – MOTOR AND FAN

1 *Nut*
2 *Washer*
3 *Rubber mounting*
4 *Housing*
5 *Nut*
6 *Threaded pin*
7 *Washer*
8 *Series resistor 2 ohms*
9 *Connector plate*
10 *Fan and motor rotor*
11 *Clip*
12 *Brush clip*
13 *Carbon brush*

WIRING DIAGRAM – 411 FROM AUGUST 1971

A	Battery
B	Starter
C	Generator
C1	Regulator
D	Ignition/starter lock
E	Windscreen wiper switch
E1	Lighting switch
E2	Turn signal switch (switch for hand dimmer and headlight flasher)
E3	Emergency flasher switch
E9	Switch for fresh air motor
E13	Heater temperature regulating switch
E15	Heatable rear window switch
E16	Heater switch
E17	Starter cut-off switch and back-up light switch
F	Brake light switch
F1	Oil pressure switch
F2	Door contact switch, left
F3	Door contact switch, right
F8	Kick-down switch
G	Fuel gauge sender unit
G1	Fuel gauge
H	Horn button
H1	Horn
J	Relay for hand dimmer and headlight flasher
J2	Emergency flasher relay
J8	Heater relay
J9	Heated rear window relay
J10	Heater. safety switch
J16	Voltage supply relay for electronic fuel injection
J17	Fuel pump relay for electronic fuel injection system
J21	To control unit, for fuel injection system
K1	High beam warning lamp
K2	Generator charging warning lamp
K3	Oil pressure warning lamp
K4	Parking light warning lamp
K5	Turn signal warning lamp
K6	Emergency flasher warning lamp
K7	Dual circuit brake warning lamp
K11	Heater warning lamp
L1	Halogen low beam headlight, left
L2	Halogen low beam headlight, right
L6	Speedometer light
L10	Instrument panel light
L13	Halogen high beam headlight, left
L14	Halogen high beam headlight, right
L19	Shift lever console light
M1	Parking light, left
M2	Tail/brake light, right
M3	Parking light, right
M4	Tail/brake light, left
M5	Turn signal light, front left
M6	Turn signal light, rear left
M7	Turn signal light, front right
M8	Turn signal light, rear right
M16	Back-up light, left
M17	Back-up light, right
N	Ignition coil
N5	Solenoid for kick-down switch
N7	Wiring for heater temperature feeler
O	Distributor
P1	Spark plug connector, No 1 cylinder
P2	Spark plug connector, No 2 cylinder
P3	Spark plug connector, No 3 cylinder
P4	Spark plug connector, No 4 cylinder
Q1	Spark plug for No 1 cylinder
Q2	Spark plug for No 2 cylinder
Q3	Spark plug for No 3 cylinder
Q4	Spark plug for No 4 cylinder
S	Fuse box
S1	Single fuse for heater (16 amp). for heated rear window (8 amp)
T	Cable adaptor
T1	Cable connector, single
T2	Cable connector, double
T5	Plug connection 6 pin
T20	Test socket
U1	Cigar lighter
V	Windscreen wiper motor
V2	Fresh air motor
V4	Heater motor
W	Interior light
W4	Parking lamp, left
W5	Parking lamp, right
X	License plate light
Y	Clock
Z1	Heated rear window
1	Ground cable from battery to frame
2	Ground cable from transmission to frame fork
4	Ground cable over steering coupling

WIRE COLOUR CODE

BLACK – BK	RED – RD	YELLOW – YW	BLUE – BL	GREY – GY	WHITE – WH
BROWN – BR	ORANGE – OR	GREEN – GN	VIOLET – VT		

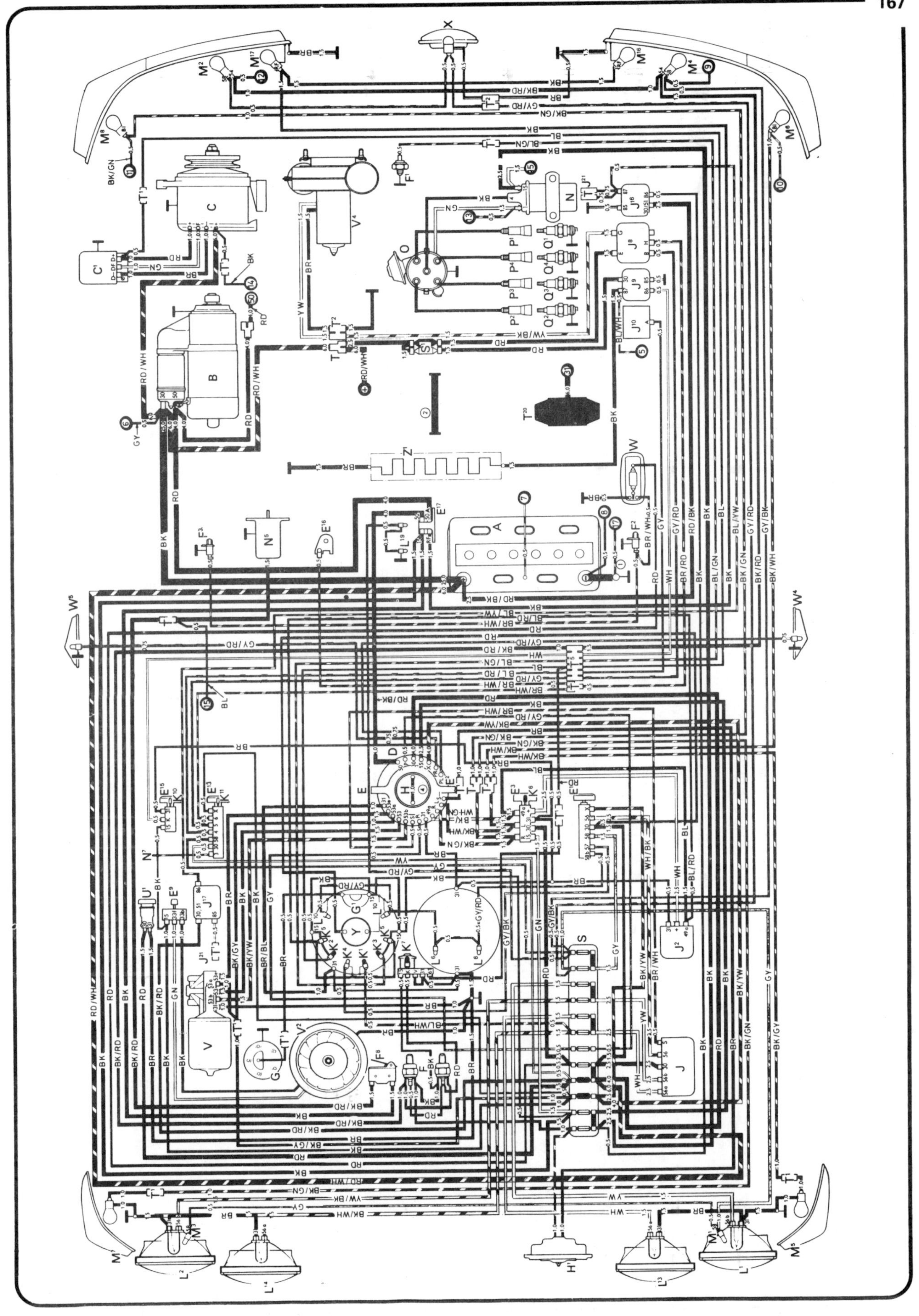

WIRING DIAGRAM – 411 US VERSION FROM AUGUST 1971

A	Battery
B	Starter
C	AC generator
C1	Regulator
D	Ignition/starter switch
E	Windshield wiper switch
E1	Lighting switch
E2	Turn signal switch and switch for hand dimmer
E3	Emergency flasher switch
E9	Switch for fresh air motor
E13	Heater temperature regulating switch
E15	Heated rear window switch
E16	Heater switch
E17	Starter cut-off switch and back-up light switch
F	Brake light switch
F1	Oil pressure switch
F2	Door contact switch, left, with buzzer contact H5
F3	Door contact switch, right
F8	Kick-down switch
G	Fuel gauge sender unit
G1	Fuel gauge
G4	Ignition timing sender unit
H	Horn half ring
H1	Horn
H5	Ignition key warning buzzer
J	Relay for hand dimmer
J2	Emergency flasher relay
J4	Dual wire horn relay
J8	Heater relay
J9	Heated rear window relay
J10	Heater safety switch
J16	Relay for electronic fuel injection
J17	Fuel pump relay for electronic fuel injection system
J21	To control unit for electronic fuel injection system
K1	High beam warning lamp
K2	AC generator charging warning lamp
K3	Oil pressure warning lamp
K4	Parking light warning lamp
K5	Turn signal warning lamp
K6	Emergency flasher warning lamp
K7	Dual circuit brake warning lamp
K10	Heated rear window warning lamp
K11	Heater warning lamp
L1	Sealed-beam unit left - high and low beam
L2	Sealed-beam unit, right - high and low beam
L6	Speedometer light
L10	Instrument panel light
L17	Sealed-beam unit, left - high beam
L18	Sealed-beam unit, right - high beam
L19	Shift lever console light
M2	Tail/brake light, right
M4	Tail/brake light, left
M5	Turn signal and parking light, front left
M6	Turn signal, rear left
M7	Turn signal and parking light, front right
M8	Turn signal light, rear right
M11	Side marker light, rear right
M12	Side marker light, rear left
N	Ignition coil
N5	Solenoid for kick-down switch
N7	Wiring for heater temperature feeler
O	Distributor
P1	Spark plug connector, No 1 cylinder
P2	Spark plug connector, No 2 cylinder
P3	Spark plug connector, No 3 cylinder
P4	Spark plug connector, No 4 cylinder
Q1	Spark plug for No 1 cylinder
Q2	Spark plug for No 2 cylinder
Q3	Spark plug for No 3 cylinder
Q4	Spark plug for No 4 cylinder
S	Fuse box
S1	Fuse for heater (16 amp)
S2	Fuse for heated rear window (8 amp)
T	Cable adaptor
T1	Cable connector, single
T2	Cable connector, double
T6	Push-on connector, 8 point
T20	Test socket
V1	Cigar lighter
V	Windshield wiper motor
V2	Fan motor, front
V4	Heater blower
W	Interior light
X	License plate light
X1	Back-up light, left
X2	Back-up light, right
Y	Clock
Z1	Heated rear window
1	Ground strap from battery to body
2	Ground strap from transmission to body
3	Ground cable for steering coupling

WIRE COLOUR CODE

BLACK	–	BK	RED	–	RD	YELLOW	–	YW	BLUE	–	BL	GREY	–	GY	WHITE	–	WH
BROWN	–	BR	ORANGE	–	OR	GREEN	–	GN	VIOLET	–	VT						

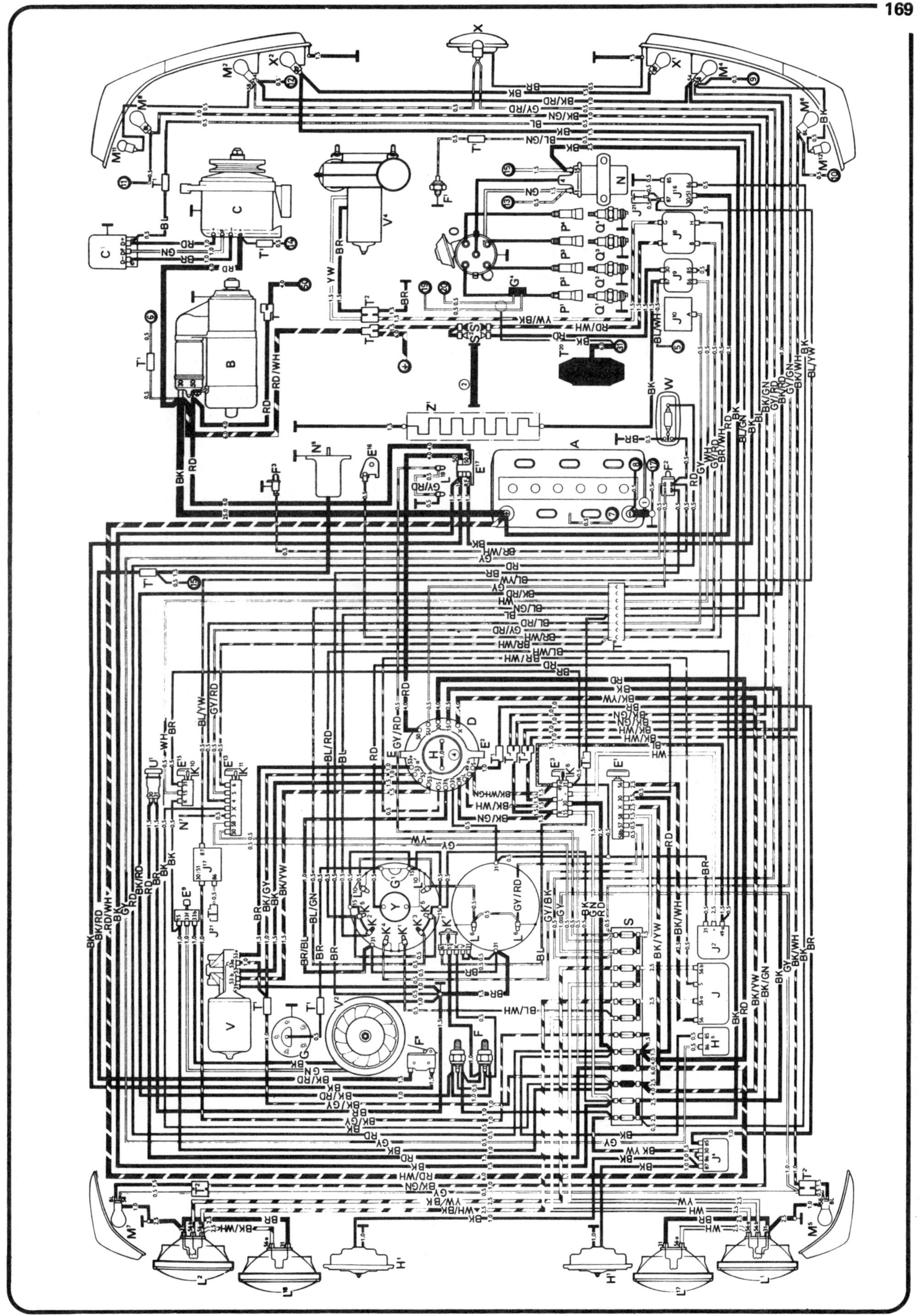

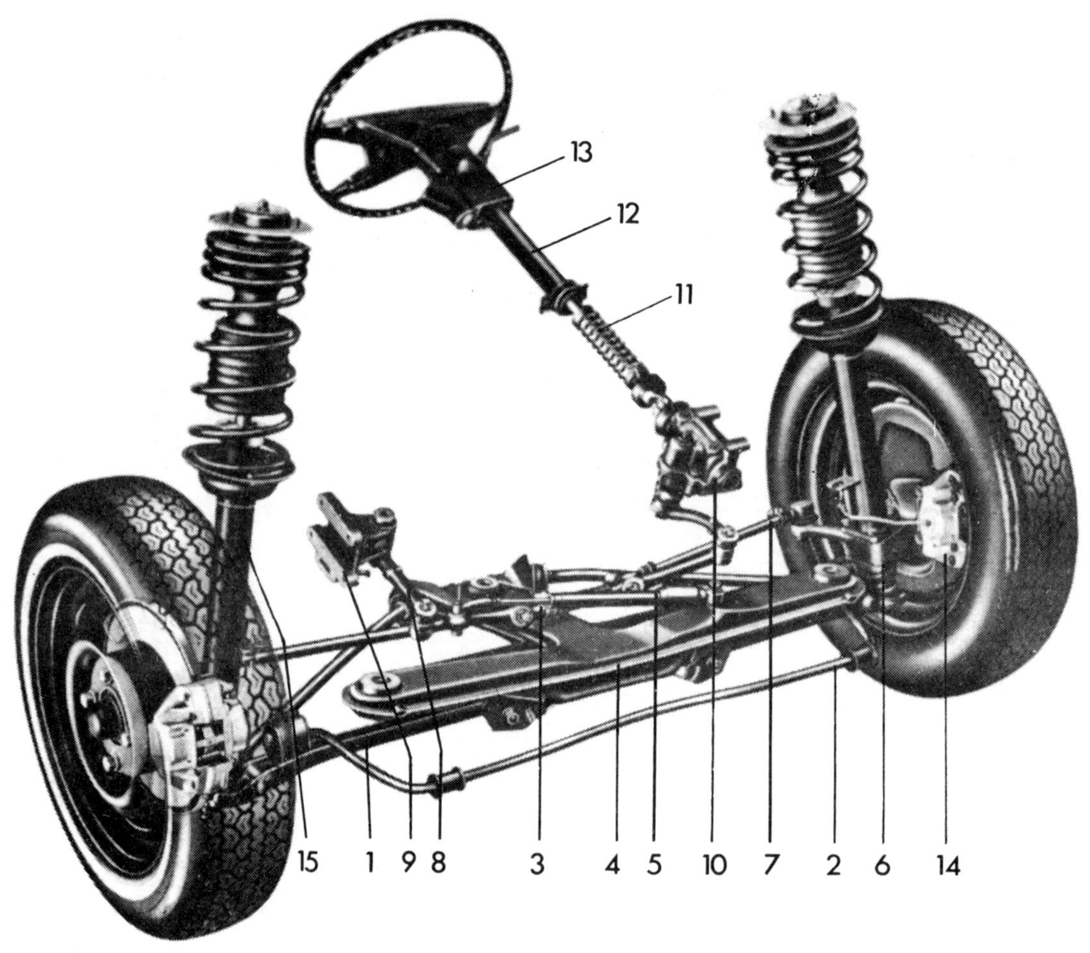

FIG.11.1. FRONT AXLE WITH SUSPENSION STRUTS

1 Track control arm
2 Stabilizer
3 Centre tie rod
4 Carrier
5 Steering damper
7 Tie rod
8 Idler arm
9 Idler arm bracket
10 Steering box
11 Steering column (plastic safety
12 Steering column tube
13 Column switch
14 Brake caliper
15 Suspension strut

Chapter 11
Front suspension, steering, tyres and wheels

Contents

Specifications

Front suspension ...	Independant McPherson strut with coil springs and hydraulic shock absorbers	
Track ...	1376 mm	
Stabilizer bar ...	15 mm diameter to August 1972, then 16.5 mm	
Coil springs:	To August 1972	August 1972 onwards
Effective coils ...	6.5	6.5
Wire diameter ...	12.35 mm	10.3 to 12.25 mm
Coil diameter ...	129 mm	129 mm
Length unloaded ...	392 mm	441 mm
Colour code ...	Yellow	Blue

Note: The coil springs must have the same characteristics on both sides of the front suspension.

Shock absorbers ...	Hydraulic piston - modified in 1972 to match new coil spring
Steering gear ...	Recirculating ball
Turns lock to lock ...	3½
Geometry:	
Toe in ...	0.6 - 4.2 mm/20′ ± 15′
Toe in with 10 kg pressure on each front wheel ...	1.8 toe in to 1.8 Toe out 0° ± 15′
Camber - straight ahead ...	1° 10′ ± 25′
Toe out on turns (20°) ...	1° 20′ ± 40′
Castor angle ...	1° 10′ ± 35′
Steering pivot inclination ...	8° 15′
Steering ball joint wear (checked with special lever) ...	Max. 2.5 mm
Wheels and tyres	
Wheels - rims ...	4½J x 15 4 hole fixing
Tyres ...	Radial 155 SR 15
Pressures ...	See Section 16.

Torque wrench settings:	**lbs ft**	**mkg**
Steering damper to axle carrier ...	32	4.5
Track control arm to axle carrier ...	65	9
Suspension strut mounting to strut ...	61	8.5
Steering knuckle and ball joint to strut ...	32	4.5
Track control arm to strut ...	29	4
Stabilizer to track control arm ...	25	3.3

Tie rod clip	14	2
Tie rod ball joint pins	22	3
Strut to body	14	2
Pitman (drop) arm to steering gear	80	11
Idler arm to bracket	22	3
Steering gear to body	36	5
Centre tie rod to drop arm and idler arm	22	3
Front axle carrier to body	47	6.5
Steering column coupling flange	14	2
Steering wheel to column	40	5.5
Worm spindle adjusting screws locknut	43	6.0
Front brake calipers to steering knuckle	60	8

1 General description

1 The front suspension is a McPherson type strut giving independant springing to the four wheels. The steering gear is a recirculating ball type with a collapsible steering column. Figs. 11.1 and 11.2 show the layout.
2 The suspension struts are located on the top in the bodyshell and in the track control arms at the bottom. At the top the spring caps are located in rotating friction washers and bonded rubber mountings so that the coil springs turn with the suspension struts. After chassis No 410 2044 405 the friction washers were replaced by ball bearings.
3 The suspension struts act as double acting shock absorbers. The lower part is a hydraulic shock absorber which fits into the track control arm and at the top of the outer case of the shock absorber is a cup which supports a coil spring. The inner part (piston shaft) of the shock absorber passes through this spring and through the spring cap holding the spring in compression. Thus as the wheel goes over a bump the spring is compressed and the resultant motion damped by the shock absorber. The lower end fastened to the track control arm, which is pivoted in a vertical plane on the front axle carrier, also carries the steering knuckle (stub axle) which in turn carries the wheel. The brake disc and wheel hub are cast in one piece and run on the stub axle in taper roller bearings.
4 A torsion bar connects the control arm to the body to minimise roll on corners.
5 The front axle carrier is a steel pressing secured by three bolts to the body. The centre mounting has allowance for movement along the axis of the car, and the two side mountings allow lateral movement, thus permitting adjustment of the front wheel camber.
6 The recirculating ball type steering box (Fig.11.2) has a worm attached to the column which turns as the steering wheel turns. The nut moves along the worm and a hemispherical boss on the nut engages in a spring loaded socket in the lug of the pitman shaft, so that as the nut moves to and fro the pitman shaft rotates. This in turn rotates the pitman arm and transmits steering motion to the wheels.
7 To reduce friction the worm and nut do not mesh directly but ball bearings run in the threads of the nut and worm. There are two circuits of these ball bearings, each circuit carrying 29 balls, and as the balls reach the end of the nut thread circuit they are fed via split tubes back to the commencement of the circuit in the thread. In this way the friction is reduced to ball race proportions and wear almost eliminated. The worm is carried in the case in two thrust bearings. Arrangement for adjustment of axial play is provided. Adjustment is also provided for the pitman shaft which is carried in bearings located in the top and bottom of the case.
8 The case is filled with grease and does not require maintenance.
9 The pitman arm outer end is attached to the centre tie rod, the other end of which is carried by the idler arm. Bosses on the centre tie rod carry ball joints which motivate the side rods and provide steering motion to the steering knuckles. The steering damper is attached between the centre tie rod and the axle carrier (Fig.11.3).
10 The steering column is fitted with safety devices so that if a head-on collision occurs the lattice work plastic safety element of the column will fracture and absorb the energy of the driver's impact on the steering wheel. Similarly sideways impact is taken care of by plastic rivets which hold the column at the top end and shear should there be an impact between the driver and the wheel in this direction. This is an excellent idea but it does mean that if the vehicle is involved in an accident however slight the column must be checked for cracks and distortion. Should there be even the smallest sign of damage the complete column must be replaced.
11 The column is mounted at the bottom in a support ring with rubber bushes which is attached to the pedal bracket and at the top to the luggage pan.

2 Maintenance and scope of repair

1 Although there are no grease nipples or oiling points this does not mean that the suspension and steering can be neglected.

Wear and damage will quickly make themselves known to the driver in the form of vibration of the steering wheel, noise from the suspension and excessive wear on the tyres. All of which can be expensive.
2 Every 10,000 miles, or sooner if the vehicle has been over rough ground check systematically round the linkages looking for perished or torn joint boots, loose nuts, and signs of impact or distortion.
3 Faulty shock absorbers will make a rumbling noise when worked but slight oil leaks from them may be ignored.
4 Where ball joint boots on tie rod ends have split the tie rod end must be checked for damage before a new boot is fitted.
5 Front wheels should be balanced whenever new tyres are fitted.
6 The scope of repair undertaken will depend upon the experience confidence and ability of the owner and the availability of equipment. When even steering linkages have been dismantled the steering geometry MUST be checked with proper equipment. However while there is nothing very different about the steering gear provided the agent is willing to check the adjustment afterwards, the dismantling of a suspension strut should be viewed thoughtfully. It has a very strong spring. The manual goes into those jobs which can be undertaken with a normal tool kit. If the owner driver is contemplating removing the axle carrier to remove the fuel tank it is strongly recommended that a time schedule be worked out before starting, and that an estimate be obtained from the agent for the job. It may alter the original plan more than somewhat.

3 Front wheel bearings - adjustment, removal and replacement

1 There are two front wheel bearings which are taper rollers, the outer one outside diameter is 40 mm and the inner one 50 mm (See Fig. 11.6.
2 To adjust the bearing, first jack up the wheel. Check that the brake linings are not rubbing and that the wheel turns freely.
3 Remove the nave plate and then the hub cap. This can be prised off or alternatively eased off by tapping from side to side.
4 This will expose the clamp nut on the end of the stub axle. Using an Allen key slack off the socket head screw which clamps

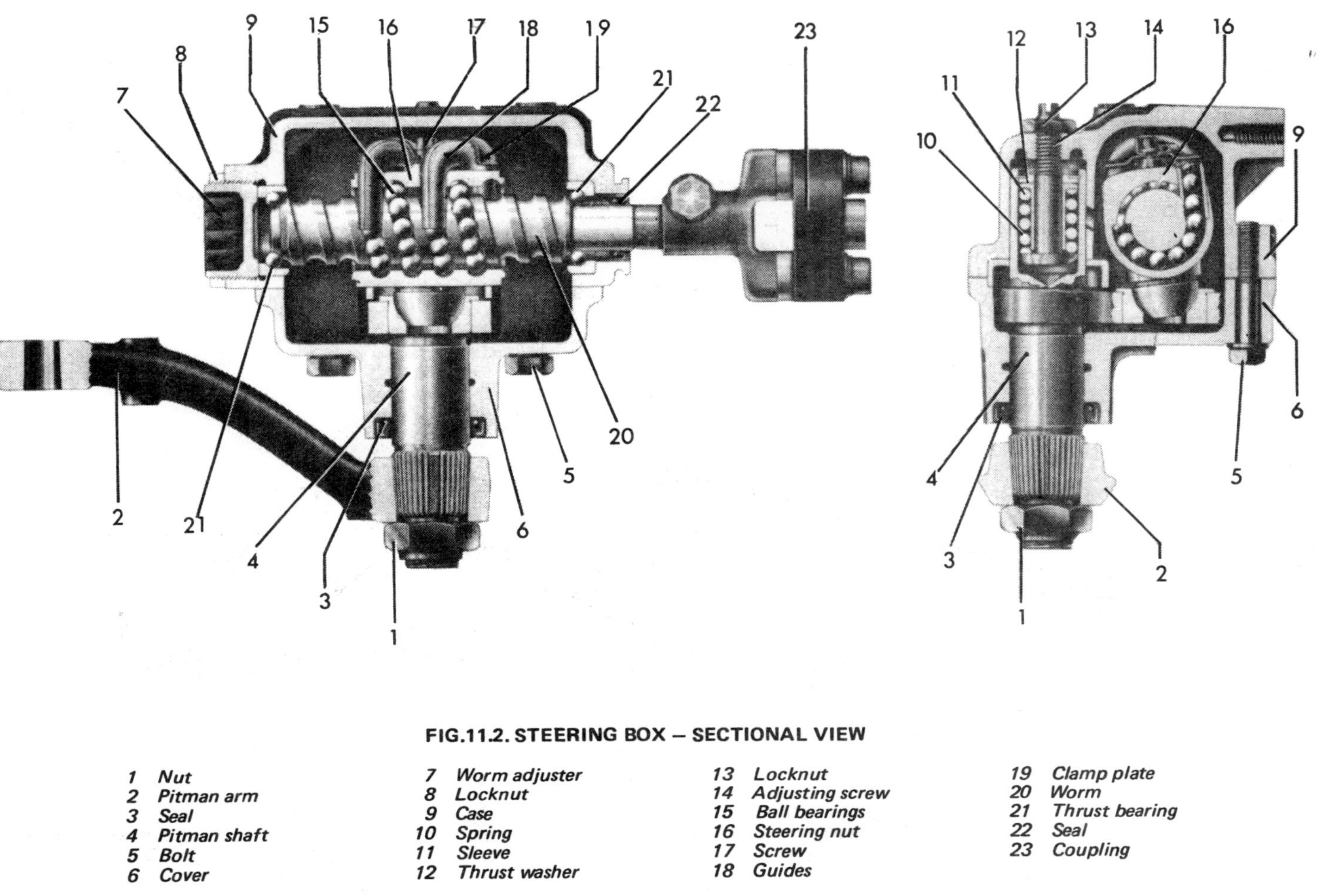

FIG.11.2. STEERING BOX – SECTIONAL VIEW

1 Nut
2 Pitman arm
3 Seal
4 Pitman shaft
5 Bolt
6 Cover
7 Worm adjuster
8 Locknut
9 Case
10 Spring
11 Sleeve
12 Thrust washer
13 Locknut
14 Adjusting screw
15 Ball bearings
16 Steering nut
17 Screw
18 Guides
19 Clamp plate
20 Worm
21 Thrust bearing
22 Seal
23 Coupling

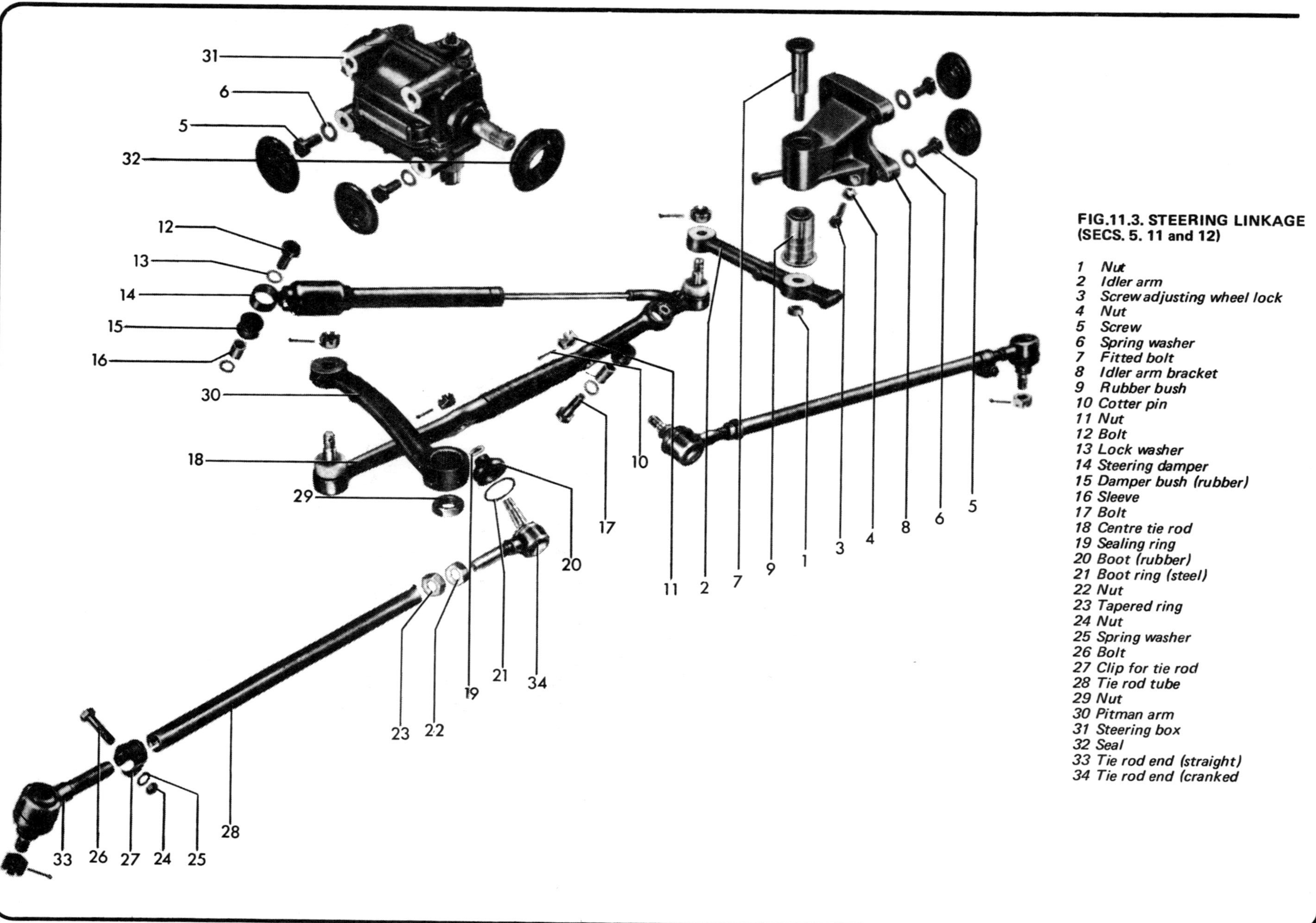

FIG.11.3. STEERING LINKAGE (SECS. 5. 11 and 12)

1 Nut
2 Idler arm
3 Screw adjusting wheel lock
4 Nut
5 Screw
6 Spring washer
7 Fitted bolt
8 Idler arm bracket
9 Rubber bush
10 Cotter pin
11 Nut
12 Bolt
13 Lock washer
14 Steering damper
15 Damper bush (rubber)
16 Sleeve
17 Bolt
18 Centre tie rod
19 Sealing ring
20 Boot (rubber)
21 Boot ring (steel)
22 Nut
23 Tapered ring
24 Nut
25 Spring washer
26 Bolt
27 Clip for tie rod
28 Tie rod tube
29 Nut
30 Pitman arm
31 Steering box
32 Seal
33 Tie rod end (straight)
34 Tie rod end (cranked

the nut. (photo).

5 The nut may now be slackened or tightened to adjust the play in the bearing. The axial play should be between 0.001" and 0.005" (0.03 - 0.12 mm). This gives quite an alarming amount of rock at the wheel rim but only if the bearing is noisy when running should adjustment be necessary.

6 To remove the bearings, first remove the wheel, take out the two bolts holding the caliper to the steering knuckle and ease the caliper out of the way. Do not remove hydraulic pipes.

7 Remove the clamp nut, take off the thrust washer and the complete hub may be removed. (Fig. 11.6).

8 The outer races of each bearing will probably remain in the hub and must be drifted out. The inner races will probably be left on the stub axle and must be pulled off.

9 Wash the bearings carefully with white spirit, fit them together, lightly oil and check for wear and roughness when spun. Check for excessive end play and if all seems well take them apart and examine the tracks for flats or signs of overheating.

10 Check the fit of the inner race on the stub axle. It should be a tight fit and should not revolve. If it does, check whether the races on the stub axle have worn. If there is only slight wear on the stub axle it is possible to make a temporary repair by marking the axle with a centre punch to enable the race to grip. Excessive wear means replacement of the steering knuckle.

11 Examine the fit if the outer race in the hub.

12 This should be repeated for both bearings and the bearings replaced if any significant wear is found.

13 To refit first replace the inner races on the shaft. The oil seal should be renewed with a new one. Drift the inner races into the hub, coat the bearings and the space between them liberally with Castrol LM Grease. Replace the hub on the axle, fit the thrust washer and clamp nut and adjust as in paragraph 5. (photos).

14 Replace the caliper and adjust if necessary (Chapter 9).

15 Replace the wheel and lower the vehicle to the ground. Tighten the wheel correctly, (torque 90 ft lbs/12 - 13 mkg) replace the hub cap and nave plate.

16 The width of the slot in the clamp ring must be 0.12" (3 mm) when slack so that the nut will clamp sufficiently tight to be safe.

3.4. Undoing the clamp screw

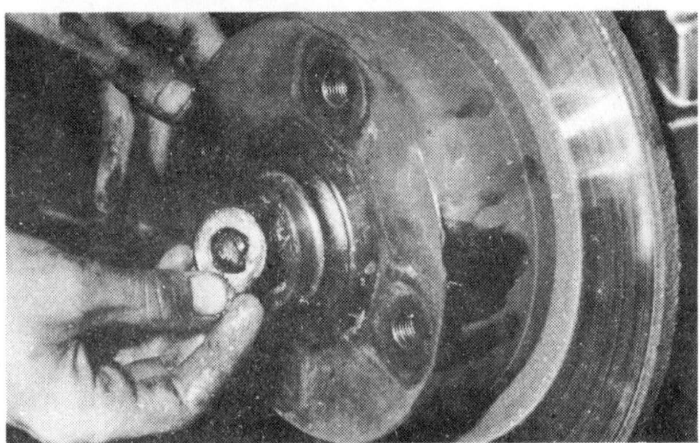

3.13a. Replace the thrust washer

3.13b. Replace the bearing adjusting nut

4 Steering ball joints - testing, removing and refitting

1 This is the joint the case of which is bolted to the front of the suspension strut, actually the shock absorber and steering knuckle, and the ball of which is bolted to the track control arm. Thus while the ball is held firmly the case rotates controlled in the vertical plane by the radius of the track control arm and in the horizontal plane by the steering linkages. (Fig. 11.6 refers).

2 Obviously there must be no play in this joint. The ball is held between two plastic shells the upper of which is spring loaded Fig. 11.4 refers. The total wear allowed is 2.5 mm. To measure the wear the spring must be compressed. Ideally Tool VW 281a should be used, which is shaped as shown in Fig. 11.5 but a suitable lever can be contrived with a little ingenuity from a piece of pipe and a short length of flat bar. The lever can be placed between the track control arm and the arm on the steering knuckle in such a way as to compress the spring of the ball joint. Play can be measured either with a vernier or a depth gauge and feelers between the control arm and the lower edge of the ball joint flange. The vehicle must be jacked clear of the ground and the wheels turned slightly to do this test.

3 Referring to Fig. 11.4 again. There is 1 mm play between the upper plastic shell and the housing. Between shells A and B there is 1.5 mm clearance. When the plastic has worn so that the 1.5 mm clearance has vanished and the 1 mm clearance has disappeared and the shell A is hard against the casing, further wear will mean that the ball is not held rigidly. The joint will now begin to rattle and the control of the steering knuckle ceases to be definite.

4 To remove the ball joint refer to Fig. 11.6. Remove the stabiliser by taking off the stabiliser clamps from the carrier and

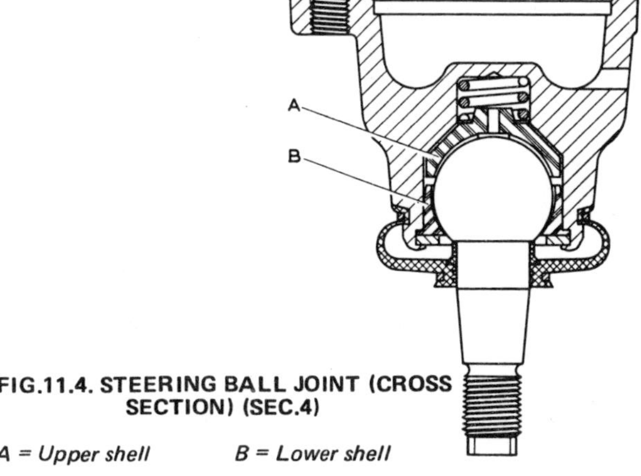

FIG.11.4. STEERING BALL JOINT (CROSS SECTION) (SEC.4)

A = Upper shell *B = Lower shell*

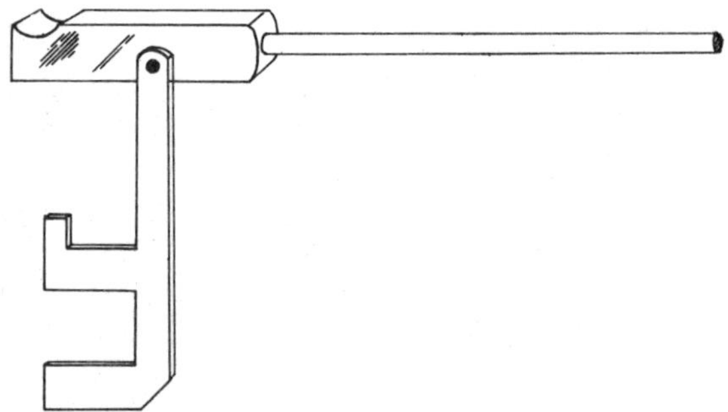

Fig.11.5. Outline shape of lever to be used when checking wear in steering ball joints (Sec.4)

the track control arm.

5 Take the nut off the ball joint and using a long armed extractor pull the track control rod off the ball joint. Now remove the screws holding the ball joint to the steering knuckle and take the ball joint off. Tie the steering knuckle out of harms way with a piece of wire.

6 Refitting a new ball joint is the reverse of removal. The ball joint pin should be free from grease or oil when it is fixed to the track control arm. Torque the ball joint to steering knuckle screws to 30 lbs ft (4 mkg) the ball joint to track control rod to 30 lbs ft, and the stabiliser to track control arm to 25 lbs ft.

7 A ball joint with an eccentric stud is available which will give extra adjustment to camber if the movement of the front axle carrier is not sufficient (ie after an accident) but it is strongly recommended that the fitting of this part for such a reason be left to the VW agent.

5 Steering knuckle - removal, refitting and checking

1 The steering knuckle should not normally need replacement. However if the front wheel bearings are slack on the stub axle (Section 3) or the stub axle has been damaged in an accident then it must come off. IT MUST NOT BE STRAIGHTENED, if it is bent it must be replaced.

2 Unless the bend is obvious it is difficult to tell whether the stub axle is out of line, a number of jigs and dial gauges are needed, so a decision as to whether to put the vehicle into the agent for the steering knuckle to be tested in the vehicle, or to chance it and take the knuckle out and ask for it to be tested with a view to replacement must be made. If it is decided to remove the knuckle the following procedure is recommended. (Fig. 11.6 refers).

3 Detach the stabiliser and press the outer tie rod end out of the steering knuckle. If no extractor is available do NOT hammer the end of the thread. Hold a heavy hammer against the ball joint and give the other side a sharp blow with a small hammer. The joint may be sprung this way. (Fig.11.3 refers).

4 Take off the brake hose retainer from the shock absorber strut, remove the screws holding the brake caliper to the steering knuckle, and take the caliper off. The caliper must be removed only when it is at room temperature to avoid distortion. (See Chapter 8). Remove the hub cap loosen the socket head cap screw in the locknut and remove the locknut and front wheel hub (Section 3).

5 Remove the splash shield (Fig. 11.6).

6 Remove the screws holding the steering knuckle to the ball joint and pull the steering knuckle off the shock absorber strut.

7 There is a further complication now. From chassis 460 2030 186 on the Varient, and on the Sedan chassis 410 2032 317 the static caster of the front wheels has been increased from 9 mm to 16 mm relative to the stub axles. This means that you must have a new steering knuckle exactly like the one taken off (but not damaged or worn). The new stub axles have been moved 7 mm to the rear of the steering knuckles. Fortunately the knuckle is marked with a B embossed or stamped near the brake caliper mounting surface.

FIG 11.6. FRONT AXLE – EXPLODED VIEW (SECS. 3, 4, 5, 7, 8, 9 and 10)

1 Lockplate
2 Bolt M.12
3 Caliper
4 Hub cap
5 Socket head screw
6 Clamp nut
7 Thrust washer
8 Outer taper roller bearing
9 Disc
10 Inner taper roller
11 Oil seal
12 Bolt M.8
13 Spring washer
14 Splash shield
15 Nut M.10
16 Spring washer
17 Washer
18 Bolt M.10
10 Stabilizer clamp
20 Nut M.10
21 Spring washer
22 Control arm mounting
23 Rubber bush
24 Stabilizer
25 Self locking nut
26 Self locking nut M.8
27 Washer
28 Self locking nut
29 Damper ring seat
30 Friction ring
31 Damper ring
32 Support plate strut bearing
33 Friction cover
34 Suspension strut bearing
35 Spring cap
36 Rubber stop
37 Washers
38 Strut bearing
39 Seal
40 Spacer
41 Cap
42 Rubber stop
43 Retaining ring
44 Tube
45 Spring
46 Damping ring (coil spring)
47 Shock absorber
48 Bolt M.10
49 Lock washer
50 Steering knuckle
51 Steering ball joint
52 Bolt M.12
53 Lockwasher
54 Bolt M.12
55 Lockwasher
56 Damper ring seat
57 Damper ring (front axle carrier)
58 Sleeve
59 Bolt M12
60 Spring washer
61 Plate
62 Ring (damping)
63 Ring (locating)
64 Nut M.12
65 Spring washer
66 Bolt M.12
67 Track control arm
68 Bush
69 Front axle carrier

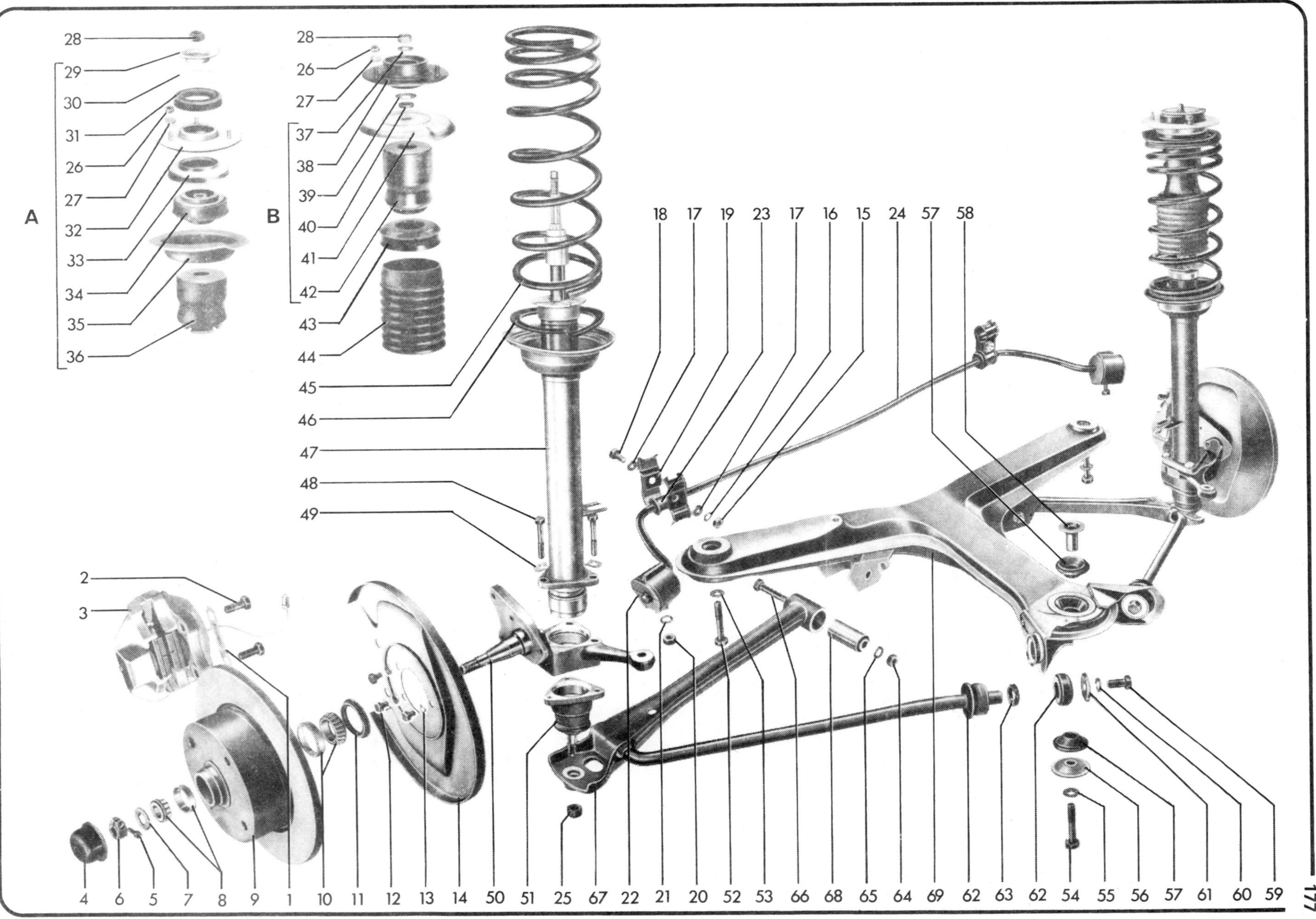
A
28
29
30
31
26
27
32
33
34
35
36
B
28
26
27
37
38
39
40
41
42
43
44
45
46
47
48
49
2
3
18 17 19 23 17 16 15 24 57 58
4 6 5 7 8 9 1 10 11 12 13 14 50 51 25 67 22 21 20 52 53 66 68 65 64 69 62 63 62 54 55 56 57 61 60 59

8 If you cannot get a steering knuckle of the old pattern to replace one of the old pattern it could involve you in an expensive and time consuming replacement of knuckles and track control arms on both sides. However VW state that old pattern spares will be available, and of course there is always the breakers yard.
9 Vehicles with 165 SR 15 tyres must be checked for clearance of the wheels if new pattern spares are fitted. The axle must be jacked clear of the ground and the clearance checked all round throughout the steering range. If the clearance is less than 15 mm (0.6") then the new type track control arm must be installed.
10 If the replacement steering knuckle is obtained satisfactorily then there is no trouble. Installation is the reverse of removal. Fit the steering knuckle to the ball joint and strut (30 lbs ft). Replace splash plate and the front hub (Section 3) and brake caliper. Do not forget the brake hose retainer. Refit the outer tie rod end to the steering knuckle (22 lbs ft/3 mkg). Refit the stabiliser arm.
11 If there was suspicion of accident damage it may be necessary to have the steering geometry checked, but if the reason for renewal was otherwise and the tie rod setting has not been disturbed, the geometry should not be at fault.

6 Track control arm - removal, replacement and repair

1 If there is reason to think that the track control arm is bent, take it off and ask the agent to compare it with a new one.
2 To take it off, remove the stabiliser arm from that side remove the self locking nut from the ball joint and pull the track control arm off the ball joint with an extractor. Undo the M12 nut from the hinge pin at the front axle carrier end and tap out the hinge. Undo the radius rod at the carrier end and remove the control arm from the car.
3 To replace the control arm in the reverse sequence. Torque both the radius arm bolt and the hinge pin nut to 60 lb ft (8 mkg).
4 The bush in the carrier end of the track control arm is renewable. It should be pressed out in a mandrel press and a new one pressed in so that the spacing on both sides is equal.

7 Stabilizer bar - removal and replacement

1 Fig. 11.6 refers. The stabilizer bar is clamped at two points to the front axle carrier and held in bushes at either end to the track control arms. As the front wheels move up and down to conform to the surface of the road the stabilizer acts as an extra damper, particularly on corners.
2 The rubber bushes are renewable. When replacing the bushes to the control arm tighten the fastening nut to 25 lb ft (3.5 mkg). This is most important.
3 Should the bar inadvertently be distorted replace it with a new one. Although it can be straightened easily the removal of the stresses so set up by annealing requires expert knowledge if the bar is to be the right shape after treatment.

8 Suspension struts - removal and replacement

1 Remove the front hub as detailed in Section 3 of this Chapter. Spend a little time making sure the car is properly supported and the wheels chocked before starting the operation. Disconnect the stabilizer bar from the track control arm.
2 Undo the nut and press the outer tie rod out of the steering knuckle.
3 Undo the nut holding the steering ball joint to the track control arm and pull the arm away from the ball joint using an extractor.
4 Undo the bolts holding the steering knuckle and steering ball joint to the bottom of the shock absorber and pull the steering knuckle away from the base of the shock absorber. Fig. 11.6 refers. The bottom end of the strut is now clear of all attachments.
5 A second pair of hands is now essential. While one person supports the strut the other should now remove the three nuts holding the top of the strut to the body (photo). DO NOT UNDO THE CENTRE NUT. The strut may now be lowered away from the vehicle.
6 At this point it may be suggested that the strut can be removed without dismantling the hub, and so it can, but the job is much more difficult that way and in any case if the strut has received treatment requiring its removal it will be a good thing for the thoughtful owner to look at the hub and steering knuckle in some detail.
7 Before reassembling the strut to the vehicle assemble the steering knuckle and steering ball joint to the shock absorber and torque the bolts to 30 lbs ft (4 mkg).
8 Offer the strut up to the body so that the studs on the top engage correctly in the holes and fit the nuts and washers. Torque these to 14 lbs ft (2 mkg).
9 Press the track control arm back onto the steering ball joint and torque the nut to 30 lbs ft. Reconnect the stabilizer arm to the track control arm and reassemble the outer tie rod to the steering knuckle. Torque the nuts to the correct amount (25 lb ft and 22 lb ft).
10 Reassemble the front hub (see Section 3 of this Chapter) replace the wheel and lower the vehicle to the ground.

9 Suspension strut and shock absorber - dismantling and reassembly

1 The suspension strut combines a strong spring with a hydraulic shock absorber. The detail is shown in Fig. 11.6. As will be seen there are two types of upper mounting. To chassis No 410 2044 405 a friction type bearing was fitted. After this chassis number, to improve straight ahead running characteristics a thrust type ball bearing has been fitted instead of the friction mounting. A sectional view of this is shown at Fig.11.7. Spare part kits are available to convert the friction type to ball bearing type but of course both sides must be done if such a course is contemplated.
2 There are two types of shock absorber for each model the later improved type fitted to the square back sedan from chassis No 460 2000 006. Neither type can be repaired, and if faulty must be replaced.
3 The only problem in dismantling and reassembling the strut is the compression of the spring. Two photographs are shown of the tools used in VW workshops. It is possible to make up similar jigs but the important thing to remember is that pressure required is a large amount and that sufficient thread must be available to allow complete decompression of the spring under complete control.
4 With the spring clamped and slightly compressed it is possible to remove the M8 self locking nut from the top of the shock absorber piston rod. (photo).
5 The spring should now be decompressed and the items at the top of the strut removed. Inspect these for wear or damage and replace as necessary. On the friction type bearing fitting a new friction disc to the damper ring may be awkward. Pinch the lips of the ring together at one point and fit the disc in there, then work the disc in all round pinching the lips as you go.
6 To check the shock absorber hold the base in a vice with the case vertical and work the piston in and out. Resistance should be uniform right throughout the stroke, particularly at the ends of the stroke. If there are any doubts as to its efficiency the VW agent must be consulted. No maintenance is possible. A slight reserve of oil is installed in the shock absorber on manufacture to allow for leakage. There is no way of topping up. A defective shock absorber usually complains bitterly in use, making a rumbling noise when operated. They also affect the steering to a certain extent and will allow the car to pitch in an uncomfortable manner at certain speeds.
7 Reassembly is the reverse of dismantling. Be careful that the

8.5. Removing the suspension strut from the body. Undo the three nuts arrowed but do not touch the centre one

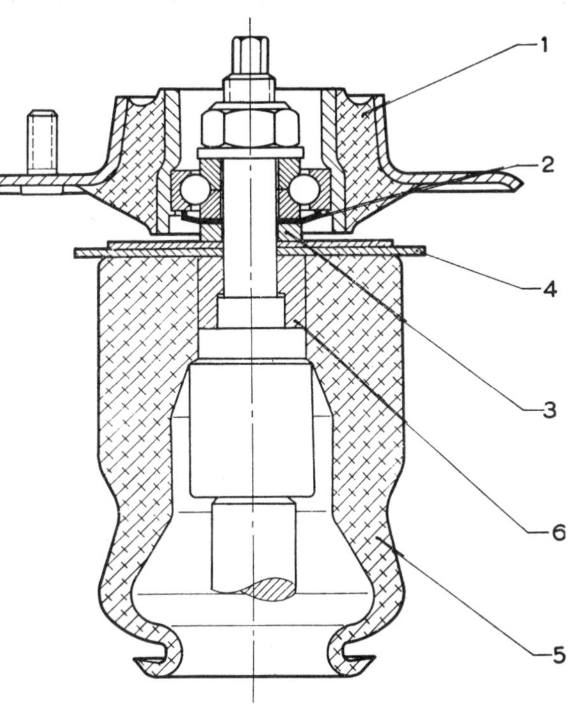

FIG.11.7. SUSPENSION STRUT – DETAILS OF TOP LAYOUT (SEC.9)

Later type with thrust ball bearing. Note: If installing with the earlier type of shock absorber the complete kit must be installed. If the later type of shock absorber is fitted item 6 is not required as the piston rod has been modified

1 Suspension strut bearing
2 Seat for damping ring
3 Spacer
4 Coil spring seat
5 Rubber stop
6 Spacer ring for shock absorber (see note above)

9.3a. Jig for removing the coil spring in position used for the strut fitted with friction ring

9.3b. Jig for removing the coil spring in position used for the strut fitted with a thrust ball bearing

9.4. When unscrewing the self locking nut (lower arrow) use a cranked ring spanner on the nut and hold the piston rod (upper arrow) with an open ended spanner or a mole wrench

spring base is located correctly in the cup. Compress the spring until the unthreaded cylindrical portion of the piston rod projects through the spring cap. The items inside the spring should of course have been installed before the spring is compressed. Now refit a NEW self locking M14 x 1.5 nut to the piston rod and tighten it to a torque of 60 lbs ft (8 mkg).

8 The strut is now ready for reassembly to the vehicle. If the steering knuckle and steering ball joint have been removed from the vehicle assemble them to the strut before assembling the strut to the vehicle.

9 Although considerable detail has been given about the work possible on the strut the author recommends assembly exchange. The strut will not have been removed unless either the spring is broken or the shock absorber weak. Whichever is the prime cause the other item is probably not far from old age and the items at the top of the strut will be better for replacement.

It is a false economy to be mean about spares at this point.

10 One final thing about suspension struts; if the strut has been damaged in an accident the vehicle MUST go to the agent for the top mounting (in the body) to be checked for alignment and distortion rectification in the proper jig.

Failure to do this may throw out the whole steering mechanism, accelerate wear of tyres and ball joints, and if the vehicle is sold in this condition render the vendor open to prosecution.

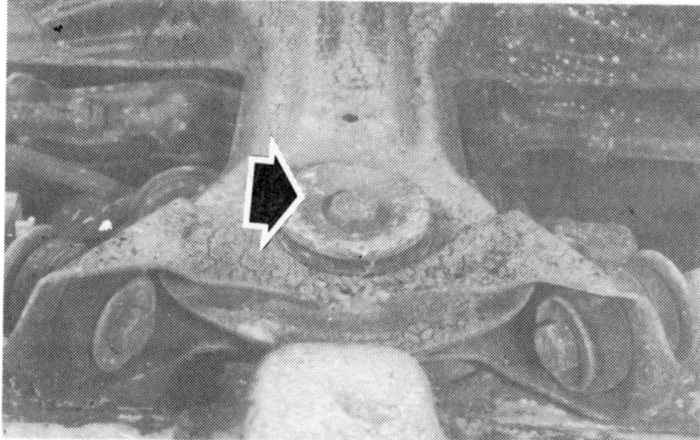

10.1a. The centre nut (arrowed) of the front axle carrier is held in a slot to allow movement along the axis of the car for camber adjustment

10.1b. The side arm nuts (one arrowed) are held in slots to allow later movement for camber adjustment

10 Front axle carrier - removal and replacement

1 Refer to Fig. 11.6. The front axle carrier is bolted to the body underframe in three places. As described in Section 1.6 the fixing bolts are located in slots in the carrier to allow for camber adjustment (photos). This means that if the necessary tools for measuring castor angle are not available (VW tool No 261 a very complicated protractor) then the job is not for the owner driver except as in paragraph 3.

2 If the damage is due to an accident then again the body frame should be checked, for an accident which bends a front axle carrier is one of some magnitude. This is a job for the VW agent.

3 If removal is required only to allow the petrol tank to be removed then mark the outline of the carrier frame in at least four places very clearly so that it can be put back in exactly the same place.

4 With the decision made and the marking done the job is not as big as it sounds but it will need two people and a pit or a ramp.

5 Remove the stabiliser bar completely from the car (see Fig. 11.6).

6 Remove the track control arms from the steering ball joint on both sides (see Section 4).

7 Detach the steering damper from the carrier (this can be seen on Fig.11.1).

8 Remove the three screws arrowed in photos 10.1a and 10.1b and lower the carrier complete with track control arms. This is where a strong assistant is essential.

9 Any damage or distortion should lead to the carrier being scrapped. Do NOT try to repair by welding or straightening. If the carrier is perfectly in order replacement is the reverse of removal. Lift the carrier into position insert the screws and tighten until the carrier can just be moved with a lever between the carrier and body frame. Move the carrier to conform with the markings giving its original position and tighten the screws to 45 lb ft (6 mkg).

10 Replace the steering damper (30 ft lbs) reassemble the track rod control arms to the steering ball joint (Section 4) reinstall the stabiliser arm; the torque to the track rod control arm for the stabiliser is critical (25lbs ft) (3.5 mkg).

11 The next time the car is taken to the VW agent ask for the camber to be checked. Checking it doesn't take long, but if it is out it will affect the steering and tyre wear badly. It is easily adjusted too, if there has been a mishap.

11 Wheel lock angle - adjustment

1 Two adjusting screws on the idler bracket (Fig.11.3) relieve the gears in the steering box from acting as a steering stop. Unless they are correctly adjusted the worm and nut may be damaged.

2 When the stops are correctly adjusted two bosses on the idler arm bear on the heads of the screws to limit the travel of the steering. (photo).

3 To adjust first jack up the front of the vehicle on both sides so that the wheels turn freely.

4 Slacken the locknuts on the adjusting screws and screw the adjusting screws into the bracket.

5 Now turn the wheels by gripping the outside of the road wheel until full left lock can be felt. The steering nut will be at the end of the worm. Do NOT arrive at this position by turning the steering wheel or you could jam the steering box. Turn the road wheel gently until this position is felt.

6 Screw out the adjusting screw until the head bears against the boss on the idler arm.

7 Turn the wheels to straight ahead until there is a gap of 1/8" between the stop and the idler arm. Screw the stop out to close this gap and lock the adjusting screw in this position.

8 Repeat for the other lock.

9 Lower the vehicle to the ground and lock hard over to the right. There should be a clearance of 5/8" between the tyres and the wheel housing. If there is not readjust the screw to obtain this clearance. Repeat for hard left lock.

12 Tie rods, steering damper and idler arm

1 Refer to Fig.11.3. It will be seen that the pitman shaft turns the pitman arm which is splined on to it. The outer end of the pitman arm carries one end of the centre tie rod. The other end of the centre tie rod is carried by the idler arm which pivots on

11.2. Steering gear - the stops screwed into the idler bracket limit travel and wheel lock angle. The correct dimension for "a" is approx 1/8 inch (3 mm)

the idler bracket, so that the three arms and body work between the steering box and the idler arm form a parallelogram three sides of which move activated by the steering gear. From the centre tie rod the side arms are connected to the steering knuckles so that as the centre tie rod is moved laterally across the car, the side rods pull or push on the steering knuckles and so turn the road wheels.

2 A steering damper is connected from the axle carrier frame to the centre tie rod. It is a hydraulic type, the outer cylinder connected to the carrier and the piston rod to the tie rod. At the carrier end the damper is located in a rubber bush. (See Fig.11.3) The bush may be removed and a new one pressed in the vice if there is too much play in the joint; otherwise there is no servicing. If the damper is removed from the car it may be tested by holding the cylinder in a vice and excercising the piston. The resistance should be uniform throughout the stroke in both directions.

3 The side tie rods have adjustable tie rod ends. If it is necessary to remove a tie rod it is important that the total length between the centre lines of the ball joints at either end is exactly the same on reassembly. If it is not the "toe-in" will be altered. Either count the threads visible before dismantling and restore that amount on assembly, or mark the tie rod at an exact distance (say 8") from the centre of the ball joint with a piece of sticky tape. On reassembly make sure this dimension is maintained.

4 The construction of the various ball joints can be seen from Fig.11.3. Make sure they are all tight, that the rubber seals are not damaged. New rubber boots may be fitted, or if the damage has gone too far new ball joints may be obtained. It is well worth while buying a proper extractor or making one up. Never hammer the threaded end of a ball joint or any other threaded end unless you want to be called a Philistine. In the absence of an extractor a taper joint can probably be "sprung" by putting a heavy hammer at the back of it and giving it a sharp rap with a light hammer.

5 Tie rods that have bent must be replaced, the stresses set up by straightening them render them liable to fracture.

6 When ever the setting of the tie rods has been disturbed it is necessary to have the steering geometry checked as soon as possible afterwards.

7 The idler arm bracket is held to the wheel housing by two screws which are covered by plastic caps. To remove it take out the plastic caps and the screws (Fig.11.3).

The idler arm is attached to it by a fitted bolt which is held in a rubber bush. The top of the bolt is shaped for an Allen key, the bolt should be held in this way while the nut is removed from below. The rubber bush may be replaced if worn by a new one. Press the old one out using a suitable mandrel and distance piece. The bush and inner sleeve come out together, then using a larger mandrel the outer sleeve. The installation is the reverse. Unless a press and suitable mandrels are available this job should be left to the VW agent.

When reinstalling the bracket tighten the scews to 30 lb ft (4 mkg) and the self locking nut (which should be a new one) to the same amount.

13 Steering wheel, column and tube - removal and replacement

1 Before commencing work remove the leads from the battery. Refer to Fig.11.8. To remove the column first remove the steering wheel. To do this turn the ignition key to "drive" and have the signal switch in the centre position. Pull the cap away from the column. Watch where the securing plugs fit. Undo the screws holding the horn operating lever to the wheel and remove the lever springs washers and bushes noting the position of each. Undo the nut holding the wheel to the column and pull the wheel off the splines.

2 Take the circlip from the top of the column remove the screws which connect the column to the steering coupling. The cap must be eased out of the way to expose the screws (photo).

3 Pull the mini plug connectors off the switch, take out the column support screws and the socket head screw for the column switch. The column may now be removed from the vehicle complete with tube and switch (photo).

4 To reinstall first check the mounting plate for the column switch between the pedal cluster bracket and the body, the closed sides of the aluminum slides must point forwards (photo).

5 Fix the column switch loosely to the column tube and slide the column tube on to the column push it into the rubber support ring mounting on the pedal cluster bracket. Attach the column to the coupling. Screw up the screws fastening the switch to the body and support ring but do not tighten them. Fit the circlip to the top of the column.

6 Make sure the wheels are in the straight ahead position and fit the steering wheel with the spokes horizontal. Tighten the steering wheel nut to 40 lbs ft (5.5 mkg).

7 Make sure the turn signal lever is in the centre position and move the column switch in the slotted holes until there is a gap 0.16" (5/32") (4 mm) between the hub and the switch. Tighten the screws securing the switch and support ring and screws holding the switch to the column.

8 Plug in the multi-pin connectors on the switch and check the operation of the turn signal.

9 Repair to the steering column is not possible. An exchange assembly must be fitted if the column is damaged.

10 A modified steering wheel containing yet another safety device was fitted in 1972. A diagram which is self explanatory is given at Fig.11.9.

14 Steering gearbox - removal and installation

1 The operation of the box is described in Section 1.7 of this Chapter. Figs.11.2, 11.10 and 11,11 refer.

2 To remove the steering box from the vehicle first remove the pitman arm from the pitman shaft. The nut has been tightened to 70 lbs ft and locked with peening into a groove so this may present a problem. The photo 14.8 shows the groove and peening. A really strong extractor is required (photo). Do NOT attempt to lever the arm away with wedges.

3 Once the arm is free go to the inside of the car and undo the two column to coupling screws and the screw holding the coupling on the worm spindle (photo). Remove the two arm

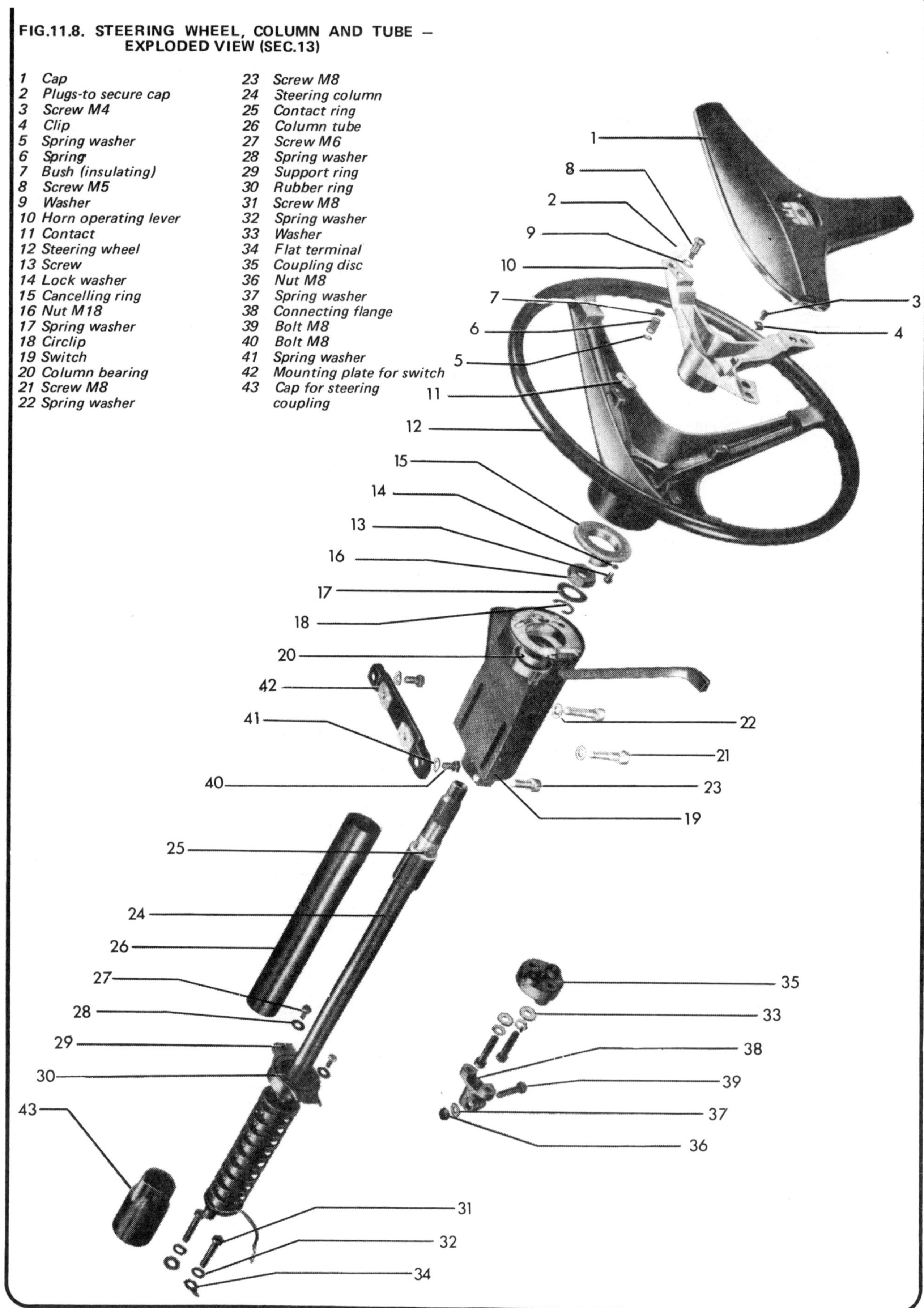

FIG.11.8. STEERING WHEEL, COLUMN AND TUBE – EXPLODED VIEW (SEC.13)

1 Cap
2 Plugs-to secure cap
3 Screw M4
4 Clip
5 Spring washer
6 Spring
7 Bush (insulating)
8 Screw M5
9 Washer
10 Horn operating lever
11 Contact
12 Steering wheel
13 Screw
14 Lock washer
15 Cancelling ring
16 Nut M18
17 Spring washer
18 Circlip
19 Switch
20 Column bearing
21 Screw M8
22 Spring washer
23 Screw M8
24 Steering column
25 Contact ring
26 Column tube
27 Screw M6
28 Spring washer
29 Support ring
30 Rubber ring
31 Screw M8
32 Spring washer
33 Washer
34 Flat terminal
35 Coupling disc
36 Nut M8
37 Spring washer
38 Connecting flange
39 Bolt M8
40 Bolt M8
41 Spring washer
42 Mounting plate for switch
43 Cap for steering coupling

13.2. With the cover removed the socket head screws which connect the column to the steering coupling are exposed (arrows) remove these and pull off the earth cable for the horn. . . . .

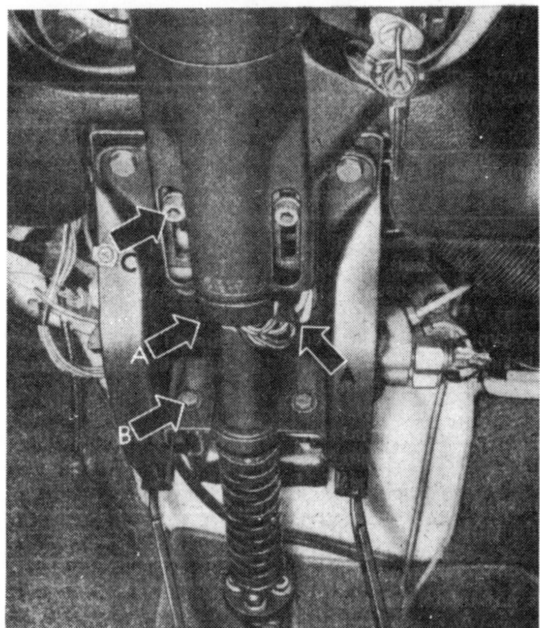

13.3. . . . . next remove the multi-pin sockets (A) and the screws for the column tube support (B). Then remove the socket head screws for the column switch (C).

13.4. When installing ensure that the mounting plates are secure. The closed sides of the slides must point as the arrows show

14.2. The pitman shaft will require a good extractor to shift it

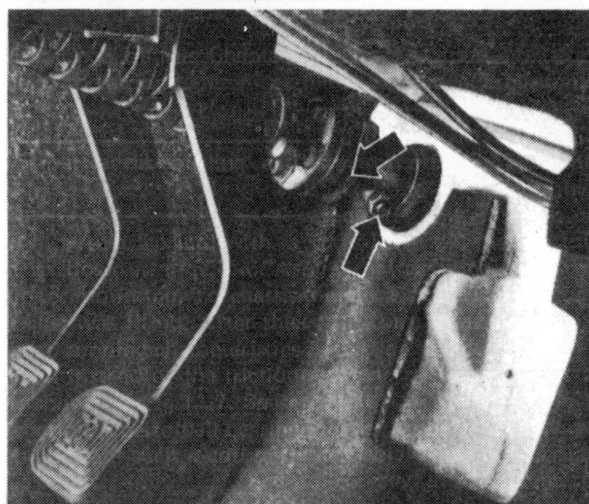

14.3. Remove the coupling screws from the flange and the worm shaft

14.4. The position of the steering box securing screws. The wheel will need to be removed to gain access

FIG.11.9. STEERING WHEEL WITH ENERGY ABSORBING HUB (SEC.13)

Note: This was introduced in 1971. It can be fitted to all vehicles from Aug 1969 having a 2 spoke deep set hub. The horn control must be modified as necessary

1 Steering wheel   2 Padded cap   3 Trim   4 Contact ring

Fig.11.10. Steering box and pitman arm. When installing the pitman arm note that one spline is wider than the others and that the shaft can be installed in one position only

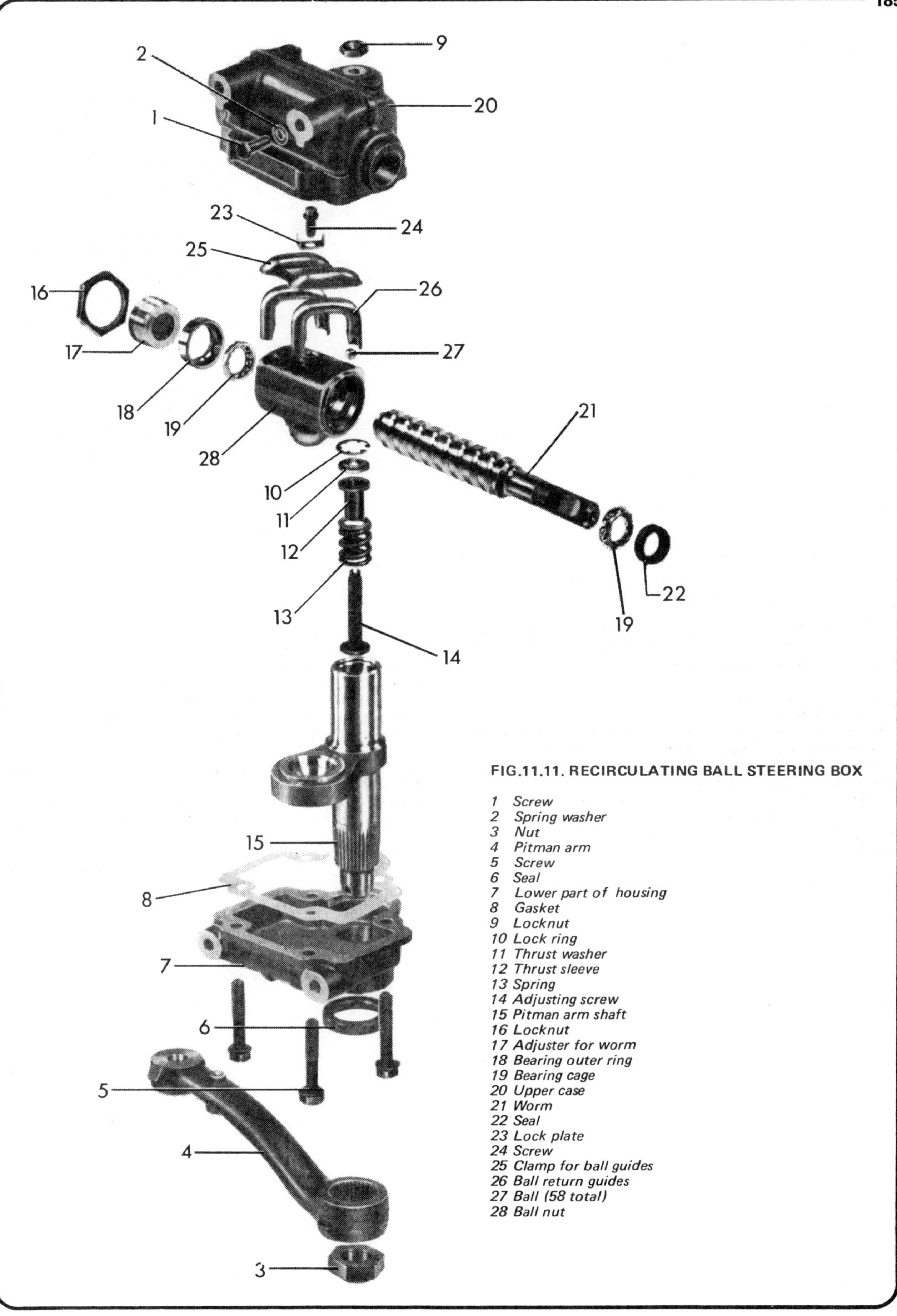

FIG.11.11. RECIRCULATING BALL STEERING BOX

1 Screw
2 Spring washer
3 Nut
4 Pitman arm
5 Screw
6 Seal
7 Lower part of housing
8 Gasket
9 Locknut
10 Lock ring
11 Thrust washer
12 Thrust sleeve
13 Spring
14 Adjusting screw
15 Pitman arm shaft
16 Locknut
17 Adjuster for worm
18 Bearing outer ring
19 Bearing cage
20 Upper case
21 Worm
22 Seal
23 Lock plate
24 Screw
25 Clamp for ball guides
26 Ball return guides
27 Ball (58 total)
28 Ball nut

flange by turning on the worm spindle as far as it will go.

4 Go to the outside of the car. Under the wheel arch at the back of the suspension strut are three plastic caps covering the steering box securing screws. Remove the caps and then take out the securing screws. (photo).

Pull the box away fom the body taking care not to damage the seal.

5 To reinstall fit the seal into the cross partition, a little glycerine will help, push the worm spindle through the hole into the two arm flange.

6 Replace the bolts attaching the steering gear to the side member, torque to 36 lb ft (5 kgm) and refit the plastic seals.

7 Refit the screws holding the steering coupling to the column and then refit the bolt holding the coupling to the worm shaft spindle and tighten the nut. Remember to position the worm spindle in the same position as it was when the clamp bolt was removed.

8 Reinstall the pitman shaft. See Fig.11.10 and photo 14.8. It would be wise to fit a new nut. Tighten to 70 lbs ft and peen into the groove.

14.8. When replacing the pitman arm tighten to 72 lb ft (10 mkg) and peen shoulder (arrows) into the groove on the shaft

15 Steering box (overhaul)

1 Fig.11.11 is supplied for interest only. The number of special tools and gauges required to dismantle and reassemble the box make it an uneconomical proposition for the owner driver. The worm and nut are supplied only in complete sets. A special torque gauge with an adaptor is required to adjust the axial play of the worm, and a considerable expertise is required to get all 58 ball bearings back into the correct place.

2 If the box is giving trouble, a suspected broken ball bearing will cause temporary jamming, too much axial play from the worm will give slack steering, then remove the box and go to the VW agent for advice and a replacement box. Avoid spares from vehicles in breakers yards. The vehicles have probably been in accidents (you only have one neck).

16 Wheels and tyres

1 The wheels of the Type 4 are of the safety type with a hump to prevent the tyres being forced into the rim well when cornering fast. (Fig.11.12 refers).

2 Whenever new tyres are fitted the wheel must be rebalanced.

3 The torque recommended for wheel nuts is 94 lb ft (13 kgm). This is as tight as you can tighten them and then a bit more using normal tools.

4 For the 411/412 with hump wheels VW definitely recommend RADIAL PLY with the designation 155SR 15. They are tubeless. Tyre pressures; front 20 - 23 psi depending on the load, rear 26 - 31 psi again depending on the load. This is checked cold before starting out. If you are going a long way in a hurry inflate the tyres to the higher pressure before starting.

5 The spare supplies pressure to the windscreen washer and should be kept between 28 to 42 psi (2 to 3 kg/cm).

6 NEVER run with crossply on the rear and radials on the front. It is best not to mix them at all but if needs must then RADIALS go on the REAR wheels. Even if you get home safely the law is very clearon the subject, and penalties can be stiff if the tyres are incorrectly fitted. It is also forbidden to run with one of each type on the same axle.

7 The front tyres are the surest evidence of trouble in the steering linkages. Feathering or wear on one side of the tread indicates incorrect steering geometry. Wear in the centre is usually due to over inflation and wear on both sides but not centre is usually due to under inflation.

17 Steering geometry

1 This is not a DO IT YOURSELF business. It requires special gauges and equipment. Adjustments are done quite easily and very exactly.

2 Failure to have the correct "toe in" and "camber" will not only make driving unpleasant but will also cost a lot of money renewing front tyres.

3 Castor angle is not adjustable, camber is adjusted by moving the front axle carrier relative to the body and measuring the camber on each wheel with a special protractor.

4 Toe in requires the use of special trammels. It is adjusted by altering the length of the side tie rods.

5 The data is given in the specification. Normally only toe in requires adjustment. If a VW agent is not available, garages having test equipment can do the job satisfactorily to this specification.

See page 188 for Fault diagnosis

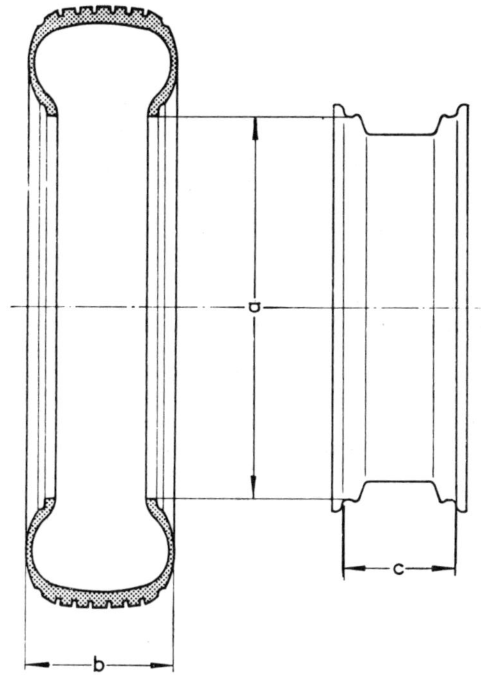

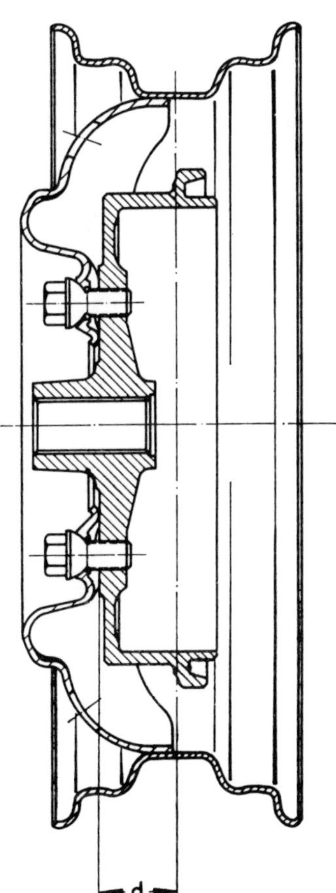

FIG.11.12. WHEEL RIMS – CROSS SECTION (SEC 15)

(a) Rim diameter (15 ins) *(b) Tyre width (6 ins)* *(c) Wheel width (4½ ins)* *(d) Pressed depth of wheel disc (46 mm)*

18 FAULT DIAGNOSIS

Before diagnosing faults in the mechanics of the suspension and steering itself, check that any irregularities are not caused by:—

1 Binding brakes
2 Incorrect 'mix' of radial and cross-ply tyres
3 Incorrect tyre pressures
4 Misalignment of the bodyframe or suspension

Symptom	Reason/s	Remedy
Steering wheel can be moved considerably before any sign of movement of the wheels is apparent	Wear in the steering linkage, gear and column coupling	Check movement in all joints, and steering gear and overhaul and renew as required.
Vehicle difficult to steer in a consistent straight line - wandering	As above	As above.
	Wheel alignment incorrect (indicated by excessive or uneven tyre wear)	Check wheel alignment.
	Front wheel hub bearings loose or worn	Adjust or renew as necessary.
	Worn suspension ball joints	Renew as necessary.
Steering stiff and heavy	Incorrect wheel alignment (indicated by excessive or uneven tyre wear)	Check wheel alignment.
	Excessive wear or seizure in one or more of the joints in the steering linkage	Repair as necessary.
	Excessive wear in the steering gear unit	Adjust if possible, or renew.
Wheel wobble and vibration	Road wheels out of balance	Balance wheels.
	Road wheels buckled	Check for damage.
	Wheel alignment incorrect	Check wheel alignment.
	Wear in the steering linkage or suspension	Check and renew as necessary.
	Castor angle incorrect	Check front axle mounting and lower clamp sleeves.

Chapter 12 Bodywork and heater

Contents

1 General description

1 The Type 4 follows the Type 3 in body style and arrangement. Introduced in 1968 the SEDAN, a normal type Saloon, and the Variant or square back estate type of body are offered as alternatives.

2 Various small modifications took place, but the conversion to fuel injection in 1969 overshadowed any change in body style until August 1972 when "extensively modified styling of the front and rear sections of the Sedan and Square back models" allowed VW the right to talk about a new model, and so the 412 came into being.

3 Although sixteen different modifications were done the main framework of the car remains the same, but what had been an alternative car now took on an even more alternative appearance without the sacrifice of any efficiency.

4 All models are fitted with a separate heater which operates without any connection with the engine. It burns petrol (gasoline), is electrically operated, and can be switched on without starting the engine. Where it is likely to be used in very cold climates a second battery may be installed in the car (Chapter 10, Section 6) to which although charged by the car engine may be used to run the heater and so prevent the primary car battery from becoming run down.

5 Following normal VW practice the more vulnerable parts of the body may be detached by undoing nuts and bolts and so come in the repair scope of the owner.

2 Maintenance - bodywork and underframe

1 The general condition of a car's bodywork is the one thing that significantly affects its value. Maintenance is easy but needs to be regular and particular. Neglect, particularly after minor damage, can lead quickly to further deterioration and costly repair bills. It is important also to keep watch on those parts of the car not immediately visible, for instance, the underside and inside all the wheel arches.

2 The basic maintenance routine for the bodywork is washing - preferably with a lot of water, from a hose. This will remove all the solids which may have stuck to the car. It is important to flush these off in such a way as to prevent grit from scratching the finish. The wheel arches and underbody need washing in the same way to remove any accumulated mud which will retain moisture and tend to encourage rust. Paradoxically enough, the best time to clean the underbody and wheel arches is in wet weather when the mud is thoroughly wet and soft. In very wet weather, the underbody is usually cleaned of large accumulations automatically and this is a good time for inspection.

3 Periodically it is a good idea to have the whole of the underside of the vehicle steam cleaned, so that a thorough inspection can be carried out to see what minor repairs and renovations are necessary. Steam cleaning is available at many garages and is necessary for removal of accumulations of oily grime which sometimes cakes thick in certain areas near the engine and transmission. The facilities are usually available at commercial vehicle garages but if not there are one or two excellent grease solvents available which can be brush applied. The dirt can then be hosed off.

4 After washing paintwork, wipe it with a chamois leather to give an unspotted clear finish. A coat of clear protective wax polish will give added protection against chemical pollutants in the air. If the paintwork sheen has dulled or oxidised, use a cleaner/polisher combination to restore the brilliance of the shine. This requires a little more effort, but is usually caused because regular washing has been neglected. Always check that drain holes are completely clear so that water can drain out. Brightwork should be treated the same way as paintwork. Windscreens and windows can be kept clear of smeary film which often appears if a little ammonia is added to the water. If they are scratched, a good rub with a proprietary metal polish will often clear them. Never use any form of wax or chromium polish on glass.

3 Maintenance - upholstery and floor coverings

1 Mats and carpets should be brushed or vacuum cleaned regularly to keep them free of grit. If they are badly stained remove them for scrubbing or sponging and make quite sure they are dry before replacement. Seats and interior trim panels can be kept clean by a wipe over with a damp cloth. If they do become stained (which can be more apparent on light coloured upholstery) use a little liquid detergent and a soft nailbrush to scour the grime out of the grain of the material. Do not forget to keep the head lining clean in the same way as the upholstery. When using liquid cleaners inside the car do not over-wet the surfaces being cleaned. Excessive damp could get into the seams and padded interior causing stains, offensive odours or even rot. If the inside of the car gets wet accidently, it is worthwhile taking some trouble to dry it out properly, particularly where carpets are involved. Do NOT leave heaters inside for this purpose.

4 Minor body repairs

1 A car which does not suffer some minor damage to the bodywork from time to time is the exception rather than the rule.

Even presuming the gatepost is never scraped or the door opened against a wall or high kerb, there is always the liklihood of gravel and grit being thrown up and chipping the surface, particularly at the lower edges of the doors and sills.

2 If the damage is merely a paint scrape which has not reached the metal base, delay is not critical, but where bare metal is exposed action must be taken immediately before rust sets in.

3 The average owner will normally keep the following 'first aid' materials available which can give a professional finish for minor jobs:

a) Matching paint in liquid form - often complete with brush attached to the lid inside. (Aerosols should only be bought for painting areas larger than 6 inches square - they are extravagent and expensive for anything less and give no better results. In fact spraying from aerosols is generally less perfect than the makers would have one expect).
b) Thinners for the paint (for brush application).
c) Cellulose stopper (a filling compound for small paint chips).
d) Cellulose primer (a thickish grey coloured base which can be applied and rubbed down in several coats to give a perfect paint base).
e) Proprietary resin filler paste (for larger areas of in-filling).
f) Rust-inhibiting primer.

4 Where the damage is superficial (i.e. not down to the bare metal and not dented) fill the scratch or chip with sufficient filler/stopper to smooth the area, rub down with paper and apply the matching paint.

5 Where the bodywork is scratched down to the metal, but not dented clean the metal surface thoroughly and apply the primer (it does not need to be a rust-inhibitor if the metal is clean and dry), and then build up the scratched part to the level of the surrounding paintwork with the stopper. When the primer/stopper is hard it can be rubbed down with wet and dry paper. Keep applying primer and rubbing it down until no surface blemish can be felt. Then apply the colour, thinned if necessary. Apply as many coats and rub down as necessary.

6 If more than one coat of colour is required, rub down each coat before applying the next.

7 If the bodywork is dented, first beat out the dent as near as possible to conform with the original contour. Avoid using steel hammers - use hardwood mallets or similar and always support the back of the panel being beaten with a hardwood or metal 'dolly'. In areas where severe creasing and buckling has occurred it will be virtually impossible to reform the metal to the original shape. In such instances a decision should be made whether or not to cut out the damaged piece or attempt to re-contour over it with filler paste. In large areas where the metal panel is seriously damaged or rusted, the repair is to be considered major and it is often better to replace a panel or sill section with the appropriate part supplied as a spare. When using filler paste in largish quantities make sure the directions are carefully followed. It is false economy to try and rush the job as the correct hardening time must be allowed between stages or before finishing. With thick application the filler usually has to be applied in layers - allowing time for each layer to harden.

Resin filler pastes are easy to work provided you use the proper tools. Having hammered in the rusted area and cleaned off all paint, prime any areas of metal which are likely to continue rusting otherwise. Then layer on the filler, onto a suitable support such as perforated zinc or wire mesh if necessary. Build it up in layers until it stands proud of the surrounding area. Do not worry about the finish at this stage. Getting the shape correct is the first job and this can only be done by cutting back with a dreadnought file or coarse rasp. Use progressively finer rasps or coarse abrasive paper until the contour conforms to the surrounding area without any lumps or valleys. Then the smoothing down operation to give the glossy finish can be attended to using varying grades of wet or dry paper.

Sometimes the original paint colour will have faded and it will be difficult to obtain an exact colour match. In such instances it is a good scheme to select a complete panel - such as a door, or boot lid, and spray the whole panel. Differences will be less apparent where there are obvious divisions between the original and re-sprayed areas.

Finally, a general word of advice. Do not expect to be able to prepare, fill, rub down and paint a section of damaged bodywork in one day and expect good results. It cannot be done. Give plenty of time for each successive application of filler and primers to harden before rubbing it down and applying the next coat.

5 Body - major repairs

1 Volkswagen owners are fortunate in that what would be relatively severe damage in some cars is not so for them. This is where wings or sills are badly damaged beyond economical repair. Being bolted on they can be removed and a new unit fitted (see subsequent sections).

2 Where serious damage has occurred or large areas need renewal due to neglect it means certainly that completely new sections or panels will need welding in and this is best left to professionals. If the damage is due to impact it will also be necessary to check the alignment of the body structure. In such instances the services of a Volkswagen agent with specialist checking jigs are essential. If a body is left misaligned it is first of all dangerous as the car will not handle properly - and secondly, uneven stresses will be imposed on the steering, engine and transmission, causing abnormal wear or complete failure. Tyre wear will also be excessive.

6 Bumpers - removal and replacement

1 Both front and rear bumpers are mounted on brackets and these in turn are bolted to the body frame. It is best to unbolt the brackets from the body and remove the bumper and brackets together.

2 With the front bumper disconnect the horn wire.

3 Replacement is this procedure in reverse. Before tightening the mounting bolts make sure that the gap between bumper and body is even all round.

4 Since August 1970 chassis No 4112000 001 the type 3 bumper has been fitted. This can be installed on models prior to August 1970, but since the curvature is different the brackets must be bent until they are parallel, the outside edges 42.5" apart and at symmetrical angles.

5 In the later type bumper there is a reinforcing strip which should only be dismantled when the bumper is off the car.

7 Front wings - removal and replacement

1 Although the wings are bolted to the body the job is not a minor operation, so allow several hours for the task.

2 Remove the cable to the turn signal, undo the connection and pull it back into the luggage compartment (disconnect the battery before starting).

3 On the right hand wing (photo) remove the clamping ring from the filler neck rubber and remove the boot from the wing. Remove the flap lock.

4 Cut the underseal between the wing and the hinge pillar.

5 Now remove the following 13 screws, one on the side member, four on the hinge pillar (2 at the top and 2 at the bottom) one near the bumper mounting and seven in the wheel housing from inside the luggage compartment. (Fig.12.1 refers).

6 Push the wing forward about ¾" and take it off the two brackets (2 more bolts) (photo).

7 The sealing tape between the wing and the hinge pillar should

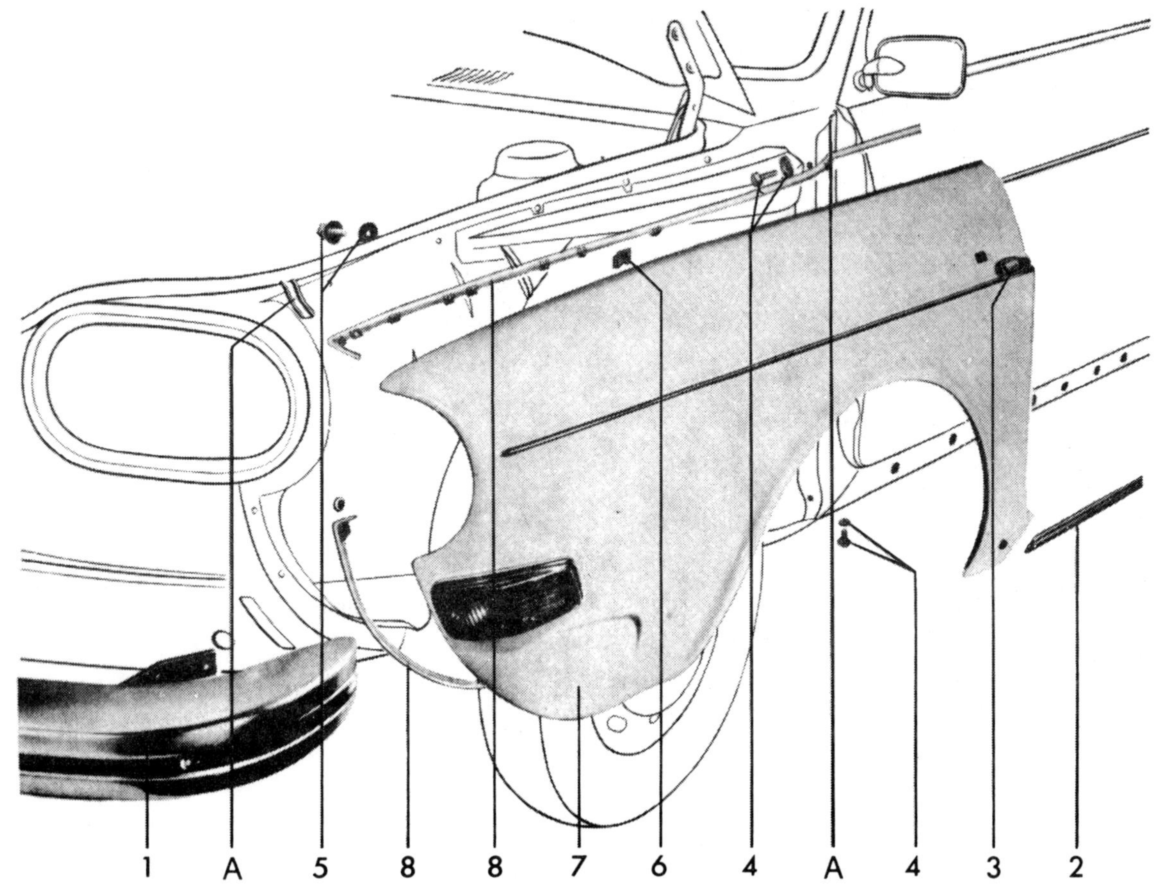

FIG.12.1. FRONT WING - REMOVAL AND REPLACEMENT
MODEL 411

1 Bumper	*4 Screw (5 off)*	*7 Wing*
2 Trim moulding	*5 Scrw (10 off)*	*8 Beading*
3 Side marker light	*6 Speed nut*	*A Retainer*

7.3. The filler cap in the right wing. The boot must be removed and the lock disconnected

7.6. Push the wing forward ¾ inch and remove the bolts from the brackets (arrowed)

be renewed.

8 To re-install align the wing with the door, bonnet and apron and replace the screws. When they are all in place finger tight, tighten them firmly, then knock the beading clips between the wing and the wheel housing into place with a wooden wedge. Connect the turn signal cable, re-install the petrol filler flap and boot and finally seal all the gaps with a PVC air drying filler.

Since August 1972 the 412 version of the front wing has changed slightly. The revised version is shown at Fig.12.1a.

8 Rear wing - removal and replacement - Sedan

1 Fig.12.2 refers. There are 10 screws to remove on the 2 door model and 12 on the 4 door model.

2 Remove the tail light and bumper. Remove the trim moulding on the 2 door model.

3 Now remove the screws from the wheel housing one on the 2 door, 2 on the 4 door; remove 3 screws from near the bumper mounting.

4 Ease the lining away in the luggage compartment and take out 2 screws. On the 4 door it will be necessary to remove the rear seat and detach the trim to get at 3 screws.

5 Undo and remove 4 screws from the engine compartment, move the wing forward and lift it up, now remove the wing from the brackets (photo).

6 Installation is the reverse of removal. Knock the beading clips in between the wing and the quarter panel with a wooden wedge.

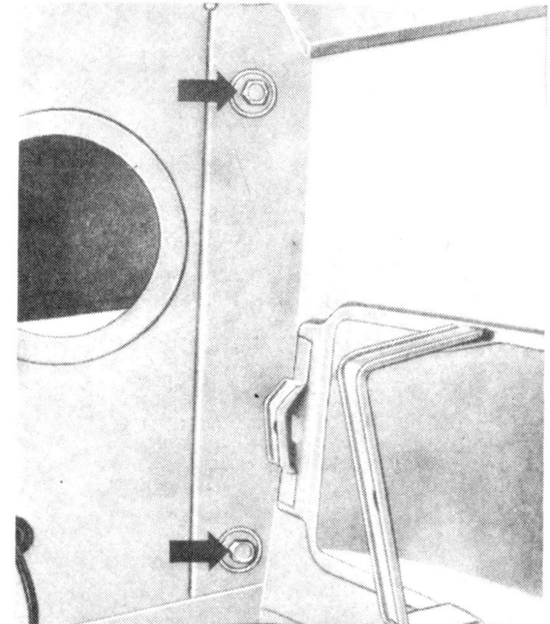

8.5. Remove the screws, (arrowed) to detach the wing from the brackets

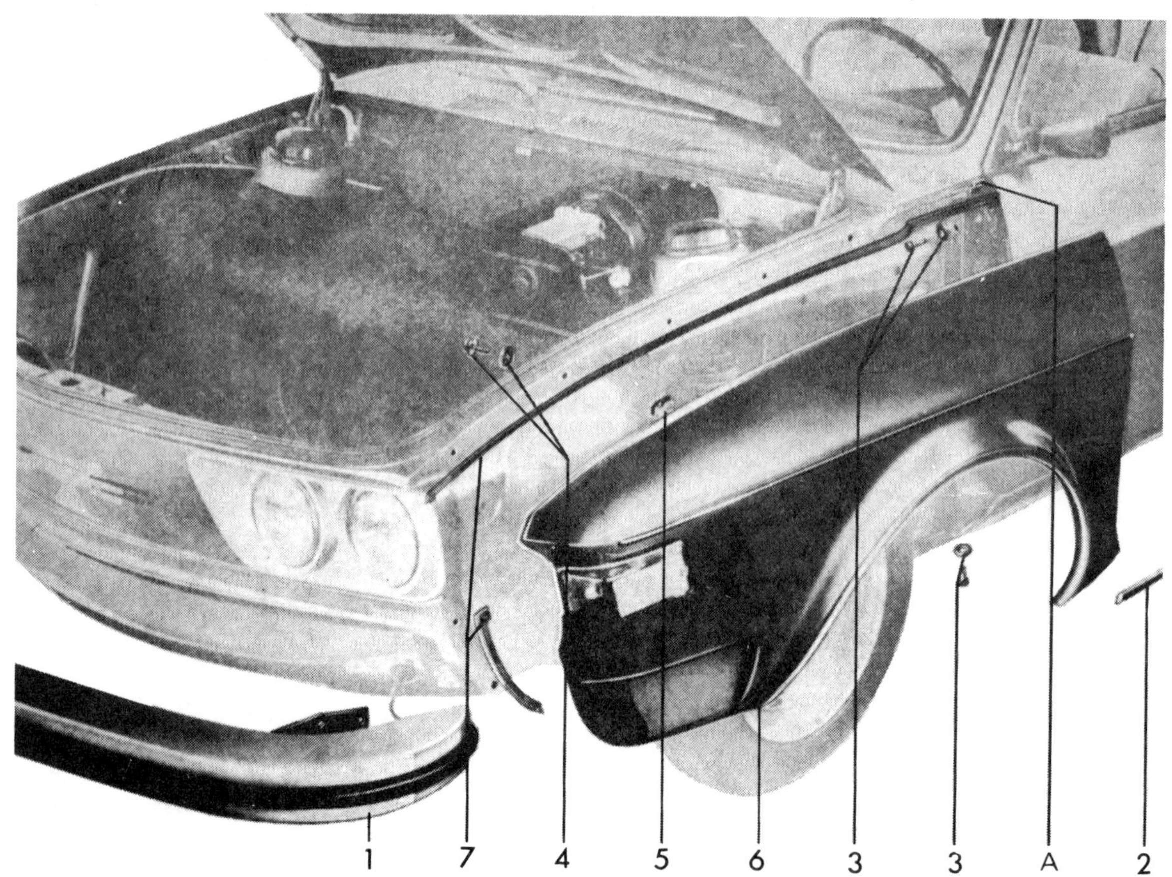

FIG.12.1a. FRONT WING REPLACEMENT MODEL 412

1 Bumper
2 Trim strip
3 Bolt
4 Bolt with washer and rubber disc
5 Speed nut
6 Wing
7 Beading
A Bracket

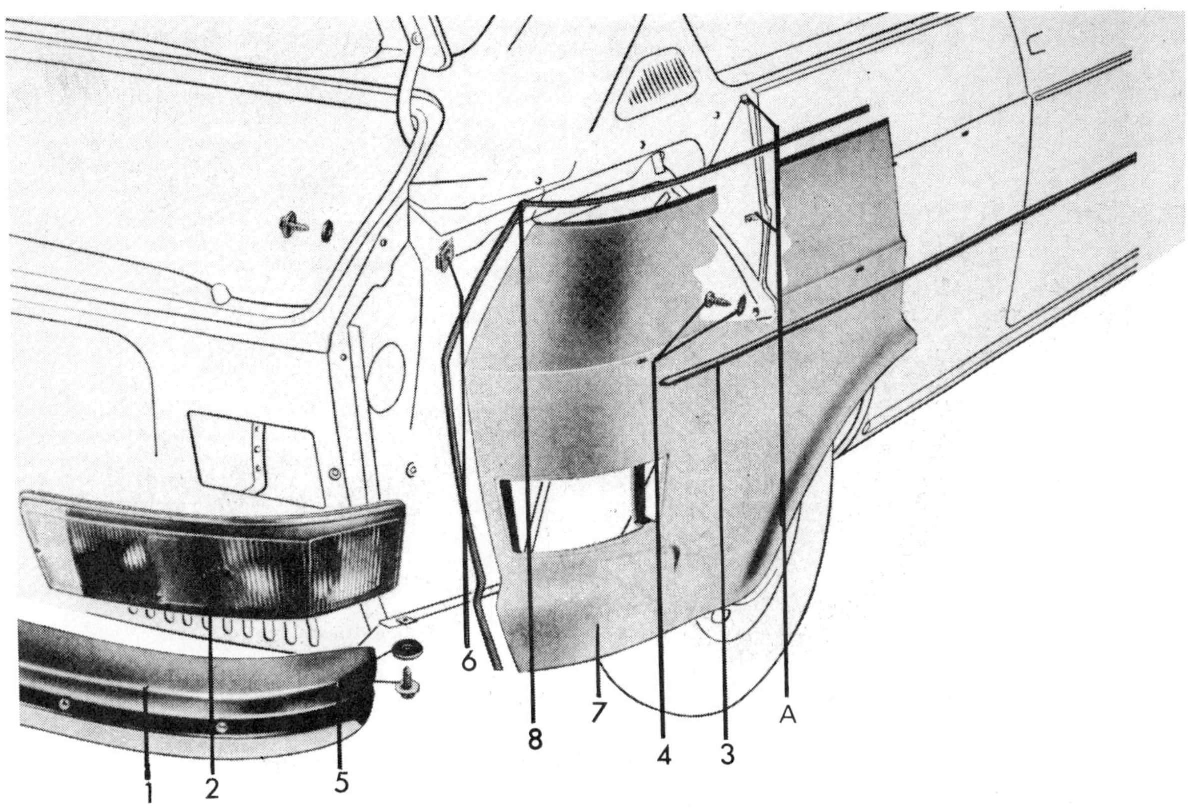

FIG.12.2. REAR WING - REMOVAL AND REPLACEMENT - SEDAN

1 Rear bumper
2 Tail light
3 Moulding
4 Phillips screw and washer
5 Tapping screw
6 Speed nut
7 Wing
8 Beading
A Retainer

Note: on the 2 door model there are 1 of part 4 and 9 part 5 and 6. On the 4 door model there is one extra of each part

9 Rear wing - removal and replacement - Variant

1 Before tackling this job make up a tool to remove the speed nuts. This can be done by brazing 8 mm nut onto a suitable holder (photo). Refer to Fig.12.3.

2 Pull off the trim moulding. Remove the 5 speed nuts and distance pieces. Remove the tail light cover and the indicator light complete.

3 Now remove the following screws, one No 7 Phillips from the wheel housing, 3 No 8 tapping bolts from near the bumper mounting 1 No 8 tapping bolt in the end panel opening for the tail light (photo).

4 Remove two screws from the rear side panel, and pull away the lining in the rear parcel compartment to remove 3 more No 8 bolts. Pull the beading off.

5 Push the wing forwards and upwards and remove from the retainer.

6 Before re-installing clean all the old rubber sealing from the side panel (and wing if the old one is to go back). Coat the places and corners so cleaned with a good sealing compound.

7 Replacement is the reverse of removal. Use a wooden wedge to drive the beading and clips into place.

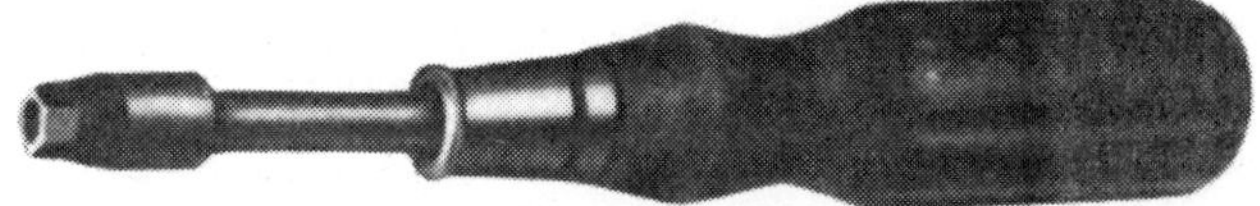

9.1. A suitable tool for removing the speed nuts may be made by brazing an 8 mm nut onto a suitable holder

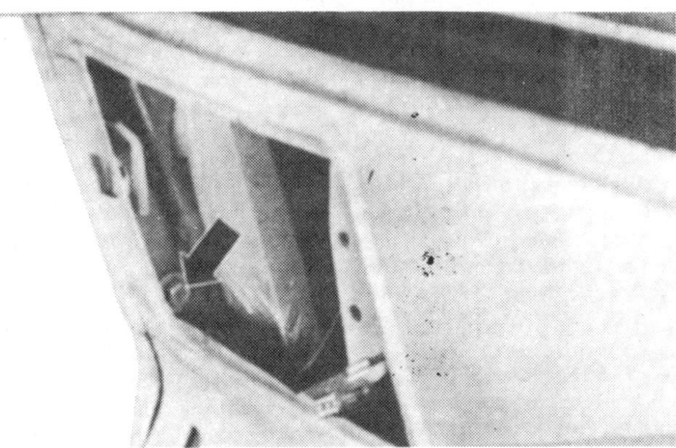

9.3. Remove one No 8 tapping bolt from the end panel opening of the tail light (arrow)

10 Windscreen and fixed glass - removal and replacement

1 Make sure you know what kind of glass is fitted. Toughened safety glass will stand a certain amount of impact without breaking but any other kind will crack at least and only carefully applied sustained pressure may be used with safety.

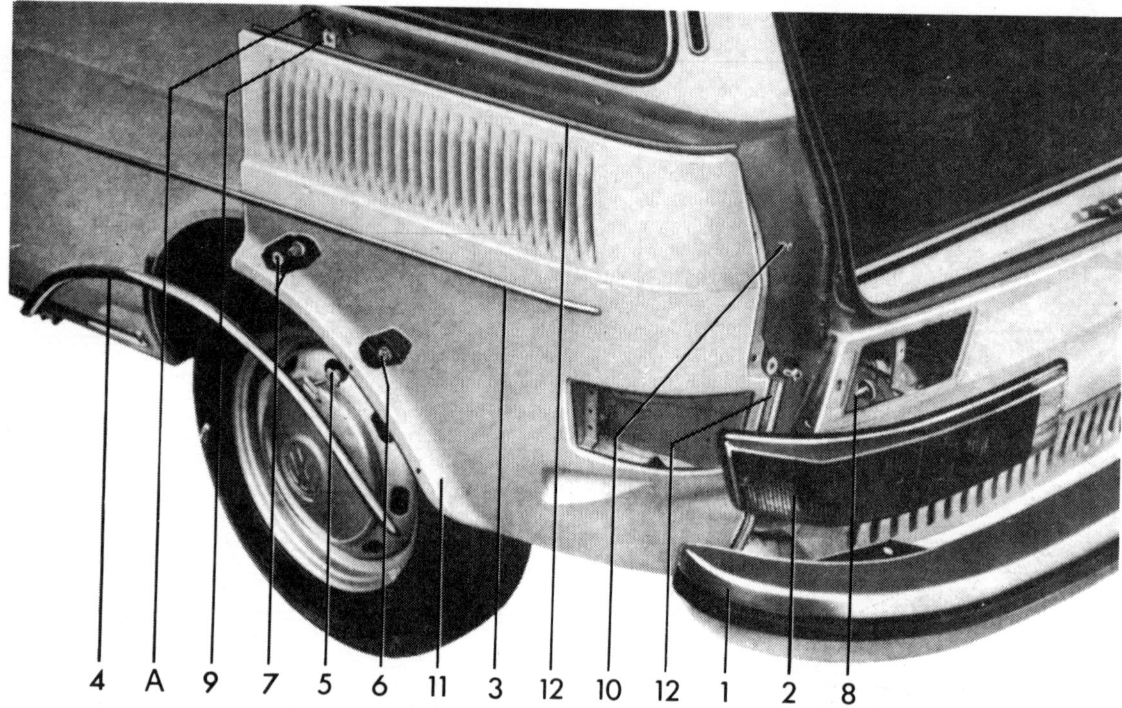

FIG.12.3. REAR WING - REMOVAL AND REPLACEMENT - VARIANT

1 Rear bumper
2 Tail light
3 Moulding
4 Wheel housing trim
5 Distance piece
6 Nuts
7 Phillips screw M6
8 Bolt
9 Snap nut
10 Screw
11 Wing
12 Beading
A Retainer

2 After taking off the windscreen wiper arms, loosen the rubber sealing strip on the inside of the car where it fits over the edge of the window frame. Use a piece of wood for this. Anything sharp may rip the rubber weatherstrip. The screen can be pushed out, weatherstrip attached, if pressure is applied at the top corners. Two people are needed on this to prevent the glass falling out. Push evenly and protect your hands to avoid accidents. Remove the finisher strip from the weatherstrip.
3 When fitting a screen first make sure that the window frame edges are even and smooth. Examine the edges of the screen to see that it is ground smooth and no chips or cracks are visible. Any such cracks could be the start of a much bigger one. The rubber weatherstrip should be perfectly clean. No trace of sealing compound should remain on the rubber, glass or metal. If the sealing strip is old, brittle or hard, it is advisable to fit a new one even though they are not cheap.
4 Fit the weatherstrip to the screen first so that the joint comes midway along the top edge.
5 Next fit the decorative moulding into the weatherstrip. This is done by first feeding fine cord into the slot (use a piece of thin tubing as a guide and time saver) and leave the ends overlapping long enough to be able to grip later. The two halves of the moulding are then put in place and the cord drawn out so that the edge of the strip locks them into place.
6 Apply suitable sealing compound to the weatherstrip where it will seat onto the metal window frame and also onto the outside faces of the frame at the lower corners.
7 Fit a piece of really strong thin cord into the frame channel of the weatherstrip as already described and then offer up the screen to the aperture. A second person is essential for this.
8 When you are sure that the screen is centrally positioned, pull the cord out so that the lip of the weatherstrip is drawn over the inner edge of the frame flange. One of the most frequent difficulties in this job is that the cord breaks. This is often because of sharp or uneven edges on the frame flange so a little extra time in preparation will pay off.

11 Doors - removal and replacement

1 An assistant is required to take the weight of the door while removing the hinges. It may be necessary to use an impact screwdriver so make sure one is available before starting the job.
2 Mark the position of the hinges on the pillar with a scriber. Take a little time over this or you may regret it when re-assembling the door.
3 Remove the two hexagon head screws holding the door check strap on the pillar.
4 Now for the difficult bit. By all means try an ordinary Phillips screwdriver on the hinge screws, but do not damage the screw heads. The screws were put in with a power driver and they are very tight. When they are all loosened get an assistant to take the weight of the door and screw them out with an ordinary Phillips screwdriver. If an impact screwdriver is not available at home ask the local garage to slacken the screws and tighten them with an ordinary screwdriver so that they can be removed easily.
5 When installing check the weatherstrip and replace if necessary.
6 If the old door is being replaced and the hinge positions were marked carefully no problem exists.
7 However a new door has to be fitted carefully. Fit the door hinges. The door should be centred in the opening, contact the weatherstrip all round, and should open and close without catching. If this is not so, remove the striker plate. The door hinges are fastened to movable plates in the brackets so that it is possible to move the door about until it does fit properly. If this cannot be done it may be necessary to move the wings.
8 Re-install the striker plate and adjust it (Section 12) so that the door conforms with the contours of the car.

12 Door latch striker plate - adjustments

1 Door rattles can often be caused by maladjusted latch striker plates. When the door closes the notch in the latch lever engages the striker post and moves into the locked vertical position. At the same time the latch plate fits tightly against the rubber cushion on the striker plate.
2 The door should not move at all when shut but it should close firmly without the need for slamming.

These two conditions are controlled by the position of the rubber buffer. If the four screws holding the striker plate are slackened the whole plate may be tilted; thus moving the rubber buffer in, to reduce closing pressure, or out, to eliminate door movement when closed.
3 Should the door still move, even when the buffer has been moved out as far as possible, then this indicates that the rubber must be replaced. As a temporary measure try putting a piece of packing under it. It is held by two screws.

13 Door rattles - tracing and rectification

Door rattles are due either to loose hinges, worn or maladjusted catches, or loose components inside the door. Loose hinges can be detected by opening the door and trying to lift it. Any play will be felt, Worn or badly adjusted catches can be found by pushing and pulling on the outside handle when the door is closed. Once again any play will be felt. To check the window mechanism open the door and shake it with the window first open and then closed. Rattles will normally be heard.

14 Door trim panels - removal and replacement

1 To remove the window winder prise off the cover at the end of the spindle and remove the cross headed screw which then becomes visible.

To remove the inner door handle lever use a screwdriver to prise out the recessed finger plate (photo) and then remove the cross headed screw which is behind it to release the escutheon, (photo).
2 Mask the door above the trim to avoid scratching the paint and carefully press out the clips which hold the trim panel to the frame. There are 22 for the two door model, 16 for the four door front and 15 for the four door rear. Go gently or the clips will tear from the panel. The panel is held in the cut out of the inner door by a sheet metal tongue on the arm rest support. This has to be lifted clear. (Fig.12.4 refers).
3 Reassembly is the reverse of removal. Bend the trim panel slightly and fit the arm rest tongue into the door, press in the clips and fit the release lever and window winder.

15 Window winders and window glass

1 The Type 4 has a different type of window winder to its predecessors. A single track cable operated window lifter is fastened firmly to the door inner panel with screws.

The cable and drive spiral are housed in a slotted tube to which the drive is fastened. At the end of the cable is a guide plate on which the locations for the window lifter channel are secured. Do not grease the drive spiral, it is coated with plastic and requires a small amount of light oil only.

On the two door models a flat spiral spring which is loaded as the window is wound down reduces the effort required to close it again.

If the window lifter is damaged a complete new assembly is required, as no repairs are possible.
2 Remove the trim panel (Section 14) and the PVC covering and the layout of the winder. The guide plate can be seen in the centre of the door opening (photo).
3 Wind the window down and take the lifter away from the channel on the window. Push the glass and lifter channel up out of the way. Undo the locating screws and the lifter can be removed out of the door.
4 Check for freeness of action. Oil the drive and if necessary straighten the tube. If the tight spots cannot be eliminated then a new winder must be fitted. If the window rattles squeeze the tube carefully at the point where the rattle occurs.
5 Re-installation is the reverse of removal, make sure the convex washers are on the right way, convex side facing the bolt.
6 It is not necessary to remove the window in order to remove the glass, detach the window lifter channel from the lifter, press door slot inner and outer weatherstrip out of the clips, pull the window glass downwards out of the front and rear guide, tilt the front of the glass upwards and take it out of the door slot. Installation is the reverse procedure. Put the glass in from the top, fit the weatherstrips, push the glass into the guides and connect up the winder.

14.1a. Prising out release lever finger plate

14.1b. Removing latch release lever ESCUTCHEON SCREW

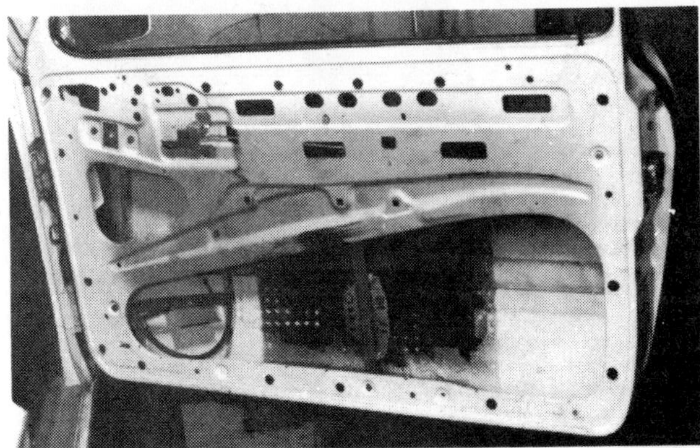

15.2. The VARIANT door with the trim panel removed. The winder mechanism is inside the door on the left. The guide plate is in the door opening

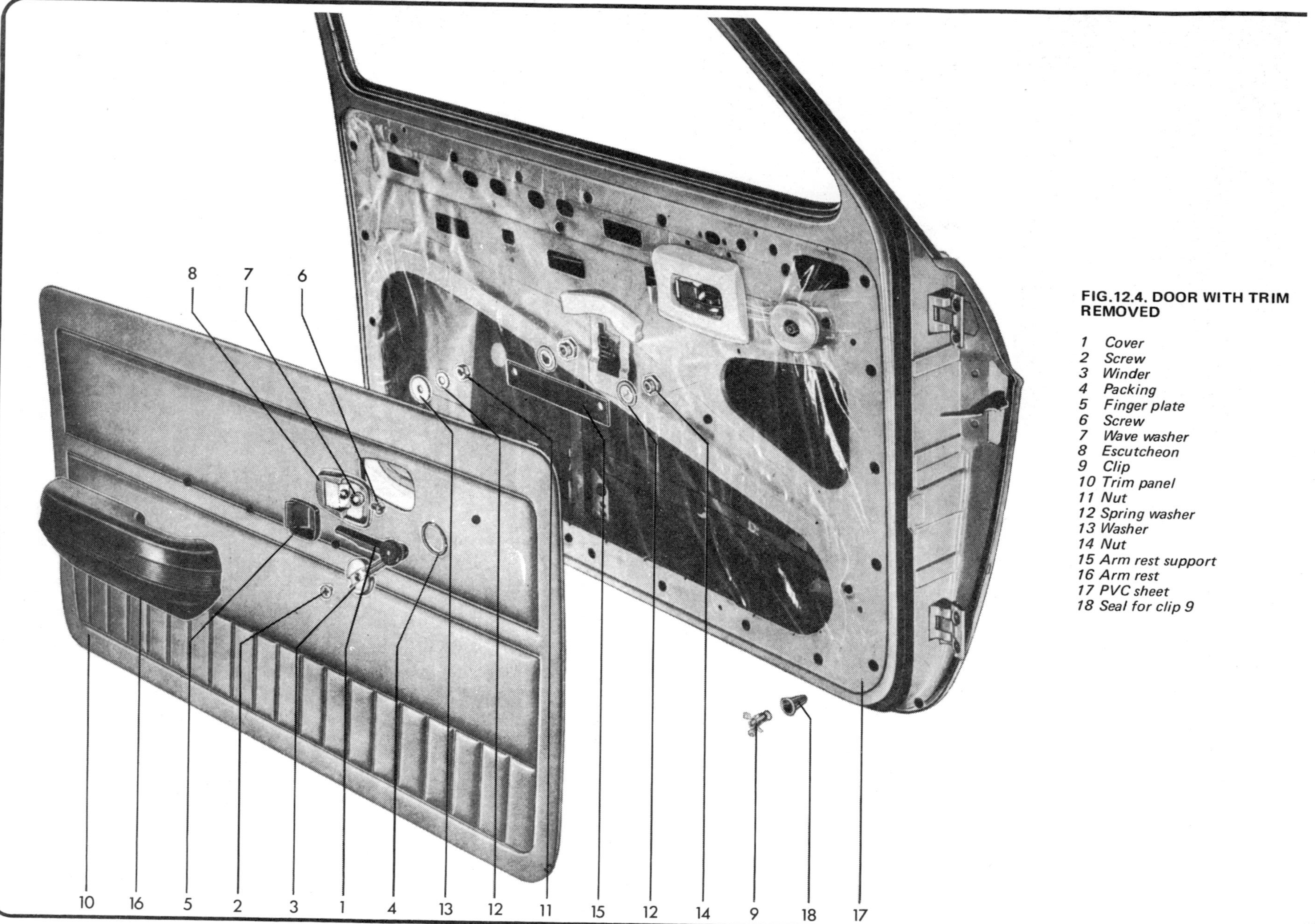

FIG.12.4. DOOR WITH TRIM REMOVED

1 *Cover*
2 *Screw*
3 *Winder*
4 *Packing*
5 *Finger plate*
6 *Screw*
7 *Wave washer*
8 *Escutcheon*
9 *Clip*
10 *Trim panel*
11 *Nut*
12 *Spring washer*
13 *Washer*
14 *Nut*
15 *Arm rest support*
16 *Arm rest*
17 *PVC sheet*
18 *Seal for clip 9*

16 Supplementary heater

1 For markets where extremely low temperatures are frequently encountered the heat exchange system is not adequate to maintain the vehicle interior at an acceptable temperature. In these cases a separate heater unit is installed at the rear in the engine compartment. These units consist of a fan/combustion unit which uses petrol as a fuel. There is a special combustion chamber and the petrol is ignited by spark and glow plugs. Hot air is blown into the regular system distribution. The combusted gases are exhausted under the vehicle.

2 The heater unit is a relatively sophisticated piece of equipment for such a mundane task. When operating it consumes approximately 0.6 litres/1 pint per hour. It is fitted with a glow plug to provide adequate warm up of the combustible mixture and a spark plug to provide continuous ignition.

The glow plug circuit is automatically switched off when working temperature is reached. Fail safe devices ensure cut off in the event of overheating and cut off in the event of non-ignition so that petrol does not continue to be pumped.

3 It is good practice to use the heater at regular intervals whether it is needed or not. Maintenance consists of checking the spark and glow plug operation if for any reason the heater has been left unused for a long time. It is also important to ensure that all electrical connections are tight and free from corrosion.

4 Do not tamper with the heater. If it fails to work have it checked thoroughly by a VW dealer. If any of the safety cut out circuits are interferred with and put out of action the consequences could be serious.

5 When the heater switch is first put on it may take anything up to a minute or so (depending on the ambient temperature) for ignition to occur - even though the fan will be running. This is because the glow plug requires a little time to warm up the combustion chamber. Similarly, after the heater is switched off the fan will continue to run on for a short time so that the combustion chamber is not left too hot.

6 The supplementary heater may be used when the engine is switched off but the power required is 220 watts on starting up settling down to 140 watts when running warmed up. For this reason it should not be used for more than about 10 minutes at most with the engine not running. If the engine is dead cold and likely to put a heavy load on the starter the heater should be used even more circumspectly.

Index

Printed by
J. H. HAYNES & Co. Ltd
Sparkford Yeovil Somerset
ENGLAND